THE KING IN LOVE

Also by Theo Aronson

THE GOLDEN BEES
The Story of the Bonapartes

ROYAL VENDETTA
The Crown of Spain (1829–1965)

THE COBURGS OF BELGIUM

THE FALL OF THE THIRD NAPOLEON

THE KAISERS

QUEEN VICTORIA AND THE BONAPARTES

GRANDMAMA OF EUROPE
The Crowned Descendants of Queen Victoria

A FAMILY OF KINGS
The Descendants of Christian IX of Denmark

ROYAL AMBASSADORS
British Royalties in Southern Africa 1860–1947

VICTORIA AND DISRAELI
The Making of a Romantic Partnership

KINGS OVER THE WATER
The Saga of the Stuart Pretenders

MR RHODES AND THE PRINCESS: a play

PRINCESS ALICE
Countess of Athlone

ROYAL FAMILY
Years of Transition

CROWNS IN CONFLICT
The Triumph and the Tragedy of
European Monarchy 1910–1918

THE KING
IN LOVE

Edward VII's Mistresses

THEO ARONSON

John Murray

First published 1988
by John Murray (Publishers) Ltd
50 Albemarle Street, London W1X 4BD

Reprinted 1988 (twice)

Typeset by Inforum Ltd, Portsmouth
Printed and bound in Great Britain by
Mackays of Chatham PLC, Chatham, Kent

British Library Cataloguing in Publication Data

Aronson, Theo
The king in love: Edward VII's mistresses.
1. Edward VII, *King of Great Britain*
I. Title
941.0823′092′4   DA567

ISBN 0-7195-4526-9

Contents

Illustrations

*For my family
the Manbys, the Pitchfords
and the Grants*

Author's Note

As much as an account of the love-life of Edward VII, as Prince of Wales and King, this book is a study of the three women with whom he was most deeply in love: his 'official' mistresses, Lillie Langtry, Daisy Warwick and Alice Keppel. It is a composite biography of these three remarkable personalities, seen in relation to their royal lover. Given Edward VII's well-merited reputation as a womaniser – and the fascinations of his three mistresses – it is surprising that no such book has been written before. There have, admittedly, been a couple of studies of his individual love affairs, but this is the first time that the King's celebrated amatory activities, including his three main liaisons, have been so comprehensively treated. And although there have been several studies of Lillie Langtry, chiefly in her role as an actress, the lives of the King's other two mistresses have been strangely neglected. It is over twenty years since Margaret Blunden's *The Countess of Warwick* was published; and there has never been a biography of Alice Keppel.

This book contains much previously unpublished material: material which has enabled me to reassess many aspects of the private lives of the four main characters, as well as to correct certain long-established myths. For this I am grateful to the Department of Manuscripts and Printed Books at the Fitzwilliam Museum, Cambridge, for permission to study the Secret Diary of Wilfrid Scawen Blunt; the Department of Manuscripts at the British Library for use of the Gladstone Papers; Mrs C. McFadyean (Lillie Langtry's granddaughter) for allowing me to study the correspondence between Lillie Langtry and her daughter, Lady Malcolm; the Société Jersiaise for permitting me to see certain letters from Edward VII and George V to Lillie Langtry; and Mr Brian Roberts for use of the letters of Abraham Hayward.

I must also thank, in alphabetical order, those many people who, to a greater or lesser extent, have helped me in the writing of this book. They are: Mrs Alison Adburgham; Mr Paul Barker, Custodian at Warwick Castle; Mr J. Black of the Mitchell Library, Glasgow; Mr Gordon Brooke-Shepherd; Miss Anne Carter; Mr G.P. Drew of the Société Jersiaise; Miss C. Easterbrook of the States of Jersey Library

Service; Miss Mary Griffith; Mrs Pamela Hamilton-Howard of Lang-
try Manor, Bournemouth; Mr Keith Killby; Mr James Lees-Milne;
Mr Michael Legat; the Countess of Longford; Mr I. Monins; Mrs
Barbara North, who arranged for me to see the Disraeli Papers at
Hughenden Manor; Mr John Phillips; Mrs R.M. Popham of the
Lansdowne Library, Bournemouth; Mr H.T. Porter of St Helier,
Jersey, who has been especially helpful; Ms Odette Rogers of the
Fitzwilliam Museum; Mrs Betty Ross; the Hon. Giles St Aubyn; Mr
Paul Sinodhinos; Mrs F. Spurrier, the Countess of Warwick's grand-
daughter, who advised me about photographs; Mr Hugo Vickers; the
Earl of Warwick; Mr Christopher Warwick; Dr N.F. Whitehead; Mr
Paul Woudhuysen of the Fitzwilliam Museum.

As always, Mr Brian Roberts has given me invaluable advice,
assistance and encouragement.

I am grateful to the staffs of the British Library, the Newspaper
Library at Colindale, the Bath Reference Library, the Bristol Reference Library, the Lansdowne Library, Bournemouth, the Library of
the Société Jersiaise and the Central Library, St Helier, Jersey. I should
like to give a special word of thanks to Mrs S. Bane and the staff of the
Frome Library for their helpfulness and patience.

Although I have listed all books consulted in the Bibliography, I am
particularly indebted to the authors of the various lives of King
Edward VII, as well as to *The Countess of Warwick* by Margaret
Blunden, *The Prince and the Lily* by James Brough and *The Gilded Lily*
by Ernest Dudley.

Prologue

THE PRINCE OF PLEASURE

1

'Whatever Is Most Seductive'

THE OCCASIONS which Queen Victoria had come to dread, almost above all others, were her audiences with Mr Gladstone. There she would sit, small, plump and high-coloured, with her white widow's veil cascading down her back, while her Prime Minister, whom she never allowed to sit, held forth in his hectoring fashion. Nothing seemed able to stop his flow. He would address her, it was said, as though she were a public meeting.

Whereas dear Mr Disraeli used to chat about water-colour painting or the third cousinships of German princes, Mr Gladstone – so runs one inimitable account of these audiences – 'harangues her about the policy of the Hittites, or the harmony between the Athanasian Creed and Homer. The Queen, perplexed and uncomfortable, tries to make a digression – addresses a remark to a daughter, or proffers a biscuit to a begging terrier. Mr Gladstone restrains himself with an effort till the Princess has answered or the dog has sat down, and then promptly resumes. "I was about to say –." Meanwhile the flood has gathered force by delay and when it bursts forth again it carries all before it.'[1]

The subject upon which Gladstone was expounding one March morning in the year 1872 was his master plan for the Queen's heir, the thirty-year-old Prince of Wales. This, in turn, was an aspect of a still more extensive subject which the Prime Minister had entitled 'The Royalty Question'.

For some time now Gladstone had been worried about the public image of the British monarchy. A dedicated monarchist, he was afraid that the institution was in danger of losing its appeal. 'To speak in rude and general terms,' he confided, with rare succinctness, to a colleague, 'the Queen is invisible, and the Prince of Wales is not respected.'[2]

About the Queen's 'invisibility' there was nothing that the Prime Minister could do. Ever since the death of her adored husband, the

Prince Consort, over a decade before, Queen Victoria had withdrawn from public life almost completely. All Gladstone's efforts to force her out of her seclusion had proved fruitless. The more robustly he insisted that the Queen show herself, the more resolutely she refused to do any such thing. Her Prime Minister's 'interference with the Queen's personal acts and movements was really abominable,' she exclaimed. Was she to be 'driven and abused till her nerves and health give way with this worry and agitation and interference in her private life?'[3]

Against this blend of obstinacy and indignation even Gladstone was powerless. In the Widow of Windsor, the Grand Old Man had met his match. 'The repellent power which she so well knows how to use has been put in action towards me,'[4] he grumbled. But, never one to abandon a cause, the Prime Minister now turned his attention to that other aspect of 'The Royalty Question': the public life of the Prince of Wales. If the Queen was not prepared to play her royal role, then the heir-apparent must be allowed to play his.

Yet the exact nature of that role was difficult to define. What was an heir-apparent supposed to do? In the past, the Prince of Wales's predecessors – those wayward Hanoverian princes – had invariably set themselves up in political opposition to the monarch. But this prince, for all his feelings of frustration, would never have done that. So the problem remained unresolved. This dilemma, sighed the Prince's private secretary, was inherent in the very nature of sovereignty. 'It has been the same thing with heirs apparent from time immemorial and I fear will continue to be so as long as there are monarchies.'[5] He was right. To this day, the question has not been satisfactorily answered. 'There is no set-out role for me,' the Prince's great-great-grandson, Prince Charles, was to complain over a century later. 'It depends entirely on what I make of it.'[6]

But Queen Victoria's heir was not *allowed* to make anything of it. The perennial difficulty was intensified by her own unyielding attitude. The Prince was left with no worthwhile occupation because this was precisely how his mother wanted it.

This had not always been her attitude. During their eldest son's boyhood, Victoria and Albert, all aglow with good Coburg intentions, had decreed that Bertie – as he was known in the family – 'ought to be accustomed early to work with [them], to have great confidence shown him, that he should be early instructed into the affairs of state.'[7] Their admirable resolve had been short-lived. In spite of – or rather, because of – a system of educational force-feeding, Bertie had never matched up to their exacting standards. He had emerged from these years of intensive study as an amiable but far from intellectual young man. Of Prince Albert's earnestness, industriousness and high-mindedness, he showed no trace. He lived, the disapproving Queen would point out, purely for pleasure.

Not even when his father had died did his mother revise her poor opinion of Bertie's abilities. In any case, the broken-hearted widow was determined that no one, and certainly not her backward heir, should play the political role that her 'adored, Angelic Husband' had once done. Not only did she consider her son to be lacking in intellect but she found him irresponsible, immature and indiscreet. The Queen would neither confide in him nor consult him. The Prince must see nothing, she warned her ministers, of a confidential nature. When one Prime Minister asked if the heir might be allowed to know 'anything of importance' that took place in the cabinet, her answer was a firm 'No'. That would be quite 'improper'. The Prince had no right, she would announce blandly, to meddle.

Nor would she dream of allowing him to represent her in public. 'Properly speaking, no one can represent the Sovereign but Her . . .' she once informed a Home Secretary. 'Her Majesty thinks it would be most undesirable to constitute the Heir to the Crown a general representative of Herself, and particularly to bring Him forward too frequently before the people. This would necessarily place the Prince of Wales in a position of competing, as it were, for popularity with the Queen. *Nothing* should be more carefully avoided.'[8]

In short, it was a hopeless situation. Denied the opportunity either of working with his mother in private or representing her in public, the Prince was obliged to lead an aimless existence. Yet the Queen would cite that very aimlessness as justification for not giving him anything worthwhile to do.

But despite his shortcomings – and there was some substance in the Queen's complaints – the Prince of Wales was not nearly as worthless as his mother imagined. He had considerable diplomatic gifts, great panache and exceptional vitality. These qualities could have been of real service to his mother. Given some active employment and some real responsibility, there was no reason why the Prince of Wales could not have been a credit to the monarchy.

This was certainly Gladstone's view. While appreciating that the Prince was no paragon, the Prime Minister was alive to his good points. The Prince's social ease and sense of showmanship were exactly the qualities which Gladstone found so disturbingly lacking in the Queen. 'He would make an excellent sovereign,' he once said. 'He is far more fitted for that high place than her present Majesty now is.'[9]

It was by making use of the Prince's social talents that Gladstone hoped to compensate for the Queen's regrettable absence from the public stage. Facing her, on that early spring day in 1872, the Prime Minister unveiled his plan for a 'remodelling' of the heir-apparent's life. The Prince of Wales must become the Queen's permanent representative in Ireland; in other words, her viceroy. In this way he would be given 'a worthy and manly mode of life'[10] and at least one leading member of the royal family would be seen to be pulling his weight. And just think of the good it would do for permanently troubled Ireland.

The Queen would not hear of it. Within a day or two of the audience she had returned the ponderously-worded memorandum with which Gladstone had backed up his arguments. The scheme was acceptable to neither Her Majesty nor His Royal Highness. The Queen had always considered it 'a stupid waste of time to try and connect the Royal Family with Ireland'[11] and the Prince of Wales would prefer some employment nearer home. The truth was that Bertie had no intention of exchanging the sophistication of London for the provincialism of Dublin.

But Queen Victoria's blunt rejection did nothing to deter the tenacious Gladstone. Warming to his task, he worked out a still more elaborate plan. This he presented, in the form of a long letter, in July 1872. Now, not only should the Prince represent the Queen in Dublin but he should deputise for her during the London season and spend one month, each autumn, with the army. To this even longer, more presumptuous and more insulting memorandum, the Queen gave an even more crushing reply. She ended by declaring that this was a question 'which more properly concerns herself to settle with the members of her family as occasion may arise.'[12] In other words, it was none of Mr Gladstone's business.

By now anyone else in the kingdom would have let the matter drop. But not Gladstone. Announcing that he had not yet 'discharged his full responsibility in the matter',[13] he ploughed remorselessly on. This time he sent the Queen two communications: a letter in which, under two headings, he again discussed his plans for a reshaping of the Prince's life, and an even longer memorandum in which, under six headings, he set out to prove that the Queen's objections to his scheme were unfounded.

Victoria was astonished. Once again she gave him short shrift. 'The

Queen therefore trusts,' she wrote firmly, 'that this plan may now be considered as *definitely* abandoned.'[14]

Incredibly, it was not. Gladstone wrote a fourth time, mercifully reducing to five the number of headings by which he refuted the Queen's arguments. A brief note from Her Majesty informed him that it was 'useless to prolong the discussion.' Finally beaten, the unconvinced Gladstone contented himself with bemoaning the fact that his views had been 'so unequivocally disapproved by Your Majesty in a matter of so much importance to the interests of the Monarchy.'[15]

The Queen's final verdict on the project was characteristically forthright. Whenever she had a strong conviction about something, she told the Foreign Secretary, 'she generally found she was right.'[16]

So the Prince of Wales remained unemployed. Never again would any serious attempt be made to find him something to do. Now and then a sympathetic Prime Minister might pass him some information but it was not until 1892, when the Prince was over fifty, that he was finally given unrestricted access to all official papers.

But not even his most dedicated apologist could pretend that his lack of any meaningful employment was the only reason for the Prince's frivolous way of life. Albert Edward, Prince of Wales, was a hedonist from the crown of his already balding head to the soles of his elegantly shod feet. Ever since his marriage – in 1863 to the beautiful Princess Alexandra of Denmark – had given him his independence, the Prince had lived in what Queen Victoria called 'a whirl of amusements'. By the 1870s he had established himself as the most fashionable figure in European society.

His lack of good looks – he was short, plump, bulbous-eyed and weak-chinned – were admirably compensated for by his stylish clothes and engaging manner. That thinning hair was invariably covered by a sharply tilted hat. His flaccid lips and receding chin were disguised by a neatly-trimmed beard and moustache. His thickening waist was minimised by superb tailoring. The fashionable cut and often daring fabric of his suits ensured that he never looked insignificant. He was regarded, in the jargon of the day, as a 'heavy swell'. He loved uniforms. Few things delighted him more than sporting the dress uniforms of those honorary colonelships and admiralships so readily bestowed on him by foreign sovereigns.

His charm and geniality were exceptional. 'Warm human kindness,' wrote one Foreign Secretary, 'were the very substance of the man.'[17] He had a genuine desire to please; he loved to be surrounded by happy faces. His thoughtfulness towards servants, his politeness towards strangers, his loyalty towards his friends were legendary. Except in the presence of his formidable mother, the Prince's demeanour was one of complete self-assurance.

The pace of his life was frenetic. Easily bored, averse to reading, wary of intellectual talk, lacking in application, hating desk-work, unappreciative of serious music or anything other than the most blandly representational painting, he flung himself into a ceaseless round of amusements. Between rising early and going to bed late, he filled every minute of his day. There were, of course, minor public duties of the foundation-stone-laying, exhibition-opening variety to be carried out, but by far the greater part of his time was spent in a relentless pursuit of pleasure. He was seen everywhere: at balls, banquets and garden parties; at Goodwood, Doncaster or Ascot for the races; at Cowes for the yachting; on country estates for the shooting; at Covent Garden or Drury Lane; at his own club, the Marlborough, which he had founded after he had fallen foul of stuffier establishments such as White's and the Travellers'; playing baccarat; attending dinner parties or more intimate supper parties; visiting pleasure gardens, music halls or night clubs.

None of this is to say that the Prince of Wales was indistinguishable from any other roistering youngish man-about-town. He never let anyone forget who he was. No matter how informal the occasion, how drunken the company or relaxed the atmosphere, he was very conscious of his dignity. Even his closest companions faced the dilemma of all those who are befriended by members of the royal family, then and now: where to draw the line between friendliness and familiarity. With the Prince, it was a very nicely positioned line indeed. While joining wholeheartedly in the pranks and practical jokes he would freeze at any undue show of presumption or disrespect. Then his pale blue-grey eyes would turn steely and his celebrated affability evaporate.

Once, when an acquaintance with whom he was playing billiards greeted a bad shot with a jocular 'Pull yourself together, Wales!', the Prince promptly sent for the man's carriage. On another occasion, when he gently reproved a badly behaved guest by saying 'Freddy, Freddy, you're very drunk', and the guest retaliated – using the Prince's forbidden nickname and imitating his rolling 'r's – with 'Tum-Tum, you're verrry fat!',[18] the Prince ordered the guest's bags to be packed before breakfast.

Yet the fear of exposing himself to over-familiarity never prevented him from choosing his friends from the widest, most unlikely circles. Quite naturally, he moved amongst the great aristocratic families, or at least, those families who were rich enough to entertain him and amusing enough to divert him. But he was just as ready to befriend anyone whom he found interesting. Both the Prince and Princess of Wales were refreshingly free of social and religious bigotry. To their homes – Marlborough House in London and Sandringham House in Norfolk – were invited a great company of the witty, the worldly or the simply attractive. The Prince had a *penchant* for rich, self-made men: Jewish bankers, South African millionaires, American manufacturers, Midlands industrialists.

'I find the company pleasant and civil,' wrote Bishop Magee of Peterborough after arriving at Sandringham one day in December 1873, 'but we are a curious mixture. Two Jews, Sir Anthony de Rothschild and his daughter; an ex-Jew, Disraeli; a Roman Catholic, Colonel Higgins; an Italian duchess who is an Englishwoman, brought up a Roman Catholic and now turning Protestant; a set of young Lords and a bishop . . .'[19]

The Prince's life, for all its variety and restlessness, was lived within a strict framework. The most punctual and punctilious of men, he insisted on a regular routine. His year followed an unvarying pattern. January and February were spent at Sandringham, shooting, and entertaining that kaleidoscopic collection of guests. From the beginning of March he spent five weeks, *en garçon*, on the French Riviera, including a few days stay in Paris at either end. During the summer he was in London for the season; in August he spent a couple of weeks yachting at Cowes. Sometimes accompanied by Princess Alexandra but more often alone, he enjoyed a much needed cure at some German or Austrian spa. By October he was grouse-shooting or deerstalking in Scotland, and by November he was back at Sandringham.

And wherever he was, either at home or abroad, he would indulge in the one activity which he preferred above all others. For more than racing, shooting, yachting, gambling or eating, the Prince of Wales enjoyed making love.

Even before the days of the long-lensed camera and the twenty-four-hour press vigil, a prince's intimate moments were the subject of close scrutiny and intense interest. There was always a companion to pass on a bit of gossip, an equerry to make a report or a diarist to jot down an entry. So even if the general public was unaware of the full extent of the Prince of Wales's amorous escapades, they did not go unnoticed in his own circles.

Bertie was not quite fourteen when his dawning interest in the opposite sex first became apparent. In 1855 Queen Victoria – accompanied by Prince Albert and their two eldest children, the Princess Royal and the Prince of Wales – paid a state visit to Paris. At the brilliant court of the Second Empire, presided over by the worldly Napoleon III and the beautiful Empress Eugenie, the young Prince first experienced a way of life which he would one day make his own. In the person of the Emperor of the French, Bertie discovered an adult who accepted him for what he was. Here was someone who seemed to take an unashamed delight in the things in which he delighted; who loved show and colour and movement; who lived, quite naturally and openly, for pleasure. To the youngster, whose life had always been narrow, repressed and dedicated to self-improvement, Napoleon III's tolerance and sense of enjoyment were a revelation. This, surely, was how life was meant to be lived.

It was during this state visit that Bertie's great love of France was born. The splendour of the French capital, the liveliness of the French people, the *bonhomie* of the French Emperor, the elegance of the French Empress, all made an indelible impression on his pleasure-hungry nature. From now on it would be towards France, rather than towards Germany (so admired by the rest of his family) that his personality was to be orientated. From the time of his first visit to Paris until the establishment, almost fifty years later, of the *entente cordiale*, he never ceased to work for an understanding between Great Britain and France.

But more, perhaps, than anything, it was the presence of the ladies of the court that set the boy's blood pounding so disturbingly. The young Empress, so beautiful herself, liked to be surrounded by equally beautiful women. In their swaying crinolines and with artificial flowers tucked into their *coiffures*, these chattering, free-and-easy *demoiselles d'honneur* were quite different from his mother's staid ladies-in-waiting. 'In the Tuileries,' notes one Frenchman, 'he breathed for the first time that *odore di femmina* whose trail he was to follow for the rest of his life. The scented, seductive women not only kissed him (was he not a child?) but also curtsied to him, and as they bent forward, their décolletage revealed delights that were veiled at Windsor.'[20]

Within two years, the fifteen-year-old boy was giving more tangible evidence of his appreciation of female attractions. In the course of what was meant to be an educational tour of his father's beloved Rhineland, Bertie, flushed with too much wine, kissed a pretty girl in public. Fortunately, news of the incident (which Gladstone described as a 'squalid little debauch'[21]) did not reach the ears of the Prince Consort. That highly moral parent would almost certainly have ordered his son home before any more Rhine maidens led him into heaven knows what depths of depravity.

Not that the Prince would have had the opportunity for the plumbing of any such depths. He was too closely supervised for that. Nor, frankly, would he have known how to take advantage of any such opportunity. For in spite of his interest in pretty women, Bertie was still sexually immature.

His parents, in their misguided efforts to shield him from tempta-tion, had never left him alone with his contemporaries. Victoria was haunted by 'a great fear of young and carefully brought up boys mixing with older boys and indeed with any boys in general, for the mischief done by bad boys and the things they may hear and learn from them cannot be overrated.'[22] Albert was even more apprehen-sive. In his conviction that boys, left to themselves, would 'talk lewdly'[23] he was determined that Bertie should associate only with 'those who are good and pure.'[24]

So the Prince was almost seventeen before he asked his tutors about the meaning of certain words; quite clearly, he was entirely ignorant about the facts of life. His answer was a lecture on 'the purpose' and, even more important, 'the abuse' of 'the union of the sexes'.[25]

To prevent the young man from being tempted into any such abuse, he was kept well away from those aristocratic young bloods who would, in the ordinary way, have been his natural companions. Both at Oxford and Cambridge, where he spent short and generally unproductive spells, he was obliged to live out of College so that he could be protected from the more rakish elements of undergraduate life. On his various cultural tours of the Continent, and even during his more exciting tour of Canada and the United States in 1860, Bertie was closely watched. His plea that he be allowed to join the army was firmly turned down by his governor, the dour General Bruce. The 'temptation and unprofitable companionship of military life',[26] warned Bruce, were to be avoided at all costs.

But the Prince of Wales could not be kept out of the army forever. In 1861, when he was nineteen, it was agreed that he should spend ten weeks attached to the Grenadier Guards at the Curragh military camp near Dublin. And it was here that General Bruce's apprehensions were confirmed. The Prince not only embraced the 'unprofitable companionship' of military life but, one night after a drunken party in the mess, found himself embracing an actress whom his companions had secretly slipped into his bed.

Her name was Nellie Clifden and she was one of those easy-going, warm-hearted girls whose cheerful promiscuity relieves the sexual act of any semblance of sin. The Prince could hardly have hoped for a better introduction into what was to be a lifetime of love-making. Very taken with Nellie, he continued to see her on his return to England. She, understandably chuffed by her relationship with the heir to the throne (they were calling her 'the Princess of Wales'), boasted about it. In time, the news reached the ears of the Prince Consort.

He was appalled. Whereas any other royal father – before or since – would simply have shrugged the matter off, regarding it, quite properly, as part of the process of growing up, Prince Albert saw it in the blackest possible light. Assuring his son that he had inflicted on him 'the greatest pain I have yet felt in this life'[27] the Prince Consort treated him to one of his most sanctimonious, if anguished, literary outpourings. Bertie was to hide himself, not only from the sight of God, but from the sight of his own father: the Prince Consort was too heart-broken, he wrote, even to see his son.

To understand Prince Albert's reaction to his son's 'evil deed', it is necessary to go back to the early years of his marriage to Queen Victoria. In order to counteract the legacy of the Queen's 'wicked uncles' – that tribe of licentious Hanoverian princes who had brought the British throne into such disrepute – and to control the rising tide of nineteenth-century democracy, the earnest Prince Albert had come up with what could best be described as the 'Coburg' solution. The monarchy must become the most highly respected institution in the land. The royal family must set itself up as an example. Not only must the sovereign be a wise, influential and impartial personality, raised high above the hurly-burly of political life, but, by their unimpeachable morals and high sense of duty, the entire royal family must win the love and admiration of the people.

What Prince Albert had in mind, in fact, was the sort of monarchy which Britain enjoys today. Not all the members of the present royal family might be notable for the unimpeachability of their morals but, by and large, the British monarchy is now a highly respected and very popular institution.

The most important of this race of paragons which the idealistic Prince Albert was hoping to raise was, of course, his eldest son, the future king. Thus far, the young man had shown precious little sign of developing into the sort of enlightened sage of his father's fond aspirations. In fact, in that tug-of-war between Coburg and Hanover for control of the boy's character, his Hanoverian ancestry was winning hands down. Every year these regrettable characteristics were becoming more pronounced.

And now here, in this incident with Nellie Clifden at the Curragh, was proof positive of what Bertie's parents considered to be his bad blood. The Prince Consort's great dream of fashioning the perfect, unsullied heir had been shattered. Not only was the Prince of Wales proving himself sadly lacking intellectually, but he was about to go the way of Queen Victoria's unspeakable uncles.

There was only one possible remedy. An early marriage, decided the Prince Consort, was essential to halt his son's drift into debauchery. Without that, he would be lost. He '*must* not, *dare* not be lost,' wailed Albert. 'The consequences for this country and for the world would be too dreadful!'[28]

Not until Bertie had expressed due contrition did his father consent to see him again. The Prince Consort travelled to Cambridge (where the young man had resumed his education) to pay him a visit. He returned to Windsor exhausted. A week later he collapsed with typhoid fever and a fortnight after this – on 14 December 1861 – he died.

That her adored husband's death had been caused by 'that dreadful business at the Curragh' the Queen had no doubt. Unbeknown to her son, the Prince Consort had told her 'all the disgusting details.' 'I never can or shall look at him without a shudder,'[29] admitted the grief-demented mother in a letter to her eldest daughter, the Crown Princess of Prussia. Indeed, she could hardly bear to look at him at all. But determined that her late husband's every wish should be carried out and believing that marriage would indeed be the only saving of her son, Victoria pushed ahead with the marriage plans.

The Crown Princess was all agreement. 'Marry early Bertie must,' wrote that serious-minded young woman. 'I am more convinced of that every day; he has not resisted small temptations, only launch him alone in London society and you will see what becomes of him . . . the chances are, if he married a nice wife that he likes, she will keep him straight; and, as he is too weak to keep from sin for virtue's sake, he will only keep out of it from other motives, and surely a wife will be the strongest?'[30]

The dispenser of this self-righteous advice was just twenty-one.

The future bride had already been chosen. It had not been an easy choice, for the field, in those days, was considerably narrower than it is today. Whereas nowadays the heir apparent could marry the most humbly-born girl in the world provided she were neither a Roman Catholic nor a divorcée (and that may well change in the not too distant future) Bertie had to marry a princess. It was unthinkable that he should marry anyone not of the Blood Royal. A tireless sifting through the Protestant princesses of Europe had left one candidate: Princess Alexandra of Schleswig-Holstein-Sonderburg-Glucksburg, daughter of the heir to the Danish throne.

Although not meeting all the criteria, Princess Alexandra did meet the most important one: she was good-looking. The Queen, and the Crown Princess of Prussia – who was playing an active part in this choosing of a bride – knew the Prince of Wales well enough to appreciate that he would never settle for a plain wife, no matter how suitable she might be in other ways. In the end, Princess Alexandra was chosen because she had a beautiful face, an excellent figure and a natural elegance.

Even the Queen, although for other reasons, approved of her. 'She is so good, so simple, unaffected, frank, bright and cheerful, yet so quiet and gentle,'[31] she assured the Crown Princess.

Victoria's astute Uncle Leopold, King of the Belgians, had a rather more penetrating remark to make on the future bride. 'There is something frank and cheerful in Alex's character, which will greatly assist her to take things without being too much overpowered or alarmed by them,'[32] he wrote prophetically.

Yet the Queen, still racked by the thought of her son's 'fall', felt that it would be less than fair for the future bride's family to be kept in ignorance about it. She insisted that they be told. But they already knew. To the worldly Danish royal family, the idea of a prince losing his virginity before marriage was neither novel nor shocking; indeed, they would have been a great deal more disturbed if he had not lost it. Whether or not Princess Alexandra knew anything about the affair is uncertain. In any case, she would not have been unduly put out. Like so many women of her day, the Princess probably accepted that there was one code of behaviour for men and another for women.

The couple were married on 10 March 1863. The bridegroom was twenty-one, the bride eighteen. 'It does one good to see people so thoroughly happy as this dear young couple are,' reported the Crown Princess to Queen Victoria after visiting the honeymoon pair at

Osborne. Bertie, she said, looked blissful. 'I never saw such a change, his whole face looks beaming and radiant . . . Love has certainly shed its sunshine on these two dear young hearts and lends its unmistakable brightness to both their countenances.'[33]

The Crown Princess, who was to be proved wrong about so many things, was to be proved wrong about this.

'All the world and the glory of it, whatever is most seductive, has always been offered to the Prince of Wales of his day . . .'[34] wrote that great analyst of the British Constitution, Walter Bagehot. This had been true for the previous Prince of Wales, that celebrated debauchee who became first Prince Regent and then King George IV; and it was to be true for the future Prince of Wales, the capricious young man who was to become King Edward VIII and then Duke of Windsor. But neither of these princes availed themselves of the world's glories and seductions with quite as much uninhibited zest as did Queen Victoria's heir.

The Prince's honeymoon idyll, which had so enchanted the sentimental Crown Princess, did not last very long. Princess Alexandra, for all her grace and beauty, was not the sort to retain the interest of a man like her husband. Perhaps she was sexually cold. Lady Antrim, who knew the Princess well, once claimed that the Prince might have been a more faithful husband if the Princess had been a more loving wife. Certainly, the beauties with whom the Prince of Wales was to enjoy long-term relationships – his mistresses, in short – were all to be voluptuous women.

Nor was Alexandra clever, or at least sharp, enough to satisfy him. She had very little brain. Although the Prince was no intellectual, he liked the company of quick-witted women. A dull-witted beauty might do for the odd amorous encounter, but she could never hope for anything more than that from the Prince. And Alexandra, if not exactly dull-witted, was too simple, too childlike, too artless for her husband's taste. 'Very clever,' noted a worried Queen Victoria not long after the marriage, 'I don't think she is.'[35] The trouble was that the Prince needed constant distraction. Having nothing worthwhile to do and lacking, almost entirely, in mental resources, he was very easily bored. An intellectually stimulating wife could have helped keep this boredom at bay; a stupid one could only increase it.

Causing Princess Alexandra to appear more stupid still was her increasing deafness. Queen Victoria noted this quite early on and, as the years went by, the Princess found it more and more difficult to follow conversation. This not only made her seem somewhat slow but it cut her off from intelligent talk; she was unable to improve or broaden her mind by hearing the opinions of others. Her tendency to avoid people whose voices she found difficult to understand gradually distanced her, not only from that scintillating company in which her husband delighted but from her husband himself. More and more she devoted herself to their five children – two boys and three girls, born between 1864 and 1869 – and to a small circle of companions.

But none of this can explain the Prince of Wales's tireless extramarital activity. It is doubtful whether even the most sensual, sharp-witted or sophisticated of wives could have kept him at home for long. He had a voracious sexual appetite and, having nothing better to do with his time, indulged it to the full. Where another man might have channelled much of that prodigious energy into work, the Prince channelled it into love-making. It was boredom, too, that was responsible for his need for constant change and variety in his sexual partners. During the first fifteen or so years of his marriage, he remained faithful to no one; he made love just as happily to duchesses as he did to prostitutes.

There were a couple of mitigating factors. One was his age. The Prince was only twenty-one when he was dragooned into marriage. Most male Victorian aristocrats married late. Their twenties and even their thirties were the years for sowing wild oats. In the ordinary way the Prince of Wales would have spent that period roistering and whoring with the other young bloods. Marriage would have illustrated a willingness to settle down. But having discovered the delights of promiscuity after marriage, Bertie could see no good reason for giving it up.

Another factor was that he was granted every opportunity for infidelity. To this day, princes are presented with the sort of chances denied to many others. Very few women would withhold their favours from the sons of the monarch. Snobbery, as one of Bertie's biographers has put it, 'is a powerful aphrodisiac'.[36] It would have needed a very strong-minded woman indeed to withstand the heir's advances, particularly when he was as accomplished, persuasive and charming a philanderer as the Prince of Wales. And he, in turn, would have had to have been a saint not to have taken advantage of the opportunities offered to him.

These opportunities were everywhere. Mid-Victorian respectability, so studiously encouraged by Victoria and Albert, was largely confined to one layer of society – the middle classes. The aristocracy, as the Queen only too frequently pointed out to her lusty heir, was anything but respectable. It was quite given over to 'frivolity, the love of pleasure, self-indulgence and idleness'.[37] It was in this happy hunting ground that the Prince of Wales was able to assuage his appetites.

There were other hunting grounds, too. London, behind the grandiose sweep of Regent Street and the imposing façades of Piccadilly, was a maze of mean alleys, ill-lit courts and shabby tenements, where every taste was catered for. More genteel areas, in St John's Wood or on the fringes of Regents Park, offered rather more discreet services. It was in this world – of actresses and chorus girls and courtesans, the world that had given him Nellie Clifden – that the Prince could satisfy his less discerning tastes. The Crown Princess of Prussia was shocked to hear that her brother was to be seen in such disreputable places as Cremorne Gardens or Evans's Supper Rooms. And the King of the Belgians, who was in no position to throw stones, professed himself pained to hear that the Prince of Wales frequented the notorious Midnight Club.

Yet another of the Prince's pleasure arenas was Paris. The periods that he spent there, *en garçon*, were very largely given over to amorous adventures. His Parisian conquests – if they can be called that – ranged from such members of *le gratin* as the Princesse de Sagan to the notorious Hortense Schneider who was known, with abundant reason, as *le passage des princes*.

How much did Princess Alexandra know about her husband's unfaithfulness? 'I often think her lot is no easy one,' wrote Queen Victoria as early as 1864, when the couple had been married for less than two years, 'but she is very fond of Bertie, though not blind.'[38] The Princess would have noticed what others noticed: how her husband was paying too much attention to a certain 'Madame von B' at Sandringham, or how he was 'spooning with Lady Filmer'[39] at Ascot. She would have heard of his involvement with various Russian beauties when he was in St Petersburg in 1866 and of his suppers with 'female Paris notorieties'[40] when he visited France the following year. She must certainly have suspected the worst when, during her long illness in 1867, the Prince stayed out night after night, often not coming home until three in the morning.

And there were things she could not have known about. On one occasion the Prince was obliged to buy back some letters which he had written to Madame Giulia Barucci, one of the great courtesans of the

Second Empire, who was pleased to describe herself as 'the greatest whore in the world'.[41] At the same time he was being asked for money, in an altogether less menacing fashion, on behalf of Lady Susan Vane Tempest who – not being the greatest whore in the world – was apparently about to bear his child.

During his serious illness in 1871, he gave so much away in the course of his fevered ravings that it was thought best to keep Alexandra out of the room. He even, at one stage of his delirium, accused *her* of being unfaithful. 'You were my wife,' he ranted, 'you are no more – you have broken your vows.'[42]

Every now and then, when her husband was involved in some major scandal, Alexandra's private misgivings would become public knowledge. He appeared as a witness in the divorce suit filed by Sir Charles Mordaunt against his wife and, although the Prince emphatically denied that there had been 'any improper familiarity or criminal act' between himself and Lady Mordaunt, the very fact of his association with the young woman (he had written her letters and paid her private calls) caused Alexandra real distress and the public pleasurable indignation.

A few years later he was caught up in an equally unsavoury scandal. In the course of a flirtation, if nothing more, with a Lady Aylesford, he had written her some indiscreet letters. When Lord Aylesford announced his intention of divorcing his wife (not because of her association with the Prince but because of her adultery with one of his friends, Lord Blandford) Lady Aylesford tried to use the incriminating letters to force the Prince to dissuade Lord Aylesford from starting divorce proceedings. In the end, the affair petered out: the Aylesfords merely separated. But by then every drawing room in London was seething with gossip about the Prince of Wales's indiscretion, while the Princess stood once more revealed as the wronged wife.

It was this public humiliation that Alexandra minded most. In private, she was quite prepared to play the game according to the rules of the time. In many upper-class Victorian marriages the husband's infidelity was taken almost as a matter of course. Wives tolerated it in the same way as they might tolerate any other of their husband's failings: extravagance or meanness, weakness or violence. Male unfaithfulness would never have been regarded as a good enough reason for breaking up a marriage, as it is today.

Divorce, in those days, was looked upon as a much greater shame than infidelity; a divorcée, no matter how blameless her own conduct might have been, always trailed an aura of scandal. She was generally regarded as an adventuress. In any case, the divorce laws were such as to discourage the contemplation of any such step. A husband was entitled to keep not only the children but any money or property that the wife might have brought to the marriage. So a divorced wife faced both ostracism and penury. It was no wonder that, during the 1870s, there were under a hundred divorces a year in England.

Even after he became King, Bertie – unashamedly employing the double standards of the period – once refused to be seen in the company of a couple who were about to be separated; and in 1909 he claimed that divorce was a subject 'which cannot be discussed openly and in all its aspects with any delicacy or even decency before ladies'.[43] Not until late in the reign of George V was the 'innocent party' in a divorce admitted to the royal enclosure at Ascot; the 'guilty party' remained barred, regardless of the fact that the enclosure might be teeming with adulterers.

So, very much an exponent of the social code of her time, Alexandra simply swallowed her pride, showed the world a smiling face ('the Princess looked lovely but *very* sad when she was not exerting herself,'[44] reported Lady Cavendish after the Mordaunt divorce trial) and devoted herself to raising her family, preserving her looks and tending to that great army of pugs, pekes and poms without which she seldom moved. 'My naughty little man' was the strongest epithet she seems ever to have applied to her errant husband. Apparently unembittered, she remained a charming, scatterbrained, unpunctual creature, the darling of the public. The Prince, by way of atonement, was always careful to treat her with great respect and courtesy.

There was, for Princess Alexandra, one consolation. Her husband, for all his unfaithfulness, had never fallen seriously in love with anyone else. Not once, in the course of all those tea-time *têtes-à-têtes*, after-theatre suppers or late night assignations in country houses, had he ever met anyone with whom he wished to establish a more lasting relationship. But in the year 1877, at the age of thirty-five, the Prince of Wales met the woman with whom he was to fall in love, and who was to be recognised as his first official mistress.

Part One

'MY FAIR LILY'

The Jersey Lily

TO THIS DAY, Lillie Langtry remains something of an enigma. Even though she lived the most public of lives – as a 'professional beauty', as a royal mistress, as an actress, as a racehorse owner, as a squanderer of fortunes and collector of lovers – she remains elusive. Opinions about her are contradictory; her personality defies definition. To some, she was simply a calculating, cold-hearted creature who used her physical attractions to further her own career; to others she appeared charming, open, with 'far more heart than she was given credit for'.[1] Contemporaries talk of her fascination, her intelligence, even of her erudition. There must surely have been something, other than her marvellous beauty, to attract so great a variety of people, and to win her so remarkable a reputation.

There can be no doubt, though, that it was her beauty that launched the young Mrs Langtry on her glittering way. For at the age of twenty-three, in 1877, she had the advantage not only of being beautiful but of having an unusual type of beauty. Hers were the looks then in favour with the artistic *avant garde*. This is a feature which is often overlooked when assessing beauty of a previous period. In that age of the Pre-Raphaelites, Lillie Langtry was the Pre-Raphaelite woman personified. Everything – the great column of a neck, the square jaw, the well-defined lips, the straight nose, the slate-blue eyes, the pale skin (she was nicknamed Lillie, she tells us, because of her lily-white complexion), even the hair loosely knotted in the nape of the neck – conformed to the artistic ideal of feminine good looks. It was no wonder that so many eminent artists fell over each other in their eagerness to paint her.

Yet, at the same time, Lillie was not one of the languid, ethereal maidens so beloved of the bohemian brotherhood of the day. Her beauty was brought to life by her vivacity. 'How can words convey the vitality, the glow, the amazing charm, that made this fascinating woman the centre of any group that she entered?', asks Daisy, Countess of Warwick, who was one day to supplant Lillie in the affections of the Prince of Wales. 'The friends we had invited to meet the lovely Mrs Langtry were as willingly magnetised by her unique personality as we were.'[2]

And there was something else. Lillie Langtry exuded an aura of sensuality. Her full-breasted, broad-hipped body held the promise of an almost animal passion; she walked, wrote one admirer, 'like a beautiful hound set upon its feet.'[3] There was an abandon about her – an entirely deceptive abandon, for Lillie was one of the most calculating of women – which men found all but irresistible.

It needed only one night, and the right setting, for Lillie's particular combination of qualities to launch her on her meteoric rise to fame. Until that evening early in 1877, she and her husband, the ineffectual Edward Langtry, whom she had married in her native Jersey three years before, had lived a life of almost total obscurity. Although they had been in London for over a year, living in apartments in Eaton Place, they were all but friendless. Their London life had certainly not been the breathless social whirl of Lillie's aspirations. But a chance meeting with Lord Ranelagh, an old roué whom she had known in Jersey, led, in turn, to their first London invitation: a Sunday evening at-home given by Sir John and Lady Sebright in their Lowndes Square house.

Olivia Sebright was one of those self-consciously bohemian hostesses who surround themselves with the cultural élite. A talented amateur actress and singer, she crammed her salon with as many of the leading professional actors, singers, writers and painters as she could muster. On this particular evening she had managed to assemble, among others, such luminaries as Henry Irving, John Everett Millais, James McNeill Whistler, George Francis Miles and that socially influential essayist and diner-out, Abraham Hayward. It was not, admittedly, an exclusively upper-class gathering ('actors and actresses were not then generally received,'[4] notes Lillie) but in Lady Sebright's crowded drawing room the aristocratic and artistic worlds overlapped. For Lillie, it was the ideal springboard.

Among the throng of sumptuously dressed, glitteringly bejewelled and toweringly coiffured women, Mrs Langtry struck a highly individual note. Her simple black dress had been run up by a Jersey dressmaker, she wore no jewels or ornaments ('I had none,'[5] she admits candidly), and she had twisted her golden-brown hair into a casual knot on the nape of her neck. The effect was dramatic. Yet, on this occasion at least, it was not studied. Lillie simply could not afford anything more elaborate.

Feeling, she assures us, 'very un-smart and countrified', she 'retired to a chair in a remote corner.' Her corner did not remain remote for long. The sight of this decorously dressed, ravishingly beautiful and curiously erotic young woman acted like a magnet on the company. 'Fancy my surprise,' continues her arch account of this memorable evening, 'when I immediately became the centre of attention and, after a few moments, I found that quite half the people in the room seemed bent on making my acquaintance.'[6] The half was, of course, the male half. And from 'the rush of cavaliers' begging to take her down to supper, Lillie chose John Everett Millais. Not only was he a fellow Jerseyman and the handsomest man in the room, but he was the most famous painter in the country.

Inevitably, over the supper table, Millais asked the enchanting Mrs Langtry to sit for him. He wanted to be the first painter 'to reproduce on canvas what he called the "classic features" of his countrywoman.'[7] After a token protest, she agreed.

That evening at the Sebrights' transformed Lillie Langtry's life. The particular *milieu* – aesthetic, arty-crafty, unconventional – into which she had just been introduced was always on the lookout for new diversions, new sensations and new faces. And there were few faces as striking as hers. Within a few days the hall table of her Eaton Place apartment was heaped with invitations – to lunch, to dine or to dance. By the end of the month the Langtrys' landlady was grumbling about the number of times she was having to answer the door as yet another liveried footman delivered yet another gilt-edged invitation.

For the gratified Lillie Langtry, her girlhood dreams were at last coming true.

On the face of it, Lillie Langtry's background was highly respectable. She had been born Emilie Charlotte Le Breton on 13 October 1853 in the Old Rectory, St Saviour, Jersey. Her father was the Very Reverend William Corbet Le Breton, Dean of Jersey, a man notable – or so she tells us – for 'his zeal and solicitous care for the poor'. Her mother, born Emilie Davis Martin, was apparently a paragon among women: poetic, musical, devoted to animals, flowers and fresh air. Both were exceptionally good-looking. The Dean was well over six feet tall, with piercing blue eyes, a head of prematurely white hair and a military bearing. 'Do you know Sir,' exclaimed one general on first meeting the stalwart Dean Le Breton, 'that when you joined the Church, there was a deuced fine sergeant-major spoilt!'[8] Lillie was convinced that the stage, rather than the army, had suffered the greater loss. For her father had, besides his commanding presence, 'the true histrionic gift' and an exceptionally good memory.

Mrs Le Breton, on the other hand, was small and fragile. But she was no less attractive. Charles Kingsley, who had known her as a girl in Chelsea, once described her as 'the most bewitchingly beautiful creature he had ever seen'.[9] This handsome couple had seven children; Lillie, the last but one, was their only daughter. The grey stone deanery, all but smothered in climbing roses and sweet-scented jasmine, was one of the most picturesque houses in Jersey. The island itself, with its mild climate and lushly-wooded valleys, was a delectable place in which to live.

But life in the deanery was not quite as idyllic as it appeared. As in many another Victorian vicarage, dark undercurrents surged beneath the apparently tranquil waters. Lillie's claim, in her discreetly written memoirs, that her father was 'widely adored for his geniality and charm of disposition'[10] was truer than she intended it to be. Her comment, made privately many years later, was nearer the mark. 'He was a damned nuisance,' she grumbled, 'he couldn't be trusted with any woman anywhere.'[11]

For Dean Le Breton was, in the polite terminology of the day, 'a ladies' man'. Stories about his rampant womanising ranged from the ludicrous to the scandalous. Amy Menzies, writing anonymously as 'A Woman of No Importance', tells one about the Dean emerging from church with a notable beauty on each arm: one was Mrs Knatchbull, the other Lady de Saumerez. At the sight of the notoriously lecherous Dean, the irate husbands, who had been waiting outside the church, set about him with their walking sticks. Le Breton, well practised, apparently, in avoiding angry husbands, managed to slip away, leaving Colonel Knatchbull and Admiral de Saumerez to continue the fight – but by this time against each other.

In the more serious battle – between Dean Le Breton's soul and his flesh – it was the flesh that usually won. Very few of the island's serving maids or flower sellers had the courage to refuse their favours to this muscular man of God. Jersey seethed with rumours about his amorous exploits. His distinctive features were said to have been reproduced time and again among the island's population. There was even a postman, in later years, who bore an uncanny resemblance to the by then long-dead Dean.

It was no wonder that Mrs Le Breton – again in true Victorian wifely tradition – took to her bed. Her frequent and unexplained illnesses could hardly have been serious for she lived to a ripe old age, having long outlasted, and apparently forgiven, her faithless husband. 'An exquisite little woman, plump and as pink and white as a baby when she was seventy years old,' runs one account of Mrs Le Breton in old age, 'with a reverent and sacredly-held fidelity to her husband, the Dean of Jersey, whom she always extolled in a quiet, proud and wifely way, speaking of him as "my dear husband, the Dean".'[12]

Lillie had good reason, it seems, to remember her father's extramarital activities. For she first learned about them in the most brutal way. Many years later, in the course of one of her highly-coloured bouts of reminiscence, she told the story. At sixteen she had fallen in love with a slightly younger, socially inferior but extremely handsome boy. So passionate, apparently, was her attachment to him that when her father asked her to break off the relationship with this unsuitable youngster, she refused. There was nothing for it but for the Dean to reveal the true reason for his objections to the association: the boy was his illegitimate son. For the adolescent Lillie, the revelation came as a double blow: not only did she suffer the anguish of a broken romance, but she suffered a disillusionment about her father whom, until then, she had 'adored to the extent of a fixation'.[13]

Perhaps, in recounting the incident, the ageing Lillie Langtry may have dramatised its details and exaggerated its impact, but it seems unlikely that she would have invented the episode.

By the age of sixteen, the young Lillie Le Breton was already developing a distinctly unconventional streak. Her upbringing – with her father so often immersed in both pastoral and sexual activities, and her mother so often confined to her couch – had been relatively unrestrained. The only girl among six brothers, she tended to take her tone from them: she was tomboyish, hoydenish, devil-may-care. There was almost nothing of the demure Victorian miss about her; she apparently did very little in the way of embroidery, flower-pressing or water-colour painting. While her brothers attended Victoria College, she was educated at home, first by a governess and then by some of her brothers' tutors. Meeting few other girls and then not really liking those she met, she joined her brothers in their pranks and practical jokes; she would do almost anything for a dare. There is even one story of her running naked, at dead of night, along a country lane.

She was determined to prove that she was her brothers' equal. 'I must steady my nerves, control my tears, and look at things from a boy's point of view,'[14] she remembered.

The result of all this was that the young Lillie Le Breton learned, early on, to make her way in a man's world. She became accustomed to the company of men. She never suffered from any feelings of inadequacy or timidity in their presence. She learned not only how to handle them, but how to dominate them.

Allied to her exceptional self-assurance was her exceptional beauty. Few could believe that this radiantly lovely, physically mature creature was still a child. Was it any wonder that she received her first proposal of marriage at the age of fourteen? Or that Lord Suffield, recently appointed lord-in-waiting to Queen Victoria and a regular visitor to Jersey, once declared, 'Do you know, Miss Le Breton, that you are very, very beautiful? You ought to have a season in London.'[15]

Yet when she did have that season in London, it was a humiliating failure. At the age of sixteen her mother took her to England and for several nightmarish weeks Lillie tried to cope with this unfamiliar world of expensive clothes, polished manners and social chit-chat. The nightmare culminated at a party given by Lord and Lady Suffield. 'When I walked into the ballroom,' remembered Lillie many years later, 'I felt like a clumsy peasant. My one "party gown", which had been made for me in St Helier, made me look like one of the serving maids. I had never waltzed, and could follow the leads of none of my dancing partners. The food was strange and never have I seen so many forks and spoons at one's supper place, I had no idea which to use. I disgraced myself so often I could scarcely wait until the evening came to its abysmal end.'[16]

But the experience did not crush her already resilient spirit. Back in Jersey, Lillie set about improving both her mind and her manners. She studied hard. 'Between the ages of sixteen and twenty,' she afterwards wrote, 'I learned the magic of words, the beauty and excitement of poetic imagery. I learned there was something in life other than horses, the sea, and the long Jersey tides.'[17]

Despite her lyrically expressed reflections, it was not by plumbing the depths of literary appreciation that Lillie was hoping to compensate for the shallowness of the long Jersey tides: her ambitions were altogether more down to earth. She wanted to establish herself in English society. 'I was possessed by a conviction that my destiny lay in London,'[18] she says. And as the only possible way for her to fulfil this destiny was through marriage, Lillie consciously set about finding herself a suitable husband. Somewhere there must be a Prince Charming who would take her away from the limitations and longueurs of life in Jersey; who would offer her a wider stage on which to display her physical charms and social talents.

Lillie was twenty before she met such a man. None of her other suitors had been considered worldly enough by her or elevated enough by her parents. Not that Edward Langtry was that brilliant a catch: a twenty-six-year-old widower (Lillie puts his age as thirty in her memoirs) whose first wife, another beauty living in Jersey named Jane Frances Price, had died a couple of years before. Plump, phlegmatic, with a drooping moustache and resigned expression, Edward Langtry was hardly the shining knight of Lillie's imaginings. His interests were confined to sailing and fishing. He was not even, by the yardstick of the day, particularly well-born: his father and his grandfather had been Belfast shipowners, pioneers of the service across the Irish Sea to Liverpool.

But there were, as far as Lillie was concerned, certain compensatory factors. Langtry claimed to have taken a degree at Oxford and to have studied, if not practised, law. He had a house in England. And, above all, he was rich. Or rather, Lillie thought he was rich. Indeed, it was a party aboard his yacht, 'Red Gauntlet', then lying off St Helier, that first awakened Lillie's interest in him. 'One day there came into the harbour a most beautiful yacht,' she is reported to have said in later life. 'I met the owner and fell in love with the yacht. To become the mistress of the yacht, I married the owner, Edward Langtry.'[19]

Perhaps, at the time, it was not quite as calculated as that. But Lillie might well have seen in Edward Langtry the sort of man whom she would be able to mould, who would be a provider without expecting too much in return, and who would, above all, enable her to establish herself in society.

With the grudging consent of her parents, both of whom thought that she could have done better for herself, Lillie Le Breton was married to Edward Langtry, by her father, in St Saviour's Church on 9 March 1874.

The first two years of Lillie's married life were a period of deep disillusion. They were spent not, as she had imagined, in London but partly in Jersey, partly on another of Edward's yachts, 'Gertrude', and partly in their first English home, Cliffe Lodge, overlooking Southampton Water. Edward turned out to be poorer, less amenable and even duller than she had imagined. While she battled with the complexities of running a home for the first time, he spent his days drinking and yarning with his yachting cronies. 'We had so little to say to one another,' she complains, 'that we began to eat breakfast separately. Edward usually went off to join friends in Southampton at noon, so we rarely spent much time with each other until we dined together in the evening.'[20]

Many years later Lillie confessed that the intimate side of her marriage had been unrewarding; Edward had never aroused her sexually. In fairness to him, no Victorian husband expected his wife to enjoy the act of love-making, any more than she expected to enjoy it. Brides approached the marriage bed in a state not only of unsullied chastity, but of almost total ignorance. At best, they would have been told by their embarrassed mothers not to deny their husbands their 'rights'. 'Now you know what has to be done, so don't make a fuss,'[21] were one husband's brisk instructions to his terrified wife as he climbed into bed on their wedding night.

What disappointed Lillie most of all was the fact that she was still no more part of the world of fashionable society than she had ever been. Not until she contracted typhoid fever, late in 1875, while living in Southampton, was Lillie able to take a step towards the realisation of her dreams. The doctor, she assures us unblinkingly, suggested that the best possible place for her to convalesce would be London.

'I have no idea,' she protests, 'what led us to select the great, smoky city as a sanatorium.'[22] But select it she did, and early in 1876 the Langtrys settled into an apartment in Eaton Place.

But another year – of visiting museums and picture galleries, of strolling through pleasure gardens, of going to Hyde Park in the hope of seeing a member of the royal family ride by ('I had never set eyes on even a minor one,'[23] says Lillie) – passed before the chance meeting with her Jersey acquaintance, old Lord Ranelagh, led to that invitation to Lady Sebright's at-home.

It was this invitation, claims Lillie, 'that completely changed the current of my life'.[24]

In the months after the Sebrights' party, Lillie Langtry developed into one of the most sought-after women in London. Swiftly and surely she progressed from the artistic salons of women like Lady Sebright to the grandest drawing rooms in the land. 'There was scarcely a great house in London that I did not visit during my first season,'[25] she boasts.

She was fortunate in her timing. Society, by the late 1870s, was undergoing a transformation. Until then, the English aristocracy had been an exclusive clan, made up of about ten thousand people who, in turn, belonged to about fifteen hundred families. A title (the older the better) or a long established lineage were two of the qualifications necessary to belong to this select group; a third was the ownership of land. The upper classes were all landowners; over ninety per cent of the land was privately owned. No one could hope to be regarded as an aristocrat unless he could boast a great country estate and a great country house. Most of this privileged group knew one another or about each other; they almost never married out of their class. And just as rarely did they welcome anyone into their ranks who did not meet these qualifications.

But in the course of the last few years things had begun to change. Much of this was due to the attitude of the Prince of Wales. With his penchant for very rich men – whether they be self-made, Jewish or foreign, or indeed all three – he extended the boundaries of the upper classes beyond the gilded stockade of the landed aristocracy. Business acumen, beauty and, to a lesser extent, brains were becoming enough to get one accepted. Men like Baron Ferdinand de Rothschild, whose recent forebears had been humble money lenders; women like Lady Waldegrave, whose father had been a Jewish singer, or Lady Molesworth, the daughter of an obscure writing master; all these were not only being accepted but were often leading social lights.

As well as acquiring vast country estates and building palatial country houses, the *nouveaux riches* were marrying off their daughters to the sons of local aristocrats. Many a crumbling mansion was being restored and many a bankrupt estate being salvaged by the uninhibited use of the dowry brought by the daughter of some industrialist from Cleveland, Ohio, or some mineowner from Johannesburg, Transvaal. Not until the Roaring Twenties or the Swinging Sixties was there again to be such a breaking down of class barriers or such a relaxation of social conventions.

It was this opening-up of society that partly explains the ease with which Lillie Langtry was accepted; partly, but not entirely. Much of her success was due to her own particular qualities. For one thing, she was not some brash *arriviste*. She was, by Victorian standards, a lady. Her husband, whatever his shortcomings, did not do anything so vulgar as work for his living. His grandfather might have been a self-made shipping magnate, but Edward was a gentleman of leisure. Then Lillie herself was the daughter of the Dean of Jersey; and clergymen's daughters, if not exactly aristocratic, were certainly socially acceptable. In the Victorian hierarchy, clergymen ranked beside the landed gentry. Indeed, one of Lillie's brothers was to marry Lord Ranelagh's daughter.

Her air, despite her vivacity and sensuality, was well-bred: she knew how to conduct herself in public. Some witnesses even talk of her 'shyness' in these early days. Lillie displayed none of the brittle, metallic self-assurance of a woman like Wallis Simpson who, over half a century later, was to set so many aristocratic teeth on edge. Her fascination was of an altogether more subtle variety.

And it says a great deal for that fascination when one remembers that she lacked the one sure entrée into this expanding upper class world: money. Edward Langtry was not anything like as rich as Lillie had at one time imagined. As so often happens, the Langtry dynasty was going from rags to riches and back to rags in three generations. Edward had no head for finance. In his efforts to keep up with the yachting fraternity, with those millionaires who raced three-hundred-ton cutters, he had squandered his inheritance. By now almost everything – Cliffe Lodge in Southampton, the stud of hunters, the coach and four, and the yachts – had gone. He was having to depend almost entirely on the rents from various properties which he still owned in Ireland. Nor was his suddenly burgeoning social life doing anything to conserve what little remained of his fortune.

Lillie, in common with most Victorian wives, knew very little about the state of her husband's finances. But she did not need to be a financial expert to appreciate that they had no country house, no town house, not even a carriage, of their own. And others, of course, appreciated it as well.

But then, in addition to her beauty and her personal magnetism, Lillie had something else to offer: her curiosity value. Within weeks of Lady Sebright's party, Lillie's had become one of the best-known faces in London.

Her meeting, at the Sebrights, with the artists John Everett Millais and Frank Miles had borne almost immediate fruit. Although Miles's sexual preference – as was the case with many another Victorian literary or artistic notability – was for little girls, he was not blind to Lillie's possibilities. He apparently sketched her there and then and, a day or two later, did another drawing of her which he sold to a printer. The picture, reproduced in its thousands, began appearing in shop windows all over London; within weeks Lillie's distinctive features had become familiar to a huge public. 'My sketches of Lillie during her first London season,' wrote Miles twenty years later, 'earned far more

than I've ever made on the largest commissions for my most expensive paintings.'[26]

There was an equally large and no less appreciative public for her
next portrait. Millais used her as the model for 'Effie Deans' in his
painting of a scene from Sir Walter Scott's famous novel, *The Heart of
Midlothian,* which he exhibited in the Marsden galleries in King Street.
'Her sweet lips are parted,' enthused one critic, 'and there seems to
linger on them a trace of the last quivering sob which made the blue,
upturned eyes glisten. It is in this sorrow-laden mouth, in the azure
depths of tenderness in her appealing eyes that the rare art of Mr
Millais is exemplified to a marked degree.'[27]

Here, in short, was the sort of sentimental story-picture to wrench
the hearts and quicken the pulses of the aristocratic patrons who
flocked to the King Street gallery. And not only them: engravings of
'Effie Deans' were soon adorning walls of middle-class sitting rooms
throughout the land.

Millais's next picture of Lillie, which he was to exhibit at the Royal
Academy of 1878, would make her even more famous. He painted
her, not as she imagined he would, 'in classic robes or sumptuous
medieval garments'[28] but in a simple black dress, with lace collar and
cuffs. She was, Millais told her, the most exasperating subject he had
ever painted. For fifty minutes of each hour, she looked only 'beautiful', but for the other ten she looked 'amazing'.

One touch of colour relieved the sombre tones of the painting: in
her left hand Lillie holds a fragile crimson flower. This was a *Nerine
sarniensis,* a species of amaryllis which grows on Guernsey and which
Millais, inaccurately, referred to as a Jersey lily. But inaccurate or not,
he titled his painting 'A Jersey Lily' and it was as the Jersey Lily that
Lillie Langtry was to be known from then on.

Winning Lillie even wider recognition were her photographic
likenesses. At a time when photography was a relatively new art and
an appreciation of feminine beauty at one of its heights, reproductions
of attractive women were being bought by a vast public. Known as
'professional beauties', these women – or ladies, for they were almost
all members of society – were photographed in every conceivable
attitude: clasping bunches of artificial flowers; lolling in hammocks
under riotously blossoming branches; gazing dolefully at dead birds;
standing swathed in furs amid fake snow-storms. The craze for
collecting these pictures – a craze foreshadowing the popularity of first
film stars and then pop stars – was not confined to the middle classes;
many an aristocratic drawing room boasted a leather-bound, brass-

locked album featuring the Junoesque charms of the Duchess of Leinster, the delicate profile of Mrs Luke Wheeler or the piquant expression of the Marquis of Headfort's daughter, Mrs Cornwallis West.

The most ardently collected pictures of all were those of Lillie Langtry. Whether the photographers 'one and all besought'[29] her – as she claims – to sit for them, or whether she suggested it herself, one does not know; what is certain is that before very long her voluptuous features were familiar all over London. And as the professional beauties, or P.B.s, were much sought after by hostesses ('*Do* come', they would scrawl on their invitation cards, 'the P.B.s will be here'[30]) Mrs Langtry soon found herself much in demand.

The society into which Lillie was being swept was a brilliant one. Her first London season, spanning the months between late April and early August, meant a succession of parties. Often she was invited to as many as three a night. 'I see striped awnings,' recalls one member of this vanished world, 'linkmen with flaring torches; powdered footmen; soaring marble staircases; tiaras, smiling hostesses; azaleas in gilt baskets; white waistcoats, violins, elbows sawing the air, names on pasteboard cards, quails in aspic, macedoine, strawberries and cream . . .'[31]

Lillie's breathless account of that first season teems with titles: the Duchess of Westminster invites her to stay in the country, Lady Rosslyn asks her to join her for a drive in the Park, Lord Hartington drenches his evening clothes as he pulls water lilies out of a marble pool to present to her.

Trailing disconsolately behind Lillie on all these occasions was her husband Edward. It would have been unthinkable, of course, for her to have been invited without him. But as much as she revelled in all this social activity, so did he loathe it. 'My husband greatly disliked all this publicity,' she reports blandly, 'sometimes losing his temper and blaming *me*.'[32] But such, apparently, was the force of Lillie's personality that Edward never actually refused to accompany her. One's heart goes out to him. Night after night this dull but inoffensive man, who asked for nothing more than a day's quiet fishing or a night's drinking with his yachting mates, was obliged to get into white tie and tails and stand awkwardly in some corner while his wife enchanted the assembly with her beauty, her vivacity and her sexuality. 'My husband,' says Lillie with a flash of that steel that was as much part of her personality as was her charm, 'felt quite like a fish out of water.'[33]

Throughout this kaleidoscopic social whirl, Lillie had appeared in her only evening dress: the black one which she had worn to Lady Sebright's party. 'I dined with Lord Wharncliffe last night,' reported Lord Randolph Churchill to his wife, Jennie, during the early days of Lillie's rise to fame, 'and took in to dinner a Mrs Langtry, a most beautiful creature, quite unknown, very poor, and they say has but one black dress.'[34]

It was not only Lillie's relative poverty that kept her in her black dress. In December 1876, her younger brother Reggie had died as the result of a riding accident in Jersey, and this meant that Lillie had to wear mourning. It was not until Lady Dudley, on inviting her to a ball some months later, 'tactfully and gracefully' asked Lillie not to wear black as Lord Dudley 'could not bear the idea of anyone appearing at his house in that sombre hue',[35] that Lillie put off her mourning.

So, instead of appearing at Dudley House in black, Lillie wore white. The effect was hardly less dramatic. The dress, of white velvet embroidered with pearls, was classically simple: its bodice was low-cut and close-fitting; its skirt, drawn tightly back into a bustle, emphasised the seductiveness of her hips and the length of her legs.

'Looking back,' she says, 'and judging from the sensation it caused, it must have been a striking creation. As I entered the ballroom the dancers stopped and crowded round me, and as I pursued my way to greet my hostess, they opened out to allow me to pass.'[36]

But it was not, for all Lillie's assertion, her dress that caused the crowd to part like the Red Sea as she entered the ballroom. Nor was it because of her fame as a professional beauty. By now the word had got out that the Prince of Wales was very interested in the delectable Mrs Langtry.

At the apex of the society up which Lillie Langtry was so resolutely climbing was the royal family. Whereas today the monarchy is a supra-national body, trying its best to stand above class and faction, then it was as much a social as a political institution; the sovereign was not only the head of state but the head of society. The royal family crowned the social pyramid; they were the star on the Christmas tree of a class structure that appeared fixed and immutable. These days, almost anyone, provided they have discharged some sort of civic duty, stands a chance of being invited to the Palace; a century ago, such an invitation would have signified that one was a member of society – of the charmed circle of aristocratic families. Not until after the First World War did the crown, in the realisation that its appeal must be to all its subjects, begin to distance itself from the great families and from the so-called ruling class.

With Queen Victoria proving herself to be, in Gladstone's phrase, 'invisible', it fell to the Prince of Wales to carry out – only too happily – those social functions which were considered a very proper part of royal obligations and duties. Not only did he preside over such official occasions as investitures and presentation parties but, as the acknowledged leader of fashion, he attended private balls, receptions and garden parties. To entertain, or be entertained by, a member of the royal family was regarded as a tremendous social triumph; even to meet one of the princes or princesses socially was to indicate that one was moving in very elevated circles indeed.

The first two members of the royal family whom Lillie Langtry met were Queen Victoria's fourth daughter, the twenty-nine-year-old Princess Louise, then Marchioness of Lorne and afterwards Duchess of Argyll, and the Queen's youngest son, the twenty-three-year-old Prince Leopold, afterwards Duke of Albany. Both these royals fancied themselves as bohemians; they moved in artistic, relatively unconventional circles. Princess Louise – handsome, emancipated, sharp-tongued – was a talented sculptress. Her marriage, in 1871, to the Marquess of Lorne, who succeeded to the dukedom in 1900, was unhappy; Lorne was said to be homosexual. Lillie first met this high-spirited princess in Frank Miles's 'dusty old studio' in his rambling house just off the Strand. Here, late most afternoons, would gather many of the leading actors, artists and writers of the day.

Prince Leopold she met in more conventional surroundings: at a dinner party given by the Marchioness of Ely. But he, too, was often to be found at Frank Miles's studio. Slim and slight, with soulful eyes, a waxed moustache and a wispy imperial beard, Prince Leopold had a romantic, almost Byronic air. Lillie talks of his artistic interests and 'marked intellectuality'[37] and certainly, to the public, he was known as the Scholar Prince. Unfortunately, Prince Leopold suffered from what was euphemistically termed 'very delicate health'; he was in fact a haemophiliac, a sufferer of the dreaded 'bleeding disease'. As such, he tended to be kept very firmly under Queen Victoria's wing. Prince Leopold's short life (he was to die, at the age of thirty, in 1884) developed into a tug-of-war between his mother's understandable possessiveness and his own, no less understandable, determination to break free.

On this score, Lillie has an amusing story to tell. Prince Leopold would often come to Miles's studio to watch the artist doing sketches of her. On one occasion he bought one of these sketches, a portrait showing Lillie in profile, with her name 'being delicately suggested by a background of faintly pencilled lines.' This the Prince hung over his bed. It remained there until one day, when he was laid up with yet another of his bleeding attacks, the Queen came to see him. At the sight of the portrait of the by now celebrated Mrs Langtry, the disapproving Queen Victoria immediately took it down; 'standing on a chair,' claims Lillie, 'to do so.'[38]

It was neither in an artist's studio nor at a grand dinner table that Lillie Langtry met her next member of the royal family. She was introduced to the Prince of Wales, on 24 May 1877, at an intimate supper party given by Sir Allen Young at his home in Stratford Place.

Sir Allen Young, known to his friends as 'Alleno', was one of those Victorian prototypes: a swashbuckling, chivalrous, clear-eyed adventurer, ready to devote himself to the cause of Queen and Empire. His particular field of endeavour was arctic exploration. Twice, in 1875 and 1876, he had, at his own expense, sailed his yacht 'Pandora' in a brave but futile attempt to discover the North-west Passage – that elusive arctic sea route joining the Atlantic and Pacific oceans. In recognition of his services, he had been knighted in March 1877.

Sir Allen was also one of that coterie of discreet and wealthy bachelors who could be relied upon to arrange the sort of evenings that the Prince of Wales enjoyed above all others: intimate, informal suppers in slightly *risqué* company. Not all his bachelor friends, though, were equally accommodating. A request, through the Prince's private secretary, that Lord Rosebery make his house in Berkeley Square available as 'a rendezvous for the Prince of Wales and the Duke of Edinburgh [his brother] to meet their "actress friends" '[39] was politely but firmly turned down by Rosebery. His home, protested his lordship, was too small.

Ten people, including Mr and Mrs Edward Langtry, had been invited to this particular supper. And although Lillie seems to have had no idea that the Prince had been invited, there can be little doubt that the Prince knew that she would be there. Perhaps that old roué, Lord Ranelagh, had told him about her; perhaps the Prince had seen her photograph or heard of her great beauty; perhaps Sir Allen, knowing something of His Royal Highness's taste in women, had decided that they should meet.

The time could hardly have been more opportune. With the Princess of Wales away visiting her brother, King George of the Hellenes, the Prince (who had himself only just returned from his annual spring holiday in the South of France) was free to indulge himself with even less restraint than usual.

As the company stood waiting for supper to be announced, the host suddenly disappeared from the room. The puzzled Lillie heard a slight commotion outside and then came the sound of a genial, guttural voice saying, 'I am afraid that I am a little late.'[40] A few seconds later the Prince of Wales entered the room.

The presence of royalty can strike panic into even the bravest of hearts and the most equable of temperaments and Lillie, despite her self-assurance, proved no exception. Her first impression of the Prince was blurred; she noticed only a dazzle of orders pinned to his chest. While Bertie, in his affable way, shook hands with the head-nodding men and curtseying women, she stood numbed. Should she escape up the chimney? But when the moment of introduction came, she executed her curtsey perfectly and then 'greatly enjoyed watching my husband go rather stammeringly through a similar ordeal.'[41]

Sir Allen had, of course, seated her beside the Prince at table and in no time Bertie was subjecting her to his practised brand of courtship: the chuckling laugh, the complimentary remarks, the caressing glance, the absorbed expression. Two things, other than his flattering attentiveness, Lillie especially noticed about the Prince. One was his great good nature; the other his dignity. 'I decided that he would have been a very brave man who, even at this little *intime* supper party, attempted a familiarity with him,'[42] she wrote.

One cannot know what the Prince said to Lillie on taking his leave but one may be sure that he would have asked whether he could pay her an afternoon call. And that she, as she sank down into her curtsey, would have known exactly what such a call signified.

The Prince of Wales, instigator of so many social changes, was in no small measure responsible for the establishment of a revised code of sexual behaviour among the aristocracy during the second half of the nineteenth century.

Until then, with upper-class girls having to remain unblemished until the wedding night, their male relations had been obliged to confine their sexual activities to women of a lower social status. These rich, idle and self-confident young – and not so young – men could always find a servant girl to seduce or a prostitute to sleep with. London alone could boast a quarter of a million prostitutes. In this way, the virginity of their sisters and daughters could be preserved and the purity of their blood lines be ensured.

'Society girls,' writes one of their number, 'if not as innocent as they were pure, were often unbelievably ignorant of the physical facts of marriage. Marriage – their goal, their destiny, their desire – was all in a rosy haze. Afterwards, as wives, they accepted the code of their day as unchanging and unchangeable. Nearly all the young men had mistresses, so most bridegrooms had a second establishment to pension off or maintain. If a society woman met a man – even her own brother – in the park or a restaurant when he was accompanied by his mistress or an actress, he would not raise his hat to her. He cut her, and she understood.'[43]

All this – the untouchability of young unmarried women and the libertinism of their brothers or fathers or uncles – remained unchanged. What the Prince of Wales did change, or helped change, was the attitude towards adultery. As it was not really practical, or advisable, for the Prince to consort too often with prostitutes or chorus girls and as he did not really want to set up a 'second establishment', he solved the problem by making love to young married women. In that way, provided the husband was either unsuspecting or complaisant, the Prince was able to have the best of all worlds. He could enjoy the favours of a beautiful young aristocrat without having deflowered her; knowledge of the liaison would be confined to a relatively small circle; and, perhaps most important of all, he was able to choose the sort of woman who could give him more than just sexual satisfaction.

For Bertie was one of those men for whom feminine company, in or out of bed, was essential. 'He was never happier,' claims one of his secretaries, 'than in the company of pretty women.'[44] He was interested in their clothes, their pastimes and their chatter. Never one for exchanging smutty jokes over the port with the other men, the Prince would far rather be in the drawing room talking to some stylishly dressed, sharp-witted beauty. 'What tiresome evenings we shall have,'[45] he once sighed, when his wife's mourning for the death of her father obliged him to hold a series of men-only dinner parties.

As London was almost entirely lacking in the sort of women who flourished in Paris – those *demi-mondaines* who were not only sexually available but witty, informed and intelligent – the Prince of Wales was obliged to seek their equivalent among the young married women of his circle. And they were only too happy to oblige the heir to the throne. Condoned by the Prince, adultery became, if not exactly respectable, certainly acceptable. Once a wife had borne her husband an heir, she was considered fair game. Provided everything was organised in a civilised manner and that certain rules of discretion were adhered to, these liaisons between married people became more and more commonplace. They had not, of course, been unknown in earlier, more rakish, periods but they were now regarded as less reprehensible.

So it was along the by now generally accepted lines that the Prince's relationship with Lillie Langtry developed. After the initial flirtation at Sir Allen Young's supper table, there would have been a letter delivered to Lillie's Eaton Place address and then Bertie would have paid her an afternoon call. These calls were very much part of the prescribed routine of courtship. No husband would be at home at that hour: he would be at his club, or else calling on some other man's wife. The visiting gentleman would leave his hat, cane and gloves, not in the hall but on a chair in the drawing room, so giving the impression that he had simply dropped in for a few minutes.

'The etiquette when the Prince called upon my aunt,' remembered the niece of one of Bertie's married amoratas, the fascinating Nina Kennard, 'was that everybody else should leave the room; sometimes we children were still in the drawing room when the butler showed him in, whereupon we had to back out of the Royal Presence as gracefully as best we could – often colliding unavoidably with the furniture on our way to the door; after our exit we could hear from the landing the Prince's laughter at our discomforture . . . It is almost unnecessary to emphasise the fact that the hostess was a singularly attractive creature.'[46]

The aproned maid, having deposited the tea tray with its sparkling silverware, gleaming china and laden, many-tiered cake stand, would bob her curtsey and take her leave, closing the door behind her in the knowledge that she must not re-enter until summoned by her mistress's tinkling brass bell.

What happened next ranged from a little flirtatious conversation, through passionate kissing, to full-scale sexual congress. Or as much congress as was possible given the restrictions of a chaise-longue and the armoury of clothes worn by the women. Under those flounced, ruched, draped, bustled and many-buttoned dresses lurked layer upon layer of underclothes, ending up with the most daunting of garments – a tightly-laced whalebone corset. Hardly less daunting would be the lady's coiffure: a fragile confection of curled fringes, false locks and strategically planted combs. A man would have had to have been as

much a ladies' maid as a lover first to undress, and then to dress, one of
these decorative creatures. To one contemporary observer, it all
seemed like 'an enterprise which would have to be organised like a
household furniture removal'.[47]

To meet this particular challenge, a special garment, known as the
tea-gown, evolved. More than a peignoir, less than a formal afternoon
dress, these filmy, lacy garments with their hint of the boudoir had
one inestimable advantage: they could be worn without corsets. While
respectable and lavish enough to be worn in public, they could very
easily be slipped out of in private. By the last decades of the nineteenth
century the tea-gown, or 'teagie', was an essential part of a society
woman's wardrobe, whether she was contemplating adultery or not.
For instance, the future Queen Mary, when Duchess of York, had a
sumptuous collection of tea-gowns and one really cannot imagine her
indulging in a little extra-marital dalliance on the chaise-longue.

Whether it was in the course of one of these tea-time *têtes-à-têtes*, or
whether it was in rather more comfortable circumstances that Lillie
Langtry first succumbed to the Prince's amorous advances one cannot
know, but it very soon became apparent that he was fascinated by her.
Quite clearly, she was not going to be just another in that succession of
young married women with whom he amused himself.

Not content to confine their meetings to the odd afternoon call or
the occasional country house weekend, he began appearing openly
with her. Hostesses soon realised that if they hoped to lure the Prince
to their dinner tables or their ballrooms, Mrs Langtry would have to
be invited as well. There was nothing clandestine about their affair.
Lillie Langtry became an openly acknowledged and apparently
permanent feature of the Prince's life. She became, in short, his first
official mistress.

Royal Mistress

NOT SINCE THE days of the Stuarts have royal mistresses played a significant part in British history. There has been no British equivalent of women like Madame de Maintenon or Madame de Pompadour. The Hanoverians might have enriched, and even ennobled, their mistresses, and their liaisons often caused great scandal, but these women never developed into national figures; they never wielded any social or political influence. For the most part, royal mistresses were content to use their unique positions to feather their nests.

The mistresses of Edward VII – both as Prince of Wales and as King – were content with even less than this. It was enough, it seems, to have become the royal favourite: they looked for neither power nor titles. Just to bask in the reflected glory of the throne, and to get some of the dress bills paid, was all they wanted.

The same was true of the mistresses of Edward VII's grandson Edward VIII, afterwards Duke of Windsor. His three mistresses – Lady Coke, Mrs Dudley Ward and Lady Furness – were all married women, content with no honours other than the honour of being the companion of the heir to the throne. Not until the arrival on the scene of Mrs Wallis Simpson (and one does not know whether she was, in fact, Edward VIII's mistress before she became his wife) did a royal romance develop into a national issue. Mrs Simpson could, of course, have settled for less than marriage; she could have contented herself with the not unenviable life of a king's mistress, in the way that others had done before her. That she did not do so was due, almost entirely, to the strength of Edward VIII's love for her: he was determined to marry her, even at the cost of losing his throne. Few royal mistresses – or, at least, objects of royal affection – can boast that.

No such overpowering passion marked Edward VII's feelings for Lillie Langtry. He was far too level-headed a man for that. But there can be no doubt that he was in love with her. During the first few years of their liaison, at least, he had eyes for no one else.

What was it about Lillie Langtry that the Prince of Wales found so fascinating? Initially, her physical attractions: her lovely face, her voluptuous body, her graceful bearing. 'Lillie Langtry happens to be, quite simply, the most beautiful woman on earth,'[1] claimed Millais. She had, in addition, the sort of animation that Bertie liked in a woman: she was vibrant, high-spirited, amusing. But then all these were qualities which he could have found, to a greater or lesser extent, among many women in the so-called Marlborough House set. Pretty, bright, sexually available women were never hard for him to find.

What set Lillie apart from them were her non-physical attributes. For one thing, she had a refreshing independence. Although she was always polite in the Prince's company, she was never subservient. She spoke her mind. Princes – indeed, any member of a royal family – are so surrounded by sycophants and conformers that they tend to welcome almost anyone from another world: anyone who is open and natural and honest. Queen Victoria's obsession with the Highlanders was in great measure due to the fact that they were 'very independent and proud in their bearing – always answering you and speaking openly, and strictly the truth, with great freedom, but ever respectful.'[2] Victoria's appreciation could be echoed in the royal family today.

So although, in old age, Lillie Langtry once told the actor Alfred Lunt that she had always been a little afraid of the Prince (she also told him that, close to, His Royal Highness smelt *very* strongly of cigars) she was clearly never overawed by him. In his company she remained, for all her charm, her usual practical self; a woman fired by an unsentimental ambition to get on in the world. In some respects, she was not unlike those self-made men for whom the Prince had so much admiration. She epitomised the new sort of person whom Bertie was welcoming into society.

Nor was Lillie one of those socially ambitious but essentially stupid women. On the contrary, she was very intelligent. And she was always eager to learn. 'Lillie's beauty has no meaning,' her friend Oscar Wilde once declared. 'Her charm, her wit and her mind – what a mind! – are far more formidable weapons.'[3] The Prince found that he could discuss things with her; she was not some doll-like creature with no opinions of her own. And here is another parallel with Wallis Simpson, in whom that later Prince of Wales always felt that he had found a confidante: Lillie was to Bertie not only a lover, but what so many princes lack – a friend.

'I resent Mrs Langtry,' joked George Bernard Shaw some years later. 'She has no right to be intelligent, daring and independent as well as lovely. It is a frightening combination of attributes.'[4]

It was a combination that the Prince of Wales found irresistible.

Indeed, the claim that King Edward VII was not as feckless and foolish a man as has sometimes been asserted is admirably borne out by the calibre of the three women whom he chose as his mistresses. Lillie Langtry, Daisy Warwick and Alice Keppel were all, in their different ways, exceptional women. By his association with them Bertie enhanced, rather than debased, the quality of his own life.

'It would be difficult for me to analyse my feelings at this time,' wrote Lillie of these early days of her association with the Prince of Wales. 'To pass in a few weeks from being an absolute "nobody" to what the Scotch so aptly describe as a "person"; to find myself not only invited to, but watched at all the great balls and parties; to hear the murmur as I entered the room; to be compelled to close the yard gates in order to avoid the curious, waiting crowd outside, before I could mount my horse for my daily canter in the Row; and to see my portrait [A Jersey Lily] roped round for protection at the Royal Academy – surely, I thought, London has gone mad, for there can be nothing about me to warrant this extraordinary excitement.'[5]

The lady was protesting too much. There was a great deal about her to warrant the excitement. Word that the alluring Mrs Langtry was the Prince of Wales's mistress soon spread beyond aristocratic circles. It was no longer only at balls that dowagers clambered onto gilt chairs to get a better look at her. People ran after her in the street. Crowds massed around her in the Park. Shopkeepers were obliged to usher her out of the back door because of the mob collecting at the front. One day in the Park a young girl bearing a striking resemblance to Lillie was mobbed to such an extent that she had to be carried 'suffering and unconscious'[6] to St George's Hospital.

Everything Lillie wore set a fashion. When she twisted a length of black velvet into a toque, stuck a quill through it and wore it to a race meeting at Sandown Park, copies of the creation appeared in milliners' windows throughout London, bearing the label 'The Langtry Hat'. When she wore a pink dress to Ascot, that particular shade of pink became the rage.

In short, the days of the one black dress had gone forever. Lillie now wore every colour in the rainbow. Instead of having her clothes made by a humble St Helier dressmaker, she went to Worth and Doucet. Hours were spent in the fitting-room; her dresses became more elaborate, her hats more striking. She had her tea-gowns bordered with silver fox, her evening dresses embroidered with pearls, her negligées edged with ermine. To a ball at Marlborough House she wore a creation of yellow tulle draped with wide-meshed gold net under which 'preserved butterflies of every hue and size were held in glittering captivity'.[7] It was left to her princely lover, the following morning, to pick up such butterflies as had been scattered all over the ballroom floor.

'Each successful season brought with it the same orgy of convivial gatherings, balls, dinners, receptions, concerts, opera etc, which at first seemed to me a dream, a delight, a wild excitement,' runs her breathless account of her new life, 'and I concentrated on the pursuit of amusement with a wholeheartedness that is characteristic of me, flying from one diversion to another, from dawn to dawn . . .'[8]

She was painted by every leading artist of the day. Edward Poynter pictured her in a 'gorgeous golden gown'[9] looking like some seductive Renaissance princess. George Frederick Watts, on the other hand, decided that her luminous quality would be better captured if she were seen in a simple black dress, as 'The Dean's Daughter'. Edward Burne-Jones, impressed by her 'healthy appearance', used her, in full face and in profile, for two of the women in his famous painting 'The Golden Stair'. To illustrate, perhaps, yet another facet of her character, the perceptive Burne-Jones depicted her as 'Dame Fortune', in which a hard-faced figure in grey draperies turns a wheel on which 'kings, princes, statesmen, millionaires and others rise, reach the top, and then fall'[10] to be crushed by a relentless Fate.

When Lillie posed for James McNeill Whistler in his studio in Tite Street, she was seen by the well-known art critic, George Smalley. 'A vision never to be forgotten,' wrote Smalley afterwards, 'the colouring brilliant and at the same time delicate; the attitude all grace. There was a harmony and a contrast all in one: the harmony such as Whistler loved; the contrast such as it pleased her Maker to arrange; between softness and strength; the lines of the woman's full body flowing gently into each other, but the whole impression was one of vital force.'[11]

As the apartment in Eaton Place was hardly adequate for her new status, Lillie – accompanied by the apparently unprotesting Edward –

moved into more appropriate premises. Not that her new home, 17 Norfolk Street, off Park Lane, was another Petit Trianon. In this more bourgeois age, kings and princes no longer set their mistresses up in palatial mansions: a discreet establishment with a conveniently private entrance was considered to be more in tune with the democratic tenor of the times.

Indeed, the Prince of Wales might not have set her up at all. His financial contribution to his lady loves usually went no further than the giving of expensive jewellery. Bertie may have paid for the odd Worth creation but to meet all her other extravagances Lillie would have to have looked elsewhere. The rents of Edward's Irish properties would hardly have kept her in the style to which she was now aspiring. Lillie would almost certainly have been earning some money from the sale of her 'professional beauty' photographs. Although some society beauties – Mrs Cornwallis West chief amongst them – protested that they received no commission on the sale of their photographs and that talk of them earning thousands of pounds was nonsense, Lillie Langtry would have made sure that at least some of this money came her way. Her claim that, at this time, she was a financial scatterbrain, is difficult to believe. Throughout her career she was known as a shrewd and hard-headed businesswoman. She might have been profligate, but she would never have settled for anything less than her monetary due.

Then, as the Prince's acknowledged mistress, she would have been granted extensive credit. There would have been very little difficulty in borrowing money or in finding some socially ambitious acquaintance to stand surety for her. And after all, her new Norfolk Street home was hardly luxurious. It was simply one of a typical terrace of red-brick houses boasting no more than eight or nine rooms, a modest staff and some stabling in the mews. Nor were its furnishings particularly lavish. They consisted, for the most part, of spurious antiques pressed on Lillie by unscrupulous dealers. Touches of advanced contemporary taste were provided by Lillie's friend Whistler: gilded palm-leaf fans to enliven the plum-coloured walls of the drawing room, a ceiling painted to represent the sky, water lilies floating in flat blue glass bowls.

It was to this modest Norfolk Street house that Bertie would come to pay his afternoon calls or, less frequently, to attend little dinner or supper parties. About these, Lillie is discretion itself. 'His affability to servants was well known to all who entertained him, for he seldom passed one without a word or a kind look,' she says in her memoirs.

'He really worked hard to make one's dinners and parties successful – an easy task with his magnetic personality.'[12]

In those more leisurely days, it was still possible for the Prince to visit Lillie, or anyone else, with a freedom that would be unthinkable for a member of the royal family today. Although his libertinism was sometimes hinted at or even openly criticised in the popular press, Bertie was never hounded by reporters.

'I recall with wonder and appreciation,' writes Bertie's grandson, the future King Edward VIII, of his youth in pre-First World War London, 'the ease with which we were able to move about in public places. The thought occurs to me that one of the most inconvenient developments since the days of my boyhood has been the disappearance of privacy . . . Because our likenesses seldom appeared in the press, we were not often recognised in the street; when we were, the salutation would be a friendly wave of the hand or, in the case of a courtier or family friend, a polite lifting of the hat.'[13]

On one occasion, when Bertie and Lillie were returning down Constitution Hill from a ride in the Park, they were held up by the preparations for a levée which the Prince was due to hold in Buckingham Palace in an hour or so's time. Sitting on their horses at the corner of the Mall, the couple were able to watch the band and the guard of honour march by and even to recognise some of the arriving guests. But the Prince himself was unrecognised by the waiting crowd. He remained so long, says Lillie, that he had a great scramble to get to the levée on time.

If Bertie was not paying for the lease and the running of the Norfolk Street house, he was apparently responsible for another of Lillie's homes. Towards the end of the year that he met her, 1877, he started building her a home in that most decorous of seaside resorts, Bournemouth. Designed in the mock-Tudor style so dear to the hearts of the late Victorians, and known, because of its red-brick lower storey, as the Red House, it was indistinguishable from the home of any successful business or professional man who had decided to retire to the South Coast. As such, it suited Bertie perfectly. With the house leased, according to municipal records, to an Emily Charlotte Langton, and with the foundation stone revealing nothing more than the date and a cryptic E.L.L. (for Emilie Le Breton Langtry), the Prince was able to avoid any direct association with the house. Travelling down to Bournemouth incognito, he was assured of the necessary anonymity whenever the two of them arranged to meet.

As a royal love nest, it may not have been a particularly romantic establishment but, in many ways, it suited this realistic, eminently practical couple to perfection. Along one wall of the high-ceilinged dining room, whose stained-glass window sported a couple of amorous swans, ran a defiant inscription: 'They say – What say they? Let them say.'[14]

It is not difficult, down the vista of the years, to picture the celebrated lovers amid the comfortable but incongruously middle-class surroundings of the Red House: the cigar-puffing Bertie in his brocade dressing-gown, the lovely Lillie in one of her frothy peignoirs, with her golden-brown hair cascading down her back. The hours spent in this Bournemouth retreat would have created an oasis of tranquillity amid the bustle and sparkle of their everyday lives. For Bertie, it would have provided a rare touch of domesticity; for Lillie, it would have meant a break in her unrelenting efforts to make her way in the world.

'My only purpose in life,' she later said of these halcyon days, 'was to look nice and make myself agreeable.'[15]

How did the two people most closely associated with the lovers – Princess Alexandra and Edward Langtry – react to the affair? For not only did they have to contend with their private knowledge of it, but with the fact that it was being widely talked about.

Alexandra, very wisely, accepted it. With customary grace and dignity, she behaved as though nothing were wrong. The blind eye which she had always turned towards her husband's casual affairs she now turned, with equal determination, towards this more serious relationship. Indeed, the Princess not only tolerated Lillie but welcomed her to both Marlborough House and Sandringham, where she always showed her great kindness. On one occasion, for instance, when Lillie was a guest at a small dinner party at Marlborough House, she was suddenly taken ill.

'The Princess, so considerate and compassionate always, immediately told me to hurry home to bed, which I thankfully did. Half an hour later the Household Physician, Francis Laking, was ushered into my room, having been sent by command of the Princess of Wales to see me and report to her on my condition. By the next afternoon I was feeling better, and was lying on the sofa in my little drawing room about tea-time, when the butler suddenly announced Her Royal Highness . . .

'The honour of the unexpected visit brought me at once to my feet, ill though I felt, but the Princess insisted on my lying down again, while she made herself tea, chatting kindly and graciously. She always used a specially manufactured violet scent and I recall exclaiming on the delicious perfume, and her solicitous answer that she feared possibly it was too strong for me.'[16]

Although Lillie was not above embellishing the incident, there can be no doubt that the Princess was never vindictive towards her. Some of this was due to Alexandra's genuine goodness of heart; she had a horror of jealousy, regarding it as one of the worst sins – 'the bottom of all mischief and misfortune in this world.'[17] Or she may have been guided by more practical motives: as there was nothing that she could do about her husband's unfaithfulness, Alexandra's best bet was to accept it. In this way she could win respect for her generous behaviour rather than pity, or even ridicule, for some less dignified response. Her attitude certainly won her the gratitude of her husband.

Or perhaps she simply did not care. With the passing years, Alexandra was becoming progressively more selfish and self-centred; she may by now have decided that as long as she was left to live her life in her own way, Bertie could do as he pleased with his.

Edward Langtry faced a somewhat different dilemma. His was the dichotomy of all husbands who are cuckolded by princes: resentment and jealousy on the one hand, pride and loyalty on the other. During the last century or so, British royal history has not been lacking in the wronged husbands of princely favourites: those silent, long-suffering, stiff-upper-lipped gentlemen whose reverence towards the monarchy forbids them to make a fuss. They bow their heads in deferential greeting while their royal guest's gaze shifts to their wife's décolletage; they eat lonely meals in the club dining room while she sips *Moët et Chandon* in some candle-lit supper alcove; they go on business trips to New York or Chicago while she is whisked off to Biarritz or Dubrovnik. Poor George Keppel was forced to go into 'trade' to earn enough to keep his wife in a manner to which her royal lover was accustomed. Ernest Simpson was forever having to find himself some work to do in another room while the scintillating Wallis entertained the Prince of Wales in the drawing room of their Bryanston Square flat.

As a *mari complaisant*, Edward Langtry was not as *complaisant* as he might have been. Although, according to Lillie, they had ceased having marital relations soon after moving into the Norfolk Street house, Edward was still capable of jealousy. Despite his apparent lethargy – unlike his wife, he was lazy, incurious, unambitious –

1. Lillie Langtry's birthplace: St Saviour's Rectory, Jersey.

2. The only known photograph of Edward and Lillie Langtry together, taken soon after their marriage.

3. The young Mrs Langtry, whose blend of simplicity and sensuality made her so irresistible to the Prince of Wales.

4. The debonnaire Prince of Wales, aged thirty-five, at the time of his meeting with Lillie Langtry.

5. 'The Jersey Lily', Millais's famous portrait, picturing Lillie holding a *nerine sariensis*.

6. Lillie Langtry, 'looking like a seductive Renaissance princess' in a painting by Edward Poynter.

7. The Red House, Bournemouth: the curiously bourgeois
'love nest' which the Prince of Wales built for Lillie.

8. Soignée and seductive: Lillie Langtry as the very picture of a
royal mistress.

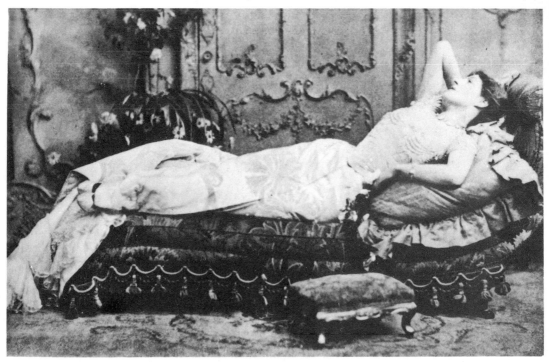

9. Queen Victoria presiding over the sort of 'Drawing Room' at which Lillie
Langtry was presented.

10. Prince Louis of Battenberg who fathered Lillie's daughter and who became, in time, great-grandfather to Charles, the present Prince of Wales.

11. Lillie at the time of her liaison with Prince Louis of Battenberg.

12. Lillie Langtry, as a celebrated actress, in one of her stage roles.

Edward had a violent temper. Every now and then he would lash out at Lillie: at her extravagance, at her frenetic socialising, even at her association with the Prince of Wales.

Once, early in Lillie's liaison with the Prince, when she and Edward were guests at Lord Malmesbury's country house, she wrote an indiscreet letter to her lover. Edward, on finding the letter reproduced on the blotting paper (every Victorian husband was adept at holding blotting paper up to the looking glass), was furious. Such was the force of his anger that even the resilient Lillie was reduced to tears. Lord Malmesbury was no less angry. But the anger of this experienced old diplomat was not directed at Lillie or Edward, but at the servants. They had strict instructions, he explained to Lillie, to renew the blotting paper throughout the house every day, in order to prevent precisely such an eventuality.

But not for a moment would Edward have expected his wife to break off her relationship with the Prince of Wales. Dutifully he continued to escort her to all those dinners and balls and country house parties which he so hated; doing it not so much for her sake but as an obligation towards the Prince and, indeed, the throne. Even he, it seems, was ready to bask in a little reflected royal glory. If one was going to be cuckolded, who better to be cuckolded by than the future King of England?

However, to make the whole business more palatable, Edward applied the customary remedy: he took to the bottle. He had always been fond of a drink; now he became fonder still. It was one way of passing the evenings on which he was left alone; or, even worse, the evenings on which he was obliged to stand about, making desultory conversation to people who he knew despised or pitied him. Sometimes, declared Lillie in later life, Edward was so drunk that he was incapable of going out. She would then be obliged to send last-minute apologies to her hostess.

Yet he consistently refused to grant her a divorce. Long after her affair with the Prince of Wales had ended, long after husband and wife had separated, long after Lillie had become a rich, world-renowned actress with a string of lovers, Edward would still not hear of divorcing her. And when Lillie was eventually able to win her freedom in an American court, it was on the grounds that Edward had deserted her.

'I have always treated Mr Langtry with affection,' she unblinkingly assured the judge, 'never giving him cause to disregard his duty to me as a husband.'[18]

★

During the first rapturous years of Lillie's romance with the Prince of Wales, she adapted her life, almost entirely, to his. There was hardly an occasion, in his crowded social calendar, on which she did not appear in his company.

One of the most public of these occasions was the daily ride, or drive, in the Park. This was one of the great rituals of society during the last decades of the nineteenth century. 'The Park' meant Hyde Park, never any of London's other great parks, and it was only the stretch between Albert and Grosvenor Gates, taking in Rotton Row, that was regarded as really fashionable. Here, after breakfast and between tea and dinner in the afternoons, during the season, would assemble a great concourse of riders and carriages. The scene was a splendid one: a kaleidoscopic pattern of lacquered carriages, high-stepping horses, gleaming harness, liveried footmen, smartly turned-out men and opulently dressed women. It was, remembers one observer, 'like a daily Society Garden Party.'[19] Highlight of the late afternoon cavalcade would be the arrival of Princess Alexandra in her claret-coloured barouche. Looking, as always, transcendently elegant, she would bow, in her inimitable way, to the hat-doffing men and the curtseying women.

Sometimes the Prince would be with her; more often he would be riding with his equerries and friends. Among these friends, of course, would be Lillie. Occasionally, arriving home at dawn from some ball, she would change straight into her riding habit and set out for the Park. By now she had a horse of her own, called Redskin, given to her by another of her new admirers, the young Morton Frewen. (The Langtrys had also acquired a carriage.) Dressed in her superbly tailored riding habit and top hat, Lillie would join the group around the Prince – whose own horse would be unmistakable in its royal red brow-band.

One day, when the two of them were out riding together in the late afternoon, Bertie showed no sign of wanting to go home. 'As etiquette demanded that I should ride on so long as His Royal Highness elected to do so,' explains Lillie, it was after nine before she arrived back in Norfolk Street. Her husband was furious. They were to dine out that evening. Having scrambled into an evening dress, and with the grumbling Edward in tow, Lillie arrived at her Eaton Square destination just before ten o'clock to find the entire company waiting for her. Her hostess was all sympathy. One of the guests, on his way over, had seen her in the Park with the Prince.

'As we knew you couldn't get away,' smiled her hostess, 'we postponed dinner indefinitely.'[20]

When the couple were not riding, they would be racing; or rather they would be attending the great race meetings which were such a feature of the Prince's social life. Bertie relished the company of racing people and revelled in the 'glorious uncertainty'[21] of the turf. He once shocked Queen Victoria by suggesting that the funeral of Dean Stanley be held a day earlier than planned to avoid a clash with the racing at Goodwood. It was, in fact, in the year he met Lillie that Bertie first ran his own horses: the Prince's colours – the purple, gold braid and scarlet sleeves – were seen at Newmarket for the first time in July 1877.

Bertie was advised in all racing matters by the manager of his stud, Lord Marcus Beresford, one of those Beresford brothers – Charles, Marcus and William – whom Lillie describes as 'the most entertaining' of the Prince's set. 'They were all handsome as paint,' she says, 'and as merry as the traditional Irishman or sandboys . . . full of native wit, charm and bonhomie.'[22] Unsuspected by Lillie at the time, Lord Charles Beresford was to be instrumental in involving the Prince with her successor – Daisy Warwick.

It was at these race meetings, at Newmarket, Ascot and Goodwood, where the Langtrys were invariably members of the Prince's party, that Lillie's own great love of racing was born. She had always been interested in horses, but from now on she was to take a far more intelligent interest. In time, she was to become an enthusiastic and successful racehorse owner, twice winning the Cesarewitch. 'As far as I am concerned,' she says, 'the pleasures of the turf do not merely consist in owning horses and seeing them win. I like the routine of racing. The fresh air, the picnic lunch, the rural surroundings, all tend to make a race meeting a delightful outing.'[23]

It could have been Bertie talking.

Lillie has a story to tell about her first meeting, just before Ascot one year, with Disraeli, then in his second term as Prime Minister.

'What can I do for you?' asked Disraeli, smiling quizzically.

'Four new gowns for Ascot,' was Lillie's pert reply.

'You are a very sensible young woman,' commented the Prime Minister. 'Many a woman would have asked to have been made a duchess in her own right.'[24]

With his sense of history, Disraeli would have appreciated the fact that, a couple of centuries before, a royal favourite would have stood a very good chance indeed of being made a duchess in her own right.

Another setting for the lovers' meetings was, of course, the Prince's London home, Marlborough House. For almost a century, from the time that the newly-married Prince and Princess of Wales took up residence in 1863, until the death of Queen Mary in 1953, Marlborough House was one of London's great royal residences. It was particularly associated with the Prince of Wales who lived in it for almost forty years until he ascended the throne in 1901; indeed, his circle of racy, pleasure-loving friends were known as the Marlborough House set. Its grey, somewhat four-square exterior belied the luxuriousness within: the rooms of Marlborough House glittered with all the richness of an Aladdin's Cave. The main reception rooms were a riot of damask wall-paper, painted ceilings, velvet curtains, gilt-framed portraits, white marble busts and Gobelin tapestries. The private apartments, reflecting Princess Alexandra's love of intimacy, were divided up by screens and curtains and potted palms, and crowded with little sofas, love-seats, pouffes, silver-framed photographs and dozens upon dozens of knick-knacks.

The Langtrys, arriving for anything from an intimate supper party to a ball (the whole of society, it was said, could be accommodated in the Marlborough House ballroom at the time of the Prince's marriage; his liberal social attitudes soon changed that), would be admitted by a gillie in Highland dress. Two scarlet-coated and powdered footmen would take Lillie's wrap and Edward's coat and give them to the hall porter, in his short red coat with leather epaulettes. A page in a dark blue coat and black trousers would then escort the couple to an ante-room. From here they would be led, by yet another page, into one of the drawing rooms.

When all the guests had assembled, the Prince and Princess would enter. 'The appearance of the Princess of Wales . . .' writes Lillie with studied generosity, 'wonderfully lovely and faultlessly dressed, seemed almost to dim the beauty of every other woman in the room, and her grace and fascination were such that one could not take one's eyes from her.'[25]

And if the guests found the Princess's flawless, almost wax-flower-like beauty remarkable, they found the Prince's energy and good nature even more so. One observer, attending a ball – not at Marlborough House but at the Prince's Norfolk home, Sandringham – watched in amazement as, in a country dance, 'the Prince and Princess set off with their partners, round and round, down the middle and up again, and so on to the end, the Prince the jolliest of the jolly and the life of the party, as he is wherever he goes. I never saw such amazing vitality . . . He is the antidote to every text and sermon that ever was preached upon the pleasure of the world palling upon the wearied spirit.'[26]

The Prince was equally in his element during the recreation that followed the close of the London season: the yachting at Cowes. At the beginning of August, society shut up its London houses and made for the Isle of Wight. The Royal Yacht Squadron, headquartered in its castle on the seafront at Cowes, was, says Lillie, 'the most exclusive club in the kingdom'.[27] Although Queen Victoria, ensconced in Osborne House, confined her participation to the occasional drive along the beflagged and bustling waterfront, or to watching the proceedings through a telescope, Bertie flung himself into the activity with customary gusto.

Yachting quickened his pulses no less than racing. The swelling of the sails, the shimmer of the sea, the tilting of the decks, the gusting of the wind – all these delighted him. He delighted equally in the less bracing pleasures of Cowes week: in dining aboard some luxuriously appointed two-hundred-foot craft belonging to one of his millionaire friends, or in dancing on deck, under a canopy of flags, to the music of Strauss or Waltaeufel.

But, as much as anything, he enjoyed being with Lillie at Cowes. In spite of her delicate beauty, she was no hot-house plant; she loved the outdoors. Lillie's tomboyish streak, so marked during her Jersey girlhood, was very much in evidence on these occasions. 'How I enjoyed the excitement of that race,' she once enthused, 'crowding on sail to the verge of danger, with a swirling spray drenching us to the skin.'[28]

Lillie and Edward would be guests of the Prince's friend – the man who had introduced them – Sir Allen Young, on board his schooner, 'Helen', while the Prince, and sometimes the Princess, would be on the royal yacht 'Osborne'. Often, to Lillie's gratification, there might be other members of Europe's inter-related royal families on board 'Osborne', and what she calls 'a favoured few' – herself, of course, included – would be invited to dine or dance.

Amongst the galaxy of royals to whom Lillie was introduced by the Prince was the widowed ex-Empress Eugenie of the French who, since the fall of the Second Empire in 1870, had been living in exile in England. She and her only child, the Prince Imperial, then in his early twenties, would take a house at Cowes each August. The Empress, although still remarkably beautiful, was no longer the stylish, insouciant creature of Bertie's first youthful visit to Paris. The Prince Imperial, on the other hand, was one of those high-spirited, devil-may-care young men in whose company the Prince of Wales delighted.

Through this irrepressible French prince, Bertie and Lillie were once involved in two of the most popular activities of the period: spiritualism and practical jokes.

A spiritual 'investigation' or 'table-turning' session had been organised at a seaside villa and was attended by, among others, the Prince of Wales, the Prince Imperial and the Langtrys. No sooner had the company around the table joined hands and the lights been put out than the furniture began crashing about. A lighted match revealed the young Prince Imperial to be the culprit. He was promptly expelled and locked out of the room. Once again the company settled down, in the dark, to await some spiritual manifestation. It came, some ten minutes later, in the shape of a ghostly white figure. Another match revealed the same culprit. The Prince Imperial had climbed up the wisteria, in through the open window and had covered himself, and several others, with flour.

But the Prince Imperial was not alone in his penchant for practical jokes. Bertie adored them. The late Prince Consort's admonition that no prince should ever indulge in anything as vulgar as a practical joke had fallen on very deaf ears indeed. Bertie's friends were spared nothing: apple-pie beds, pockets stuffed with sticky sweets, water squirted from bicycle pumps, pies full of mustard. And Lillie, no less a child of her time, was equally addicted to them. She tells of the occasion when the two princes hoisted a donkey into a bedroom, clothed it in a nightdress and somehow put it into the bed of the son of the house: the son being that notorious lecher, Harry Cust.

Another of her stories concerns that other celebrated lover and dashing naval commander, Lord Charles Beresford. On the occasion of Lillie's first visit to Cowes, Beresford was in command of HMS Thunderer. One afternoon, during an impromptu dance on board, Lillie, accompanied by someone she calls 'royalty' – we must assume she means the Prince of Wales – slipped away to one of the cabins. As all the ship's cabins lay below the water line, they had to rely on shafts for ventilation. Lord Charles, having noticed the couple slip away, and imagining, only too vividly, what they were up to in the cabin, switched off the supply of air.

'Very soon our faces became scarlet, our breathing grew difficult, and we began to go through the uncomfortable sensation which must be experienced by a fish out of water.' Beresford's prank, in other words, very quickly put a stop to whatever was going on.

'Fortunately,' continues Lillie, 'Lord Charles did not go beyond the frightening limit, or the Beresford joke might have developed into the Beresford tragedy.'[29]

Or – if the Prince of Wales had been discovered suffocated to death in the arms of Lillie Langtry – the Beresford scandal.

Of all the social occasions shared by the Prince of Wales and Lillie Langtry, none was more characteristic of the period than the country house weekend; or, as they were more properly termed, 'Saturday-to-Monday', with the use of the word Monday emphasising the fact that one did not need to return to town at the start of the week to earn one's living. These mammoth house parties, at which sport – hunting and shooting – was combined with entertainment – dining and dancing – were very much to Bertie's taste. And by the late 1870s no host could hope to entertain the Prince if the guest list did not include Mrs Edward Langtry.

The Prince was willing to accept the hospitality, not only of such grandees as the Duke of Devonshire at Chatsworth, the Duke of Beaufort at Badminton, the Duke of Sutherland at Dunrobin, the Duke of Westminster at Eaton Hall or the Duke of Portland at Welbeck, but of almost anyone rich enough to entertain him. To claim that the Prince of Wales had been a guest at one's country house was the ambition of almost every aristocratic or would-be aristocratic host. Many an enterprising socialite crippled himself financially in his determination to prove worthy of the favour bestowed by the presence of the Prince of Wales.

The photograph of one of these autumn gatherings, with His Royal Highness seated plumply and confidently in the middle of a group of tweed-suited men and elaborately hatted women, was a greatly treasured possession: incontrovertible proof that one had been granted the supreme social accolade.

The routine at these country house parties was unvarying. Between twenty and forty guests would be invited, with no introductions ever being made, on the assumption that all people in society knew one another. With the exception of the hostess's private wing, the entire house would be open to the guests; they could wander through the lushly furnished rooms and galleries as they wished. The hardly less luxurious bedrooms would be provided with every facility except a bathroom. In each room was a metal tub, discreetly screened, which would be filled and emptied by a housemaid. The grounds, with their walled gardens, pleached avenues, sloping lawns, winding paths, woods, belvederes and view sites, would be equally at the disposal of the guests.

These house parties involved, as Disraeli once complained to Queen Victoria, 'a good deal too much both of eating and dressing.'[30] And, of course, of shooting. Meals were gargantuan. At breakfast guests would help themselves from a row of silver chafing dishes on the sideboard: the fare would consist of fried, poached or scrambled eggs, bacon, sausages, mushrooms, tomatoes, kedgeree and cold ham. Luncheon sometimes took the form of a picnic but was none the less lavish for that: every conceivable type of hot and cold food, particularly varieties of game pie, and of course wine, would be provided. Tea, in the drawing room, meant bread-and-butter, scones, tarts, cakes, sandwiches, muffins and crumpets. At dinner there were often ten courses, each with a different wine. And, later that evening, there would be yet a fifth meal to be eaten – supper, which usually included a cold chicken or lobster salad. And in the unlikely but by no means unheard-of event of anyone feeling peckish during the night, sandwiches were provided in every room.

While the men usually changed their clothes only three times a day – tweeds, velvet smoking suits and full evening dress of white tie and tails – the ladies were expected to change at least four times. For breakfast there would be morning dresses. If they were picnicking out of doors with the men they would wear tweeds; if not, they would change into another dress for luncheon. For afternoon tea they would wear elaborate tea-gowns. In the evening they would appear in low-cut dresses with trains, wearing jewellery and carrying ostrich-feather fans.

As the men's daytime activities were confined to shooting, or talking about shooting, the women had to entertain themselves as best they could. Between changing their clothes, they could gossip with the 'darlings' – those non-sporting men who were especially invited to keep them amused – or write letters.

Lillie, despite her gratification at being included in these house parties, did not enjoy them unreservedly. She disapproved of hunting and shooting: 'I was once persuaded to see a stag stalked,' she says, 'but I felt so sick and sorry for the fine beast that I have never forgotten it.'[31] Nor did she much enjoy the company of other women. Too lively to sit about gossiping all day, and not really a member of this milieu, she found other amusements.

At Heron Court, the home of Lord Malmesbury, for instance, she would continue her process of self-improvement. She had always been one for keeping her eyes and ears open; now, guided by old Malmesbury, she would wander through the rooms, asking, listening, remembering. 'It was in these rooms that I learned to distinguish the different periods of French furniture, china, etc, for they contained quantities of beautiful examples, including some lovely signed buhl tables. It was, moreover, a pleasure to their owner to explain the most minute characteristics of each chair, cabinet, table or vase. The library was a vast one, and among its treasures were many portfolios filled with rare engravings and cartoons by Raphael, Bartolozzi, Angelica Kauffmann and others . . .'[32]

Nor did she ever hesitate to put this new-found knowledge to practical use. On one occasion Alfred de Rothschild drew her aside at the end of an evening and murmured, 'What shall I give you, beautiful lady?' Lillie promptly picked up a lavishly bejewelled Louis XVI snuff box. 'This will do,' she said crisply. 'He had a weak heart,' she afterwards wrote, 'and for a moment I thought I had stopped it. But when he got his breath he promised me something "much prettier" and out came one of the well-known gift boxes.'[33]

But not all Lillie's country house activities were devoted to self-enrichment, of whatever variety. Her natural effervescence was never far below that composed surface. One host was obliged to lock up his largest silver tray because she insisted on tobogganing down the stairs on it; another had to chide her for her 'disregard of conventionalities' for dismissing the groom who had been following her and Lord Manners as they rode through the park. Once, after she had burned her tongue with a forkful of *gratin à la Grammont,* she complained to her host about it being too cold; furious with his chef, the poor man gulped down a large mouthful, to the intense, if puerile, amusement of the company.

Such spirited behaviour delighted the Prince of Wales. He would roar with laughter at her antics. It was this dash, this boldness, this invincible *joie de vivre,* so closely resembling his own, that Bertie found so attractive in Lillie.

Late at night, the house party would offer amusements of another nature. For notable as these gatherings were for the sport, the food and the dressing up, they were equally notable for their adulterous

liaisons. It was chiefly at country house parties that the new code of
sexual behaviour was put into practice. On arrival – at teatime on the
first day – the men would eye the married women with a view to what
was euphemistically called 'amusing' one of them during the next two
or three days. An elaborate, if speedy, courtship would follow:
glances across the candle-lit dinner table, a touch of a hand on a gloved
elbow, a whispered suggestion of a private meeting, a note on a
breakfast tray, a walk to the summer house, a poetry reading in the
conservatory. All this led, inevitably, to a late-night assignation.

The experienced hostess, in allotting bedrooms to her guests,
would ensure that their current romantic attachments were taken into
account, or that sudden sexual attraction was allowed for. A reading
of the names on the cards slipped into the little brass frames on the
bedroom doors would tell the informed observer a great deal. The
hostess would see to it that Mr and Mrs Langtry were given separate
rooms and that Mrs Langtry's room was not too far from the suite set
aside for His Royal Highness. Well known Romeos would never be
placed in rooms beside happily married couples.

Yet everything was arranged with great discretion. An open scandal
was to be avoided at all costs. 'Everything was all right,' claimed one
such errant wife, 'if only it was kept quiet, hushed up, covered.'[34] A
married woman could conduct an affair more easily and in greater
safety within the closed circle at a country house party than she could
in a hotel or restaurant; even if she were prepared to risk the social
stigma of being seen in such an establishment.

The corridors of country houses must have been alive with the
sounds of padding feet, swishing dressing-gowns and gently closing
doors. A six o'clock warning bell would ensure that everyone was
back in his or her own bed long before the maids arrived with the
morning tea tray.

These late-night assignations gave rise to a litany of anecdotes about
miscarried plans. There was the one about the husband who, feeling
hungry, carried off the plate of sandwiches which his wife had left
outside her bedroom door as a sign to her lover. Or the irrepressible
Lord Charles Beresford who, having tiptoed into a dark room, leaped
lustfully into the arms, not of his lady-love, but of the astonished
Bishop of Chester. There was even one about the Prince of Wales,
who was assured by the lady on whom he was pressing his, for once,
unwelcome attentions, that she would mark her bedroom door with a
rose: when His Royal Highness duly crept into the room, it was to find
a kitchenmaid planted in the lady's bed.

Not that the Prince, or any other upper-class gentleman, would have hesitated to bed a kitchenmaid. They were considered to be there for the taking. When Edward Horner seduced a parlourmaid after a drunken lunch, a woman guest thought it 'eighteenth century and *droit de seigneur* and rather nice.'[35] She would not have been anything like as approving if he had seduced an unmarried woman of his own class. That would have been regarded as a major scandal.

Nor did the upper classes permit, among their servants, the sort of moral laxity which they — provided the women were married — enjoyed at these country house weekends. When Lord Curzon discovered that one of his housemaids had allowed a footman to spend the night with her, he was incensed. 'I put the little slut out into the street at a moment's notice,'[36] he boasted. And his guests, secure behind their façade of double standards and regardless of whose bed they had spent the night in, would have agreed that their host had acted most honourably.

But one may be sure that, for the first two or three years, the Prince would have been satisfied with Lillie by his side and in his bed. When they were not together, he would write to her. The tone of his letters was touchingly solicitous. Quite clearly, Lillie was constantly in his thoughts. He would give her the sort of news that a devoted husband gives a wife; he would write about the weather or the shooting or the racing. In describing the society beauties at Cowes, during a season that she was not with him, he would hasten to add that, somewhat to his own surprise, he was not flirting with any of them. Sometimes his letters were accompanied by a brace of pheasant; at others he would enclose the ticket to Ascot which she had wanted for a friend.

Such was the depth of Bertie's regard for Lillie that long after the first flush of his infatuation had faded and they had gone their separate ways, he would continue to see her and to write her his tender, concerned, affectionate letters; always signing them with a simple A.E. (for Albert Edward) and always opening them with the words 'My Fair Lily'.

'Dreams of Fairyland'

INDISPUTABLE PROOF of Lillie Langtry's social acceptability came in her second season. She was presented at court; presented, not to the Prince of Wales who sometimes deputised for Queen Victoria on these occasions, but to the Queen herself.

Until the late 1950s, when the young Queen Elizabeth II finally abolished the by then meaningless ceremony, presentation at court was regarded as the *sine qua non* of social recognition. No debutante was considered fully 'out' – out, that is, of girlhood and into society – until she had been formally presented to the monarch. The ritual was enacted at special presentation parties, as soon after a girl's eighteenth birthday as possible. Together with putting up her hair and letting down her skirts, being launched at her own coming-out ball and attending a prodigious number of other balls and parties, presentation at court was part of a young woman's initiation into society.

But presentation was not confined to debutantes. Married women – colonials, foreigners, women who had married Englishmen, who had been out of the country at eighteen or who had gained prominence in national life – could also be presented. Provided they had a 'presenter' or sponsor, usually a woman who had herself been presented, any aspiring socialite could make her curtsey to the sovereign. Some of these sponsors were not above making the necessary introductions for a cash consideration. An occasion which, in early days, had been confined to exclusively aristocratic circles, became progressively less select. 'We had to stop it,' said one member of the royal family recently, 'every tart in London was being presented.'[1] A more valid reason was that, in a more egalitarian age, the whole concept of 'society' had become outdated.

For a century or more, however, presentation at court remained the goal of every socially ambitious woman. What should she do, asked one desperate American matron of one of the young Vanderbilts, to get her daughter presented?

'Don't you know anything about presentation at the court of St James's?' he asked.

'No, but I do know that it would be marvellous for my girl,' she answered.

The young man, more enlightened than most, did his best to dissuade her. In graphic detail he outlined the disadvantages of the whole business: the months of learning how to conduct oneself, the expense of the clothes, the strain on the nerves, the tedium of waiting – first in the carriage procession in the Mall and then in the palace ante-chamber – and all for the dubious thrill of curtseying to a person who would never recognise one again.

In silence, the mother heard him out. 'I see,' she said when he had finished this grim catalogue of drawbacks. 'And now tell me what I should do to get my daughter on the list of presentees?'[2]

Whereas the Prince of Wales, on ascending the throne as Edward VII, reintroduced evening Presentation Courts, Queen Victoria held them in the afternoons, when they were known as Drawing Rooms. These Drawing Rooms (at which, noted one debutante tartly, 'Her Majesty does not offer any refreshments to the guests'[3]) might have lacked the glamour of the evening courts, but the ceremonial was no less exacting. So it was on a May afternoon in 1878 that Lillie Langtry found herself, stiff with nerves, waiting to make her curtsey to Queen Victoria at Buckingham Palace.

The Prince of Wales had prepared the ground thoroughly. Earlier that season he had presented Edward Langtry to the Queen at a levée. He had arranged for Lillie's sponsor to be Lady Conyngham, whose credentials, as a member of the Queen's household, were impeccable, and for her actual companion on the day to be Lady Romney. On the morning of the presentation he sent Lillie a huge bouquet of pale yellow Maréchal Neil roses.

This choice of flowers had not been arbitrary. They complimented her dress perfectly. Lillie was wearing, for this great occasion, a dress of ivory brocade with a long court train which hung, à l'Impératrice Joséphine, from the shoulders and which was lined with the same pale yellow of the artificial Maréchal Neil roses which garlanded the dress. As the Queen had recently expressed disapproval of the smallness of the obligatory three white feathers which the presentees wore in their hair, Lillie had chosen three of the largest ostrich plumes she could find. It was with some difficulty that she secured these three towering feathers and the customary tulle veil, for she still wore her hair coiled in a simple knot low on her neck.

Although gratified at the idea of being presented, Lillie was in two minds about the actual presentation to Queen Victoria. By now, the Queen would almost certainly have known about the Prince's relationship with Mrs Langtry ('Who is it *tells* her these things?'[4] wailed one of Her Majesty's secretaries) and Lillie was, she admits, 'rather afraid'[5] of the Queen. But as Queen Victoria, who now hated all public appearances, was known to spend no more than an hour or so at a Drawing Room and then hand over to the Prince and Princess of Wales, Lillie decided to delay her arrival. In this way she would still be presented at court but without having to face the probably disapproving Queen.

She could not, though, escape the waiting which was such a feature of these presentation days. The Mall was one solid line of carriages: a picturesque river of gleaming coaches, caparisoned horses, bewigged coachmen and powdered footmen, their liveries glittering with gold and silver braid. A good-natured mob of bystanders peered into the carriage windows, hoping for a glimpse of the bejewelled and befeathered occupants.

'It was certainly anything but agreeable,' grumbled Lillie, 'to sit in full costume, with low neck and arms, in bright sunlight, for the edification of the surging crowd.'[6] The fact that many of the presentees had not eaten since early morning, and were obliged to nibble their sandwiches and sip from their flasks in full view, made it less agreeable still.

Things were hardly less tedious in the palace itself. With infinite slowness, the line inched forward. Finally, 'after hours of waiting in the crush room, penned like sheep, with a heavy train folded on one's arm, and a constant dragging at one's tulle veil,'[7] the moment of presentation arrived. Although Lillie's late arrival meant that she would be the last but two to be presented, she was disconcerted to hear that the Queen was still receiving. She was more disconcerted still when, having handed her train to the pages but before having handed her card to the Lord Chamberlain, she heard him say, 'Mrs Langtry comes next, Your Majesty.' Quite clearly, the Queen had been waiting for her.

'It seems,' writes Lillie, 'that she had a great desire to see me, and had stayed on in order to satisfy herself as to my appearance. It was even added that she was annoyed because I was so late in passing.'[8]

True or not, Queen Victoria certainly looked annoyed as Lillie approached. Yet, to the trembling Lillie, this merely added to her air of majesty. The simplicity of the Queen's low-necked and short-sleeved black dress was enlivened by the blue ribbon of the Garter and by her many sparkling jewels: the diamond orders and decorations on her corsage, the rows of pearls about her neck, the rings on her podgy fingers and the small diamond crown on her head. It seemed almost unbelievable that someone so small and plump could look so awe-inspiring. 'I was thrilled with emotion, loyalty and pride,'[9] enthuses Lillie.

Her mind filled with stories of misadventures – of fat women over-balancing as they made their obeisances, of others tripping over their trains or clutching the outstretched royal hand for support – Lillie sank into her curtsey. The Queen seemed to show no interest in her whatsoever. Extending her hand in a 'rather perfunctory manner', Victoria stared straight ahead. 'Not even a flicker of a smile crossed her grimly set lips.'[10]

That ordeal over, Lillie dropped a series of curtseys to the other members of the royal family – including a no doubt beaming Prince of Wales – lined up beside the Queen, and then faced her final test. This was the catching of her train, thrown to her by a nimble page, over her left arm and then exiting backwards. She executed this complicated ritual perfectly.

That evening, as a relieved Lillie danced with Bertie in the Royal Quadrille at a ball at Marlborough House, he confirmed that the Queen had remained so late expressly in order to see her. What, wondered Lillie, had the Queen thought of her three outsize ostrich feathers? The Prince had certainly been amused by them. Perhaps he appreciated their symbolism. Were they not a reminder of his own coat of arms, with the accompanying motto *Ich dien* – I serve?

Lillie just missed an opportunity of meeting Queen Victoria socially later that year when the royal family descended, *en masse*, on Scotland for their annual autumn sojourn. With the Queen and some of her family at Balmoral and the Prince and Princess of Wales at Abergeldie, it was arranged that the Langtrys should be the guests of one of the Prince's friends, the 'commercial magnate' Cunliffe Brooks, at Glen Tanar. Although Lillie could not approve of the mass slaughter of game which so enthralled the men of the house party, she loved Scotland. She was not the first southerner to succumb to the fascina-tion of the Highlands: the colourful national dress, the vigorous dancing, the virile men, even the determined drizzle guaranteed, she says, 'to bring roses to a woman's cheeks'.[11]

In his Stuart tartan ('Something a little more *Scots* tomorrow,'[12] the Prince would instruct his valet as the ship bringing him north approached the Scottish coast) even Bertie managed to look somewhat less Hanoverian. As for Alexandra, Lillie had to admit that she looked as radiant in her 'blue serge workmanlike costume'[13] and deerstalker cap as she did in one of her shimmering court dresses.

One afternoon, accompanied by two other members of the house party – Lord Strathnairn and Lady Erroll – the Langtrys drove over to Balmoral. Designed by the late Prince Consort, Balmoral Castle is a mixture of German Schloss and Scottish baronial hall: a jumble of pepper-pot turrets, crenellated parapets and stepped gables. Lillie, who had never seen it before (and was never to see it again) found it 'bleak and uninteresting', utterly lacking in the romance of Scotland's older, less *ersatz* castles.

The party had not come, of course, to call on Queen Victoria (no one would have dared do that, uninvited; and invitations to call on the Queen were rare) but to pay their respects by signing their names in the visitors' book. Lillie hesitated to do even this, imagining that it would be an act of presumption. But Lady Erroll assured her that, as Lillie had been presented to the Queen earlier that year, it would be perfectly proper, indeed imperative, for her to sign. So they duly wrote their names and left.

Later, Lillie heard from Lady Ely, one of Queen Victoria's ladies-in-waiting, that some twenty minutes after the party had driven away, the Queen had paged through the book and, on noticing their names, had said, 'I should like to have seen Mrs Langtry.'[14] A rider was promptly despatched to try and overtake them but it was too late. So history was denied the intriguing little scene of these two disparate women – the squat, dowdy, imperious Queen Victoria and the svelte and alluring Mrs Langtry – discussing who knows what subject provided it was not the one responsible for bringing the two of them together.

Although Lillie makes no mention of it in her circumspect memoirs, Balmoral was the chief setting for the juxtaposition of Queen Victoria with another unlikely personality: her gillie, John Brown. By the time of Lillie's visit, Brown had become a permanent, and much discussed, feature of the Queen's life.

What exactly was the nature of the relationship between this oddly assorted pair? On one level, Brown was Victoria's devoted servant.

The Queen had always had a soft spot for Highlanders – those handsome, muscular, plain-speaking, utterly honest 'children of nature' – and in Brown she saw embodied all these stalwart Scots qualities. He had been in her service for many years but it was not until some years after the Prince Consort's death that Brown was promoted from chief gillie to 'the Queen's Highland Servant', a position which made him part-servant, part-secretary, part-confidant. In time, she could hardly bear to be parted from him. She relied on him more and more, not only for his services but for his support, sympathy and companionship. He was constantly at her elbow. When she sat working, he kept guard over her; when she drove out he sat, sturdy and impassive, on the box of her carriage.

He treated her – this most intimidating of women – in an extraordinarily irreverent manner. 'What's this ye've got on today?' he would grumble if he disapproved of her dress. 'Hoots, then, wumman', an astonished tourist once heard him shout as he pinned together the Queen's cloak, 'can ye no hold yerr head up?'[15] Indeed, when they were alone, he almost always called her 'wumman'.

Some, in an effort to explain away the puzzling intimacy between the Queen and the gillie, claimed that the link between them was supernatural. They said that Brown had second sight, that he was a spiritualist medium through whom the Queen kept in touch with her late husband, that the Prince Consort's spirit had actually passed into John Brown. But others were only too ready to believe that the relationship was sexual: that the rugged, good-looking, undeniably masculine gillie was the Queen's lover, possibly even her husband. In some circles she was referred to as 'Mrs Brown' or 'the Empress Brown'.

Was this Bertie's view? The Prince certainly made no secret of his aversion to his mother's favourite. He deeply resented the bluntness and insolence with which Brown conveyed the Queen's often peremptory instructions to him, and for years he was reluctant to visit Balmoral because it meant shooting with the gillie. When, in 1884, the Queen sent him an advance copy of her book *More Leaves from a Journal of Our Life in the Highlands,* with its fulsome references to John Brown, the Prince was appalled. The worldly Bertie knew exactly how sophisticated readers would interpret the relationship. He held, he told the Queen, very strong views on the subject of this exposing of her private life to the general public and urged her to restrict the book to private circulation. Victoria, of course, ignored his advice.

Whatever Bertie's private thoughts on the nature of the relationship might have been, one of his intimate associates certainly regarded it as sexual. This was the famous Victorian courtesan, Catherine Walters, more usually known as 'Skittles'.

For many years the bewitching Skittles had been kept by the eldest son of the 7th Duke of Devonshire, the young Marquess of Harting- ton (the same 'Harty-Tarty' who had recently ripped the water-lilies out of an ornamental pool at a Devonshire House ball to present to Lillie Langtry) but this had never prevented her from distributing her favours among other young men-about-town. One of them was the Prince of Wales. In the years before he met Lillie, Bertie often visited Skittles and he was to remain friendly with her into her old age, frequently writing to her and even paying her an annual allowance. Whenever she was ill, his own doctor would attend her. During the course of this long and intimate association, the two of them apparent- ly discussed many royal secrets.

Yet another of Skittles's lovers was that colourful contemporary personality, the poet and traveller Wilfrid Scawen Blunt, and it was to Blunt that Skittles revealed what she knew about the Queen and John Brown. Blunt, in turn, transmitted the astonishing revelations to his secret diary: a confidential record which was not opened until 1972, fifty years after his death. Although both Blunt and Skittles tend to be unreliable witnesses, there seems to be no good reason why either of them should lie about facts that were not to be revealed until long after both of them were dead. In fact, Skittles did not even know that Blunt was recording her memories and, 'because the story is so important historically', Blunt cross-questioned her closely.

'Brown,' repeats Blunt in his secret diary, 'was a rude unmannerly fellow . . . but he had unbounded influence with the Queen whom he treated with little respect, presuming in every way upon his position with her. It was the talk of all the household that he was 'the Queen's Stallion'. He was a fine man physically, though coarsely made, and had fine eyes (like the late Prince Consort's, it was said) and the Queen, who had been passionately in love with her husband got it into her head that somehow the Prince's spirit had passed into Brown, and four years after her widowhood, being very unhappy, allowed him all privileges. It was to be with him, where she could do more as she liked, that she spent so much of her time at Balmoral, though he was also with her at Osborne and elsewhere . . . She used to go away with him to a little house in the hills where, on the pretence that it was for protection and "to look after the dogs", he had a bedroom next to hers, the ladies-in-waiting being put at the other end of the building

. . . [There was] no doubt of his being allowed every conjugal privilege.'[16]

Perhaps the truth was more complicated than this. That Victoria was infatuated with, indeed besotted by, John Brown, there is little doubt. But there were many factors, other than the sexual, to account for this obsession. In the first place, John Brown was a link – a tangible and not a spiritual link – with Prince Albert. The gillie had known the Queen's adored husband in the Prince's happiest periods: on holiday in their beloved Highlands. He was a living reminder of those unclouded days. Then, in this simple, trustworthy, dependable man were embodied all the peasant virtues which the Queen was coming to champion so ardently. How stalwart he seemed when set against the frivolous, immoral, self-indulgent members of the aristocracy – the Prince of Wales chief amongst them.

Queen Victoria had always been shy in sophisticated or intellectual society; with the Highland peasants, and with John Brown in particular, she could be utterly natural and relaxed. Royals do not easily make friends; they can never be quite certain of their disinterestedness. The result is that they quite often form close attachments with their personal servants. One of Queen Elizabeth II's most trusted confidantes is said to be her long-serving dresser, Miss Margaret ('Bobo') MacDonald. So, in John Brown, Queen Victoria felt that she had a friend who appreciated her for herself alone.

But, for all that, it was his masculinity she found so attractive. Brown not only gave her the physical protection she needed (time and again he saved her from danger, even death) but he gave her the masculine attention she so ardently craved. The real secret of Brown's success was that he treated Queen Victoria as a woman first, a queen second. He was not overwhelmed by her status; he was not afraid of her. He knew, by instinct rather than by calculation, that in that dumpy and intimidating figure there beat an intensely feminine heart. She was simply a woman who needed cherishing.

Whether or not Victoria allowed the relationship to develop to its obvious, sexual conclusion, one cannot know. It seems unlikely. Like Brown himself, the Queen was without guile. She never dissembled, she could never live a lie. There is no doubt that Victoria was a passionate woman, but her cravings were emotional rather than physical.

Had Skittles discussed the affair of the Queen and John Brown with the Prince of Wales? The two of them certainly discussed other intimate topics concerning members of the royal family. And did

Bertie appreciate the complexity of his mother's feelings for John Brown? Possibly not. Bertie was not much given to analytical or metaphysical thought. But some indication of the depth of his detestation of John Brown – for whatever reason – came on his accession to the throne. One of King Edward VII's first commands was for the destruction of all those statues, busts, cairns and plaques which Queen Victoria had had erected to the memory of her gillie. For an exceptionally kind-hearted man, who seldom bore a grudge, this was a significant gesture.

No account of the Prince of Wales's association with Skittles can be complete without reference to one of his most famous practical jokes. Once, on an official tour of Coventry, the Prince was accompanied by Lord Hartington who had by now discarded Skittles for the more aristocratic but equally available charms of Louise, Duchess of Manchester. Unsuspected by Hartington, the Prince had instructed the mayor of Coventry to make a point of showing the royal party, and more particularly Lord Hartington, the town's bowling alley.

When, to the mayor's discomforture, his lordship seemed to be showing no interest in the bowling alley whatsoever, his worship decided to draw his attention to it.

'His Royal Highness asked especially for its inclusion,' explained the mayor in all innocence, 'in tribute to your lordship's love of skittles.'[17]

Presentation to Queen Victoria had unlocked the last, and most important, of the great London doors for Lillie Langtry: she could now be invited to balls and receptions at Buckingham Palace itself.

Although the Queen no longer attended state balls, having long since handed over the responsibility to the Prince and Princess of Wales, these Buckingham Palace dances remained the most important of the season. Their atmosphere was, not unnaturally, a little staid. Whereas, at other great houses, waltzes, gallops and even the occasional Highland schottische ('as an extra ebullition of hilarity,'[18] says Lillie) made up the programme, stately formation dances were still the rule at the palace. Everything tended to be more formal, more restrained.

But none of this could detract from the brilliance of these occasions. The Prince of Wales never looked anything less than regal; Princess Alexandra, in her glittering fabrics, pearl choker and diamond tiara, never anything less than breath-taking. Uniform or court costume –

the knee breeches and stockings that can occasionally be seen at court to this day – were *de rigueur* for the men. The women, 'lovely beings in diaphanous frou-frous of tulle and chiffon'[19] as one lyrical guest put it, blazed with 'historic' family jewels. Most dazzling of all was the scene at the supper table: the footmen resplendent in scarlet coats and powdered wigs, the damask cloth laid with gold plate and silver cutlery, the tazzas laden with fruit and flowers from the royal gardens at Frogmore.

'These balls at Buckingham Palace,' enthused Lillie, 'completely realised my girlish dreams of fairyland.'[20] She found it hard to believe that she had once felt nervous mounting the palace steps. She had, indeed, come a long, long way from St Saviour's vicarage, Jersey.

Her circle was becoming ever more elevated. She could hardly move, these days, for royal friends and acquaintances. One year at Cowes she was presented to Princess Alexandra's parents, King Christian IX and Queen Louise of Denmark. Another of Alexandra's relations, Prince Wilhelm of Glucksburg, gave her a signed photograph of himself, 'with cap on head' as he scrawled under his signature. Yet another signed photograph came from King Oscar II of Sweden. At an intimate dinner party at Marlborough House she met the future German Emperor and Empress, at that stage still Crown Prince and Princess; the Princess being the Prince of Wales's elder sister, Princess Victoria.

Lillie also met Bertie's two sons, Prince Albert Victor – always known as Eddy – and Prince George. When, in September 1879, the fifteen-year-old Eddy and the fourteen-year-old George set off, as midshipmen, on board HMS Bacchante for a series of cruises, Lillie was able to give them each a small gift. Prince Eddy who was, to put it kindly, a little backward, but who was already developing an eye for a pretty face, was particularly pleased with the trinket Lillie had bought him at Bensons, the jewellers in Cowes. He immediately attached it to his watch-chain.

'I had to take off my grandmother's [Queen Victoria's] locket to make room for it,'[21] he told the gratified Lillie. What Queen Victoria would have thought of this substitution is another matter.

One apparently uninvited royal caller was that notorious lecher, Queen Victoria's first cousin, Leopold II, King of the Belgians. The tall, spade-bearded King, who found his Belgian kingdom too provincial by half, was given to paying incognito visits to London and Paris. Here he could assuage that seemingly insatiable sexual appetite in ways undreamed-of in unsophisticated Brussels. Whether, on the theory that what was available to one royal lover would be as readily available to another, Leopold II imagined that Lillie Langtry would grant him her favours is uncertain, but he one day presented himself at her house at nine in the morning.

Woken from sleep, Lillie scrambled into a dress and rushed downstairs. There stood the stork-like figure of King Leopold, sopping wet from having trudged through the rain from his hotel. The two of them sat making polite conversation – although conversation, polite or not, was hardly King Leopold's forte – for 'an interminable period'[22], and he left. At nine the following morning, the King called again. This time Lillie sent down a polite excuse. Or so she tells us.

An even more determined caller was Crown Prince Rudolph of Austria. Only son of the stolid Emperor Franz Josef and the beautiful but wayward Empress Elizabeth, the twenty-year-old Crown Prince Rudolph had inherited much of his mother's fascination and still more of her emotional instability. The arrival in London, in 1878, of this handsome and headstrong heir to the Austro-Hungarian throne was regarded as a significant social event, and he was lavishly entertained.

One of the first private dances in his honour was given by Baron Ferdinand de Rothschild at his home in Piccadilly. Determined that his famous white and gold 'Louis XVI' ballroom would be the setting for an occasion of unparalleled magnificence, the Baron invited a dozen celebrated beauties – Lillie amongst them – to a special luncheon party at which he offered to buy them each a new Doucet dress for the ball. Needless to say, the offer was snapped up. For Lillie, Doucet created a dress in pale pink crêpe-de-chine, subtly draped and richly fringed. It was delivered to Norfolk Street, together with a petticoat which the couturier considered essential for the hang of the gown.

Months later, Doucet sent Lillie a bill for the petticoat. Although the sum was trifling, Rothschild had refused to pay it. He was responsible for the dress only, explained the multi-millionaire.

At the ball, one look at Lillie – so seductive in her clinging silk and with her loosely-knotted hair – was enough for the impressionable young Crown Prince. He insisted on dancing almost every dance with her. And ten minutes after the royal party had processed into their own supper room (where Rudolph was seated beside his host's sister, Alice Rothschild) the Baron came hurrying back into the ballroom. The Crown Prince, he explained to Lillie, had demanded that she be put next to him at table. Rudolph had not addressed a single word to poor Alice Rothschild, an amused Bertie afterwards told Lillie.

After supper, Rudolph again monopolised her. So vigorous,

apparently, was his dancing that his hands were leaving sweaty imprints on her dress. Politely, Lillie asked him to put on his gloves. His reply was singularly graceless.

'It is you who are sweating, madam,'[23] he said.

In the days that followed the Rothschilds' ball, the Crown Prince was a persistent caller at Norfolk Street. One cannot know how much Lillie led him on, or whether she led him on at all, but there can be no doubt that the young man was infatuated by her. In later years, she is said to have told Somerset Maugham that their association ended when Rudolph one day made his 'dishonourable intentions' so apparent that, 'in disgust', she pretended to throw a magnificent emerald ring he had just given her into the fire. With a 'horrified cry he fell to his knees and desperately scrabbled out the burning coals in an effort to retrieve the jewel.'

'I couldn't have loved him after that,'[24] shrugged Lillie.

But she kept the emerald ring.

Almost ten years later, Crown Prince Rudolph shocked the world by shooting first his mistress, young Mary Vetsera, and then himself in what has been described as a suicide pact, at the imperial hunting lodge at Mayerling.

Would Lillie have considered a sexual liaison with Crown Prince Rudolph? It is doubtful. She would hardly have risked a possible break-up of her affair with the Prince of Wales. Her position was too precarious for that. She might have been tickled by the thought of adding the name of the future Emperor of Austria-Hungary to that of the future King of England as a royal lover, but it would have remained a thought only.

Yet in spite of her circumspection, there is some recently unearthed evidence that Lillie was indeed involved in a clandestine love affair throughout this period. A cache of sixty-five love letters, written by Lillie to Arthur Henry Jones, was discovered in a battered green box in an attic in a Jersey farmhouse. The box had apparently been brought there by Arthur Jones's niece, many years ago. The tone of these letters is passionate; the relationship between Lillie Langtry and Arthur Jones was undoubtedly sexual. Always addressing him as 'My Darling', she often tells him when it will be safe for him to visit her. 'Please, please, hurry back,' she writes on one occasion. 'I want you so much.'[25]

The ardent nature of these letters gives the lie to the frequent assertion that Lillie Langtry was asexual, cold-hearted, incapable of love. On the other hand, they reinforce the theory that no matter how passionately she might be in love, she would never allow her heart to rule her head. With Lillie, love always came second to ambition. Not for a moment would she have considered the world well lost for love: nothing must be allowed to interfere with her liaison with the Prince of Wales. She kept her three-year-long love affair with Arthur Jones secret; to this day he remains a shadowy figure.

In any case, she had given the gossips quite enough to be getting on with. News of Lillie Langtry's spectacular success had by now crossed the Atlantic. 'Lovely Lillie Langtry,' trumpeted the New York *Tribune, à propos* her friendship with Crown Prince Rudolph, 'has added another royal scalp to her fast-growing collection.'[26]

And when Moreton Frewen, one of her earliest admirers, who was soon to marry the sister of Jennie Jerome (wife of Lord Randolph Churchill and mother of Winston Churchill) arrived in New York, he was immediately quizzed on his friendship with Lillie by a reporter on the New York *Post*.

Would he call himself an intimate friend?

'Unfortunately, no,' replied Frewen.

Would he have wanted to become her good friend?

'I believe she is otherwise occupied,' was his circumspect answer to that one.

Was Mrs Langtry as beautiful as was claimed?

'Yes, I suppose she is.'

Had there been just a hint of hesitation in that reply?

'Not really,' said Frewen. 'She is lovely, but I've found her a bit dull, since she's always surrounded by people. A lily, to bloom as it should, must be planted in its bed.'[27]

This was hardly guaranteed to turn the swelling tide of gossip.

Foreshadowing, in a way, the turn her career would ultimately take was Lillie's friendship with someone still far removed from these royal and aristocratic circles: the young Oscar Wilde.

They met towards the end of 1879, after Wilde had come down from Oxford and had moved into the 'untidy and romantic house'[28] just off the Strand belonging to Lillie's artist friend, Frank Miles. Here, in a fittingly fashionable setting – white panelled walls, blue and white china, peacock feathers and sunflowers – Wilde entertained what he described as 'beautiful people' to tea. The most beautiful, in his opinion, was Lillie Langtry.

'The three women I most admired,' wrote Wilde a year before his death, 'are Queen Victoria, Sarah Bernhardt and Lillie Langtry. I would have married any one of them with pleasure. The first had great dignity, the second a lovely voice, the third a perfect figure.'[29]

Whether any one of the three women would have married him with an equal degree of pleasure is another matter.

Lillie's opinion of Wilde, at this early stage of his career, is rather less flattering. She professes herself 'astounded' at his strange appearance: she describes him as 'grotesque'. His face was too large, his skin too pale, his hair too long, his lips too coarse, his teeth too discoloured, his nails too dirty and his clothes too *outré*. But she had to admit that he had a certain fascination. She found his voice alluring and his enthusiasm infectious. In those days, she says, he was truly ingenuous: 'his mannerisms and eccentricities were then but the natural outcome of a young fellow bubbling over with temperament, and were not at all assumed.'[30]

For Wilde, Lillie's chief attraction was her notoriety. He might pay elaborate homage to her arresting appearance and her sharp mind, but it was her position as *maîtresse en titre* of the Prince of Wales that attracted him more. Determined to hitch his wagon to this dazzling star, Wilde announced himself in love with her. There was nothing like an unrequited love affair with a celebrity to win a budding poet some public attention.

A poem which he had originally written in praise of a youth was slightly altered to fit her ('A fair slim boy' was easily metamorphosed into 'A lily-girl') and an even more fulsome tribute, entitled 'A New Helen', was published in Edmund Yates's magazine, *The World*. 'To Helen, formerly of Troy, now of London', ran Wilde's florid inscription on the white vellum-bound copy which he presented to Lillie.

On his way to visit her, he would stroll along Piccadilly holding in his hand, for all to see, a single lily. He even, so she tells us, once fell asleep, like a devoted dog, on the doorstep of her Norfolk Street house. On another occasion, after the two of them had had a tiff, Wilde, on suddenly spotting her in a box at the theatre, had to be led out of the house in tears.

Lillie, of course, was too shrewd to be taken in by all these flowery gestures. Just as shamelessly as Wilde used her to draw attention to himself, she used him in her continuing quest to improve her mind. He took her to Professor Newton's celebrated lectures on Greek art at the British Museum; he introduced her to that great artistic arbiter, John Ruskin; he set about teaching her Italian; he tried to instil in her something of his own 'wild worship of beauty'.[31] He even advised this most soignée of women on clothes.

'I wanted to ask you how I should go to a fancy dress ball there,' she once wrote, 'but I chose a soft black Greek dress with a fringe of silver crescents and stars, and diamond ones in my hair and on my neck, and called it "Queen of the Night".'[32]

But she was not always ready to take his advice.

'The Lily is so tiresome,' he once sighed, 'she *won't* do what I tell her.'

'Indeed?' answered a friend.

'Yes. I assure her that she owes it to herself and to us to drive daily through the Park dressed entirely in black, in a black victoria drawn by black horses, and with "Venus Annodomini" emblazoned on her black bonnet in dull sapphires. But she won't.'[33]

What, one wonders, would the Prince of Wales have said if she had? What, indeed, did he think of Lillie's exotic new admirer? There is no record of his having met Oscar Wilde until some years later, in Homburg in 1892. The by then successful playwright, together with his new young friend, Lord Alfred Douglas, was in Homburg to recover from his unsuccessful battle with the Lord Chamberlain over the proposed London production of his play *Salomé*, in which Sarah Bernhardt was to have appeared. The worldly Prince, who had a more than passing interest in the Divine Sarah, was all sympathy.

Not until the autumn of 1879 did word of the Prince of Wales's two-and-a-half-year affair with Lillie Langtry appear in the British press. The respectable newspapers would have been too deferential to mention it, and the popular papers, without today's intrusive reporters, would have lacked enough hard evidence to risk carrying the story. That would have been the only reason for their reticence. In the ordinary way, popular journals never hesitated to criticise or lampoon members of the royal family.

From the days of Gillray's and Cruikshank's ribald cartoons to the usually apocryphal stories in today's tabloid press, royals have been regarded as legitimate targets. The press might not, in Queen Victoria's time, have kept such a relentless watch on every waking – or, indeed, sleeping – moment of a member of her family, but there was no lack of critical comment. And nothing is guaranteed to cause the royal family more annoyance, or anguish, than adverse press publicity.

Throughout his adult life, Bertie had been the subject of considerable newspaper abuse. Journals like *Fun, Puck, Moonshine, Tomahawk*
and *Reynolds Newspaper* never hesitated to take advantage of the
opportunities with which his hedonistic lifestyle provided them.
Every fresh scandal brought forth its crop of cartoons, caricatures and
comic verses. *Reynolds Newspaper* was particularly harsh in its editorial
comment. 'If the Prince of Wales is an accomplice in bringing dishon-
our to the homestead of an English gentleman,' it lectured at the time
of the Prince's involvement with Harriet Mordaunt in the Mordaunt
divorce scandal, 'if he has assisted in rendering an honourable man
miserable for life; if unbridled sensuality and lust have led him to
violate the laws of honour and hospitality – then such a man, placed in
the position he is, should not only be expelled from decent society, but
is utterly unfit and unworthy to rule over this country.'[34]

It was the scurrilous magazine *Town Talk,* edited by the young
Adolphus Rosenberg, that first mentioned the Prince of Wales's name
in connection with Lillie Langtry; a mention that was to lead to a
titillating court case. Curiously enough, not one of Edward VII's
major biographers, in cataloguing the various court cases in which he
was involved, has mentioned the *Town Talk* affair.

Rosenberg's first salvo came in the issue of 30 August 1879, when he
claimed that, 'A petition has been filed in the Divorce Court by Mr
Edward Langtry. HRH The Prince of Wales, and two other gentlemen whose names up to the time of going to press we have not been
enabled to learn, are mentioned as co-respondents.'

Even today, with society's more lenient attitudes towards sexual
behaviour, an announcement that the Prince of Wales was to be cited
in a divorce case would cause a sensation; it certainly caused one then.
The circulation of *Town Talk* soared as the public, in the pleasurable
anticipation of another royal exposé, rushed to buy copies. Whether
Rosenberg was acting on firm evidence or whether he was simply
chancing his arm is uncertain; but as there was no denial from the
Langtrys, he pushed ahead.

Each issue fed the hungry public another titbit. 'When we have a
lady's name paraded before the public in a thousand different ways,'
railed Rosenberg against Lillie, 'when we see her photographs displayed in almost every stationer's window: when we see that photograph side by side with bishops and lawyers, and in conjunction with
facial representations of well-known harlots, the question arises,
"Who is Mrs Langtry?" '

He lost no time in supplying the answer. In a sentence heavy with *double entendre*, he claimed that 'there was something not very pleasing to the loyal mind to see, in a dozen shop windows, Mrs Langtry side by side or else beneath the Prince of Wales . . .'

In one issue his readers were told that the Home Secretary had forbidden the cracking of any Langtry jokes in music halls. In another they were enlightened as to the names of the two men who would be appearing, along with the Prince of Wales, as co-respondents: they were Lord Lonsdale and Lord Londesborough. In a third they were informed that the divorce case was to be held *in camera*.

Adopting that stock-in-trade of the popular press – a tone of mock outrage at the spreading of tittle-tattle – *Town Talk* applauded the fact that the case was to be heard *in camera*, so depriving 'scandalmongers of a fine opportunity'. 'Mrs Langtry has, I understand, filed an answer, denying the adultery [with the Prince of Wales and lords Lonsdale and Londesborough] and, as far as I can learn, the petitioner [Mr Edward Langtry] will find it exceedingly difficult to make good his case.' Of course, continued Rosenberg in the same sanctimonious vein, 'there will be a great outcry against the case being tried privately, but I don't see why anyone need be dissatisfied, especially as the details are not likely to be at all creditable to us as a nation.'

In case his readers had not understood the significance of this last phrase, Rosenberg went on to say that he would not like to be 'more explicit' on this point.

Why did the Langtrys not deny Rosenberg's assertions? Were they true? Or had the Prince, in his anxiety to prevent the affair developing into a full-scale scandal, advised Lillie against taking any action against Rosenberg? Or was royal pressure being brought to bear on *Town Talk?*

For some reason or other Rosenberg, in the issue of 4 October, suddenly changed direction. 'I am now informed on authority which I have no reason to doubt,' he announced, 'that Mr Langtry has withdrawn the petition which he had filed in the Divorce Court. The case of Langtry vs Langtry and others is therefore finally disposed of and we have probably heard the last of it . . . I am told also that it is not unlikely that Mr Langtry will shortly be appointed to some diplomatic post abroad. It is not stated whether his beautiful consort will accompany him.'[35]

But Rosenberg had not heard the last of it. In the same issue of *Town Talk,* he foolishly moved his sights from Mrs Langtry to that rival beauty, Mrs Cornwallis West. This celebrated 'professional beauty', known always as 'Patsy', had been another of the Prince of Wales's paramours. There is a story that when the little daughter of one of the Duke of Westminster's estate workers told her father that she had seen the Prince of Wales 'lying on top of' Mrs Cornwallis West in the woods, the girl's father struck her 'a violent blow and told her she'd be killed if she repeated the story'.[36] Indeed, it was rumoured that the Prince was not only the godfather of Patsy Cornwallis West's son George, but his actual father.

Yet it was on quite another score that Rosenberg now attacked her. He accused Patsy Cornwallis West of co-operating with the photographers of 'professional beauties' to such an extent that she had rigged up no less than four photographic studios and fifteen darkrooms in her Eaton Place home; that she had all but exhausted herself in her eagerness to give sittings; and that she was making thousands of pounds a year in commission on the sale of her photographs.

Mrs Cornwallis West's husband proved to be not nearly as long-suffering as Mrs Langtry's husband appeared to be. Within a week Cornwallis West had sued Rosenberg for defamatory libel. Rosenberg was arrested, and at the preliminary hearing he was astonished to learn that he was to be tried not only for his defamation of Mrs Cornwallis West, but also for his libelling of Mr and Mrs Langtry.

The trial, which opened in the Central Criminal Court on 25 October 1879, turned out to be a *cause célèbre*. But the crowds that flocked to it in the hope of seeing the notorious Mrs Langtry were disappointed. They had to be content with the distinctly less beguiling figure of her husband, Edward Langtry. The court was assured, by the Langtrys' orotund counsel, that the couple lived in the best and highest society and that they had been honoured with the acquaintance, nay, friendship, of Their Royal Highnesses, the Prince and Princess of Wales, who had frequently visited them. That His Royal Highness had visited her a sight more often than Her Royal Highness (who had, in fact, visited her only once, when she was ill) was a point not stressed by counsel.

'The lady of whom this libel has been published is of great personal attractions and beauty. Hence it has been that the defendant [Rosenberg] and those who are associated with him, have thought fit for the purpose of profit, and for the sake of their vile publication, to make her the subject of obloquy and defamation.'

Edward Langtry assured the court that there was no truth whatsoever in Rosenberg's assertions; that he had never contemplated divorce; and that he and his wife lived on the most affectionate terms.

Was there any truth, asked counsel, in Rosenberg's claim that Mr

Langtry had been offered a diplomatic appointment?

'Not a word,' replied Langtry.

'I am very glad to hear it,' said counsel, a shade ambiguously.

Rosenberg, pleading guilty to having published the libels, denied that he had known that they were false. The judge was not impressed. He sentenced him to eighteen months in prison.

The Prince of Wales had been saved from another major scandal. Yet it must have been with more than a flicker of amusement that the crowded court heard Rosenberg's counsel declare that it was far from him 'to suppose that the Prince of Wales could for one moment depart from that morality which it is his duty to exhibit . . .'[37]

Quite obviously, said the wags, there was nothing between the Prince of Wales and Lillie Langtry; not even a sheet.

The End and the Beginning

BY THE SPRING of 1880, three years after she had first met the Prince of Wales, Lillie Langtry was riding the crest of her self-created wave. By a deliberate exploitation of her physical attractions, she had managed to achieve all her girlhood ambitions. At twenty-six, she was one of the most celebrated women in society. She had been presented to Queen Victoria, she could claim the friendship of kings and princes, she was the guest in some of the grandest houses in the land, she had been painted by the world's most famous artists, her photographic likenesses were familiar throughout the country, her movements were reported in the press, she was the centre of interest whenever she attended a ball and in danger of being mobbed whenever she appeared in the street. 'Jersey Lily' was one of the most famous sobriquets in the kingdom. When the ancient Egyptian obelisk – Cleopatra's Needle – was re-erected on the banks of the Thames in 1878, Lillie Langtry's photograph was among the various articles buried, for posterity, in its foundations.

Yet more than anyone Lillie appreciated the precariousness of her social position. It depended, entirely, on the patronage of her royal lover. Without that neither her beauty, her vivacity, nor her drive could guarantee her a place in society. Lillie was no fool. She knew well enough that those who entertained her most readily were those most eager to gain, or retain, the Prince's friendship. In the main, it was the Prince's *nouveaux riches* friends, people like the Rothschilds and the Sassoons, who opened their doors to her, while the doors of truly aristocratic establishments, such as Hatfield House, home of the Salisburys, remained firmly closed. In short, if she had not been the Prince's mistress, Lillie Langtry's curiosity value would not have lasted for more than a season.

At the same time, she realised that she could not hope to hold

Bertie's interest forever. He was too fickle, too restless, too self-indulgent a man to remain faithful to one woman for long. After all, he was not yet forty. Already he had enjoyed the occasional peccadillo and he was often to be seen, these days, with another professional beauty, Mrs Luke Wheeler. In fact, the Prince was so often in the company of Mrs Wheeler – and, for appearance's sake, of her husband Luke – that Luke's father, a naive old clergyman, was once heard to remark, 'It is strange how fond the Prince of Wales has become of my son. He and Luke are inseparable.'[1]

The year before, Lillie had had to compete with the attractions of an altogether more formidable rival – Sarah Bernhardt.

The already famous actress had arrived in London with the Comédie Française in the summer of 1879. Lillie was among the first people to meet her. She was invited, with other members of 'the fashionable world'[2], to a welcoming breakfast given by Sir Algernon Borthwick, proprietor of *The Morning Post*.

The Divine Sarah looked, to say the least, extraordinary. 'Her beauty,' as Lillie somewhat gingerly puts it, 'was not understood by the masses.'[3] Whereas Lillie, with her sloping shoulders, small waist, generous breasts and hips, conformed to the contemporary ideal of womanhood, Sarah was an exponent of the new 'aesthetic' style. Together with other unconventional women such as the actress Ellen Terry, and William Morris's wife, Jane, Sarah Bernhardt spurned the constraints of Victorian couture and dressed in a free, flowing, uncorseted fashion. Instead of disguising her thin, angular figure, Sarah emphasised it by wearing waistless dresses with bold vertical trimmings. Everything was designed to accentuate her sinuous seductiveness. The gauzy bow at the neck, the tight, transparent lace sleeves, the sensuous velvets or slithery silks, the 'tantalising' front fastenings – all these were regarded as highly provocative in less bohemian circles.

Even more provocative was Madame Sarah's face. The forerunner of the 'vamp' or the 'It' girl of a later period, she painted her face in a manner that shocked those users of a little surreptitious rice powder or a few geranium petals. Her lips were brightly coloured, her eyes – with their famous 'drugged stare' – were outlined in kohl, her tufts of frizzy hair were dyed, even her earlobes were rouged. 'I went,' admitted the actress, 'to extremes in everything.'[4]

This was no less true of her private life. The illegitimate daughter of a Jewish cocotte, with an illegitimate son of her own, Sarah Bernhardt cheerfully flouted every convention. 'London has gone mad over the principal actress in the Comédie Française . . .,' wrote an appalled Lady Frederick Cavendish, 'Sarah Bernhardt, a woman of notorious character. Not content with being run after on the stage, this woman is asked to respectable people's houses to act, and even to luncheon and dinner, and all the world goes. It is an outrageous scandal.'[5]

But it was, of course, as an actress that Sarah Bernhardt should have been judged and here Lillie Langtry, so soon to become an actress herself, showed admirable discernment. 'This great and overwhelming artist was almost too individual, too exotic, to be completely understood or properly estimated *all at once*. Her superb diction, her lovely silken voice, her natural acting, her passionate temperament, her fire – in a word, transcendent genius – caused amazement . . .' Bernhardt's personality was 'so striking, so singular that, to everyday people, she seemed eccentric; she filled the imagination as a great poet might do.'[6]

Sarah's opinion of Lillie was more succinct. 'With that chin,' she snapped after first meeting her, 'she will go far.'[7]

Lillie was being remarkably generous in her assessment of Sarah, for not least among the actress's admirers was the Prince of Wales. In a way, this is surprising. Bertie's taste in women, as in so much else, was conventional. He liked dressy, well-groomed, curvaceous women. So punctilious himself, he disapproved of any sloppiness in dress; with the freedom affected by the so-called 'new women', he had very little sympathy. When Lady Florence Dixie appeared at Ascot in one of her 'rational' garments – a shapeless white boating dress – he icily asked her whether she had, by mistake, come in her nightgown. On the other hand, Bertie admired spirit, and Sarah Bernhardt was certainly spirited. Nor would he have been shocked by her unashamed hedonism.

The two had met, some years before, in Paris, and on his frequent visits to the French capital, the Prince always made a point of seeing the actress, both on and off stage. He even, on one occasion, appeared on stage with her. During a performance of Sardou's *Fédora,* the irrepressible Bertie doubled as the corpse in the scene in which the distraught heroine weeps over the body of her murdered lover. One can only hope that Queen Victoria did not hear about this unseemly behaviour on the part of the forty-year-old Heir Apparent.

During this 1879 London season, Bertie seems to have paid the visiting actress a great deal of attention. He not only reserved a box for each of her opening nights in her different roles but let it be known that she was to be received in society. He even entertained her at

Marlborough House. After one such visit, Sarah scrawled a note of apology to the doyen of the Comédie Française. 'I've just come back from the P. of W. It is twenty past one. I can't rehearse any more at this hour. The P. has kept me since eleven . . .'[8]

Quite clearly, Bertie was fascinated by the piquant-faced French-woman. Whether or not they became lovers is uncertain. Given their shared sexual appetites and moral attitudes, it is not unlikely. Sarah had a seductive, smouldering quality that the Prince would have found hard to resist, and few women, least of all Sarah Bernhardt, would have turned down the opportunity of sleeping with a future king who also happened to be a man of great charm and considerable amorous expertise.

What did Lillie Langtry make of all this? She would have realised that the Prince was fascinated by the actress but she would have been far too astute to have mentioned it, let alone to have reproached him for it. She was, in any case, in no position to throw stones. Not only was Lillie carrying on her clandestine affair with Arthur Jones, but her public behaviour was becoming increasingly indiscreet. Daisy, Countess of Warwick, then in her first season, has a story to tell on this score. Daisy was being courted by a young lord whose protestations of undying love she was more than ready to believe until she one night happened to overhear him call Lillie Langtry 'my darling'. He then went on to make an assignation with Lillie. 'Naturally I was furious,' says Daisy, 'and never looked at him again.'[9]

Margot Asquith, too, has her youthful memories of Lillie's tendency to cause scandal. 'In a shining top-hat and skin-tight habit, she rode a chestnut thoroughbred of conspicuous action every evening in Rotten Row,' she remembers. 'One day when I was riding, I saw Mrs Langtry – who was accompanied by Lord Lonsdale – pause at the railings in Rotten Row to talk to a man of her acquaintance. I do not know what she could have said to him, but after a brief exchange of words, Lord Lonsdale jumped off his horse, sprang over the railings and with clenched fists hit Mrs Langtry's admirer in the face. Upon this a free fight ensued and to the delight of the surprised spectators, Lord Lonsdale knocked his adversary down.'[10]

This adversary was Sir George Chetwyn, who had accused Lillie of breaking her promise to go riding with *him*.

And then there was the story of her obsession with 'young Shrewsbury, a boy of nineteen'. It appears that the young man's worldly mother, hoping that 'an attachment to a married woman would keep him out of mischief', encouraged the liaison. So conscientiously, apparently, did Lillie fulfil her duties of keeping the young man out of mischief that she one day sent a note to the Prince, asking him not to call, as arranged, that afternoon. The Prince, not having received the note, duly arrived to find her with Shrewsbury. What they were doing one does not know, but His Royal Highness, reports Wilfrid Scawen Blunt, was 'very miffed'.[11]

Yet, at the same time, Lillie seems to have been anxious to affirm her hold over her royal lover. In doing so, she came dangerously close to överstepping the bounds of propriety. Lillie had once claimed that it would need a bold man to attempt any public familiarity with the Prince, and on a couple of occasions she seems to have proved herself very bold indeed.

Once, at a charity fête held in the Royal Albert Hall, Lillie had been asked to grace the refreshment stall. Gentlemen were obliged to part with five shillings for the thrill of being served a cup of tea by her and with a guinea for the even greater thrill of having her take the first sip. When the Prince of Wales, accompanied by Princess Alexandra and their three daughters, approached the stall, Lillie poured the Prince a cup of tea and, without being asked, put her lips to the rim of the cup. The Prince put it down, untouched.

'I should like a clean one please,'[12] he said politely. In silence he accepted another cup, drank it, paid a couple of sovereigns, and walked away.

There was also the occasion on which Lillie is said to have dropped a piece of ice down the Prince's back at a fancy dress ball. Down the years the story has been so altered and embroidered upon that its authenticity is impossible to prove. Some say that it was a dollop of ice cream that Lillie slipped down the neck of Bertie's pierrot costume; others that it was not Lillie at all, but a pretty little actress by the name of Kitty Munro who put the ice down the Prince's back in – of all places – the foyer of the Folly Theatre; in the United States, cartoons showed Lillie dousing her royal lover with a bottle of iced champagne.

Lillie, who always denied the incident, claimed that it was actually an 'audacious Irish beauty' (by whom she apparently means Patsy Cornwallis West) who 'popped a spoonful of strawberry-ice' down the spine of her irate husband.

But however vigorously she protested her innocence, dismissing the story as 'a vulgar fabrication . . . in which there is not a grain of truth,'[13] Lillie was pursued by it for the rest of her life. And, true or not, the story's significance lies in the fact that it was so widely reported and so readily believed. Mrs Langtry, it was now said, was getting beyond herself. Many of the Prince of Wales's other companions had discovered, to their cost, that there was a limit to his familiarity. Had Lillie Langtry over-stepped that limit?

It was at this time, in the spring of 1880, that Lillie embarked on a relationship that was to run parallel with the gradual ebbing of her affair with the Prince of Wales. In March that year she met the twenty-five-year-old Prince Louis of Battenberg.

Prince Louis was a member of the Battenberg family that was just then beginning the extraordinary climb that was eventually to take it to some of the highest pinnacles in the world, including the British throne. The origins of the family had been, by royal standards, both humble and scandalous. The dynasty had come into being as recently as 1851 when the third son of the Grand Duke of Hesse had shocked his royal relations by marrying a commoner. The children of this morganatic marriage, excluded from the Hessian line of succession and addressed only as *serene* as opposed to *royal* highnesses, had been given the surname of Battenberg.

Only gradually, and exceedingly grudgingly, had the Battenbergs been admitted into the golden stockade of royalty. That they were accepted at all was in no small measure due to their exceptional qualities; for not only were the four Battenberg princes – Louis, Alexander, Henry and Franz Josef – extremely handsome young men but they were all talented, high-spirited and intelligent.

Prince Louis, the eldest, had joined the British navy at the age of fourteen in 1868. In the dozen or so years since then, he had proved himself to be an accomplished and conscientious sailor, treating his career with a seriousness that astonished many of his aristocratic shipmates. They found his cultural and intellectual interests puzzling and his abstinence from alcohol positively alarming. In one area, though, they found him reassuringly conformist. The tall, well-built, dark-bearded and handsome Prince Louis had a reputation not only as a 'good sport', but as a Lothario. 'If it was not quite a girl in every port,' writes one of his biographers, 'it was, for Louis, a girl in every other anchorage, island and naval establishment.'[14] Women found his particular qualities – his gentle voice, his engaging manners, even his foreign accent – irresistible.

The Prince of Wales was very fond of his young relation (Louis was a cousin-by-marriage to Bertie's late sister Alice, Grand Duchess of Hesse) and entertained him lavishly whenever he was home on leave.

In earlier days, the Prince of Wales had often given the homesick young naval cadet sensible advice (and Bertie was more sensible than Queen Victoria ever gave him credit for) and during the winter of 1875–6, Louis had accompanied Bertie, as an orderly officer, on the Heir's spectacular tour of India.

'You would do much better to get a little half-pay and spend the season with me at Marlborough House,'[15] wrote Bertie to him on one occasion; while Louis, describing the periods he spent in the company of the ebullient Prince, claimed that 'theatres and balls were the daily fare'.[16]

Queen Victoria was not anything like as ecstatic about Louis's frequent sojourns in England. It was not that she minded the morganatic 'taint' in the young man's blood (she once castigated her daughter, the German Crown Princess, for accusing the Battenbergs of not being *Geblüt* – pure bred – as though they were animals) but with her appreciation of virile good looks, she was afraid that her youngest daughter, Princess Beatrice, might fall in love with Prince Louis. The Queen had no intention of losing her daughter to a foreign prince: she wanted Beatrice to remain by her side.

It was during a period of unemployment (the Admiralty were proving strangely tardy about finding him another appointment) that Prince Louis met Lillie Langtry. True to form, he fell passionately in love with her. Quite possibly, the Prince of Wales encouraged the liaison. Tiring of Lillie himself, and devoted to his young kinsman, he would have been amused by the idea of these two attractive young people enjoying each other's company.

Ever a snob and pleased to have her powers of attraction confirmed, Lillie would have been delighted by the ardent attentions of yet another royal suitor; particularly one as personable as Prince Louis. Not only was he handsome and entertaining, but he also shared her taste for amusing, artistic and intellectually stimulating people. Through her, Louis met many of the leading cultural personalities of the time.

The affair was conducted with great discretion. With Edward Langtry invariably away on what Lillie calls 'fishing trips', the couple would meet in the Norfolk Street house or in the country houses of sympathetic friends. That Louis was infatuated by Lillie there can be no doubt; but he could never have imagined that he might be able to marry her, even if she were to divorce her by now all–but–invisible husband. For a gentleman, let alone a prince, to marry a divorcée would be unthinkable. It would have meant, for Louis, dismissal from the navy, rejection by his family, social ostracism and a life of penurious exile on the Riviera. The Battenberg morganatic marriage had been bad enough: a Battenberg marriage to a divorcée would be considered disastrous.

'Even the loss of a dear person is better than the general disgrace of a divorce,' declared the Princess of Wales's sister, the Empress Marie Feodorovna of Russia, on one occasion. And when, in 1912, one of the Empress's sons married his long-standing mistress who was a divorcée, she was thunderstruck. 'It is unbelievable!' she wailed. 'I can hardly understand what I am writing – it is so appalling in every way that it nearly kills me!' Unless the marriage were kept 'absolutely secret'[17] she would not be able to show her face in public.

Indeed, not until 1978 (after Edward VIII had abdicated his throne to marry the twice-divorced Wallis Simpson, and Princess Margaret had renounced the once-divorced Peter Townsend) was a divorcée allowed to marry into the British royal family. Having received the permission of Elizabeth II and renounced his own rights to the throne, Prince Michael of Kent married the divorced Baroness Marie-Christine von Reibnitz.

But even without the question of marriage ever seriously being considered, Lillie found herself facing a royal closing of ranks. By the autumn of 1880 she suspected that she was pregnant by Prince Louis. 'My own darling,' she wrote, not to Louis but to the faithful Arthur Jones with whom, throughout all the turbulence of her love life, she had kept up a loving relationship. 'I am not yet . . . I am sure there must be something wrong or what I took would have made me. Please go to a chemist and ask how many doses one ought to take a day as I must go on taking it . . .'[18]

Once Lillie's suspicions were confirmed, she told Louis. He, in turn, told his parents. They acted with that instinct for self-preservation characteristic of all royal families. Louis was informed that there was no possibility of a marriage; an aide-de-camp was despatched from Hesse to arrange a financial settlement with Lillie; and the Admiralty, having kept Louis hanging about for months, suddenly found him an appointment. On 16 October 1880, he was sent away on the longest voyage he was ever to undertake.

The man-o'-war on which he sailed had the unfortunate, if entirely appropriate, name of 'Inconstant'.

All at once, Lillie's whole shiny, elaborate, painstakingly assembled house of cards began to collapse. The Prince of Wales was losing interest in her; society was beginning to cold-shoulder her; she was five months pregnant by Prince Louis who had deserted her; even her husband had all but disappeared. And, most immediately disastrous of all, her creditors were starting to close in.

For years, as one of society's darlings, Lillie had lived well beyond her means. The Prince of Wales had usually paid her in kind rather than in cash. What with that, with Edward's financial fecklessness and with diminishing rents from the Langtry properties in perennially troubled Ireland, her income had reached, as she says, 'vanishing point'.[19] No longer was she able to stave off her creditors with airy promises or pretty entreaties: more acutely than anyone, they sensed the way the wind was blowing. In the end, the bailiffs moved into the Norfolk Street house; the contents of her home were to be auctioned off to pay her debts.

Although her maid, Dominique, who had been with her, as she puts it, 'through all my astonishing London experiences',[20] managed to save a few pieces of jewellery by slipping them into the pockets or handbags of visiting friends, the rest of her possessions went under the hammer. 'Everything went for immense prices –' reported Lady Lonsdale to Lillie, 'your little tea-table with your initials on down to your skates – so I hope your horrid creditors are satisfied.'[21]

For Lillie had not been there to witness this humiliation. With the sherriff's 'carpet flag' – the 'dismal emblem' of an auction – hanging from the drawing room window, she had fled the house forever.

She made for Jersey. But not even here could she find the anonymity she so desperately needed. 'Mr and Mrs Langtry have given up their London residence,' reported the New York *Times* that November, 'and for the present Mrs Langtry remains in Jersey. Is beauty deposed, or has beauty abdicated?'[22] And if beauty had indeed lost her throne, who, wondered the Jersey gossips, was responsible for beauty's thickening waistline? Edward Langtry was certainly nowhere to be seen. Was the Prince of Wales the culprit?

'I really don't know why we should blackguard the memory of Harry the Eighth,' wrote the indefatigable Adolphus Rosenberg, recently out of jail for his previous libelling of Lillie Langtry. 'True, he had a great weakness for the fair sex, but, unless history lies, he *married* all the women he fancied, which is not a bad trait in a prince.'[23]

Nor was Lillie the only member of her family to be providing material for gossip. By now, apparently, the lecherous behaviour of her father, the Dean of Jersey, had so outraged his parishioners that he had been obliged to leave the island. Although he remained Dean of Jersey until he died, in 1888, his duties were taken over by the vice-dean. It was given out that, for the sake of his health, the Dean had been obliged to move to London. Not with the best will in the world, though, could anyone believe that the air of Kennington was so much more salubrious than that of Jersey. While claiming that the shame of her bankruptcy had forced her to seek sanctuary with her parents in Jersey, Lillie makes no mention of the fact that one of these parents was no longer there.

Nor, of course, does she mention the birth of her illegitimate child. This event was wrapped in all the mystery characteristic of a Victorian melodrama. As the child could clearly not be born in Jersey (the birth certificate alone would present problems) Lillie made for the less restrictive atmosphere of France. With arrangements having been made, one assumes, by the Prince of Wales, Lillie gave birth to a daughter, in Paris, on – or about – 8 March 1881. She named the girl Jeanne-Marie. The child was handed over to the care of Lillie's mother and was brought up to believe that the dazzling creature who moved in and out of her life was her aunt. Jeanne-Marie was fourteen before she realised that Lillie was in fact her mother, and not until she was twenty-one was she told that her father had not been Edward Langtry but Prince Louis of Battenberg.

By that time Prince Louis had married, very properly, one of Queen Victoria's many granddaughters, Princess Victoria of Hesse. The couple had four children and, in time, Lillie's illegitimate daughter found herself half-sister, not only to Lord Louis Mountbatten, but to Princess Andrew of Greece, the mother of Prince Philip, Duke of Edinburgh who, in turn, married the future Queen Elizabeth II.

By this route are the descendants of Lillie Langtry, mistress of Albert Edward, Prince of Wales, related to Charles, the present Prince of Wales and Britain's future King.

Lillie Langtry was nothing if not resilient. 'Being young and of optimistic tendency,' she says, 'my nature quickly rebounded from the shock of misfortune . . .'[24] Within a month of Jeanne-Marie's birth she was back in London. This time, accompanied by the faithful Dominique, she took a modest flat in Victoria Street. Resolutely, she began to rebuild her life. Although Lillie was without any income, things could have been worse. She still had the Red House in Bournemouth, which the Prince of Wales had given her and into which she now put her mother and Jeanne-Marie. The dramatic death of her brother Maurice (he had been mauled by a tiger in India) did bring one advantage: it allowed her to go into mourning. So it was back to the days of the black dress, enlivened with a white collar in the mornings and with a little jet trimming at night. Had she felt so disposed, she says meaningfully, she could have had many more dresses for the asking, but she did not. Her pride, in other words, would not allow her to ask the Prince of Wales for money.

What was she to do? Her few remaining friends were full of advice. Frank Miles, the artist, suggested market gardening, but Oscar Wilde professed himself appalled at the idea of the lovely Lillie 'tramping the fields in muddy boots'.[25] Wilde's own advice was that she go on the stage. Whistler encouraged her to take up painting; others urged her to try millinery or dressmaking.

In the end, her mind was made up, and her course set, by the redoubtable Mrs Henry Labouchère. Wife of the famous 'Labby' Labouchère, Radical member of parliament and founder of the out-spoken magazine *Truth*, Henrietta Labouchère asked Lillie to take part in an amateur theatrical production which she was organising in cause of some charity. As far as the general public – and indeed Mrs Labouchère herself – was concerned, Lillie Langtry was still a celebrity. Her name on the bill would act as a powerful magnet. After a show of reluctance, Lillie agreed.

Her performance, in the Twickenham town hall, was judged a great success (*The World* described her voice as 'full, round and vibrant'[26]) with the result that Henrietta Labouchère had very little difficulty in persuading Lillie to tackle something more ambitious.

That well-known pair of actor-managers, Mr and Mrs Bancroft, lessees of the Haymarket Theatre, were talked by the enthusiastic Mrs Labouchère into giving Mrs Langtry a part in the charity matinée which they were planning in aid of the Royal General Theatrical Fund. She would play Kate Hardcastle in Oliver Goldsmith's *She Stoops to Conquer*. Any reservations the Bancrofts might have had about the 'startling proposition' of allowing a celebrated but complete amateur to appear in an otherwise professional cast melted in the face of two major considerations. 'The extraordinary career of popularity which has been Mrs Langtry's lot for several London seasons,' decided Bancroft, 'must have destroyed all fear of complete failure, for the ordeal of "facing the public" had already been often and gracefully passed through.'[27] The second consideration he left unsaid. This was that the inclusion of Mrs Langtry would ensure, not only a large and fashionable audience, but the attendance of the Prince of Wales.

Bancroft was proved right on all counts. Lillie's performance won high praise (the critic on *The Times* expressed himself astonished 'at the ease with which she glided into the part, the accuracy of the conception, and the felicity of the execution throughout'), the theatre 'overflowed with rank, fashion and celebrity'[28] and the Prince and Princess of Wales were in the royal box.

'Yesterday,' reported the Prince to his sixteen-year-old son, Prince George, then serving as a midshipman aboard HMS Bacchante, 'we went to a morning performance at Haymarket Theatre and saw Goldsmith's comedy, *She Stoops to Conquer,* in which Mrs Langtry acted with a professional company. It was her début, and a great success. As she is so very fond of acting, she has decided to go on the stage and will, after Christmas, join Mr and Mrs Bancroft's company at the Haymarket.'[29]

Quite clearly, Lillie was still in close touch with the Prince of Wales. For it had been only a week or so before that charity matinée that she had decided to accept the Bancrofts' offer of a contract. Having watched her rehearsing, the couple felt that she had the makings of an actress. And although Lillie was not as 'fond of acting' as Bertie suggests ('after all the adulation and social *éclat* that had fallen to my lot',[30] appearing in public held, she protests, no especial thrill for her) she could not afford to turn down the chance of making some money. So she accepted the Bancrofts' offer.

One thing, though, still bothered her. By becoming an actress, she would jeopardise whatever chance she had of regaining her social standing. Amateur acting was one thing; professional acting quite another. Actresses, in mid-Victorian society, were never ladies. Often synonymous with prostitutes, they certainly ranked no higher than tradespeople. Actors were received neither at court nor in society. The days of actors actually being knighted still lay in the future and even this would not give them an automatic entrée into aristocratic circles. 'The only actress at that time to be received in the "inner circle" of Society'[31] says Lillie, was Madge Robertson – Mrs Kendal. The rest had to be content with being entertained in what Lillie dismisses as the 'pleasant' enough houses of the *nouveaux riches* or by such unconventional society hostesses as Lady Sebright. Even when, in 1882, the Prince of Wales took the unprecedented step of inviting several members of the acting profession to a banquet at Marlborough House, it had to be an all-male occasion. And the meal was cut down, it was noted, to a mere nine courses.

So not only had Lillie lost the protection of her royal lover, she was in danger of becoming a social outcast. What she needed, to bolster her position and to counteract the faintly disreputable aura associated with treading the boards, was the patronage of some important figure whose respectability was beyond question.

Who better than that pillar of Victorian respectability – the Prime Minister, William Ewart Gladstone?

Hitherto, Lillie Langtry's biographers have assumed that her intriguing relationship with Gladstone dated from the early days of her rise to prominence and that throughout her years of social success (and at the request of the Prince of Wales) Gladstone had been her friend and 'mentor'. The assumption is inaccurate. It is true that they had once met, briefly and casually, at Millais's studio, but from then on, until January 1882, after Lillie had joined the Bancrofts' company, there was no personal contact between them. Nor, when they again met, was it Gladstone who sought her out; the approach came from Lillie.

Her approach was made through that influential contemporary figure, the essayist and raconteur, Abraham Hayward. In many ways, Hayward was typical of the sort of person – now largely forgotten but then socially powerful – who pervaded Victorian society. Relatively humbly born, he had, by virtue of a lively mind, an amusing tongue and an informed interest in cultural and political affairs, gained admittance into the grandest salons in the land. Few social gatherings were complete without the slight, sprightly figure of Abraham Hayward.

It was, in fact, Hayward who had given Lillie Langtry that glowing review in *The Times* for her performance in *She Stoops to Conquer*. (His private opinion was somewhat less effusive; his review may well have been written with one eye on Marlborough House.) Lillie had then, on the advice of another society gossip, Lord Torrington, written to thank Hayward for his kind words. And not only to thank him but to ask him to do her a favour. Or so it appeared.

Among Gladstone's papers in the British Library is this letter from Abraham Hayward, dated 8 January 1882.

'My dear Gladstone,

'Mrs Langtry, who is an enthusiastic admirer of yours, told me this afternoon that she should feel highly flattered if you would call on her, and I tell you this, although I fear you have other more pressing overtures just at present. Her address is 18 Albert Mansions, Victoria Street, and she is generally at home about six.'[32]

It seemed, on the face of it, to be an extraordinary imposition on Lillie's part. Why should the Prime Minister of Great Britain bother himself with the likes of her? But Lillie, as always, knew exactly what she was doing. For Gladstone was not nearly the moral paragon of popular imagination. A small circle of his intimates were only too aware of this: they knew all about the Prime Minister's bizarre sex life. And Lillie, through her liaison with the Prince of Wales, would have known about it too. It was this knowledge which emboldened her to write to Gladstone.

Even in his seventies Gladstone remained a robust, energetic, full-blooded man. Tall and craggy-featured, the Prime Minister still had the body, reported his doctor in 1882, 'of some ancient Greek statue of the ideal man'.[33] By nature impetuous and passionate, he had all his life exercised an iron self-control. In this he was helped by two things: his exceptional strength of character and his unquestioning belief in God. All instincts towards self-gratification had to be repressed, he maintained; humility and self-mortification must be the ideal.

To few aspects of his life did Gladstone apply this belief more rigorously than to his sex life. Faced with a sexual drive no less vigorous than his other drives, he did his utmost to sublimate it. In the main, this sublimation took an unexpected form: a lone campaign against prostitution. Throughout his long life, Gladstone set himself the task of rescuing and reforming prostitutes.

There was no shortage of possible candidates. The field in which he so zealously carried out his self-imposed mission – an area bounded by Soho, Piccadilly and the Thames Embankment – was swarming with street-walkers. Late at night, armed with a stick for protection, Gladstone would roam the foggy, gas-lit pavements. Sometimes waiting to be accosted, sometimes making the first advance himself, sometimes even going into brothels, he would endeavour to talk the women into giving up their way of life. He might offer to take them home for a meal, he might give them gifts of money, he might send them to some institution for 'fallen women'. Not only did he make generous contributions to rescue homes but he was instrumental in founding several of these institutions.

Inevitably, his strange behaviour led to gossip. From time to time he was spotted in conversation with a prostitute, or entering a brothel, and on one occasion an attempt was made to blackmail him. Few men – the worldly police among them – could believe that his interest was purely philanthropic. Occasionally his parliamentary colleagues would warn him of the dangers, both to his career and to his Party, but Gladstone refused to listen. So candid, so innocent, so honest seemed his reaction to these warnings, that his friends could not believe that his behaviour was inspired by anything other than the highest motives.

And so it may have been, but in not quite the way that they imagined. For Gladstone took his determination to be humbled and mortified very far indeed. To control his sexual torment, to master temptation, he is said to have read pornography and to have resorted to what he himself called 'strange and humbling' acts with the prostitutes whom he visited. And if he felt that his mortification at the hands of these women had not been severe enough, then, on reaching home, he would flagellate himself.

'Has it been sufficiently considered how far pain may become a ground for enjoyment?' confided Gladstone to his diary. 'How far satisfaction and even an action of delighting in pain may be a true experimental phenomenon of the human mind?'[34]

Such admissions were for his eyes only (each act of flagellation he marked with a little whip in the margins of his diary) and it is unlikely that anyone else would have guessed the lengths to which Gladstone was prepared to go in search of this pleasurable humiliation. But enough was known of his strange habits to cause deep misgivings.

Causing his colleagues even more unease than his prostitute-hunting was his friendship with various well-known courtesans. Talking to anonymous street-walkers was one thing; visiting some of London's more notorious 'scarlet women' in their homes was quite another. One of these women was the famous Laura Thistlethwayte. This theatrical-looking beauty, having spent half her life as a courtesan, suddenly underwent a religious conversion. And although this conversion seems to have interfered very little with her former occupation, Mrs Thistlethwayte became an evangelical preacher. This gave her, for Gladstone, a double appeal: reformed prostitutes with a taste for religion were exactly up his street.

Another of his associates was that ubiquitous contemporary figure, Skittles. Much to the amusement of the Prince of Wales, whom she kept fully informed, Skittles – having heard of Gladstone's interest in 'ladies of light character' – invited him to visit her. 'Saturdays and Sundays were his evenings out,' she explained to Wilfrid Scawen Blunt. Carrying a bunch of narcissi and having sent her a twelve-pound tin of Russian tea in advance, the Prime Minister duly arrived.

'I have not come to talk politics,' he announced (not even in her most self-important moments, surely, had Skittles imagined that he would) and remarked, more properly, on the smallness of her waist. He then went on to measure it, she says, by putting his hands around it.

What else they discussed or, for that matter, measured, is not known, but when he left, Gladstone asked her to write to him. She 'should mark the envelope private, followed by a little cross, thus "Private X".' Skittles afterwards heard that the Prime Minister had been 'much struck with all my go and charming ways . . .'[35]

It was no wonder that Lillie who, for 'go and charming ways' could match Skittles any day, decided to approach Gladstone. Or that it should have been through Abraham Hayward that she did so. Hayward (sometimes referred to as 'the Viper') knew all about Gladstone's sexual activities; in fact, he was not above doing what amounted to a little discreet pimping. Having insisted that he replace the usual reviewer for Lillie's theatrical début, Hayward had quickly appreciated that she would be just the type to interest Gladstone. Between them, then, Lillie and Hayward concocted the letter to the Prime Minister. And Gladstone, reading between the lines, would have known exactly what Hayward's letter implied.

Within days, the Prime Minister had become a frequent caller at her little flat and she was soon making use of the 'double envelope system' whereby her letters to him were kept out of the hands of his secretaries. Abraham Hayward had reassured him that although there was no formal separation between Lillie and her husband, 'they are but little together and he has as good as told her to shift for herself.'[36] In other words, Gladstone was unlikely to run into an irate husband during his calls.

The Prime Minister's colleagues were no less worried about his relationship with Mrs Langtry than they were about his other friendships. 'She is evidently trying to make social capital out of the acquaintance she has scraped with him,' his private secretary, Sir Edward Hamilton once complained. 'Most disagreeable things with all kinds of exaggeration are being said. I took the occasion of putting in a word and cautioning him against the wiles of the woman, whose reputation is in such bad odour that, despite all the endeavours of H.R.H., nobody will receive her in their house.'[37]

Hamilton could have saved his breath; Gladstone took no notice.

Yet, granted the fact that the Prime Minister's underlying interest in Lillie Langtry was sexual, their relationship – on a superficial level – was probably innocent. As much as by her erotic aura and scandalous reputation, Gladstone would have been attracted by her independent spirit.

With characteristic discretion, she refers to the 'uplifting effects' of his visits. How wonderful, she gushes, 'that this great and universally sought-after man should give me and my work even a passing thought.' He gave her advice, he brought her books (including his favourite, *Sister Dora,* a biography of a high-born woman who worked as a nurse among the poor), he read aloud his favourite passages from Shakespeare, he interested himself in her financial affairs (Hayward kept him informed on these) and they discussed, of course, religion. 'One could not be in his company without feeling that goodness emanated from him,'[38] says Lillie piously.

One piece of advice she always remembered. 'In your professional career, you will receive attacks, personal and critical, just and unjust. Bear them, never reply and, above all, never rush into print to explain or defend yourself.'[39]

The advice could have applied, equally well, to himself.

'I may have my faults,' the Prince of Wales once said. 'No one is more alive to them than I am; but I have held one great principle in life from which I never waver, and that is loyalty to one's friends . . .'[40]

This was true. And it was certainly true of the Prince's relationship with Lillie Langtry. Although the white heat of his love for her had cooled, he remained as fond of her and as loyal to her as ever. Throughout her stage career, which was to burgeon as spectacularly as her social career had once done, she could count on the interest and support of the Prince of Wales. He could always be relied upon to exert a little pressure here and to use a little influence there. Bertie loved the theatre; often his presence alone was enough to ensure the success of a play. And there were few of Lillie's London opening nights on which the plump, bearded and immaculately dressed figure of the Prince of Wales was not to be seen in the royal box. Often, to the consternation of the rest of the cast, he would leave his seat after the first act and spend the rest of the evening in Lillie's dressing room, eagerly awaiting her stage exits and chatting, in his affable way, to her dresser as he waited.

On a less professional level, too, the couple kept in touch. They wrote to each other, they exchanged photographs, they paid little visits, they went racing together. And there was still the occasional candle-lit supper at Rules or Kettners at which His Nibs, as she affectionately called him, would respond anew to the quick mind, spirited manner and enduring beauty of the Jersey Lily.

In fact, far from having ended, their relationship had merely entered a different phase.

Part Two

'MY OWN DARLING DAISY WIFE'

The Heiress

IN NOVEMBER 1881 the Prince of Wales turned forty. This milestone brought with it neither a relaxation in his exclusion from affairs of state nor any prospect of more worthwhile employment. He knew as little as ever, says one observer, 'about the contents of those boxes that were piled upon his Mother's desk. There was the tree of knowledge, there the fountain of wisdom; they were just out of reach; and occasional confidences made his predicament all the more tantalising.'[1]

Earlier that year the Prince, on meeting Sir Charles Dilke – then Under-Secretary for Foreign Affairs – at a dinner party, had spoken to him about his 'anxiety to be kept informed of foreign affairs'.[2] Dilke promised to do what he could. But a few years later, at another dinner party, the Prince was obliged to raise the matter yet again; this time with Gladstone's private secretary, Sir Edward Hamilton. 'He complains of being kept too much in the dark by the Government,' reported Hamilton, 'and I think not without reason. He would like important decisions of the Cabinet communicated to him.'[3] Hamilton promised to speak to Gladstone about it.

Gladstone, very wisely, felt that he could take no such step without having first consulted Queen Victoria. He did not feel very optimistic. Gladstone had not forgotten his previous attempt, made over a decade before, to talk the Queen into giving her eldest son some responsible job.

He was no more successful on this occasion. The Queen would not hear of it. She, and she alone, would decide what papers, if any, should be passed on to the Prince of Wales. 'She is very jealous of anything tending to derogate her Sovereign Powers,'[4] noted Hamilton.

That was one reason for her attitude; another was that she considered her son to be notoriously indiscreet. The Prince was never to be shown anything, she would warn her ministers, of a *confidential* nature; she 'deprecated the discussion of national secrets over country house dinner tables.'[5] Writing at this time to one of her many granddaughters, Princess Victoria of Hesse, the Queen ventured to make what she called 'a very *private* little *observation*': this was that 'Dear Uncle cannot keep anything to himself – but lets everything *out.*'[6]

Rendering the Prince of Wales's position even more galling was the fact that his youngest brother, the artistic and scholarly Prince Leopold, was being entrusted with precisely the sort of job at which Bertie himself would have excelled. It had been Disraeli, at that stage still Prime Minister, who had suggested the employment for Prince Leopold. As Leopold's haemophilia prevented him from treading the traditional princely path – a career in one of the armed services or a governor-generalship – Disraeli had suggested that he assume the cloak, or one of the cloaks, once worn by the late Prince Consort: that he become Queen Victoria's assistant and adviser in her dealings with foreign affairs. He could read official despatches, correspondence with ambassadors and ministers, and letters to and from the Queen's fellow sovereigns.

It was, in short, the sort of job that would have suited the Prince of Wales to perfection. Bertie's frequent visits to the Continent, and particularly to France, had greatly strengthened his interest in, and knowledge of, foreign affairs. Not quite all his time in Paris was spent at the *Jardin de Paris* or the *Chat Noir*. In the salons of women like the Princesse de Sagan or the Comtesse de Pourtalès, he absorbed a great deal of political information; and he had several meetings with that fiery and significant figure in French political life, Leon Gambetta. Indeed, of all aspects of government business, foreign affairs were guaranteed to hold the Prince of Wales's otherwise flickering attention.

How harmoniously Bertie would have worked beside his exacting mother is another matter. In any case, he was never given the opportunity. Queen Victoria, who always looked kindly on dear Mr Disraeli's suggestions, agreed that the job should be entrusted to Prince Leopold. And so, for half a dozen years, from 1877 to 1882, Prince Leopold acted as part personal assistant, part confidential secretary and part go-between to Queen Victoria.

Just how valuable Leopold proved himself to be is difficult to assess. Ministers were careful to consult him, to include him and to make use of his services. And the Queen seemed well enough pleased. So, of course, did Prince Leopold. Proudly, he once showed a key to Sir Charles Dilke's secretary, James Bodley. 'It is the Queen's Cabinet key which opens all the secret despatch boxes,' he explained. 'Dizzy gave it to me, but my brother the Prince of Wales is not allowed to have one.'[7]

In the face of this humiliating situation (Leopold was twelve years younger than Bertie) the Prince of Wales showed remarkable forebearance. Never a vindictive man, he did not allow it to sour his relations with his brother. 'Uncle Bertie,' wrote Prince Leopold's daughter, Princess Alice, Countess of Athlone, in later life, 'was, of course, aware of the assistance which my father was giving to the Queen and knew that his younger brother had access to State papers which he, though Prince of Wales, was not allowed to see. He was understandably indignant at such treatment, and I cannot help being filled with admiration for his magnanimity, for he bore no grudge against my father and was always kindness itself to my mother and me . . . I consider he showed real greatness of spirit in his attitude.'[8]

Disraeli, having applied his astute mind to one aspect of Prince Leopold's life, now applied it to another: the Prince's marriage. Queen Victoria's confidant in so many matters, Disraeli appreciated that the Queen was no longer thinking in terms of great royal matrimonial alliances for her children. These had brought nothing but trouble. Wars on the Continent had invariably split her family into violently opposed camps, while the marriage of yet another minor and usually impoverished German prince or princess into the British royal family always led to public grumbling. Some well-born, well-heeled British spouse was a much better bet. Already, in 1871, the Queen had allowed her daughter Louise to marry the wealthy Marquess of Lorne. So why not, thought Disraeli, a similar arrangement for Prince Leopold?

He had a candidate to hand. This was a young woman blessed, apparently, with every advantage: birth, beauty, brains and great wealth. Disraeli had once taken her to the theatre and had been charmed. She would, he imagined, make the perfect wife for Prince Leopold. And so, just before the young lady's eighteenth birthday in December 1879, the Queen commanded her parents, Lord and Lady Rosslyn, to bring her to Windsor for inspection.

Lord Rosslyn was, in fact, the girl's step-father, her mother's second husband. Her own surname was Maynard and her first name Frances. But just as Emilie Le Breton had always been known as Lillie, so Frances Maynard was always known as Daisy.

*

Daisy Maynard's background was very different from Lillie Langtry's. For one thing, it was indubitably aristocratic. Frances Evelyn
Maynard had been born, on 10 December 1861, into a world of
wealth, position and privilege. Her father, the Honourable Charles
Maynard, was the only son and heir of the third Viscount Maynard,
whose family seat was the palatial Easton Lodge near Dunmow in
Essex. Her mother was a Fitzroy, doubly descended from Charles II
through the Dukes of Grafton and the Dukes of St Albans.

Charles Maynard was one of those splendid Victorian swashbuck-
lers; a *beau sabreur* straight out of the pages of an Ouida novel, whose
escapades, real or imagined, were to become legendary. A big man,
red-haired and blue-eyed, he became colonel of that most fashionable
of regiments, the Royal Horse Guards (the Blues) where he was
chiefly distinguished for his bravado, his quick temper and his addic-
tion to drink. He was a superb horseman. 'He could leap his charger to
and fro over the mess table ready laid for a banquet,' boasts Daisy,
'without disturbing a single wine glass.'⁹ And once, while attending a
bull-fight in Spain, he astonished his companions – and infuriated the
crowd – by leaping over the barrier, vaulting onto the bull's back and
galloping the rampaging animal round the ring. That Daisy had
inherited a somewhat wild streak is not to be wondered at.

Her mother was very different. Twenty years younger than her
ebullient husband, Blanche Maynard was a woman of more restrained
behaviour but more sterling qualities. She was a forceful character:
strong-willed, resourceful, ambitious.

She needed to be all these for, in 1865, when her daughter Daisy was
three and her second daughter not yet one, Charles Maynard died. His
death was followed, less than five months later, by that of his father,
Viscount Maynard.

But whatever losses Charles Maynard's widow might have suffered
by way of death were handsomely compensated for by way of
inheritance. For her eldest daughter, the three-year-old Daisy
Maynard, now inherited the entire Maynard estates. Suddenly the
golden-haired, blue-eyed little girl had become an heiress. Not only
would she one day be mistress of Easton Lodge and its vast acreage,
but she would enjoy an income of over £30,000 a year, equivalent
today to something like three-quarters of a million. It was no
wonder that her Maynard relations, eagerly gathered round the
breakfast table to hear the reading of the will, were so incensed that

they flung pats of butter at the portrait of the late Lord Maynard.

Two years later, in 1866, Daisy's mother remarried. Her second husband, the thirty-three-year-old Lord Rosslyn, was very different from her first. No vaulting onto the backs of bulls for him. Sophisticated, cultivated and intelligent, Lord Rosslyn was far happier composing poetry or discussing politics. Very much the courtier, he was a great favourite with Queen Victoria. Like Disraeli, he had the Queen's measure exactly. He handled her with just the right blend of reverence and impudence. Lord Rosslyn was the only man in the kingdom, claims Daisy, who could tell the Queen a risqué story and go unrebuked.

'I have been at dinner in Windsor Castle and heard Lord Rosslyn spinning a daring yarn to the Queen, while the Princess Beatrice looked as though she were sitting on thorns, and other guests were quaking. I have seen the Queen's lips twitching with suppressed laughter and . . . I might go so far as to state that I have seen her most gracious Majesty shaking like an agitated jelly.'[10]

Yet for all his worldliness, Lord Rosslyn had a taste for family life and simple country activities. It was, therefore, in an atmosphere both cultured and loving that Daisy Maynard grew up. As her mother bore her second husband five children, there were seven children in all – five girls and two boys – growing up at Easton.

Their upbringing, in spite of Lord Rosslyn's cultural interests, was very much that of the average Victorian upper-class family. 'Except for escapades prompted by the natural high spirits of a group of healthy, happy children, in a beautiful country place, who had ponies to ride and animals to caress,' says Daisy, 'the story of our childhood was the story of our training and education.'[11]

The children saw their parents at set hours, usually in the late afternoon, after tea. 'Children in my early days,' remembered one of them in later life, 'were looked upon partly as a nuisance and partly as a kind of animate toy, to be shown, if they were sufficiently attractive, to callers. We were always brought down and shown after lunch, but were never expected to utter, and were consequently all abominably shy.'[12]

The rest of the time was spent in the care of nurses, governesses and tutors. Although the boys might be sent away to school, the girls were always educated at home. This education was designed to give them a veneer of culture: just enough to meet the not very exacting conversational demands of aristocratic society. They learned history, languages (French, German and sometimes Italian) and literature, with the study of literature being largely confined to memorising great chunks of the classics. Geography meant little more than 'the use of globes for young ladies'[13]; science was all but ignored. Religious instruction was limited to the study of the concepts of right and wrong, good and evil, heaven and hell; an uncompromising doctrine reinforced by the habitual gloom of the Victorian Sunday.

Considered equally important were such things as deportment (a straight back would serve one better than a thousand remembered pages of Molière or Schiller), dress, which must always be modest and subdued (heiress to a vast fortune, Daisy spent her girlhood in her mother's cast-off clothes), piano lessons, riding lessons, drawing lessons and visits to concerts and exhibitions. Even as late as the 1930s, the then Duchess of York, mother of the future Queen Elizabeth II, could maintain that all girls needed was plenty of fresh country air, the ability to dance and draw and appreciate music, good manners, perfect deportment and feminine grace.

It says a great deal for young Daisy Maynard's strength of character that her individualism was not stamped out by this unimaginative curriculum. On the contrary, she seems to have overcome its many limitations and to have benefited from its few advantages. It left her, she assures us, with a great love of reading, an interest in history and a talent for languages. She even goes so far as to claim that it gave her 'a just sympathy and an open mind'.[14]

By no means, though, could her education have been responsible for the telling observation she has to make on one aspect of her Easton girlhood. This concerned that sacred Victorian ritual – Sunday church-going. For the young Daisy, the ritual underlined, more strongly than anything else, the inequalities between masters and servants, rich and poor. The gentry or 'quality', in their determination that nothing should sully the sanctity of the Sabbath, kept it as a day of rest; they saw no inconsistency in the fact that a similar day of rest was denied to those who worked for them: the no less pious maids and valets who dressed them, the cooks, maids and footmen who served them their huge meals or the stablemen, coachmen and grooms who ensured that they were driven to and from worship.

Within the church itself there was a strict separation of the classes. Among the gentlefolk who sat, of course, at the front, there was even a separation of the sexes. Apparently, this sexual separation was not considered necessary among the lower orders. The service over, the congregation would file out in order of precedence: the Rosslyn family first, then the estate steward and his family, then the farmers and finally the cottagers. There was even some curtseying as the 'quality' processed down the aisle.

'I used to wonder, even as a child,' remembers Daisy, 'how God viewed this "table of precedence" in His church, where all men were supposed to be equal.'[15]

If such unorthodox observations serve as a pointer to the direction Daisy's life would one day follow, another girlhood memory is linked to a very different phase of her future career.

Daisy was still in her teens when, on going to Frank Miles's studio for the last sitting of a pencil drawing of her head, she met Lillie Langtry. Lillie was then on the threshold of her years of social success and to the young Daisy she was simply the most beautiful creature she had ever seen. 'How can any words of mine convey that beauty?' she gushes: those dewy eyes, that peach-like complexion, that 'mass of lovely hair drawn back in a soft knot at the nape of her classic head.' Even more remarkable was Lillie Langtry's charm; it was almost tangible.

Lord Rosslyn, who had accompanied his step-daughter to Miles's studio, was hardly less captivated. He immediately invited this lovely young woman to dine the following evening at the family's London home, in Grafton Street. Lillie came, accompanied by her husband (Daisy described Edward Langtry as 'an uninteresting fat man whose unnecessary presence took nothing from his wife's social triumph') and 'magnetised' the rest of the company.

After that, Lillie was often invited down to Easton. Here Daisy and her younger sisters, with all the ardour of adolescence, became her 'admiring slaves'. Uncomplainingly Lillie allowed herself to be led about on a fat cob, or to have her hats amateurishly trimmed by the adoring girls. 'My own infatuation, for it was little less, for lovely Lillie Langtry, continued for many a day,'[16] admits Daisy.

Or, at least, until the day when Daisy took her idol's place as the Prince of Wales's mistress.

'In my teens,' writes Daisy, 'it came as a deep and almost incredible surprise and delight to me to find in men's eyes an unfailing tribute to a beauty I myself had not been able to discern.'[17]

This is understandable. Victorian girls, with their long, tortuously frizzled hair and their short-skirted versions of adult fashions (the hip-hugging, bustled fashions of the late 1870s were particularly unsuitable for immature girls), needed to be exceptionally good-

looking to convince even themselves that they might one day be
beautiful. And, in any case, Daisy did not have the sensuous, striking,
untamed beauty that had been Lillie Langtry's from childhood; her
looks were altogether more refined. Daisy Maynard was slight,
small-boned, sharp-featured. Lillie in the simplest of dresses and the
most casual of hairstyles still looked arresting; Daisy needed the adult
aids of elegant clothes and carefully coiffured hair to set off her more
subtle looks.

But there were some features – her dark-lashed, dark-blue eyes, her
golden hair and her good bone-structure – which set her apart, even in
girlhood, and which won her those admiring male glances. The most
admiring of all, it seems, came from the young Lord Brooke. Francis
Greville, Lord Brooke, heir to the fourth Earl of Warwick, was
twenty-three when he first met the sixteen-year-old Daisy Maynard.
He immediately fell in love with her. Within weeks he had asked her
parents' permission to propose.

In the ordinary way, Lord and Lady Rosslyn would have welcomed
the match. Lord Brooke was a handsome, well-made, dependable
young man who would one day inherit an ancient and respected
earldom. Many a parent would have been only too anxious to snap
him up. But the Rosslyns, somewhat to the surprise of the love-lorn
Lord Brooke, begged him to say nothing to Daisy until she 'came
out', at eighteen. Reluctantly and uncomprehendingly, Lord Brooke
agreed. He was not to know that the Rosslyns had more ambitious
plans for their daughter.

Lord Rosslyn was friendly with Disraeli, then in his second term as
Prime Minister, and it was Disraeli who first drew Queen Victoria's
attention to Lord Rosslyn's step-daughter, Daisy Maynard, as a
possible bride for Prince Leopold. Daisy, oblivious both of Lord
Brooke's interest in her and of her parents' hopes of a royal marriage,
was astonished to be told, one day in December 1879, when she was
not yet eighteen, that she was to be taken to Windsor for inspection by
Queen Victoria with a view to her becoming the Queen's daughter-
in-law.

It was an intimidating prospect. But not for a moment would
Daisy, or any other aristocratic young girl, have defied her parents'
wishes in this matter. Most Victorian society marriages were arranged
and, in any case, few young women would have turned down the
chance of becoming a princess. Daisy had already met Prince Leopold
(he was friendly with Lord Brooke) and rather liked him. One
suspects, from her description of him, that she found him a little too

tame ('too delicate in health to ride or to take part in any sport': 'a sincere lover of art and music'[18]) but she admits that he was always very amusing company.

The evening at Windsor was as unnerving as she had feared it would be. For three-quarters of an hour the company waited in the huge, draughty corridor for the Queen to appear. When she did, she rushed in, a tiny, black-clad figure followed by Princess Beatrice, and with quick nods to left and right, disappeared into the dining room. The party was small and intimate, but no merrier for that. Everyone, including the Queen, spoke 'in undertones', and no one dared laugh. Daisy felt the Queen's eyes on her all the time. Dinner was served, she says, 'in hot haste' and in less than half an hour, the Queen rose from her chair and, followed by the docile Princess Beatrice, 'seemed to run from the room'.[19]

Reassembled in the freezing corridor (Queen Victoria always felt the heat, never the cold) the company stood about stiffly while the Queen addressed a few words to each of them. Suddenly, it was Daisy's turn. How did she like the idea of coming out? Was she fond of music or of drawing? After addressing two or three more questions to the 'agonisingly shy and overrawed' girl, the Queen passed on. These innocuous exchanges having, apparently, convinced the Queen that Daisy would make a suitable wife for her haemophilic, cultivated and complex son, negotiations moved on to the next stage.

But it was now that the one element for which no one had made any allowances – love – asserted itself. Once Daisy turned eighteen, on 10 December 1879, Lord Brooke felt less obliged to hide his feelings for her ('in Lord Brooke's eyes I had recognised something that told me, in mute appeal, that his happiness and destiny were inseparably linked with mine,'[20] she claims) while she found herself attracted far more strongly to the stalwart Lord Brooke than to the frail Prince Leopold. As it happened, Leopold was no more in love with her than she was with him. He had lost his heart to someone else whom, says Daisy, 'he took great care not to name.'[21]

The impasse was resolved in the spring of 1880. During the course of a house party at the Prince's home, Claremont House in Surrey, Leopold 'opened his heart' to Daisy. As he was in love with someone else and as his friend Lord Brooke had told him of his love for her, Leopold suggested that Daisy turn him down in favour of Lord Brooke. No sooner suggested than accomplished. The following day, as Daisy and Lord Brooke were sheltering under a large umbrella on the muddy road between Claremont and Esher, he proposed and she accepted.

Lord and Lady Rosslyn, their hopes of a great royal alliance dashed (they had spent the previous weeks in insisting that, once married to Leopold, Daisy would be given the full rank and privileges of a royal princess) were obliged to resign themselves to the situation. Queen Victoria was not nearly so resigned. According to Disraeli's secretary, she was 'furious'.[22] Daisy was sent for but throughout her interrogation by the Queen 'she stood her guns'.[23] In the end, it was the fear of a public loss of face that stopped Queen Victoria from making too much of a fuss.

Within two years Prince Leopold had married, more conventionally, Princess Helen of Waldeck-Pyrmont. And in less than two years after this, he bumped his knee while climbing some stairs and died from the resulting internal haemorrhage. 'Prince Leopold's death was a great loss to my husband and myself,'[24] says Daisy.

For by this time, of course, Daisy had become Lady Brooke. Their engagement was officially announced at a ball in Grosvenor House, Park Lane in June 1880, in the middle of Daisy's first season. This season was her introduction to the sort of frivolous and frenetic life she was to lead for the following fifteen years. 'I was fêted, feasted, courted and adored, in one continual round of gaiety, and I lived in and for the moment,'[25] runs her account of the social whirlpool into which she now plunged. For not only was Daisy a great heiress, she had developed into a great beauty. All those 'thronging admirers',[26] all those moustache-twirling officers from the Guards and the Blues, were attracted as much by her looks and personality as by her immense wealth. It was as well, perhaps, that the stolid Lord Brooke was too overwhelmed by his love for her to feel any apprehensions about the number of young men whom Daisy seemed not only to attract, but to encourage.

The couple were married in Westminster Abbey on 30 April 1881. The ceremony was described as 'the most brilliant wedding of a dozen seasons'.[27] Heading the galaxy of royal guests (Prince Leopold was best man) was the Prince of Wales.

Although Queen Victoria who had, by now, forgiven the bride for turning down her son, did not attend the ceremony, she did what she imagined to be the next best thing. The newly-married couple were commanded to break into their honeymoon in order to dine at Windsor Castle. The bride was instructed to wear her wedding dress, 'orange blossom and all'.[28]

Victoria professed herself enchanted with Daisy's appearance and asked not only for a photograph of her in her dress but for a spray of orange blossom to keep as a souvenir. First love, the sentimental Queen had once pronounced, was sacred: 'the divinest thing in the world'.[29]

With their marriage, Lord and Lady Brooke became, if not exactly members of the Marlborough House set, certainly representatives of the sort of society that took its tone from the Prince of Wales.

Marriage meant that Daisy could at last come into her inheritance and that until her husband, in turn, became the fifth Earl of Warwick, they could move into Easton Lodge. Considering Easton's combination of Elizabethan and mock-Elizabethan styles to be not nearly impressive enough for her new position in society, Daisy commissioned alterations that would transform it into 'a flamboyant pseudo-Gothic palace'.[30] With all the gusto of youth and good health, and bolstered by Daisy's fortune, the couple now embarked on a life of uninhibited enjoyment.

'It sufficed,' claimed Lord Brooke in later life, 'to be an agreeable young man, well-mannered, equipped with a modest independence and real skill at some sport, to have the very best of times.'[31] By 'the best of times' he meant that state of highly organised idleness in which the upper classes passed their days. From the start, the lives of Lord and Lady Brooke followed the by now well established pattern: the London season with its rides in the Park, its afternoon calls with their complicated ritual of card-leaving, its balls and receptions and dinner parties; the great race-meetings ('I could find all the stimulus I needed in the movement, the glitter, the skill and, of course, the beauty of the animals themselves,'[32] enthuses Daisy); Cowes Week; the country house parties with their hunting and shooting; the holidays in the South of France.

Of all these diversions, it was hunting that afforded Daisy the most pleasure. There was something about the dash, danger and exhilaration of the chase that accorded well with her own increasingly headstrong nature. Very soon Daisy developed into a skilful and fearless rider, following some of the smartest hunts in the country. Dressed in her tight-fitting side-saddle costumes, and with a bowler hat perched on her fashionably fringed and ridged hair, she presented a striking figure on the hunting field.

It was this love of hunting – allied to her determination to have her own way – that once caused Daisy to offend Queen Victoria. The Brookes had been commanded to dine and sleep at Windsor, but as her husband was to be away from home and as Daisy was anxious to attend the Essex hunt races, she made her excuses. But the Queen was not to be put off: Lady Brooke must attend alone.

Not one to be balked, Daisy worked out a plan whereby she could attend both the Queen's dinner and the day's hunting. The dinner, an intimate occasion with only six guests in addition to the Queen and the inevitable Princess Beatrice, went well enough, and the guests retired to their rooms on the understanding that they would leave the following morning, after breakfast. But by first light Daisy was up and, having put on a hunting coat of brilliant pink ('a fashion innovation of my own,'[33] she claims), she requested a carriage to take her, 'breakfastless', to the station to catch the earliest train. The lord-in-waiting, whom etiquette obliged to see her off, was both shocked and annoyed at her unorthodox behaviour.

So was Queen Victoria. The Queen, having heard the carriage draw up below, got out of bed and, standing by the window in her night-gown, peeped through the curtain to watch Lady Brooke, in her vivid coat, climb into the carriage and drive off. She was appalled.

'How fast! How very fast!'[34] she muttered to her lady-in-waiting.

The incident must have confirmed the Queen's view that Lady Brooke, whom she had so recently considered as a suitable wife for her son Leopold, had by now quite given herself over to 'the frivolity, the love of pleasure, self-indulgence and idleness (producing ignorance)' of the 'Higher Classes'.[35] The tone and style of contemporary society, grumbled the Queen, was '*repulsive*, vulgar, bad and frivolous *in every way*.'[36]

In later years, when Daisy's opinion of the aristocracy had come to echo Queen Victoria's (although from a different standpoint), there was one aspect of this upper-class way of life which she found especially regrettable: its philistinism. 'The majority of the people who made up society were not taught to use their brains; they disliked making the effort necessary to appreciate books, pictures, music or sculpture, and what they disliked they distrusted,'[37] she says. 'We acknowledged that it was necessary that pictures should be painted, books written, the law administered; we even acknowledged that there was a certain class whose job it might be to do these things. But we did not see why their achievements entitled them to our recognition; they might disturb, over-stimulate, or even bore.'[38]

She was equally oblivious, at the time, to a far more serious aristocratic failing: the inability to comprehend, or even notice, the injustices of the social system in which they lived. 'Social problems

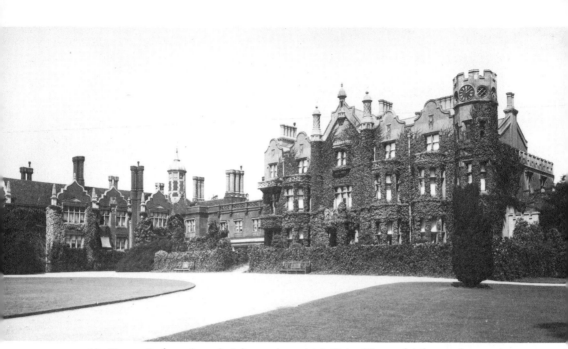

13. Easton Lodge, the palatial mansion which Daisy Maynard (afterwards Warwick) inherited at the age of three.

14. A 'shooting luncheon' at Easton Lodge. The Prince of Wales stands in the centre; below him, in a white hat, sits Daisy Warwick, at her feet sits her husband, the Earl of Warwick.

15. Daisy, when still Lady Brooke, before her momentous meeting with the Prince of Wales.

16. The always immaculately dressed Prince of Wales, at Homburg in the 1890s.

17. The Wales family. From the left, standing: Prince George, the Princess of Wales, the Prince of Wales, Princess Victoria. Seated: Princess Maud, Prince Albert Victor (Eddy), Princess Louise.

18. Warwick Castle, one of the settings for the liaison between Daisy and the Prince of Wales.

19. Royal Mistress: Frances (Daisy),
Countess of Warwick.

20. A sketch of the Prince of Wales setting out from Marlborough House on his way, no doubt, to an amorous assignation.

21. Princess Alexandra, the beautiful, elegant and frequently betrayed wife.

22. Daisy Warwick in fancy dress,
as the Queen of Assyria.

23. Daisy's cuckolded husband, the
long-suffering Earl of Warwick.

24. A German cartoon showing the Prince of Wales 'comforting the wives and widows' of the men away fighting in the Boer War.

25. Daisy Warwick, 'the Socialist Countess', on the hustings.

were apparently unknown,' wrote a bemused Lord Brooke in his memoirs. 'I hadn't heard of any, and the right of a young man to make the most agreeable use of the May-morn of his youth went unchallenged.'[39] Most members of the Victorian upper classes simply accepted things as they were: they never reflected on the causes of the poverty and misery and inequality of their day. Their contacts with the lower classes were mainly with their servants (and, goodness knows, they seemed happy enough); poverty was personified by the cap-doffing stable-lad, the ruddy-cheeked farmhand or the aproned housewife on her cottage doorstep. Of the grinding penury and the seething discontent in the great industrial cities they knew very little and understood even less.

Just occasionally, as she rode back from a pleasurable day's hunting and passed the exhausted labourers trudging home after working in the fields since dawn, Daisy Brooke might feel a pricking of the conscience she had sometimes felt as a child but, for the most part, she was happy enough to accept things as they were. She was always ready to dole out money to any of her tenants who were in trouble or to overlook non-payment of rent, but it never occurred to her that there might be something wrong – or immoral – with the system itself.

For the upper classes, nothing was ever so wrong that it could not be put right by an act of charity. Dutifully, the ladies of the manor would instruct the housekeeper to send coal and blankets to the elderly, broth and jellies to the sick, old clothes to the needy. Self-righteously, they would organise bazaars, run needlework guilds or collect donations. Unblinkingly, they would maintain that their tenants and dependants were more like friends, and their servants almost part of the family. Social divisions, they would claim, were just as prevalent among their servants; this was the natural order of things.

Over eighty years later Prince Leopold's daughter, Princess Alice, Countess of Athlone, remembering her own girlhood in the 1880s, could boast that 'class distinctions permeated the whole social structure and could be as rigid in the servants hall and in the village as they were in the castle. There distinctions were, however, tempered by gracious manners; and, in general, a courteous consideration for others, alas so rare today, governed the relationship between all ranks of society.'[40]

On Sunday mornings, across country churchyards, would float the reassuring lines of the hymn which, more perhaps than any other, reflected the Victorian upper-class view of their world: 'The rich man

in his castle, the poor man at his gate; God made them high and lowly,
He ordered their estate.'

What better way of confirming the fact that all things were indeed
bright and beautiful?

Only occasionally, during the first half a dozen years of her marriage,
did Daisy Brooke come into contact with the hub about which this
idle, unthinking, self-confident society revolved – the Prince of
Wales. Lord and Lady Brooke were invited to shooting parties at
Sandringham and they once entertained the Prince and Princess of
Wales at Easton Lodge. On one occasion, during a ball given by the
Prince's brother, Alfred, Duke of Edinburgh at Eastwell, Bertie had
asked Daisy to dance and had spent some time in the corridor talking
to her. But for all her attractions – her big blue eyes, her fashionably
straight nose, her alert expression, her ruby-red velvet dress with its
low neckline and huge bustle – she seemed, for some inexplicable
reason, unable to hold his attention. 'He doubtless found me shy and
stupid,' she writes, 'for he spent most of the evening with Mrs
Cornwallis West, then in the zenith of her beauty.'[41]

Nor was Mrs Cornwallis West the only beauty with whom the
Prince was spending his evenings. Throughout the 1880s his name
was linked, briefly, with this or that society figure. For a while he
adopted what the Duke of Cambridge called 'a strange new line of
taking to young girls and discarding married women'. Gladstone's
secretary spoke of 'H.R.H.'s virgin band' and Lady Geraldine Somerset claimed that he was 'more or less in love' with, in turn, such
'reigning young ladies' as 'Miss Stonor, Miss Tennant and Miss
Duff'.[42] Then there was the lovely American debutante, Miss Cham-
berlayne, with whom, for a while, the Prince 'occupied himself
entirely', and whom the Princess of Wales, with what passed for wit at
Marlborough House and Sandringham, nicknamed 'Miss Chamber-
pots'.

Not all the Prince's indiscretions were conducted within closed
aristocratic circles. His public behaviour could be equally improper.
In Paris, there was hardly a music hall in which his portly figure was
not familiar.' '*Ullo Wales,*' shouted La Goulue, the raucous star of the
Jardin de Paris as he one night entered the establishment, '*tu paies le
champagne!*'[43]

The French police needed all their ingenuity to keep track of his
amorous meanderings through the capital. There were his afternoon

calls on various society hostesses, his leisurely meetings with famous beauties in the Jardin des Plantes, his hour-long stays with celebrated courtesans, his clandestine visits to unidentified women in shady hotels, the evenings spent in his favourite brothel, the luxurious *Le Chabanais*. Its *fauteuil d'amour,* a curious double-decker chair especially designed, it is said, to accommodate the Prince's considerable paunch, has recently been sold for £20,000.

There were times when even the Prince's fellow royal rakes were embarrassed by his indiscreet behaviour. One evening he took a party of friends to a London restaurant. Among them was Crown Prince Rudolph of Austria, the young man who had once been infatuated by Lillie Langtry. At about two in the morning Bertie asked the orchestra to play the famous can-can from *La Belle Hélène.* With the beautiful but notorious Duchess of Manchester as his partner ('the Duchess of Manchester *is not a fit companion for you,*'[44] Queen Victoria had long ago warned the Princess of Wales), he flung himself into the dance with embarrassing abandon.

The far from priggish Crown Prince Rudolph was shocked. 'Tell the waiters to go,' he whispered to one of the company, 'they must not see their future King making such a clown of himself.'[45]

The easy-going attitude of the Prince of Wales's set towards extra-marital affairs was one which Daisy Brooke lost no time in adopting. 'From the beginning of our life together,' she admits airily, 'my husband seemed to accept the inevitability of my having a train of admirers. I could not help it. There they were. It was all a great game.'[46] In the first four years of marriage, Daisy gave birth to three children, but even during this period she was playing 'the great game' with all the ardour of her nature. As the novelist Elinor Glyn once explained, 'it was quite normal in Society circles for a married woman to have a succession of illicit love affairs, during the intervals of which, if not simultaneously, intimate relations with her husband were resumed.'[47]

Beautiful, flirtatious, passionate, 'with little responsibility and no driving need other than to satisfy each impulse as it arose',[48] Daisy gave herself over to the febrile excitements of these love affairs. She delighted in the established ritual of such courtships, from the first meaningful glance to the final sexual fulfilment; followed by what Mrs Patrick Campbell – who was in a position to know – used to call 'the deep, deep peace of the double bed after the hurly-burly of the chaise-longue'.

Lord Brooke, like Edward Langtry, was obliged to make the best of things. He was, in any case, a more complacent, better-natured man than Lillie Langtry's husband. There were no outbursts of temper, no bouts of drinking with him; he was far too much of a gentleman to make a fuss. His own five-year obsession with the young Daisy Maynard had not long outlasted their wedding. It had been killed both by Daisy's feverish infidelity and by a certain incompatability between husband and wife. Daisy, although an enthusiastic rider to hounds, could not share her husband's passion for shooting; she found those long sporting house parties, when the women were left to amuse themselves for most of the day, 'intolerably boring'.[49] For his part, Lord Brooke maintained that 'a good day's fishing or shooting is second in point of pleasure to nothing on earth'.[50]

Daisy's most serious love affair during these years – and the one which was to lead her directly into the arms of the Prince of Wales – was with the Prince's great friend, Lord Charles Beresford.

This dashing naval commander, one of whose pranks had been to switch off the supply of air to the cabin in which the Prince and Lillie were apparently making love, was one of the great adulterers of the period. Handsome, energetic and charming, Beresford had very little trouble in seducing the bored wives of the Marlborough House set. His own wife offered very little competition. Older than her husband, Lady Charles Beresford made gallant attempts to project a youthful image. Bright spots of rouge enlivened her otherwise white-painted face; a toddler once pulled off one of her false eyebrows in the misapprehension that it was a butterfly; and Daisy Brooke used to repeat, with obvious relish, the story of how once, while out driving with Lady Charles, a sudden gust of wind lifted, not only her hat but her yellow wig, and deposited them both on the grass verge. 'How lucky we were not on the high road!'[51] exclaimed Lady Charles.

Lord Charles, with or without his wife, had been visiting Easton Lodge since the Brookes first moved into it, and by 1886, when Daisy was twenty-five and he thirty-nine, the couple had become lovers. In Daisy's eyes, Lord Charles Beresford possessed all the glamour so conspicuously lacking in her own husband. In fact, so besotted was she by her lover that one day, while the Beresfords were staying at Easton, Daisy marched into Lady Charles's room, told her of the liaison (in spite of the fact, sniffs Lady Charles, that 'the circumstances of the affair were at the time well known, and commented on, in Society') and announced her intention of eloping with Beresford. The reckless Daisy was quite ready, apparently, to abandon her husband

and three children and to subject both her lover and herself to public disgrace.

Lady Charles was not anything like as ready 'to sacrifice Lord Charles's career to such an insane project'. She took him home, she declared, 'on the spot'.

It was a wise move. From this point on Lord Charles's love for Lady Brooke began to die a natural death; a death hastened by his discovery that she was 'not content with his attentions alone'.[52] But Daisy, however much she might be amusing herself elsewhere, was not prepared to let him go. Her resolve turned to rage when she heard, late in 1886, that Lord Charles's wife was pregnant. As Lady Charles's morals were above reproach, there could be no doubt that the child had been fathered by her husband.

Infuriated by this indisputable evidence that her lover had deserted her for, of all people, his wife, Daisy wrote him a blistering letter. In it, she instructed him to leave his wife at once in order to join her on the Riviera; she claimed that one of her children was his; and she insisted that he had 'no right' to beget a child by his wife. This letter was regarded, by those who saw it later, as utterly shocking. Lord Charles's brother, Lord Marcus Beresford, maintained that 'it ought never to have seen the light of day'.[53]

But see the light of day it certainly did. For the letter was opened, not by Lord Charles who was away from home at the time, but by his wife. She was horrified. Lady Charles promptly passed it on to the well-known London solicitor, George Lewis. One of the key figures in late Victorian society, George Lewis enjoyed, according to one source, 'for more than a quarter of a century, the practical monopoly of those cases where the sins and follies of the wealthy classes threaten exposure and disaster.'[54] The astute George Lewis was chiefly celebrated, in fact, for keeping things *out* of court.

Acting on Lady Charles's instructions, Lewis now wrote to Lady Brooke, telling her that her letter was in his possession and warning her against causing any further annoyance to his client. Daisy was furious. She wrote to Lewis, demanding the return of her letter. 'It is my letter. I wrote it,'[55] she declared. Lewis explained that she was wrong. Legally, the letter was the property of Lord Charles Beresford, to whom it had been addressed.

Thwarted, Daisy turned to the only person she knew who was influential enough to give her some practical help: the Prince of Wales. Appreciating that he was a close friend of Lord Charles Beresford and knowing that he would do anything to avoid a public scandal in his set, Daisy hurried to Marlborough House. She begged the Prince, as Lady Charles scathingly put it, 'to help "Beauty in Distress"!'[56]

She did not beg in vain. Indeed, from out of this meeting with the Prince of Wales, Daisy got not only what she had come for, but a good deal more.

In the mind's eye, one can still see the two of them in the flaring gaslight of the Prince's overcrowded study on that evening in 1889: the plump, predatory, beard-stroking Bertie, all attentive sympathy as the distraught and lovely Daisy, her long-lashed eyes brimming with tears, spills out her story.

'He was charmingly courteous to me,' she afterwards said, 'and at length he told me he hoped his friendship would make up in part, at least, for my sailor-lover's loss. He was more than kind.'

And suddenly, she continues, 'I saw him looking at me in a way all women understand.'[57]

That very night, or rather, at two the following morning, the Prince of Wales went to see George Lewis. Any annoyance Lewis might have felt at being hauled out of bed was more than compensated for by the illustriousness of his caller. So gratified was he, in fact, that he took the highly unprofessional step of acceding to the Prince's request to be shown Lady Brooke's incriminating letter. The sight of it confirmed the Prince in his opinion that the letter should be destroyed at once. But as not even the sycophantic Lewis was prepared to do so himself, the Prince went to see Lady Charles.

She proved to be not nearly as overawed by the Royal Presence. She had no intention, she declared, of destroying the letter. She then, through Lewis, spelt out the terms on which she was prepared to return the letter to Lady Brooke. Read today, these terms seem ludicrous; at the time, they appeared draconian. Lady Brooke was to stay away from London for the entire season.

Lady Brooke was, as Lady Charles knew she would be, appalled at the prospect of so drastic a punishment. Again she flew to the Prince for help and again he, who was by now falling in love with her, went to see Lady Charles. This time His Royal Highness was far less conciliatory. In fact, he gave Lady Charles a dose of her own medicine. If she did not hand over the letter, it would be she, and not Lady Brooke, who would have to leave London for the season. Her 'position in Society!!' exclaimed Lady Charles with a forest of exclamation marks, 'would become injured!!!'[58]

The redoubtable Lady Charles held firm. Conveniently forgetting that it was she who had first threatened social blackmail, the lady now declared that she would refuse to give in to it. But the Prince's threat had not been an idle one. Within days he was ensuring that Lord and Lady Brooke were being invited to the same houses as himself. 'And when that sign of the Prince's support didn't stop the angry little cat,' wrote the triumphant Daisy, 'the Prince checked her in another way. She [Lady Charles] had been put down as one of the house party of a great lady to meet him. He simply cut her name out and substituted mine for it . . .'[59]

Into the teacup in which this storm was raging, there now plunged the errant husband, Lord Charles Beresford. Until then he had been trying, with uncharacteristic diplomacy, to get his wife to give up the letter. But the Prince's interference, followed by his social ostracism of Lady Charles, had proved too much for the notoriously short-tempered Beresford. On 12 January 1890, he called on the Prince. Tempers flared, with Lord Charles not only calling the Prince a blackguard but forgetting himself to the point where he very nearly hit the Royal Person.

The tangled situation was prevented from becoming more tangled still only by the fact that Lord Charles was obliged to leave England to take command of his ship. Just as the vessel on which Lillie Langtry's lover, Prince Louis of Battenberg, sailed away had borne the appropriate name of 'Inconstant', so Lord Charles Beresford's ship was distinguished by an equally appropriate name: 'Undaunted'.

For Lord Charles had by no means been beaten by the combined machinations of the Prince of Wales and Lady Brooke.

'The Babbling Brook'

ONCE AGAIN, nine years after his liaison with Lillie Langtry had ended, the Prince of Wales was in love. But this time he regarded the object of his passionate love as more than a mistress: Daisy Brooke became, in the Prince's infatuated eyes, his 'wife'. This, at least, is how he always addressed her. She was his 'darling Daisy wife', his 'own lovely little Daisy wife', his 'own adored little Daisy wife'. She had, as far as he was concerned, everything he admired in a woman: beauty, elegance, vivacity and a quick mind. He felt able to discuss with her, in addition to the usual social trivia, what she calls 'the affairs of the greater world outside'.[1] The Prince of Wales might not have been a particularly astute man but he very soon came to realise that there was more to Daisy Brooke than met the eye. She was far from being just a social butterfly with a tendency to land herself in trouble: the better he came to know her, the more he came to appreciate her many capabilities.

In these early years, he could hardly bear to have her out of his sight. Whenever they were apart, he would write to her, often three times a week, and would feel hurt if she failed to answer him. His letters were full of affectionate chit-chat, news about the weather and the shooting and the amateur theatricals with which country house guests entertained themselves in the evenings. 'Now my loved one,' ends a typical letter from Chatsworth, grandiose home of the Dukes of Devonshire, 'I bring these lines to a close, as I must dress and breakfast. God bless you, my own adored little Daisy wife . . . For ever yours, Your only Love.'[2]

She found him extraordinarily sentimental. He was a great keeper of anniversaries and sender of birthday and Christmas cards. He remembered significant shared experiences and delighted in exchanging little gifts. He once sent her a travelling clock, chosen especially because of 'a certain little gadget that added to its sentimental value'.[3] German, with its many diminutives and romantic imagery, was the language they most often used in talking to each other. One of Daisy's most treasured souvenirs was the ring he gave her: a plain gold band, like a wedding ring, on which was inscribed: 'To Bertie from his affectionate parents A. and V.R., July 9th 1860.'[4]

One must presume that Queen Victoria knew nothing about the fate of what should have been a sacrosanct token of parental love.

'He had manners and he was very considerate,' said Daisy in later life, 'and from a woman's point of view that's a great deal. Then he was remarkably constant and adored me exceedingly. I grew to like him very much. I think anybody would have been won by him . . .'[5]

For her part, Daisy was only too delighted to be swept into the brilliant world that revolved around the Prince of Wales. If she had not been a full member of the Marlborough House set before, she certainly became one now. 'Of course,' she remembered in her old age, 'the Marlborough House set had glamour; indeed, glamour was its particular asset. It created the atmosphere which intrigued the public. I can feel something of the same sense of enchantment, in recalling it, that children experienced when they watched the trans-formation scene at the pantomime. For them, the girls in their spangles were beautiful fairies, and the scene a glimpse of fairyland . . .'[6]

She went sailing with him at Cowes; she went racing with him at Goodwood, Newmarket and Epsom; she attended the same balls, receptions and house parties. In a very short time not only society, but those journals that so faithfully chronicled society's doings, knew all about the Prince's obsession with Lady Brooke. 'At the Opera,' reported *The World* with a knowing juxtaposition of their names, 'the Prince of Wales with his two younger daughters. Lady Brooke was in the pit tier, and the writer craned her neck to catch a glimpse of the goddess whose fame had penetrated even to the dim recesses of the placid country. Her profile was turned away from an inquisitive world, but I made out a rounded figure, diaphanously draped, and a brilliant, haughty, beautiful countenance.'[7]

Some of their happiest times together were spent in Paris. Travell-ing as 'Baron Renfrew' (a Wildean alias which fooled no-one: that corpulent figure was unmistakable) the Prince would always stay at the Hotel Bristol, just a few yards from the Hotel Vendôme in which, for propriety's sake, he would install Lady Brooke. They went to the theatre where they watched risqué plays; they went up the Eiffel

Tower from where they saw magnificent views; they visited Edouard Detaille's studio where they admired the sort of battle scenes which Bertie regarded as true art; they enjoyed superb food and wines at the Voisin and the Café Anglais. She was almost afraid to admire anything in the shops, protests Daisy, because gifts were 'showered' on her 'at the slightest excuse'.[8]

The Prince introduced her to his Parisian friends, the Marquis de Breteuil, the Marquis de Jaucourt, the Comtesse de Pourtalès. They went to the great autumn race-meetings at Longchamps and Auteuil, although Daisy was interested to note that the Prince once refused to attend a Sunday race-meeting with the Breteuils; he dared not offend Queen Victoria.

His deference to the sensibilities not only of his mother but of the Established Church has an echo today. 'If it were not for my Archbishop of Canterbury,' his great-granddaughter, Queen Elizabeth II, has said, 'I should be off in my plane to Longchamps every Sunday.'[9]

And, of course, the Prince accompanied Daisy to the two leading couturiers of the day, Worth and Doucet. To Doucet Daisy went for her day dresses and lingerie; to Worth, son of the founder of the firm, for her evening dresses and gala clothes. She never paid less, she claims, than a hundred guineas for a Worth dress, which is something like three thousand pounds by today's standards. Often she paid half as much again. Bertie, who was always interested in women's fashion, would sit watching while the dapper Mr Worth would study his subject 'as a painter would study a woman sitting for a portrait'.

'Suddenly inspiration would come! He would call for specially woven brocade from the looms of Lyons, or other rare and costly fabric. Instantly it would appear, and with his wonderful hands he seemed to evoke the powers of Beauty.

' "This," he would murmur, "is the colour. This the outline – this – and this –"

'With each "this" the gown would grow under the image of his fingers.'[10]

Daisy had always been well-dressed but now, as the favourite of the Prince of Wales, she blossomed into one of the most elegant women in society. Her years of triumph spanned the 1890s, a decade which saw the end of the bustle and the development of bell skirts and huge, puffed sleeves. Society journals were full of her spectacular dresses: the 'gauzy white gown beneath which meandered delicately shaded ribbons' which she wore to a dinner party attended by the Prince of

Wales; the 'splendid purple-grape-trimmed robes and veil of pearls on white' which she wore to a Drawing Room presided over by the Prince of Wales; the 'violet velvet with two splendid turquoise-and-diamond brooches in her bodice' which she wore to a hunt ball at which, inevitably, the Prince of Wales was present.

Even his clothes – for he was an arbiter of male elegance – were mentioned on this last occasion: the Prince introduced a new fashion for men, 'dogskin tan gloves with black stitching'.[11]

In the country, the couple could be together at Easton Lodge or at country house parties; in London they could use Daisy's town house or, if the Princess of Wales were away, Marlborough House. Then there were always those private rooms in London restaurants where a gentleman could entertain his lady friends. Rules, off Maiden Lane, was one of the Prince's favourite restaurants, but as it boasted only one private room, he would more often take Daisy to other restaurants, such as the Café Royal and Kettners, where the private supper rooms were furnished not only with table and chairs, but with sofas. There were even some where the touch of a button would part the panelling to reveal a double bed. The Prince of Wales, said Daisy, was 'a very perfect, gentle lover'.[12]

Rendering the Prince's prodigious love-making a little less hazardous was the availability, by the late 1880s, of a more reliable means of contraception. Until then, contraception had been very much a hit and miss affair. Pregnancy had been avoided by various means: by *coitus interruptus,* by limiting sex to so-called 'safe periods', by the insertion of a sponge on a narrow ribbon, even by the fitting of a diaphragm. Crude sheaths or condoms, made first of linen, then of sheep's intestines or fish skin, had been in use since the eighteenth century. In London, a Mrs Philips had done a brisk trade in supplying condoms to 'ambassadors, foreigners, gentlemen, and captains of ships &c going abroad'.[13] But such condoms had never been simple to make, cheap to buy or easy to put on. And as recently as 1877 a seriously-written study of contraceptive practices had been condemned, in court, as obscene literature. The case had merely emphasised the fact that contraception remained an obscure and rarely-employed practice.

But the discovery of vulcanisation in the 1840s led, eventually, to the manufacture of crêpe rubber, and by the 1880s rubber condoms were being widely used. Victorian wives, relieved of their fears of repeated pregnancies or of being infected by their husbands, many of whom may have slept with prostitutes, could only welcome the development. It led to a decline in the birthrate and a more relaxed attitude towards marital sex.

And giving the whole question of the use of condoms an aura of reassuring respectability was the box in which they were sold. In those happy-go-lucky days before the introduction of any advertising codes of practice, the manufacturers had no hesitation in illustrating their new product with portraits of the two most irreproachable Victorian notables they could think of: staring stonily at each other across every box of condoms were Queen Victoria and Mr Gladstone.

One can only hope that the Prince of Wales did not feel inhibited by the frequent sight of this formidable pair.

Easton Lodge, Daisy's country home in Essex, was the chief background against which the royal affair was enacted. Although Daisy's plans to turn Easton into a mock-Gothic palace never materialised, it remained an impressive pile: a rambling mansion set in twelve hundred acres of parkland, among whose giant oaks herds of deer roamed freely. The interior of the house was the usual high Victorian amalgam of good and bad: of beautifully proportioned rooms covered in brightly flowered wallpaper; of superb old masters alongside indifferent family portraits; of priceless *objets d'art* mixed up with worthless knick-knacks. The hall was crammed with hunting trophies – witness to Lord Brooke's shooting skills – among which, rearing up higher than a man, rose the stuffed neck and head of a giraffe.

In this luxuriant setting, Lady Brooke played the *grande dame* to perfection. She was, enthused one guest, 'the loveliest woman in England, of high rank, ample riches and great intelligence, and blessed with a charming husband who adored her.'[14]

Whether, in truth, Lord Brooke 'adored' his wife to the extent he had once done is a moot point, but if adoration means never standing in the way of one's beloved's happiness, then Lord Brooke certainly adored his wife. In the matter of her liaison with the Prince of Wales, he proved admirably accommodating. Daisy claimed that the Prince liked her husband's 'repose of temperament' – as well he might – and that 'they shared a great liking for sport, which drew them close together'.[15]

Lord Brooke's published view of his wife's royal lover could hardly have been more bland. 'He delighted in performing kind actions, they may be said to have been his hobby; and while as a host he could anticipate every possible want of his guests, as a guest he was most affable, courteous and responsive. He appreciated everything that was done for his comfort, and had the gift of setting everybody, whether prince or ploughman, at their ease.'[16] No hint of the cuckolded husband here.

As a matter of fact, Lord Brooke was not above indulging in a little extra-marital dalliance himself. On one occasion, a lady guest, having been invited by Lord Brooke to inspect a newly-planted rose garden, was astonished to find herself – just as she was bending over to look at some particularly choice bloom – being enfolded in her host's arms with the poetic assurance that she was the 'fairest rose' in the garden. Saved by the arrival of some other garden-inspecting guests, she fled into the house to report the incident to her husband.

'Did he, by Jove!' exclaimed her husband with admirable *sang froid*. 'Good old Brookie!'[17]

Daisy paints an idyllic picture of the Prince on one of his private visits to Easton: of his throwing aside 'the heavy trappings of his state to revel in his love of nature'[18]; of their walks across the park to the little church on Sunday mornings; of their conversations as they strolled through her famous 'Garden of Friendship' with its 'Border of Sentiment'. The Prince found that Daisy was very interested in political gossip, in foreign affairs and, increasingly, in social problems. Like Lillie Langtry before her, Daisy Brooke was not just a pretty face.

Even on these intimate visits, the Prince of Wales was incapable of moving without a retinue of people. He would feel obliged to bring with him not only a gentleman-in-waiting and a couple of equerries but two grooms for his horses, two loaders for his guns and two valets for the trunkloads of clothes which he considered essential for even the shortest, most informal of visits. For if the late Prince Consort's complaint – that the only thing his eldest son was interested in was clothes – was not quite accurate, clothes certainly did come high on Bertie's list of priorities. Few things were guaranteed to irritate him more than a wrongly chosen outfit.

Stories of the Prince's obsession with correct dress are legion. To a guardsman who entered the Marlborough Club wearing a new-fangled dinner jacket, the Prince said severely, 'I suppose, my young friend, you are going to a costume ball.'[19] To a secretary about to set out before luncheon to an exhibition of pictures wearing a tail coat, His Royal Highness remarked, 'I thought *everyone* must know that a *short* jacket is always worn with a silk hat at a private view in the morning.'[20] And when a diplomat in mourning asked the Prince if it would be possible for him to go to the races, his reply was unhesitating. 'Not to Ascot, where one must wear a top hat, but Newmarket is all right because you can wear a soft hat there.'[21]

Large house parties, or what Daisy calls 'more brilliant gatherings', had to be organised on the scale, and with the precision, of a military operation. Often the royal suite had to be entirely redecorated. The Prince almost broke one poor hostess's heart when, quite unaware that his suite had just been expensively refurbished, he merely replied – in answer to her eager enquiries as to whether or not he was comfortable – that his bathroom could do with a hook for his dressing-gown.

Daisy would have to submit a list of guests for his approval and often he would suggest names of his own. Sometimes she would run a special train from London and back for her guests, and there would have to be a fleet of carriages and wagonettes to transport them and their mountains of luggage (the women always travelled with huge domed, brassbound and padlocked trunks) from the station to the house. Extra servants, in addition to the maids and valets brought by the guests, would have to be employed; a band would have to be organised; and there was always the specially ordered food – the caviar, the larks, the ortolans, the ptarmigans, the wines and the champagnes. Quite often, the usual chef had to be replaced by a specialist whose skill, sighs Daisy, 'was equalled only by his wastefulness.'[22]

A telling pen-picture of Daisy Brooke at this period is given by the equally controversial woman who became a neighbour in 1892. This was Elinor Glyn, the white-skinned, green-eyed and red-haired beauty who was to become, in time, the famous romantic novelist. Like Lillie Langtry, Elinor Glyn (or Elinor Sutherland as she then was) had once lived on the island of Jersey. In fact, as a child, Elinor and her sister Lucy, who became Lady Duff Gordon, had once hidden under the skirted dressing-table of the room in Government House in which the celebrated Mrs Langtry, on a visit home to Jersey, was to leave her cloak before going down to dine. A giggle from Lucy gave them away. Far from being annoyed, Lillie was flattered by the girls' obvious interest, while they were overwhelmed by her beauty.

And now, fifteen years later and newly married to Clayton Glyn, Elinor found herself living near the Prince of Wales's latest mistress, Lady Brooke. She was no less overwhelmed. 'No one who stayed at Easton ever forgot their hostess and most of the men fell hopelessly in love with her,' remembered Elinor Glyn. 'In my long life, spent in so many different countries, and during which I have seen most of the beautiful and famous women of the world, from film-stars to Queens, I have never seen one who was so completely fascinating as Daisy Brooke. She would sail in from her own wing, carrying her piping bullfinch, her lovely eyes smiling with the merry innocent expression of a Persian kitten that has just tangled a ball of silk. Hers was that supreme personal charm which I later described as "It" because it is quite indefinable, and does not depend on beauty or wit, although she possessed both in the highest degree. She was never jealous or spiteful to other women, and if she liked you she was the truest, most understanding friend.'[23]

It was from Lady Brooke that Elinor Glyn learned many of the social nuances of the day. Entertaining beyond strictly aristocratic circles was as hazardous as negotiating a minefield. To luncheon or dinner one could invite army or naval officers, diplomats and clergymen. If, but only if, the local vicar was a gentleman, he could be asked to Sunday supper. Otherwise he joined the doctors and solicitors at a garden party; *they* were never invited to luncheon or dinner. As for anyone in trade or commerce, or in the arts – well, they could not be asked under any circumstances.

Elinor Glyn was full of admiration for the adroit way in which Lady Brooke organised the sexual liaisons, or 'amusements', which were so important a feature of these country house parties. 'Supposing,' she explains, 'you had settled to meet the person who was amusing you in the saloon, say, at eleven, you went there casually at the agreed time, dressed to go out, and found your cavalier awaiting you. Sometimes Lady Brooke would be there too, but she always sensed whether this was an arranged meeting or an accidental one. If it was intended, she would say graciously that Stone Hall, her little Elizabethan pleasure house in the Park, was a nice walk before lunch, and thus make it easy to start. Should some strangers who did not know the ropes happen to be there, too, and show signs of accompanying you on the walk, she would immediately engage them in conversation until you had got safely away.'[24]

If all these manoeuvrings cost a great deal of effort, then all this entertaining cost a great deal of money. Although hosts like the Rothschilds or the Devonshires (who were known to have up to as many as 470 people, guests and servants, at Chatsworth on occasions) could afford it, others could not. But this seldom stopped them. 'I could tell stories of men and woman who had to economise for a whole year, or alternatively, get into debt,' says

Daisy, 'that they might entertain Royalty for one weekend.'[25]

A member of this unhappy band was Christopher Sykes. One of the Prince's closest companions, the affable Sykes was a notorious snob. His reverence for his royal friend was so obsequious as to be ludicrous. His servile response – 'As Your Royal Highness pleases' – when, in one of his more boorish moods, the Prince emptied a glass of brandy over Sykes's head, became a catch-phrase with the Marlborough House set. In fact, so often had poor Sykes done as His Royal Highness pleased – so often had he given parties at the Prince's bidding or entertained the Prince's friends at Brantingham Thorpe – that, by the end of the 1880s, he was almost bankrupt. Declaring this to be a 'thoroughly bad business'[26] (bankruptcy was regarded as the most heinous of crimes) the Prince paid off some of his more pressing debts.

Time did, though, bring in some of its revenges when, in September 1890, the Prince of Wales paid his customary visit to Doncaster for the St Leger races. In the ordinary way he would have stayed with Sykes at Brantingham Thorpe, but as his friend could no longer afford this dubious honour, the Prince was put up by one of his new acquaintances, the rich ship-owner, Arthur Wilson, at his huge, 'Italianate' home, Tranby Croft.

And it was at Tranby Croft that the Prince became embroiled in a gambling scandal that was to cause him some of the greatest unhappiness he had ever known.

The country, Queen Victoria once said, 'could never bear to have George IV as Prince of Wales over again.'[27] The particular profligacy of that profligate Prince and King to which the Queen was referring was gambling. But alas, in this matter, as in so many others, Queen Victoria's heir fulfilled her apprehensions: Bertie was an enthusiastic gambler. He bet heavily on horses and played cards for high stakes, with baccarat having recently become his favourite game. Wherever he went, he took his own set of baccarat counters, engraved with the Prince of Wales's feathers and varying in denomination from five shillings to ten pounds: ten pounds being equivalent to five months' wages for an agricultural labourer on Daisy Brooke's estates, or two hundred and fifty pounds today.

This fondness for baccarat was to lead, directly, to one of the most celebrated trials of the Victorian age; a trial in which the Prince, and to a lesser extent Lady Brooke, were involved.

The Wilsons of Tranby Croft, in their ecstasy at having landed the

Prince of Wales as their guest for the Doncaster races, quite naturally invited his friends as well. Chief amongst these were Lord and Lady Brooke. But unhappily, the death of Daisy's step-father, the cultivated Lord Rosslyn, on 6 September 1980, prevented them from accepting the invitation. Another of the guests, who *was* able to accept, was Sir William Gordon-Cummings, of the Scots Guards, a man whom Daisy describes as 'the smartest of men about town'.[28]

Sir William was not quite smart enough, apparently, to conceal the fact that he was cheating at baccarat on the first evening of the Prince's stay. The next evening he was again caught cheating and, on being accused, agreed to sign a document to the effect that he would never again play cards as long as he lived. He was signing it, he made clear, without admitting guilt and on the understanding that the affair would be kept strictly secret. This somewhat schoolboyish pact having been concluded, the house party broke up.

To expect a dozen or so guests at a house party to keep their mouths shut on such a matter was being very optimistic, particularly when one of the guests was prone, as Queen Victoria put it, 'to let everything *out*'.[29] Indeed, no sooner had the Prince of Wales met Lord and Lady Brooke at York station, on their way north to her step-father's funeral in Scotland, than he was telling Daisy all about it. Daisy, in turn, passed the story on to her relations at the funeral. Or so rumour has it. But true or not – and Daisy always vigorously denied having spread the story – everyone believed that it was Lady Brooke who let this particularly vicious cat out of the bag. For the rest of her days, Daisy was to be branded as 'The Babbling Brook'.

Once the pact of secrecy had been broken, Sir William Gordon-Cumming instructed his solicitors to bring an action for libel against his accusers. Chief among them, of course, was the Prince of Wales. Frantic efforts were made to keep the Prince out of court – some suggested a private military inquiry, others an inquiry at the Guards Club – but, in the end, a civil action became inevitable.

The trial, which opened on 1 June 1891 and lasted for nine days, was sensational: it was almost as though the Prince of Wales were on trial. For all nine days he sat in court under the critical gaze of a huge crowd who listened avidly to the description of what sounded to them like very dissolute goings-on; when he did finally give evidence, he cut a very poor figure. And although in fact Gordon-Cumming lost his action, it was the Prince who emerged, in the eyes of the public, as the guilty party. The jury, who had declared against Gordon-Cumming, was hissed; the Prince was loudly booed at that month's Ascot; and the newspapers gave themselves over to an orgy of pious moralising.

The *Review of Reviews* – reflecting, it claimed, the opinions of various country gentlemen – condemned the Prince not only as a gambler but 'as a wastrel and whoremonger'.[30] *The Times* 'profoundly regretted that the Prince should have been in any way mixed up, not only in the case, but in the social circumstances which prepared the way for it.'[31]

Queen Victoria, needless to say, was appalled. 'It is a fearful humiliation to see the future King of this country dragged through the dirt . . .' she wailed to her eldest daughter, now the Empress Frederick. 'I feel it a terrible humiliation, and so do all the people. It is very painful and must do his prestige great harm. Oh! if only it is a lesson for the future.'[32]

In an attempt to limit the damage to the Prince's reputation, various courses of action were proposed. Could not the government make some sort of pronouncement in the Prince's favour? This suggestion was scotched, very firmly, by Lord Salisbury, who had by now succeeded Gladstone as Prime Minister. The private morals of the Prince of Wales were not the concern of the British government, he said. His worldly advice was for the Prince to avoid baccarat for six months and for him then to write a letter to some indiscreet friend – who would immediately publish it – to the effect that the trial had shown him the error of his ways and that he no longer allowed baccarat to be played in his presence.

The Queen had a less devious proposal. The Prince should write an open letter to the Archbishop of Canterbury, expressing his strong disapproval of gambling. This ingenuous idea was rejected by both the Prime Minister and the Prince of Wales.

In the end, Bertie wrote a private letter to the Archbishop in which he blandly expressed his 'horror of gambling' which he considered to be, along with intemperance, 'one of the greatest curses that a country can be afflicted with'.[33]

And from then on, instead of playing baccarat for money, His Royal Highness played bridge for money.

The Tranby Croft trial finished poor Gordon-Cumming. He was dismissed from the army, expelled from all his clubs and socially ostracised. He lived on, in unhappy seclusion, until 1930. Daisy Brooke, whose babbling was said to have led directly to the trial, afterwards claimed that she considered him 'more sinned against than sinning' and that 'after he had cut us all off in his retirement', she 'often had sad thoughts of him' but that she 'always kept a warm corner in my heart for him'.[34]

As a refuge from the storms of public opinion there was always Sandringham. Nowhere did the Prince of Wales feel more at home than on his Norfolk estate. He had bought the property at the time of his marriage and, until his death almost fifty years later, he remained devoted to it. Indeed, for almost a century it was the royal family's favourite country home. George V and his son, George VI – who died at Sandringham in 1952 – both loved the estate; the entire royal family would gather there for Christmas. But Queen Elizabeth II, who spent her wartime girlhood in Windsor Castle, tends to regard that ancient fortress-castle as home, with the result that Sandringham has slipped in popularity and importance as a royal residence. The great royal Christmas jamboree now takes place at Windsor.

But in its heyday – during the Prince of Wales's years as king-in-waiting and his reign as Edward VII – Sandringham was one of the country's great social centres. No home better mirrored Bertie's particular lifestyle; it was here that he was seen at his most typical.

Not everyone, though, shared the Prince's uncritical devotion to Sandringham. Many of his guests found the Norfolk countryside flat and featureless. Victorians dearly loved a dramatic, romantic landscape; Swiss scenery, with its mountains and its lakes and its waterfalls, was their ideal. But failing that, they liked rolling, pretty, heavily wooded countryside, with a glitter of water between the trees.

There was, sighed one of Princess Alexandra's ladies, 'no attraction of any sort or kind. There are numerous coverts but no fine woods, large unclosed turnip fields, with an occasional haystack to break the line of the horizon. It would be difficult to find a more ugly or desolate-looking place . . .'[35] The wind off the Wash was like a knife. The house, too, was hideous. The original Georgian mansion had been completely reconstructed in what was loosely termed the 'Elizabethan style': the result was a vast, sprawling, many-gabled pile of dark orange brick, looking more like a station hotel or the home of some *nouveau riche* industrialist than the country seat of a future king. 'As there was all England to choose from,' wailed the same lady-in-waiting, 'I do wish they had had a finer house in a more picturesque and cheerful situation.'[36]

Even Disraeli, who could usually be relied upon to make some flattering comment, confined himself to saying that visiting the Prince at Sandringham was rather like visiting one of 'the Dukes and Princes of the Baltic: a vigorous marine air, stunted fir forests . . .'[37] But then, as much as Queen Victoria hated the heat, Disraeli hated the cold.

The interior of the house was, if anything, worse. There were no really impressive rooms; arriving guests would be led directly into the main hall in which, more often than not, the royal family would be sitting down to tea. The house was furnished in the worst contemporary taste: the rooms were a cheerful clutter of sentimental paintings, plush-covered furniture, mounted animals' heads, suits of armour, display cabinets stuffed with china, tables crammed with ornaments and photographs, what-nots loaded with bric-à-brac. One had to look very closely, claims one of the Prince's biographers, to appreciate 'that those toy figures of animals were not trinkets from a parish bazaar but Fabergé creations sent by the Tsar of all the Russias'.[38] There was even a big stuffed baboon standing beside the front door supporting, on its outstretched paws, a silver salver for visitors' cards.

But what Sandringham might have lacked in elegance it made up for in warmth. Its atmosphere was welcoming, cheerful and relatively informal; one was always made to feel at home. 'While a very spacious house, Sandringham is not palatial,' wrote Lillie Langtry, 'but, what is far better, it gives one the idea of being thoroughly liveable and comfortable . . .'[39] And Daisy Brooke claimed that guests, no matter how illustrious, were always treated as personal friends. The Prince 'would impose no restraint upon those who came to visit him in his capacity as a country gentleman.'[40]

Quite often, guests would be shown to their rooms by the Prince or the Princess themselves. On one occasion Lord Fisher, wanting to avoid the other arrivals in the hall, slipped upstairs and started unpacking. As he stood with a boot in each hand, he heard someone fumbling with the door handle. Assuming it to be a footman, he shouted, 'Come in, don't go humbugging with the door handle!' But in walked his host, 'with a cigar about a yard long in his mouth'.

'What on earth are you doing?' he asked.

'Unpacking, Sir,' answered Fisher.

'Where's your servant?'

'Haven't got one, Sir.'

'Where is he?'

'Never had one, Sir; couldn't afford it.'

'Put those boots down; sit in that armchair.'[41]

So the two of them sat, one on each side of the fire, chatting so animatedly that they were almost late for dinner.

The kaleidoscopic nature of the company never ceased to amaze the Prince's more conventional guests. He flung them all together: aristocrats, clergymen, politicians, sportsmen, diplomats, financiers, soldiers, industrialists. The young Tsarevich, afterwards Tsar Nicholas II, visiting Sandringham at this time, wrote home to St Petersburg to complain about the composition of the house party. 'Most of them were horse dealers, among others a Baron Hirsch [to meet a Jew socially was regarded as unthinkable in the Russian imperial family]. I tried to keep away as much as I could, and not to talk.'[42]

Sandringham saw the introduction of other social changes as well. Lady Brooke says that it was the Prince, with his preference for female company, who set the example of leaving the table almost immediately after dinner to join the ladies. His introduction of cigarette smoking after the meal 'killed the claret habit'. After the first whiff or two it was difficult, she says, 'to tell a good wine from bad, and champagne speedily took the place of Bordeaux'.[43] Yet when a newspaper once castigated the Prince for giving champagne suppers to his lady friends, his scathing comment was that champagne was for the *demi-monde*; what he gave his ladies at night was whisky and soda.

Bridge was another of the things he helped popularise. 'Your brother Rosslyn is trying to introduce a new form of whist, called Bridge,' the Prince once wrote to Daisy. 'It does not appear to be particularly interesting, and I do not think it will be popular.'[44] Yet, within a few years, he had developed into an enthusiastic and skilful bridge player.

Life at Sandringham was permeated, above all, by the Prince's undiminished sense of fun. Few people, noted Daisy's half-sister, Lady Angela Forbes, had more *joie de vivre* than the Prince of Wales. 'He enjoyed himself with the infectious gaiety of a schoolboy. That indefinable, but undeniable, gift of youth remained with him all his life.'[45] It remained, to an even greater extent, with the Princess of Wales. Not only did Princess Alexandra look untouched by time, she acted as though she were still a young bride. The rooms rang with laughter as the company, led by their host and hostess, played their childish games: tobogganing down the carpeted stairs on silver trays, racing their tricycles round the ballroom, crouching behind sofas for hide-and-seek.

Practical jokes were especially popular; humour was always of the slap-stick variety. 'If anyone caught his foot in a mat, or nearly fell into the fire or out of the window,' sighs one long-suffering observer, 'the mirth of the royal family knew no bounds.'[46] Why bother thinking up a witty remark when a finger caught in the door will bring forth gales of laughter?

The Prince was particularly fond of dancing. (And so, more surprisingly, was Queen Victoria; the public would have been astonished at the vigour with which the Widow of Windsor danced with John Brown at the Gillies' Ball at Balmoral.) At the three annual Sandringham balls – the County, the Farmers' and the Servants' – Bertie enjoyed himself immensely. 'He was his own Master of Ceremonies,' noted one guest, 'signalling and sending messages to the band, arranging every dance and when to begin and when to leave off . . . he looked as if he could have gone on all night and into the middle of next week.'[47]

But it was for its shooting that the Prince of Wales enjoyed Sandringham most. It was a sport which, in the nineteenth and early twentieth centuries, was practised to an extent which seems hardly credible today. For most Victorian and Edwardian gentlemen, not least among them Lord Brooke, shooting was almost a *raison d'être*; their lives were organised around the shooting seasons. The 'glorious twelfth' of August, which marked the opening of the grouse season, was regarded as almost sacrosanct. Fortunes were spent on improving the game on the great estates; records were solemnly kept and achievements endlessly discussed; the daily 'bags' of slaughtered birds and animals could be enormous; gun rooms were like shrines.

The Prince of Wales's brother, Prince Alfred, on a colonial tour, once took part in a hunt of wild animals which an officer in attendance describes as 'that glorious day when we killed six hundred head of game, all larger than horses'. Firing into the bewildered and stampeding herds, Prince Alfred alone shot over twenty-five head of game. 'Most of the sportsmen looked more like butchers than sportsmen, from being so covered in blood,' wrote the same exhilarated officer. 'His Royal Highness was red up to the shoulders from using the spear . . .'[48]

That there might be something distasteful about this wholesale killing would never have occurred to them as they stood there, blazing away for all they were worth. 'What my friends and I were doing,' remembered Lord Brooke in a more enlightened age, 'we thought our children would do after us, and the only possible alteration in conditions appeared to lie in the direction of higher birds and new sporting powders.'[49] Yet a man like the Prince of Wales's son, the future George V, who was as dedicated a shot as the rest of them, could dissolve into tears at the sight of a dead garden bird.

Almost every weekday morning at Sandringham, the Prince of Wales would set out, correctly dressed in tweed suit, flat cap, heavy boots and swinging cape, with half a dozen or more of his male guests, to devote his day to shooting partridge, pheasant, woodcock and wild duck or rabbits. He was particularly fond of the *battue*: the Continental concept of a vast semi-circle of beaters driving the birds towards the sportsmen. The Prince spent tens of thousands of pounds improving the shooting at Sandringham. By the 1890s the amount of game killed each year was enormous: a single day's shooting could add up to 3000 birds or 6000 rabbits. 'At Sandringham,' wrote the Prince's eldest grandson, afterwards Duke of Windsor, 'everything, including, I regret to say, the interests of the farmer, was subordinated to the shooting.'[50]

At the time, though, very few members of the public would have been any more offended by this mass slaughter than the sportsmen themselves. It is true that some voices of protest were being raised. Even aristocrats like Lady Florence Dixie, daughter of the 7th Marquess of Queensbury, an enthusiastic shot in her time, were beginning to campaign against the barbarism of blood sports. For this she was dismissed as, at least, eccentric and, at worst, mad. In the eyes of the majority of the Prince's countrymen, he had every right to shoot as much as he pleased. It all helped confirm his image as a country squire.

For, in spite of his cosmopolitanism and his hedonism, it was as an English country gentleman that the Prince of Wales was generally regarded. He might have suffered periodic bouts of unpopularity but, for most of the time, he was admired for his quintessentially British qualities. With his love of sport – hunting, shooting and racing – and his interest in the land – the crops, forests, pigs and horses of his Sandringham estate – the Prince of Wales was looked upon as the very personification of that 'Merrie England' of so many of his countrymen's imaginations. He was, in many ways, a John Bull figure.

The day's sport at Sandringham over, the Prince's guests would assemble for tea at five o'clock in the hall. For this, the ladies would have changed, for the third or fourth time that day, into tea-gowns. They would then change again, into elaborate evening dresses with trains, while the gentlemen would wear full evening dress with decorations. As they waited downstairs for the arrival of the Prince and Princess, an equerry would move among them with a plan of the dinner table, to explain to each gentleman which lady he would be leading in to dinner and where exactly they would be sitting. The punctilious Prince disliked any hesitation in the finding of seats. The wait for their hosts might be a long one, as Princess Alexandra was invariably late, but as soon as she arrived, looking her usual soignée, charming and unflustered self, the Prince would lead the company in, 'each lady in turn having the privilege of being taken in by her royal host'.[51]

A typical dinner would consist of hot and cold soup, whitebait, trout, quail, pullet, roast mutton, cold ham, ortolans, asparagus, *gâteaux, pâtisseries,* a savoury and assorted ices. With this there would be sherry, madeira, two wines, champagne, port, more sherry and then brandy. No dish was too rich for the Prince of Wales. Quails packed with *foie gras*, pheasants stuffed with truffles, snipe crammed with forcemeat, and all of them garnished with truffles, mushrooms, prawns and oysters and served in thick, creamy sauces, he gobbled down with great relish. And if one still felt peckish after dinner, there were always plates of sandwiches or lobster and chicken salads available.

Not everyone approved of these lavish menus. For a perfectly adequate dinner, maintained the Earl of Dudley, one needed only 'a good soup, a small turbot, a neck of venison, ducklings with green peas, chicken with asparagus and an apricot tart.'[52]

Late at night, after the ladies had retired to bed, the Prince and his close friends would indulge in what were generally regarded as more masculine recreations: cards, bowls or billiards. Hazily, their pungent cigar smoke would drift across the famous billiard-room screen decorated with likenesses of such irreproachable contemporary figures as Lord Salisbury or Matthew Arnold. Only on closer inspection did one appreciate that these worthies were pictured, in extremely compromising attitudes, with naked women.

No sooner had the Tranby Croft scandal died down than the Beresford scandal flared up once more. Indeed, it might have been the fact that the Prince of Wales stood publicly disgraced by the Baccarat Case that encouraged Lord Charles Beresford to renew his attack on the Prince and Lady Brooke. This attack threatened to expose the Prince to even greater public humiliation.

Lady Charles Beresford, still smarting at having been cold-shouldered by the Marlborough House set, had been watching the triumph of her arch-enemy, Lady Brooke, with increasing fury. In letter after letter to her husband, aboard HMS Undaunted in the Mediterranean, she railed against the iniquities of the Prince and Daisy

Brooke. And when the person she scathingly refers to as 'that "Lady" ' was publicly received by the Princess of Wales at Marlborough House in the summer of 1891, Lady Charles felt that she could stand no more of this humiliation. Rouged cheeks flushing even redder, she wrote yet again to her husband, demanding that he take action.

In what was an extremely intemperate letter even for that intemperate man, Lord Charles Beresford attacked the Prince for behaving like 'a blackguard and a coward'.[53] The days of duelling might be over, he threatened, in what was the nub of his letter, 'but there is a more just way of getting right done than can duelling, and that is – *publicity*.'[54]

This inflammatory letter was sent by Beresford, not to the Prince, but to Lady Charles, with instructions that she was to send it on to the Prime Minister, Lord Salisbury. This Lady Charles lost no time in doing. One would have thought that the Prime Minister of Great Britain, with its vast empire covering over a quarter of the earth's surface and accommodating over a quarter of the world's population, would have had more pressing concerns than a squabble between two society ladies. But no. Lord Salisbury attended to the matter without delay.

He had good reason for doing so. For, in a letter of her own, Lady Charles made it clear that not only was her husband in a position to blacken the Prince of Wales's reputation, but her sister, Mrs Gerald Paget, had already written a pamphlet on the Prince's affair with Lady Brooke which, if published, would blacken his reputation still further. Several people, she continued darkly, 'wanted to make use of the story at the next General Election for purposes of their own'.[55]

What Lady Charles wanted was 'a *public* apology' from the Prince of Wales. She would not be fobbed off with some minor concession, such as an invitation to Marlborough House.

Sighing, one feels certain, a great sigh, Lord Salisbury wrote conciliatory letters to both Lord and Lady Charles Beresford. According to 'the social laws of our class',[56] the Prime Minister pointed out to Beresford, it would not be seemly for a gentleman to disgrace his former mistress. Swayed by this apparently unanswerable argument, Lord Charles agreed to send the Prince a less violent letter.

And there the matter might have ended had not Lady Charles's sister, Mrs Gerald Paget, begun circulating her threatened pamphlet. Called *Lady River*, which everyone knew meant Lady Brooke, this typewritten exposé of Daisy Brooke's various activities, not least her affair with the Prince of Wales, caused a sensation. A hostess had only to announce a public reading of the scurrilous pamphlet for her drawing room to be crowded to capacity.

News of this titillating pamphlet eventually reached the ears of the Princess of Wales, at that stage holidaying with her family in her native Denmark. She was horrified. Princess Alexandra never minded – or, at least, she could cope with – her husband's infidelity in private; what she hated was being exposed to public humiliation. This latest gossip, coming hot on the heels of the Tranby Croft scandal, was more than she could bear. Instead of returning home to celebrate her husband's fiftieth birthday on 9 November 1891, she went to visit her sister Dagmar, the Tsarina Marie Feodorovna of Russia, in the Crimea. Her gesture did not go unnoticed.

And now things got worse. In December, following an urgent telegram from his wife, Lord Charles Beresford arrived home. He promptly issued an ultimatum. Unless the Prince of Wales apologised publicly to his wife and unless Lady Brooke withdrew from society for a year, Beresford would have no alternative but to publish the full details about the Prince's private life.

There followed four frantic days in which Lord Salisbury negotiated not only with the Prince and the Beresfords but with Queen Victoria herself. On the last day, with Beresford on the point of calling a press conference at which he planned both to expose the Prince and announce his own resignation from the navy, a settlement was reached. The Prince and Beresford exchanged conciliatory letters (drafted by Lord Salisbury) and Lady Brooke agreed to a temporary withdrawal from court. By the end of the year 1891, the crisis was over.

Her withdrawal from court did not, though, mark the end of Daisy Brooke's troubles. Lord Brooke, no less than Princess Alexandra, felt that this time things had gone too far. There were limits, it seems, to even his celebrated tolerance. The Beresford affair led to a major crisis in Daisy's marriage, with divorce being widely rumoured. It was said that Lord Brooke planned to name no less than fourteen co-respondents, including the Prince of Wales, Lord Charles Beresford, the Duke of Marlborough and Lord Randolph Churchill.

In the end, though, the action was not brought. The social stigma of a divorce, with the intimate details being published for all to see, was considered much worse than an illicit love affair, no matter how scandalous. The gallant Lord Brooke could not put his wife – nor his family's good name – through that.

The one thing that had not been affected by the sensational, complicated and long-running Beresford affair was the Prince's love for Daisy. He was as infatuated by her as ever. So powerful, in fact, was her hold on his affections that he – the most forgiving of men – would not hear of a reconciliation with Beresford. Not until five years after the quarrel – in June 1897, when the Prince's horse Persimmon won the Ascot Gold Cup – would the Prince speak to him. And his first thought, after doing so, was to write to Daisy to apologise for what he had done. His letter to her is worth reproducing in full.

'My own lovely little Daisy, I lose no time in writing to tell you of an episode which occurred today after you left – which was unpleasant and unexpected – but I hope, my darling, you will agree that I could not have acted otherwise, as my loyalty to you is, I hope, a thing that you will never think of doubting!

'Shortly before leaving Ascot today, Marcus B. [Lord Marcus Beresford, Lord Charles's brother and manager of the Prince's stud] came to me, and said he had a great favour to ask me, so I answered at once I should be delighted to grant it. He then became much affected, and actually cried, and said might he bring his brother C. up to offer his congratulations on Persimmon's success. I had no alternative but to say yes. He came up with his hat off, and would not put it on till I told him, and shook hands. We talked a little about racing, then I turned and we parted. What struck me more than anything, was his humble attitude and manner! My loved one, I hope you won't be annoyed at what has happened, and exonerate me from blame, as that is all I care about. . .

'Goodnight and God keep you, my own adored little Daisy Wife.'[57]

8

Independent Women

IN THE DECADE since her liaison with the Prince of Wales had ended, Lillie Langtry had become an even greater celebrity. If her relationship with the Prince had helped launch her on her acting career, it was her own colourful behaviour that ensured its continuing success. Lillie Langtry might not have been much of an actress but she certainly knew how to fill a theatre.

Her contract with the Bancrofts had not lasted long. Once she had come to appreciate that it was her notoriety that was attracting such enthusiastic audiences, she decided to form a company of her own. A successful tour of ten British cities encouraged her to accept an offer to take her company to the United States. The boast – by Henry Abbey, the sharp-witted American impresario who had made the offer – that he never haggled about terms, proved to be an idle one as far as Lillie was concerned. She haggled until he agreed to give her the same terms as he had given Sarah Bernhardt the year before. Abbey knew that she would be worth it. The denunciation of Sarah Bernhardt from almost every pulpit in the United States had filled Abbey's pockets most gratifyingly; there was no reason, he reckoned, why the appearance of the Prince of Wales's mistress should not prove equally rewarding.

And so it did. The crowds that flocked, not only to see Lillie's arrival in New York on 23 October 1882, but to theatres throughout the country, came to satisfy their prurient curiosity, not to pay homage to great art. Lillie might parry journalists' questions about her relationship with the Prince of Wales but this never stopped newspaper cartoonists from depicting the two of them in suggestive situations. A particularly telling cartoon showed Lillie downstage, with the footlights throwing her shadow, shaped like the Prince of Wales, on the curtain behind. 'The shadow that draws the American dollars' ran the caption.

But the American public had no need to rely on reminders of her past romance for their thrills. Before many weeks had passed, Lillie was supplying New Yorkers with fresh grounds for gossip. Never one to turn her back on a wealthy admirer, the twenty-nine-year-old Lillie took up with a dark, good-looking, twenty-two-year-old multimillionaire named Freddie Gebhard. For the next few years Gebhard was her constant companion. They were seen everywhere together. 'He became famous in two continents,' Lillie afterwards announced, 'because I loved him.'[1] The boot, in fact, was on the other foot: it was Freddie Gebhard who was in love with Lillie. There was apparently nothing that the besotted young man would not do for her. He bought her expensive jewellery, he paid for her sumptuous clothes, he set her up in a luxurious house in West Twenty-third Street and, most generously of all, he provided the means of travel with which she was to become most closely associated in the minds of her vast public: the $250,000 railway carriage known as 'Lalee' which carried her across the States on her many tours.

The word 'Lalee', Lillie assures us, means 'flirt' in some unspecified Indian dialect (one would have described Lillie herself as something more than a flirt) and 'Lalee' was certainly the last word in luxurious travel. The carriage was seventy-five feet long, with a white roof, a 'gorgeously' blue exterior decorated with wreaths of golden lilies, polished teak platforms, a salon with walls covered in green and cream brocade, a bedroom whose *eau de nil* walls, ceiling and furniture were padded to resist the shock of a collision, a bathroom with silver fittings and rose-coloured curtains, two guest compartments, a maid's compartment, a pantry and a kitchen. Underneath were ice chests, big enough to accommodate a whole stag. With Lillie travelled her English butler and several maids.

In this palace-on-wheels (the rest of her company were accommodated in much humbler carriages) Lillie travelled the length and breadth of the country, bringing to many far-flung communities if not exactly culture, then certainly excitement. During the six years that she spent touring the United States, Lillie played everything from Shakespeare (one tactful critic described her Lady Macbeth as 'astounding') to contemporary drawing room comedies. Mr Bancroft had long ago told her, Lillie would say airily, to ignore all reviews: 'it is always best to await the criticism which is supplied by the box-office receipts.'[2]

Whatever her limitations, Lillie always gave value for money. If the town had no theatre, she would act on some rigged-up stage. She played to audiences of gold miners and cowboys just as happily as she did to overdressed socialites in New York, Chicago or San Francisco. In her elegant clothes and with her increasingly regal manner, she processed through the country like a princess. Babies were named after her, fans begged for autographs, her Worth hats and dresses were assiduously copied, strangers proposed marriage, the self-styled 'Judge' Roy Bean even changed the name of his Texan town from 'Vinagaroon' to 'Langtry'. Her subsequent visit to Langtry was conducted with all the formality and split-second timing of a royal occasion. When Freddie Gebhard bought her a 7500 acre ranch in California, she toyed with the idea of calling it Sandringham.

With the rest of her company, Lillie's manner was forbiddingly imperious. Although she paid them as little as she could get away with, she expected unquestioned loyalty and dedication. Deception appalled her. 'She would be hurt,' said one manager of her company, 'for she had far more heart than she was given credit for, but she could not and would not endure stupidity or incompetence.'[3] In short, Lillie Langtry had developed into a thorough-going professional: hard-headed, businesslike and with a strong sense of showmanship.

In between these mammoth tours of the United States, Lillie would return home. Backed by the faithful young Gebhard, she would lease a London theatre for a season. And whatever the play, she could always be sure that if the Prince of Wales were in town, he would be in the royal box on opening night. If he were away, he would send her a message. 'I am glad to hear that you are in harness again and most sincerely wish you all possible success in your tour though I fear you have hard work before you,' he once wrote from Stockholm where he was the guest of King Oscar II of Sweden. As the Swedish King had also been one of Lillie's many admirers, the Prince was able to add that 'he particularly begged to be remembered to you and wish you success in your profession.'

A few months later, on 19 January 1886, when Lillie was rehearsing *Enemies* at the Prince's Theatre, Bertie wrote asking her to reserve a box for him for the opening night. He would have liked to have seen a dress rehearsal as he might have been able to give her a few hints, he wrote. Would the rehearsal be on Monday, Tuesday or Wednesday? He was anxious to know because of his evening engagements; or would it be in the daytime?

Having seen the play (and having, in the meantime, arranged a time and date for their next meeting) the Prince writes 'just two lines to tell you again what a success I thought your piece was. You have certainly acted better tonight than I have ever seen you.'[4]

These visits home also allowed Lillie to see her daughter, Jeanne-Marie, who was still living, in the care of Lillie's mother, in the Red House, Bournemouth. But after one of her visits, Lillie took little Jeanne-Marie back to the States with her. For the following few years the child, attended by a governess and a maid, lived in a bewildering variety of places: aboard the luxurious 'Lalee' as it went rocketing across the States, in Lillie's even more luxurious New York home, in the state rooms of ocean liners, in flower-filled hotel rooms. To her, Lillie was still *ma tante*. The girl's father, so Lillie would sigh, had been her brother Maurice, so tragically mauled to death by a tiger in India. Who then, Jeanne-Marie must surely have wondered, was Freddie – the young man with the curling black moustache who paid all the bills?

The one person whom Jeanne-Marie knew nothing about was Edward Langtry. For years Lillie had been trying her best to divorce him, but Edward would not hear of it..Perhaps he was still hoping for a reconciliation with his now rich and famous wife. Not even the persuasive skills of the celebrated solicitor, George Lewis, could get Edward Langtry to change his mind. In the end, Lillie took matters into her own hands. In 1887 she applied for and was granted American citizenship ('without losing my love for the Union Jack, I coupled with it a great affection for the Stars and Stripes,'[5] she explains) and this eventually enabled her to have her marriage dissolved.

Yet there must have been many who guessed Lillie's secret; who knew that Jeanne-Marie was her child by Prince Louis of Battenberg. Was Oscar Wilde one of them? She and Wilde had remained in touch through all her vicissitudes; indeed, he had been in the States, on a lecture tour, when Lillie first arrived in New York. Armed with a great bunch of lilies, he had greeted her on the quayside. When a reporter asked him if it were true that he had 'discovered' Mrs Langtry, Wilde's reply was gratifyingly in character. 'I would rather have discovered Mrs Langtry,' he drawled, 'than have discovered America.'[6]

And Lillie was not above using the occasional Wildism herself. Handing back the proofs to an American photographer who had obtained exclusive rights to take pictures of her, she said, 'You have made me pretty – I am beautiful.'

'As for the love-smitten Oscar Wilde,' wrote one wide-eyed Chicago reporter, 'he is head over heels in love with the much-discussed grass widow, Mrs Langtry.'[7]

A story which Lillie tells about one of her encounters with Oscar Wilde seems to confirm that he knew the truth about Jeanne-Marie being her daughter, not her niece. One afternoon, after she had returned permanently to Britain from the States, he called to see her. Flinging a manuscript onto the table, he announced, 'There is a play which I have written for you.'

'What is my part?' asked Lillie.

'A woman,' he replied, 'with a grown-up illegitimate daughter.'

'My dear Oscar,' she exclaimed, 'am I old enough to have a grown-up daughter of any description?' She refused to open the manuscript or to have him read it to her. 'Put it away for twenty years,' she advised.

Why, she protested many years later, 'he ever supposed that it would have been, at the time, a suitable play for me, I cannot imagine.'[8]

The play was *Lady Windermere's Fan.*

By the end of 1888, there were indications that Lillie's long affair with Gebhard was turning sour. Perhaps he was beginning to regret the fortune that he had squandered on her; perhaps she was tired of him. Whatever the reason, they broke up: Gebhard to marry, first an heiress and then a chorus girl, Lillie to return to London.

She sailed from New York on 13 July 1889, having shipped thirty trunks, her horses, carriages and everything movable from the West Thirty-third Street house and having managed to save, from her theatrical and other earnings, a sizeable sum of money.

The Prince of Wales, never one to shirk a cliché, had once written – as she was about to set off on yet another American tour – that she was 'probably right to "make hay while the sun shines" '.[9] She *had* been right. Not only had she made a great deal of hay but the sun would be shining on her for many years yet.

As the Prince of Wales liked his women either stylishly dressed or naked, it is hardly surprising that he had very little sympathy with the movement for the emancipation of women. Later, as King, he dismissed the suffragettes as 'dreadful women' and was once extremely annoyed to be told that the names of two women had been put forward to serve on the Royal Commission for Divorce. He even hesitated to award the Order of Merit to the aged Florence Nightingale, on the grounds that it was not right 'to give it to a woman'.[10]

Given this attitude, and given the generally accepted idea of a mistress as a rich man's pampered plaything, it is paradoxical that both Lillie Langtry and Daisy Brooke should have been, in their different ways, examples of emancipated women.

The modern feminist movement, with all its ramifications, had its beginnings in the 1850s. It was then, as one historian has so graphically put it, that 'in women of all classes there was a stir . . . the stir of adventure and new ideas, comparable with the agitation which may be noted in a flock of migrants impelled by the lure of new worlds'.[11] In medicine, education, social conditions, the franchise, women were beginning to agitate for reform. By the late 1880s the movement was gathering strength and importance. To the names of pioneers like Florence Nightingale were being added those of Lydia Becker, Barbara Bodichon, Josephine Butler, Elizabeth Garrett – all fighting, in different fields, for a woman's right to lead her own life as a self-sufficient individual. Their bible was *The Subjection of Women*, written by that great theorist of feminism, John Stuart Mill.

Although at first glance Lillie Langtry – with her extravagant tastes, feminine guile and cultivation of rich male protectors – seems to fit awkwardly into this regiment of militant females, there is no doubt that she had many of the qualities of a feminist. A practical, independent, liberated and self-confident woman, she was yearly proving herself equal to any man. More than one theatrical manager and, in later years, racehorse trainer, professed himself astonished at her grasp of what were generally regarded as 'masculine' concerns.

'Mrs Langtry was ever an absorbing study,' wrote Edward Michael, one of her managers. 'Possessing in a marked degree every feminine charm – wiles, fascination and moods – she was at the same time possessed of an iron will power, immense courage and a gift of instant decision which the captain of a 50,000 ton liner in a critical situation might envy. Remarkably well-read, it was with me always a surprise that she found time for reading, for I have never known any topic – and I use the word "any" deliberately – literature, science, arts or any other subject which she was not able to discuss with specialists. Hers was always a big and broad mind which could not tolerate anything commonplace or futile and her favourite phrase is indicative of her nature: "Don't let's fuss, please", spoken in a soft plaintive voice, was a danger signal to those who knew her.'[12]

Hardly had Lillie arrived back in Britain from her profitable years in the United States than she had formed another company and, in her capacity as actor-manager, was starring in a series of plays. In short, in an age when the majority of women were forced to confine themselves to their homes and families, and a minority were still campaigning for the right to be admitted into the professions, Lillie Langtry had carved out a highly successful career of her own.

Daisy Brooke was proving herself equally independent-minded. In spite of her reputation as a social butterfly and mischief-maker, she had always had a good heart. That conscience, which in girlhood had caused her to question the fairness of the existing social order, had never been quite stilled. Lady Brooke was 'ever eager', wrote one neighbour, 'to be doing a good turn for somebody and not always quite knowing what it ought to be'.[13]

Another neighbour, Elinor Glyn, has a story to bear this out. One day, while she was visiting Lady Brooke, a self-righteous curate came to call. 'During conversation about the parish,' she writes, 'he mentioned that some ungodly people, non-churchgoers, were in trouble, and that the husband was very ill. It was God's judgement, he said, and they did not deserve help. Daisy listened with a faraway look that I know well, and while carrying on the conversation with the curate about a new church hall which she was building, she leant over and rang the bell. When the footman appeared she told him to send the housekeeper, and she still went on talking sweetly to the curate. When the housekeeper arrived she looked up casually and telling her the name and address of the "ungodly wretches" she said, "I hear they are in great trouble. Please have beef tea and jellies and port sent round to them at once, and say that I will drive over and see them this afternoon." Then she went on talking to the dumb-founded curate about the erection of the church hall, as if nothing had happened.'[14]

How far Daisy Brooke imagined this setting in train of footman, housekeeper, kitchenmaid and groom to deliver 'beef tea and jellies and port' would go towards nourishing a labourer's family one does not know; but then not all her philanthropic activities were quite so impractical. In 1890, in an effort to alleviate the poverty in the neighbourhood of Easton Lodge, she started a needlework school, where local women could work for wages. In other words, instead of applying the customary Victorian palliative – the giving of alms – Lady Brooke organised proper employment. Although not above making use of her influential connections (the lingerie for the trousseau of the bride-to-be of Prince Eddy, the Prince of Wales's eldest son, was embroidered by her needlewomen) Daisy did her best to run her school in a businesslike, non-charitable fashion. When she could no longer market the needlework personally, she opened a shop in Bond Street.

This move, so daring by contemporary standards, caused consternation in society. For Lady Brooke to have gone into 'trade' was
considered too *outré* for words. Her protestations, that her needlework school meant independence and a sense of pride for women who
would otherwise have to rely on charity, made very little sense to
sneering society matrons.

Daisy's well-intentioned venture was not, in fact, a great success.
Unlike Lillie Langtry, Daisy Brooke had no business sense. Nor,
indeed, was the scheme a sufficient outlet for her abundant energy,
considerable intelligence and awakening social conscience. Her philanthropic interests had yet to be channelled. When they were, they
would sweep her away into a different world: a world far removed
from society balls, country house parties and the Prince of Wales. But
not yet.

'Queen Alexandra, in her younger years,' remembered Daisy, 'was
full of fun and the joy of life. She enjoyed entertaining and being
entertained, while beneath her placid exterior there was a shrewd judgement that expressed itself now and again in no uncertain terms.'[15]

Daisy was in a position to know. For about few people did
Alexandra's shrewd judgement express itself in less uncertain terms
than about Lady Brooke. Princess Alexandra disliked her intensely.
Whereas the Princess had always been ready to tolerate her husband's
previous mistress, Lillie Langtry, she resolutely refused to have
anything to do with Daisy Brooke. Once Daisy had become the
Prince of Wales's recognised mistress, Alexandra would not receive
her at Marlborough House or Sandringham.

There were several reasons for Alexandra's unyielding attitude. For
one thing, she had sympathised with Lady Charles Beresford during
the turbulent Beresford affair. For another, the furore surrounding the
affair had publicly revealed Alexandra as the betrayed wife in a way
that her husband's more discreetly conducted liaison with Lillie
Langtry had never done. Then, where the humbly-born Lillie had
always been careful to treat the Princess with great deference, the rich
and aristocratic Daisy was far more assured in Alexandra's company.
After all, if Daisy had married Prince Leopold, she would have been
Alexandra's sister-in-law. Daisy was the sort of vain, outspoken,
trouble-making woman that the Princess did not like. Nor were
matters helped by the fact that she was eighteen years younger than
Alexandra.

There were, of course, no scenes or recriminations on the Princess's part: she simply set her face against Lady Brooke and, as Alexandra was the most stubborn of women, nothing would induce her to change her attitude. Not until the affair had run its course would the Princess of Wales have any contact with Lady Brooke. And even then, it remained minimal.

Increasingly, the Prince of Wales's restless, scandal-racked way of life caused his wife to retreat into a private, almost make-believe world of her own. She spent more and more time at Sandringham in the company of those with whom she felt most at ease, particularly those two long-serving and unmarried companions – Charlotte Knollys, her woman-of-the-bedchamber, and Sir Dighton Probyn, comptroller of the Prince's household. Enhancing the aura of unreality that was enveloping Alexandra was the fact that she still looked so extraordinarily young; it was almost as though time had passed her by. With her unlined skin, she looked twenty years younger than her age; with her figure of a girl, she dressed in the height of fashion. This enduring beauty, this bandbox elegance, was giving the Princess of Wales an almost artificial look. 'There was something about Aunt Alix,' wrote one of her nieces, 'something invincible, something exquisite and flowerlike. She gave you the same joy as a beautiful rose or a rare orchid or an absolutely faultless carnation. She was a garden flower that had been grown by a superlative gardener who knew every trick of his art.'[16]

And when one added to the Princess's youthful appearance her youthful manner – her childish sense of fun, her scatter-brained charm, her impulsive generosity – one could hardly believe that she was a woman of almost fifty by the early 1890s.

If Princess Alexandra was virtuous, it was not because she was lacking in masculine admirers. Even to Dighton Probyn, who knew her in every mood, she remained always the 'Beloved Lady'. But her most devoted admirer was the Honourable Oliver Montagu, a younger son of the Earl of Sandwich and an officer in the Blues who had been appointed as an extra equerry to the Prince and Princess of Wales in 1868. Tall and handsome, Oliver Montagu gave a first impression of being just another rollicking, sporting young blade, one of those 'wicked boys' in whose company the Prince of Wales delighted. But there was more to him than this. Behind the dashing façade, Oliver Montagu was a serious-minded, deeply religious man, imbued with a strong sense of chivalry. On first meeting the Princess of Wales, when they were both twenty-four, Oliver Montagu fell deeply in love with her, and he remained in love with her until the day he died, twenty-five years later.

For year after year Oliver Montagu, who never married, devoted himself to the beautiful Princess of Wales: attending to her needs, providing her with constant companionship, shielding her – as one observer has put it – 'in every way, not least from his own great love'.[17] That the affair remained platonic, there is no question. Even Skittles, always quick to sniff out any sexual scandal, was forced to admit that Oliver Montagu had never been Alexandra's lover. When Wilfrid Scawen Blunt asked her if the Princess had ever had a lover, she answered, 'Oh no. She is not made that way. She disliked even having her hand kissed. She submitted to her conjugal duties but never liked it. She was very fond of Oliver Montagu but it was only as a friend. She went to bed and cried for three days when he died. The Prince of Wales said he knew there was nothing in it.'[18]

Platonic love affairs such as this were as much an aspect of Victorian upper-class life as the adulterous liaisons of country house parties. Love without sex was regarded as a perfectly natural state of affairs. There had been, during the nineteenth century, a great resurgence of medievalism, not only in art and architecture but in attitudes: a revival of what were somewhat naively regarded as the knightly qualities of idealism, chivalry and gallantry. Allied to this was the sentimentalism of the Victorian age: the love poems, the pressed flowers, the exchanged tokens, the fan language, the piano duets.

It is in this light that Princess Alexandra's relationship with Oliver Montagu should be seen. It must have been no small consolation for the frequently betrayed Princess to be so blamelessly but ardently courted by this 'perfect, gentle knight'.

.

Oliver Montagu was not, though, Princess Alexandra's only consolation. She derived even more pleasure from her children. Neglected by her husband and increasingly cut off from his social world by her deafness and her domesticity, the Princess devoted herself to her five children. In those days, reminisced Lady Brooke, 'we preferred to keep our children young, for the younger generation, we knew, would date us.'[19] That might have been one reason for the Princess's determination to keep her children as childlike as possible for as long as possible, but an equally valid reason was her own immaturity. To the Wales children their mother – so gay, so spontaneous, so impractical and unpunctual – was always 'darling Mother-dear': a delightful companion hardly more grown-up than themselves. Long after their childhood was over, the Wales children still spoke and behaved like adolescents. One of the princesses celebrated her nineteenth birthday with a children's party; in manhood, the second son would sign himself 'your little Georgie'.

The three Wales princesses – Louise, Victoria and Maud, all in their early twenties by 1889 – looked very alike: carbon copies of their mother but without her marvellous beauty. All three were pale and long-faced, with protruding eyes and tightly curled poodle fringes. Boisterous in private but diffident in public, they were often referred to as 'the whispering Wales girls'. They always talked, claimed one of their cousins, about people as 'the dear little thing' or 'the poor little man'. They 'spoke in a minor key, *en sourdine*. It gave a special quality to all talks with them, and gave me a strange sensation, as though life would have been very wonderful and everything very beautiful if it had not been so sad.'[20] Their rooms were like those of little children: crammed with an accumulation of tiny, pretty, dainty but far from aesthetic *objets* – miniatures, shells, little vases, diminutive paintings, tiny china ornaments.

A letter written by the three of them when the eldest was already eighteen to their father's private secretary, Sir Francis Knollys, perfectly illustrates their enduring childishness. Addressed to 'Dear old Thingy' and enclosing drawings of themselves as animals, they hope that 'the pictures will put you in mind of your little friends Toots, Gawks and Snipey. You must notice that Toots is practising her steps for the tiresome Court ball, that Gawks is going to bed instead like Cinderella, and that Snipey is trying to console herself with a song instead of singing her hymns in Church as she ought to do . . . We are afraid you won't be at all glad to see us *country bumpkins* again, as we shall have nothing to talk about but cows and cowslips. Now good-bye, old thingy and hoping you will appreciate the *works of art* we send you. Your affectionate little friends: Toots, Gawks and Snipey.'[21]

How much, one wonders, did the Prince of Wales long for three beautiful and sophisticated daughters of whom a father could be proud?

Prince George, the second Wales boy, who turned twenty-five in 1890, was revealing himself to be more mature, not only than his three younger sisters, but than his elder brother, the twenty-six-year-old Prince Eddy. Much of this was due to the many years he had spent in the navy. Alone among Princess Alexandra's children, Prince George had inherited something of her good looks. Blue-eyed, sun-tanned, with a neatly trimmed nautical beard and moustache, he had none of the pallid, inbred appearance of his brother and sisters. And although he may have been an unimaginative and unintellectual young man, Prince George had – for his position – the more valuable characteristics of self-discipline and conscientiousness.

Yet no less than his brother and sisters was he still very much enmeshed in his mother's web. To read the letters between mother and son is scarcely to believe that she was the middle-aged future Queen of England and he a fully adult naval officer. How he wished, he had written to her two or three years before, that he were going to Sandringham for the holidays. It almost made him cry to think of it. 'I wonder who will have that sweet little room of mine, you must go and see it sometimes and imagine that your little Georgie dear is living in it.'[22]

Wrenched apart by so many things during the early 1890s – the Tranby Croft scandal, the Beresford affair, the Lady Brooke romance – the Prince and Princess of Wales were brought together by the problem of their eldest son, Prince Eddy; or, to give him his correct title, Prince Albert Victor, Duke of Clarence and Avondale.

Having turned twenty-seven in 1891, Prince Eddy remained the negative, lethargic, apathetic creature he had always been. Even allowing for the fact that all the Wales children were immature, Prince Eddy was, in his mother's telling word, exceptionally 'dawdly'. Nothing – his years in the navy, his time at Cambridge, a career in the 10th Hussars or a tour of India – had been able to shape his amorphous personality. Although not the imbecile he is sometimes made out to be, Prince Eddy was certainly backward. With his elaborate uniforms, waxed moustaches and sleepy-eyed stare, he had about as much animation as a tailor's dummy. The only activities for which he showed any trace of enthusiasm were shooting, fishing, playing cards and making love.

A personable, well-mannered enough young man, without arrogance or conceit and with an air that some women found seductive, Prince Eddy was utterly lacking in the qualities of a future king. Anyone further removed from the late Prince Consort's ideal of an intelligent, enlightened, influential and unsullied monarch would have been difficult to imagine. Indeed, even more than his father, the Prince of Wales, Prince Eddy seemed like a throwback to those dissolute Hanoverian princes whose bad blood the Prince Consort had been at such pains to get rid of.

Prince Eddy's bizarre personality and dissipated habits have given rise to two persistent rumours: that he was involved in the Cleveland Street homosexual scandal and that he was Jack the Ripper.

The story of the Jack the Ripper murders, in which five, and possibly eight, prostitutes were murdered and hideously mutilated in London's Whitechapel district during the late 1880s, is too well known to bear repeating here. In spite of several well-argued theories, the identity of the famous mass murderer has never been conclusively established. But in November 1970, an article in *The Criminologist*, by a Dr Thomas Stowell, implied that Prince Eddy had been responsible for the horrific killings. Having studied the papers of Queen Victoria's personal physician, Sir William Gull, Stowell hinted that the murders had been committed by Prince Eddy during a fit of insanity brought on by his alleged syphilis. The syphilis had been contracted by the Prince in the course of one of his voyages on HMS Bacchante.

The claim – that the Prince was syphilitic – may or may not be true. What seems more certain is that he at one stage suffered from a gonorrhoeal infection: a prescription found among the papers of one of his doctors apparently confirms this. If nothing else, this indicates that Prince Eddy led as active a sex life as any other fashionable young man.

Dr Stowell's theory, despite its deliberate vagueness, was eagerly taken up by the world's press. The Jack the Ripper story had always been an intriguing one; how much more intriguing was the possibility that the sadistic mass murderer might have been the prince destined one day to sit on the British throne.

Fascinating though the theory might be, it is patently absurd. In the first place, Prince Eddy had alibis for several of the nights on which the murders took place: for one he was in Scotland, for another at Sandringham, for a third on a tour of the Midlands. And, secondly, the Ripper must have been, above all else, an astute, quick-witted, fast-moving man; by no stretch of the imagination could poor, 'dawdly' Prince Eddy be described in those terms. He was simply not intelligent enough. And would such a kindly, good-natured, impractical oaf have been the type to slit a woman's throat, expertly eviscerate her body and carry off her uterus? Hardly.

About Eddy's possible involvement in the Cleveland Street scandal one is on firmer ground. Of the many male brothels, homosexual clubs and pubs that flourished in late Victorian London, one of the busiest places was the brothel in Cleveland Street, not far from Tottenham Court Road. The arrest, in July 1889, of several telegraph messenger boys, who seemed to have suspiciously large sums of money to spend, led the police not only to 19 Cleveland Street where the boys earned their money, but into a larger hornets' nest than they could ever have imagined. For among the many 'toffs' that frequented the brothel was Lord Arthur Somerset, third son of the eighth Duke of Beaufort, who was not only a distinguished soldier and an enthusiastic sportsman but an equerry to the Prince of Wales.

That Lord Arthur Somerset had not actually committed sodomy, but had only indulged in what was charmingly described as 'gentle dalliance with the boys',[23] was neither here nor there. He had broken the law. The Prince of Wales, on hearing the accusation, refused to credit it. 'I won't believe it any more than I would if they had accused the Archbishop of Canterbury,'[24] he exclaimed. If it were true, then Lord Arthur Somerset must be 'an unfortunate Lunatic'.[25]

But there was worse to come. No sooner had Lord Arthur Somerset fled the country to avoid prosecution than the press began to hint at what was already common talk in the London clubs: that Prince Eddy had also visited 19 Cleveland Street. Lord Arthur's solicitor had apparently warned that if his client were to come to trial, 'a very distinguished person will be involved (PAV)'[26] – the initials PAV standing, of course, for Prince Albert Victor. And Lord Arthur's sister, Lady Waterford, was very anxious to quash any notion that it might have been her brother who had taken Prince Eddy to the Cleveland Street house. 'Please correct any impression that Arthur and *the boy* ever went out together,' she instructed one of her brother's friends. 'Arthur knows nothing of his movements and was horrified to think he might be supposed to take the Father's money and lead the son into mischief of *any* kind. I am sure the boy is as straight as a line . . .'[27]

But Lord Arthur seems to have known rather more about Eddy than he was prepared to admit to his sister. Not long after he had fled to the Continent, Lord Arthur was accused, by Princess Alexandra's admirer, Oliver Montagu, of pretending that he had left the country only in order to avoid implicating others in the scandal. His silence on the real reason for his flight – that is, his own guilt – merely strengthened the rumours that he was keeping quiet for the sake of others, chief amongst them Prince Eddy.

But that, answered Lord Arthur, *was* one of the main reasons for his silence. 'I cannot see what good I could do Prince Eddy if I went into Court,' he explained. 'I might do him harm because if I was asked if I had ever heard anything against him – from whom? – has any person mentioned with whom he went there etc? – the questions would be very awkward. I have never mentioned the boy's name except to Probyn, Montagu and Knollys when they were acting for me and I thought they ought to know. Had they been wise, hearing what I knew and therefore what others knew, they ought to have hushed the matter up, instead of stirring it up as they did . . . Nothing will ever make me divulge anything I know even if I were arrested.'[28]

None of this, of course, is irrefutable proof that Prince Eddy visited 19 Cleveland Street. Those who agree with Lady Waterford that he was 'as straight as a line' point to the fact that his name, in the years ahead, was to be coupled with those of several women and that he would eventually become engaged to be married. But being 'straight as a line' does not preclude a man from having sex with the odd telegraph boy, any more than getting married proves him to be incontestably heterosexual.

Prince Eddy may well have been one of those over-sexed, easy-going and pliable young men who are ready to try anything once – or, if they enjoy it, twice or three times – without letting it become a way of life. Or he might, as has been suggested, have been taken to Cleveland Street on the understanding that he was to see some of those *poses plastiques* which were 'the Victorian equivalent of striptease'.[29] The owner of the establishment certainly advertised *poses plastiques;* these might well have been performed by girls or by boys dressed as girls. Eddy is said to have been accompanied by Lord Euston who later professed himself incensed at being offered naked boys instead of stripping girls.

'I have never even mentioned Euston's name,' wrote Lord Arthur, 'nor have I ever told *anyone* with whom Prince Eddy was supposed to have gone there. I did not think it fair as I could not prove it, and it must have been his ruin.'[30]

Whether any of this gossip reached the ears of the Prince and Princess of Wales is unknown. But there is no doubt that it was at that time that the parents decided that some sort of action was necessary to halt their son's all-too-possible drift into depravity. The only possible solution for Prince Eddy's many problems was, they agreed, the conventional one: marriage. So between the years 1889 and 1891 the names of several candidates for the post of a future Queen of England were bandied about (with Eddy falling in love with the only really unsuitable one, Princess Hélène of Orleans, the daughter of the Roman Catholic Pretender to the French throne) but in the end it was decided that he must marry Princess May of Teck. Although Princess

May's pedigree was not, by royal standards, impeccable (like the Battenbergs, there was a morganatic marriage in the background) she was, as the approving Queen Victoria put it, '*very* sensible and well-informed, a *solid girl* which we want . . .'[31]

Prince Eddy, who could usually be relied upon to do as he was told, not only agreed to the match but obliged everyone by falling in love with Princess May. The couple became engaged, at one of those inevitable house parties, on 3 December 1891. Both the Prince and Princess of Wales were delighted; 'this time I do hope that dear Eddy has found the *right bride,*'[32] wrote a relieved Alexandra to the Queen.

This mood of general gratification did not last long. Just over a month later, when Princess May and her parents were at Sandringham to celebrate Prince Eddy's twenty-eighth birthday, he fell ill. It was influenza. This quickly developed into pneumonia and for six days, in his tiny bedroom, the Prince lay dangerously ill. By the dawn of 14 January 1892, it was realised that he was dying. Soon after half-past nine that morning, surrounded by the shocked and exhausted members of his family, he died.

The Prince and Princess of Wales were desolate. The faithful Oliver Montagu, on hurrying to Sandringham, found them shattered by their loss. 'The Prince broke down terribly at our first meeting; as did also the poor Princess, but they all got calmer after and took me to see the boy three different times before I left again,'[33] reported Montagu.

For a while, their shared sorrow brought husband and wife very close together. On a booklet containing the sermon preached at Sandringham Church on the Sunday after Prince Eddy's funeral, the Prince of Wales wrote an inscription. 'To my dearest Wife, in rememberance of our beloved Eddy, who was taken from us. "He is not dead but sleepeth." From her devoted but heart-broken husband, Bertie.'[34]

Given her opinion of Daisy Brooke, Princess Alexandra would no doubt have been astonished to hear the assertion, made in 1891, 'that since the Prince had taken up with Lady Brooke, he had led a much better life . . . and that her influence had been distinctly and visibly for the better, and had terminated all the late hours and generally fast living that had prevailed before.'[35]

These were not the views of Daisy Brooke herself, but of two people in the Prince's circle. One was his private secretary, Sir Francis Knollys; the other was Lady Henry Somerset, sister-in-law of the now disgraced Lord Arthur Somerset and President of the British Women's Temperance Association. Their views had been given to W.T. Stead, the editor of *Review of Reviews,* in the course of his research for a character sketch of the Prince of Wales.

There was a great deal of truth in what Stead had been told. Daisy Brooke might have been all that Princess Alexandra thought she was – showy, flighty, amoral – but she disapproved strongly of heavy gambling and excessive drinking. In this, she was undoubtedly a good influence on the Prince of Wales. And, after Daisy's meeting with W.T. Stead in the spring of 1892 – the year after he had published his piece on the Prince – she became fired with an ambition to become an even better influence on her royal lover.

William Thomas Stead was one of the great crusading journalists of the late Victorian age. Bushily bearded and burning-eyed, this son of a Congregational minister brought to his journalism a powerful blend of moral indignation and sensationalism. Tirelessly, he flung himself into cause after cause; devoting to each, in turn, all his energy, enthusiasm and idealism. He originated what was to be known as 'the new journalism' of the late nineteenth century: the journalism of frankness, conviction and vision.

One of his most celebrated journalistic exposés was the series of astonishing articles entitled 'The Maiden Tribute to Modern Babylon' which he wrote for the *Pall Mall Gazette* in 1885. The number of male brothels in Victorian London was as nothing compared with the number of female brothels; and of all forms of prostitution, none was more reprehensible than child prostitution. Girls as young as eight or nine were readily available and, with virgins (or what were passed off as virgins) being especially highly prized, these young girls were in great demand. The widely-held belief that the taking of a girl's virginity could cure venereal disease made them even more sought after. One of the clients of the notorious Mrs Jeffries, who ran a child brothel, was said to have been another of Lillie Langtry's admirers, the lecherous old King Leopold II of the Belgians.

Determined to expose the evils of child prostitution, Stead bought a thirteen-year-old girl. His accounts of this transaction, and of the sordid world in which such trade flourished, ran for weeks in the *Pall Mall Gazette*. Whereas today such investigative journalism would be applauded, in the late nineteenth century it was deplored. The Victorians were far more shocked by the writing of the articles than by the circumstances which caused them to be written. On the grounds that Stead had not secured the consent of the girl's father when buying her (and regardless of the fact that the incident had been stage-managed and that Stead had no intention of having sex with the girl) he was charged with criminal abduction and sent to jail for two months.

Stead's imprisonment did nothing to quench his crusading ardour. His campaigning, after he moved from the *Pall Mall Gazette* to the editorship of *Review of Reviews,* remained as fervent as ever. And when, at a dinner party in the spring of 1892, he met Lady Brooke, Stead immediately saw in her the means whereby he could further yet another of his causes: the moral and intellectual uplifting of the Prince of Wales.

In researching his article on the Prince the year before, Stead had clearly come to appreciate something of his subject's potential. If only the Prince had been given a chance, if only he had been entrusted with some of his father's responsibilities, claimed Stead, 'he might have developed somewhat more of his father's virtues.'[36] The tone of Stead's article had come as a pleasant surprise to the Prince. Knowing all about Stead's high-mindedness and outspokenness, Bertie had been afraid to read it.

'I am told that there is an awful article in here about me,' he had said to Daisy, handing her a copy of *Review of Reviews.* 'I dare not open it, I want you to do so, read it, and tell me what it says.'

She had been able to put his mind at rest. Daisy considered it 'a very good article, very just, and that it gave him good advice and was very fair.'[37] In fact, Stead had succumbed to a bout of that deference which afflicts even the most hard-bitten of journalists, then and now, when writing serious articles about princes of Wales.

On meeting Lady Brooke, Stead lost no time in interesting her in his scheme for 'improving' the Prince. And who more suitable to undertake this important task, he asked her, than herself? She must use what he tactfully called her 'friendship' with the Heir to influence him for the better. Daisy was only too ready to oblige. Already she had recognised in Stead a soul-mate and a mentor: someone who could both share and direct her as yet unformed yearnings to lead a more useful life. So his suggestion that she help lift her royal lover's eyes towards more worthwhile goals, that she interest him in philanthropic causes and moral issues, was very well received. Few women, and least of all Lady Brooke, would have turned down the opportunity of using her powers to mould a great public figure.

Just how anxious the Prince was to be moulded is another matter. To date, his interest in what were then described as 'social questions' had been, at best, fitful. Although always careful to cultivate leading

Radical figures such as Sir Charles Dilke and Joseph Chamberlain (partly, as has been suggested, 'from a perverse desire to know those of whom his mother disapproved'[38]), he would issue dire warnings against 'the lower classes getting the upper hand'.[39] But this, too, might have been in reaction to Queen Victoria's championship of the hard-working 'lower orders' against the frivolous 'higher classes'.

Some years before, in 1884, the Prince had agreed to sit on a Royal Commission concerned with housing the working classes. This had entailed a tour, incognito (a slouch hat and an off-the-peg ulster) through the slums of Holborn and St Pancras. What he saw appalled him. He had had no idea that people lived in such squalor and misery. His immediate reaction – to start handing out money to ragged beggarwomen – was prevented by his companions: that was hardly the wisest way to alleviate poverty.

In a subsequent speech to the House of Lords, the Prince spoke out strongly in favour of legislation to improve these 'perfectly disgraceful'[40] conditions, while admitting that his own London properties – the estates of the Duchy of Cornwall – were in just as disgraceful a condition. He would not be the last Prince of Wales to find himself embarrassed by the state of his own back yard. To this day, even as altruistic a landlord as the present Prince of Wales is occasionally attacked for some example of exploitation or neglect in his Duchy properties.

Again, in 1892, the Prince sat on another Royal Commission, this time concerned with the problems of destitution in old age. And although, on both commissions, his colleagues found him to be affable and sympathetic, his attendance was intermittent. His frequent absences were as often due to social engagements as they were to public duties.

For Daisy Brooke, though, he was always prepared to make the effort. In 1894 she decided to stand for election as a trustee of a local workhouse. If standing for public office were not innovation enough, Daisy also beat a resoundingly feminist drum in her election message. She spoke of 'the great principle, which is gradually gaining recognition, of the joint and mutual responsibility of man and woman, which is equally important in the administration of the affairs of the community as in the management of the home.'[41] In the 1890s, that was very progressive thinking.

Daisy was duly elected and among the first visitors she showed over the workhouse was the Prince of Wales. 'I did everything that was in my power to let him know the truth about such places as workhouses and prisons,' she afterwards wrote, 'and I told him all I knew of the lives of the poor he would one day govern.'[42]

How much *she* knew at that stage of her life is debatable. But Stead must have felt very gratified.

The Socialist Countess

IN DECEMBER 1893 Daisy's father-in-law, the Earl of Warwick, died, which meant that her husband became the fifth Earl of Warwick and that after being known for twelve years as Lady Brooke, Daisy became the Countess of Warwick.

With her new title came a new home: Warwick Castle. Towering cliff-like over the wooded banks of the River Avon as it flows through Warwickshire, Warwick Castle is one of the most picturesquely sited and architecturally impressive castles in the country. Dating back to the Normans, it is, after Windsor Castle and the Tower of London, the best known and oldest continuously inhabited castle in Britain. Even the new Earl of Warwick, who tended to wax lyrical only about hunting and fishing, claimed that to stand by the banks of the River Avon 'in the earliest light of a June morning, when the colour of the castle walls was luminous pearl grey, when a full choir was wakening in the woods and great fish were leaping from the water, was to have sense of a beauty that remained secure against all the assaults of time and change.'[1]

During the time of Daisy's father-in-law, the modest and frugal fourth Earl of Warwick, the castle had been a singularly cheerless place, but with the arrival of the energetic young Countess, fresh life – and a great deal of uncertain taste – was introduced into the ancient family seat. Among the many changes made by Daisy was the organising of a special suite for the Prince of Wales – a bedroom with a recessed and elaborately painted ceiling, a dressing room, a bathroom and a lavatory – situated a few yards from the door of her own 'Chinese' bedroom.

Nothing, perhaps, better reflected the new chatelaine's love of gaiety and display than the great costume ball which she gave, in February 1895, to celebrate the end of the year of mourning for the late

Earl and her own husband's entry into his inheritance. The Victorians dearly loved a fancy-dress ball; the more elaborate and expensive the costumes, the happier they were. Lady Warwick had stipulated that Louis XVI dress was to be worn, and with a colour scheme of white and gold (as it was mid-winter, arum lilies and lilies of the valley had to be brought from the South of France) she planned to create, for one night, the splendours of eighteenth-century Versailles.

Daisy appeared, of course, as Queen Marie Antoinette. Her dress was of turquoise velvet brocade embroidered with real gold thread in *fleurs-de-lis* and roses. Diamonds flashed on her shoulders, about her neck and in her powdered hair. On her head towered a confection of pink, white and turquoise ostrich plumes, fastened by sapphires set in yet more diamonds.

No fewer than four hundred guests, some accommodated in the castle and others arriving by special trains from nearby country seats, attended the great ball and banquet. With every well-known hairdresser in London already roped in for the dressing and powdering of the guests' hair, more hairdressers had to be brought over from Paris. Not even during the famous visit of Queen Elizabeth I, three centuries before, had Warwick Castle seen such a show of wealth, colour and beauty. 'The effect of the throng of splendidly gowned and costumed men   and   women   in   the   setting   of   the   noble   rooms of the Castle seemed *at the time* to make the gathering worth while,'[2] remembers Daisy.

At the time, yes; but within a couple of weeks Lady Warwick was seeing it very differently. For the famous *bal poudré* at Warwick Castle – and its immediate aftermath – marked, she tells us, a dramatic turning point in her life. It became, in a way, her light on the road to Damascus.

Extremely gratified by the various newspaper accounts of her ball, Daisy one morning came across an article, in a weekly journal, that was anything but complimentary. In a left-wing paper called the *Clarion* she read, in mounting indignation, a violent attack on herself. How, asked the writer, could the spending of thousands of pounds on a 'few hours silly masquerade'[3] possibly be justified when so many people were forced to live in grinding and degrading poverty?

Daisy could hardly believe her eyes. Her rage on reading the article was so violent, she wrote over thirty years later, that she could feel it still. For she considered the attack to be completely unjustified. Was she not known for her sympathy for anyone in distress? Had she not started a needlework school to help the unemployed; had she not become a trustee of the local workhouse? Had her ball not provided work for dozens of dressmakers, hairdressers, decorators, gardeners, cooks, maids and footmen?

Always impulsive, Lady Warwick got out of bed, dressed, and without a word to her guests, took the first train to London. By midday she was in Fleet Street, looking for the editorial offices of the *Clarion*. On finding them, on the top floor of a dingy old building, she burst into the editor's office unannounced. If Robert Blatchford – for that was the editor's name – was surprised by the sight of this beautiful and fashionably dressed woman standing opposite his desk, he did not show it.

'Are you the editor of the *Clarion?*' she demanded.

He merely nodded,

'I came about this,' she continued, thrusting the paper at him.

Still he said nothing.

'How could you be so unfair, so unjust? Our ball has given work to half the county, and to dozens of dressmakers in London besides.'

At last Blatchford spoke. 'Will you sit down,' he asked, 'while I explain to you how mistaken you are about the real effect of luxury?'[4]

And this is what, with great eloquence and persuasiveness, Blatchford proceeded to do. He told her, in no uncertain terms, what he thought of 'ladies bountiful'. He explained to her the differences between productive and unproductive labour. He made clear to her that the making of expensive costumes for the wealthy, the providing of rich delicacies for the overfed, and the erection of temporary pavilions for the already well-housed was so much wasted effort: it was like digging holes in the ground and then filling them up again. 'The great ball and all its preparations,' realised Daisy, 'had not added one iota to the national wealth.'[5]

Although Daisy could not take in everything that Blatchford was saying, she was profoundly shaken by his arguments. Quite forgetting about lunch, she sat listening to him all through the winter's afternoon. When, finally, she left to catch her train home, she felt dazed. 'During the journey home I thought and thought about all that I had been hearing and learning. I knew that my outlook on life could never be the same as before this incident . . . I was as one who had found a new, a real world.'[6]

Perhaps Daisy Warwick's conversion to socialism had not been quite as dramatic as she claimed when she came to write about this incident many years later. After all, she had already shown signs of a stirring social conscience and for some years now W.T. Stead had been channelling her yearnings towards a more productive existence. Nor did the falling of the scales from her eyes mean the sudden end of her extravagant social life, or of her love affair with the Prince of Wales. Lady Warwick's socialism was always to be of an unorthodox, highly individual brand. But her meeting with Blatchford did set her fashionably shod feet on a different course.

'It would be idle,' she says frankly, 'to try to follow the often circuitous path I trod, but it was Robert Blatchford's honest talk on that memorable day that gave me a vision of how it would be possible to change and modify the unjust conditions of our modern life.'[7]

And who could tell: might she not be able to take her royal lover by the hand and lead him along that same, enlightened path?

In the meantime, the Prince's previous mistress, Lillie Langtry, had acquired yet another rich protector.

Back permanently in Britain after her years in the United States, Lillie had taken a house in newly fashionable Pont Street, off Sloane Street. In pride of place among her many souvenirs, most of them brought from America – the white fur rugs, the embroideries from San Francisco's Chinatown, the huge stuffed grizzly bear – was a large photograph of the Princess of Wales. Lillie was always quick to point out that the picture, signed 'Alexandra', had been presented to her by the Princess herself.

It was in the course of a luncheon party in this Pont Street house in 1892 that Lillie began to take a serious interest in the man whom she calls 'an eccentric young bachelor, with vast estates in Scotland, a large breeding stud, a racing-stable, and more money than he knew what to do with.'[8]

What this eccentric young bachelor was doing with his superfluous money, before very long, was spending it on Lillie. Thirty-one to Lillie's thirty-nine, George Alexander Baird was the son of a Scottish ironmonger who, on coming of age, had inherited – as well as those 'vast estates in Scotland' – three million pounds. Racing was his passion; Baird lived for the turf. Under the *nom de course* of 'Mr Abington' or 'the Squire', this stooped, slender young man was one of the best amateur jockeys of the day. But in spite of his great wealth, Baird detested the racing gentry; he was far happier among the 'race-course riff-raff'.[9] Never moving without a gang of thugs – ex-boxers, petty crooks, drunks – he was forever in the police station or the law courts. As dedicated a philanderer as he was a fighter, he was involved in countless marital scandals.

Baird seemed, on the face of it, an odd choice of lover for the socially ambitious Lillie Langtry. But she needed his money. Since returning to Britain she had had a run of bad luck: not even her still undiminished attractions were able to overcome a series of theatrical failures. Illness, bad weather, poor plays, over-extravagant productions – all these had swallowed up a great deal of her ready cash. At one time she had to apply to Alfred Rothschild for what she calls 'temporary help'.[10]

So when, one day at Epsom, Lillie was introduced to the tough, wiry and wealthy Baird, she was immediately interested. At luncheon in her Pont Street house the following day, he made his reciprocal interest only too apparent by offering to present her with a two-year-old colt named Milford. 'My life,' she would like us to believe, 'had been consecrated to the theatre for so many years that any extraneous interest seemed superfluous.'[11] But, in the end, she allowed herself to be 'persuaded' into accepting the gift.

This luncheon marked the start of the most turbulent love affair of Lillie Langtry's amorous career. When Baird was not showering her with gifts, he was beating her up. In the course of one violent quarrel, he is said to have given her a black eye, ripped her clothes to shreds and thrown her jewellery out into the street. To atone for this particular bout of brutality, he bought her a 220-foot steam yacht, 'White Ladye'. ('Black Eye', said the wags, would have been a more appropriate name.) Costing £100,000 and twice the tonnage of the Prince of Wales's yacht 'Britannia', 'White Ladye' was a superbly appointed vessel. She was perfectly happy, Lillie would maintain, to sit reading on deck with her little dog beside her; one would have imagined that sitting aboard one's own yacht, with its crew of thirty and its dining saloon that could seat forty, counted among life's simpler pleasures.

In 1893, the year after they met, Baird set off for New York with the intention of seeing a certain prize fight. When it was cancelled, he made for New Orleans; his route marked, it is said, 'with drinking bouts, bar brawls and street fights'.[12] One more drinking bout finished him. Baird caught pneumonia and died, two days later, in the St Charles Hotel, New Orleans. He was thirty-two.

Amongst Baird's many tangible legacies to Lillie were several race horses, including the first one that he had given her, Milford. Milford's string of successes encouraged her to take up racing more seriously. At one stage, she had over twenty horses in training.

Choosing fawn and blue as her racing colours and assuming the *nom de course* of 'Mr Jersey' (she did not want the gallery audience shouting to her on stage for racing tips, she explains) Lillie very quickly made a success of her new career. She bought what she calls 'a tiny cottage', Regal Lodge, at Kentford, near Newmarket: it was, in fact, a sizeable, sprawling, mock-Tudor house, surrounded by stables and paddocks and staffed by twenty people.

All this racing brought Lillie, once more, into the orbit of the Prince of Wales. Not long after she had bought Regal Lodge, the Prince was advised by Lord Marcus Beresford, his stud manager, to move his racing stables to Egerton House, which backed on to Newmarket racecourse. This meant that he and Lillie would often meet, not only on the racecourse and in neighbouring houses, but at Regal Lodge itself.

During these years the Prince was invariably accompanied by Lillie's successor, Lady Warwick. 'Life,' remembers Daisy in a honeyed description of the scene at Newmarket, 'was simple, pleasant and unadorned in Cambridgeshire in those days. One rose early and rode out in the brisk morning air, in order to see the horses at exercise. Then we came home to breakfast – a jolly, social meal – and later on changed, but always into country clothes, and, in due course, went to see the races.

'At the Summer Meeting there would be picnic lunches in marquees. Where the Grand Stand dominates the countryside today, there was then a pleasant wood, where, in July, one could enjoy an alfresco meal and a quiet ramble with a friend . . .'[13]

Much as she enjoyed the atmosphere of Newmarket – 'where one was surrounded by one's best friends, the best horses and the best jockeys'[14] – Daisy could not pretend to be very interested in the racing itself. This is where she differed from Lillie Langtry. The always practical Lillie was fast becoming a knowledgeable and enthusiastic owner, well able to discuss, not least with the Prince of Wales, all the finer points of the sport.

The move to Newmarket seems to have brought luck to both the Prince and Lillie: during the 1890s each enjoyed a string of successes and earned a great deal of money. Lillie's horse Lady Rosebery won, among others, the Lanark Cup and the Jockey Club Cup; and among the many wins for her most famous horse, Merman, were the Cesarewitch, the Ascot Gold Cup, the Jockey Club Cup and the Goodwood Cup. The Prince of Wales's most celebrated win was the Derby, with Persimmon, on 3 June 1896. Few things guarantee the

British monarchy more popularity than a royal win at the races, and the Prince of Wales went to bed that night, says one of his biographers, 'the happiest as well as the most popular man in the kingdom'.[15]

Unlike Daisy Warwick, and in spite of her outrageous private life and unconventional attitudes, Lillie Langtry always managed to keep on good terms with the Prince's family. Years after the liaison had ended, she was still being entertained by the Fifes (the Prince's eldest daughter, Louise, had married the Duke of Fife in 1889) and when, in 1893, the Prince's second and only surviving son, Prince George – by now Duke of York – married his late brother's fiancée, Princess May of Teck, Lillie kept in touch with them as well. They wrote occasional letters to each other, they exchanged photographs; in one note the Duke of York even hopes that 'the stuff I gave you for your hay fever will do it good'.[16]

It says a great deal for Lillie Langtry's unfeigned charm and social adroitness that she – who was often regarded as a scheming adventuress – was able to sustain this friendship, not only with the future King Edward VII, but with that far more straight-laced couple, the future King George V and Queen Mary.

Seldom was Lady Warwick's tendency to involve the Prince of Wales in her histrionic acts better illustrated than during her blaze of jingoism in the early months of 1896. This blaze was sparked off by the Jameson Raid. The incident, in which an apparently unsanctioned British force secretly invaded the Boer republic of the Transvaal with the intention of overthrowing its government, was a manifestation of imperialistic and capitalistic buccaneering at its least defensible. Yet it was stoutly defended by, among a multitude of others, Lady Warwick.

Viewed today, her attitude seems inexplicable. To the late-twentieth-century mind, imperialism and liberalism make strange bedfellows. And the fact that someone like Daisy Warwick could reconcile her – admittedly idiosyncratic – socialism with such fervent jingoism seems stranger still. But at the time it did not look so odd; in fact, it did not look odd at all.

During the last decades of the nineteenth century, imperialism was generally regarded as a noble, romantic, almost mystical creed. It had none of that stigma of racialism and exploitation of which it was subsequently to stand accused. Its aim – to bring the benefits of peace, religion, enlightenment, trade and education to the uncivilised areas of the world – was regarded as highly praiseworthy. Interpreted by the socialist John Ruskin at his famous Inaugural Lecture at Oxford in the 1870s, and embraced by radical liberals such as Daisy's mentor, W.T. Stead, British imperialism had all the appeal of a latter-day crusade.

Stead was particularly enamoured of that quintessentially imperialistic figure of the age, Cecil John Rhodes. To Stead, Rhodes's self-appointed mission of spreading 'Anglo-Saxon civilisation' not only throughout his own sphere of influence – Southern Africa (Rhodes was the Prime Minister of the Cape Colony) – but throughout the world, appeared wholly admirable. Regarded today, not entirely accurately, as the very personification of a grasping, power-hungry megalomaniac, Rhodes was, to the altruistic Stead, a hero. And he was no less of a hero to the Prince of Wales and Lady Warwick.

When, on 29 December 1895, Dr Leander Starr Jameson invaded the Transvaal with a detachment of men from Rhodes's South Africa Company, Lady Warwick was all approval. She took Jameson's reasons for invading the Boer republic – published in the form of a letter to *The Times* – at face value. She was quite ready to believe that he had answered an appeal from the largely British, largely gold-mining contingent living in the Transvaal, for protection against the iniquities of the Boer government. In the event, the raid failed and the invading force surrendered.

As far as Daisy was concerned, the capture of the British invading force by the Boers was bad enough, but when certain British newspapers condemned the raid, she was incensed. She was more incensed still when, on 4 January 1896, it became known that the German Emperor, Wilhelm II, had sent President Paul Kruger a telegram of congratulation for having repulsed the raiders.

She immediately sat down and wrote an impassioned letter to *The Times*. Knowing nothing about the raid – that it had been an extremely dishonest and foolhardy adventure – she defended it with all the vigour of her nature. Writing, she claimed extravagantly, on behalf of all Englishwomen, she castigated the press for its lack of patriotism, praised the raiders for their noble motives, and ended with a veiled attack on the German Emperor for sending his telegram.

The publication of her letter, with its criticism of the Kaiser, gave rise to the rumour that Lady Warwick had written directly to the German Emperor, complaining about his telegram. Daisy's mother, Lady Rosslyn, first heard about this from her brother-in-law, Count Münster, at that time German ambassador in Paris. 'I hear Daisy has written a most impertinent letter to the Emperor,' he complained.

'She ought to have dressed in black, and held her tongue and her pen.'[17]

Although Daisy claims that she was quite ready to laugh the whole thing off, the Prince of Wales was not. In fact, he was furious about the rumours. Not trusting Daisy to write a strong enough reply to Münster, the Prince drafted one himself.

'Dear Count M,' wrote Daisy, following his draft, 'Mamma has shown me your letter in which you state you hear *I* had written an impertinent letter to the German Emperor. I cannot get over my astonishment at so unwarrantable a statement, which is likely to do me harm, and from one who has known me since a child it is doubly hard to bear.

'I have not the honour of His Majesty's acquaintance nor is it likely I should write to him, and I certainly should have thought you would have been the first to disbelieve so palpable a lie!

'This is, however, not the first time you have said unkind things about me to Mamma, as a few years ago you asked her at Homburg when I was going to get divorced!

'I feel your unkindness very deeply, and so much so, that should I be passing through Paris I shall be obliged to give the German Embassy a wide berth.'[18]

To this, Count Münster wrote a grudging apology. But he could not resist one more jibe. 'I must say,' he wrote to Lady Rosslyn, 'I found her letter about Jameson to *The Times* uncalled for. Ladies ought not to be jingoes.'[19]

But a jingo this particular lady continued to be. Since Rhodes's involvement in the Jameson Raid had forced him to resign the premiership of the Cape Colony, both Lady Warwick and Stead began working for his reinstatement. The early spring of 1896 found the Prince and Lady Warwick on the French Riviera and from here Daisy wrote to Stead offering to get the Prince to write letters for Stead to use on Rhodes's behalf.

The Prince did not need much prompting. Indeed, he showed his support for Rhodes more publicly than this. When, in 1897, the disgraced Rhodes came to London to face a Parliamentary Committee of Inquiry into the raid, the Prince not only attended some of the hearings but frequently entertained him, both at Marlborough House and Sandringham. To the Prince, Rhodes was 'a very remarkable' man. 'I hardly know any man who has impressed me more than he did,'[20] he once claimed.

As for Daisy, she revered the Empire builder. On first meeting him,

through Stead, Daisy found this big, untidy, shambling man somewhat unimpressive to look at. But to listen to him, she says, was quite
another matter. 'Cecil Rhodes was that strange, unmistakable thing, a
man of genius,' she wrote. 'His big ideas lifted him right out of the
common, well-worn paths.'[21]

Although Rhodes was, in the expression of the day, a 'woman
hater' ('Oh, I don't think that can be so,' protested Queen Victoria,
'because he was very civil to *me* when he came here'[22]) Daisy claims
that he had a 'genuine liking' for her. 'I reciprocated this friendship
with all my heart,'[23] she says.

In December 1896 Lady Warwick arranged what she fondly imagined
was to be a momentous meeting between the two most important
men in her life: the Prince of Wales and W.T. Stead.

Until then she had acted as the link between Stead and the Prince;
she, as Stead somewhat archly put it, was 'the priest of the parish' and
the Prince 'the parishioner'. 'Mr Stead and I,' says Daisy grandilo-
quently, 'were mainly concerned with benevolently co-opting, com-
mandeering and enlisting the sympathies of the Prince of Wales in the
various schemes we nursed for bettering the race, or the country, or of
allying him with some cause or movement that beckoned to our
idealism.'[24] In short, alone of King Edward VII's mistresses, Daisy
Warwick fancied herself as an *éminence grise*, a woman of influence, if
not power.

The three of them met for luncheon in the South Audley Street
house that Daisy had taken for the winter. Faced with the prospect of
meeting the Prince, even the self-assured and politically radical Stead
found himself suffering the usual apprehensions of those who are
about to be shown into the royal presence. What, he asked Lady
Warwick, should he talk about? South African affairs? His proposed
character sketch of Queen Victoria? Or might it not be better for him
to talk about the one subject in which he was quite certain the Prince
was interested: Lady Warwick herself? Should he sing her praises as
soon as she left the room?

'She laughed very much at this,' reports Stead, 'and said she had no
doubt it would please him as much as anything I could do.'[25]

But as soon as the Prince was ushered in, Stead's journalist's eye,
and ear, got the better of his nerves. He found himself able to come to a
dispassionate assessment of his fellow guest. As Lady Warwick sank
into her 'extremely pretty curtsey, prettier than any I had seen

before,'[26] Stead studied the Prince. He was smaller than Stead expected, both in height and in girth, and much simpler in his manner. This, again, is the usual reaction on meeting a royal figure; their status, their inaccessibility, the aura of pomp and deference with which they are always surrounded, lead one to expect something more majestic, in both looks and manner. Stead got the impression that the Prince had a slight squint and that one of his front teeth was crooked.

The conversation at luncheon was wide-ranging – old age pensions, Cecil Rhodes, society small talk – with the astute Stead noticing that the Prince was like 'the type of Society hostess who contrives to give the impression to every one that she is much interested in what he is saying, and five minutes afterwards forgets all about it'.[27] Diplomats and politicians noticed something rather similar about the Prince: that his opinions often reflected those of the last person to whom he had been speaking, and could very easily be changed.

Luncheon over, Lady Warwick left the men to their coffee, cigars and still more talk. When they rejoined her in the drawing room, she was lying down. A fall on the hunting field some weeks before had left her feeling unsteady. But she had the satisfaction of believing that the meeting between the two men had been a great success. The Prince, in his letter to her the following day, thanked her for giving him the opportunity of meeting a 'remarkable man who made a far more favourable impression on me than I ever believed possible'.[28] One day he would like to hear from her the impression that he had made on Stead.

In repeating all this to Stead, Daisy expressed her delight in the fact that the two men had 'mutually pleased' each other; she intended that 'mutual feeling' to grow into 'a mutual friendship some day'.[29]

But it would have needed more than Daisy Warwick's remarkable beauty and formidable powers of persuasion to turn this ill-assorted couple into friends. The Prince's political interests were in foreign – and particularly European – affairs; despite his natural kindheartedness, he could not really work up any enthusiasm for the sort of domestic politics or social conditions that so obsessed Stead. And as, in the years ahead, Daisy's hold over the Prince weakened, so in turn did Stead see the ebbing of his hopes of influencing 'the parishioner'.

As Lillie Langtry became steadily wealthier and more self-sufficient, her husband, Edward Langtry, sank ever deeper into poverty and obscurity. They had not set eyes on each other for years. Lillie's only contact with him was through her solicitor, the famous George Lewis. Each quarter Lewis sent Langtry Lillie's £25 cheque, most of which he spent on drink; and every so often Lewis passed on her request for a divorce, which he resolutely refused to consider. The days when Edward Langtry had stood behind his radiant wife in the grandest drawing rooms in the land – including Buckingham Palace and Marlborough House – had long since gone. Shambling, unkempt and invariably drunk, he shifted from one lodging house to another, leading an utterly purposeless existence.

Yet he was still abjectly in love with the woman who had treated him so shamefully. For a while he lived in Holyhead through which his celebrated wife would often pass on her way to and from some theatrical engagement in Dublin. He always knew exactly when she was due and for hours beforehand would be at the station, pacing up and down the platform in mounting excitement. But half an hour before she was due to appear, in a flurry of feather boas, veiled hats and fur muffs, he would lose his nerve.

'Boy,' he would say, summoning a young porter. 'I can't stick it any longer. Watch her for me. Look closely at her; tell me how she looks; does she look well? Is she as beautiful? What she wears. Be careful about her dress, and tell me all about it.' Then he would dart out of the station.

'After the train or boat had gone,' reported a Detective-Inspector Perkins who was stationed at Holyhead and who knew Langtry well, 'he would come back and question the porter most minutely, and sob as if his heart would break as he learned the details, and walk off the station sobbing, and apparently dazed. I have seen tears come into the eyes of the porters at this exhibition of his emotion.'[30]

Since 1893 Edward Langtry had been lodging in the home of Cornelius Collins, a valet, in Southampton. Sometime in 1897 Langtry heard, presumably from George Lewis, that Lillie had finally been granted a divorce. On 13 May that year a judge in Lakeport, California (where Lillie, an American citizen, owned property) decreed that Mr Langtry, having failed to answer a summons, was in default and that the marriage was dissolved. It was generally believed, though, that the divorce applied only in the state in which it had been granted. 'It certainly would not apply in England,' claimed one report. 'So strong is the opinion on this point that it is held that if Mrs Langtry had married again in this country, she would have been liable to have been prosecuted for bigamy'.[31]

The news of the divorce upset Langtry considerably. According to a friend, he became 'extremely unhappy'.[32] On 29 September that year, the fifty-year-old Langtry suddenly left Southampton for London, telling Collins, his landlord, that he was going to join a Mr Arthur Greenwood for a journey first to·Belfast and then to Glasgow.

From this point on, the story becomes extremely curious. In London Langtry joined Greenwood and the two of them travelled to Liverpool from where they caught the ferry to Belfast. In the course of the crossing between Liverpool and Belfast, a steward came across Langtry sprawled out on the deck, badly cut and bruised. His nose had been fractured. How exactly he sustained the injuries, no one knew, least of all Langtry. It was thought that he had stumbled on entering the smoking room and had fallen, hitting his head on a step. The steward claimed, though, that Langtry was not drunk.

Arriving in Belfast, Greenwood took the injured Langtry to the Royal Hospital, summoned Collins by telegraph and then disappeared. Collins, on reaching Belfast from Southampton, found that Langtry had already discharged himself from hospital and was on his way back to London. He never saw him alive again.

At three o'clock on the morning of 3 October 1897 Edward Langtry shuffled into the Station Hotel at Crewe, some thirty miles south of Liverpool. His face was bandaged, according to the night porter, 'from his moustache to his eyes' and he was 'very unsteady on his feet'. On asking for accommodation he was shown into an empty bedroom, but he soon came down again, to complain that there were two other people in the room. When he was refused a drink on the grounds that it was too late at night, he asked, 'Oh, is it night?'

Having had enough of him, the night porter suggested that he continue on his journey to London and led him back to the station. But by eight the following morning Langtry was back at the hotel. Again he asked for a drink (two bottles of bitter was what he wanted) and again it was refused.

At ten that morning Detective-Inspector Perkins, who was now stationed in Crewe, found him wandering along the station platform. He looked so disfigured and acted so strangely that Perkins barely recognised him.

'Langtry, how did this happen?' asked Perkins.

Langtry then gave him a very strange answer. 'They thought they knocked me out this time, but they didn't.'[33]

Perhaps he was too drunk, or too dazed, to know what he was saying. But in the days ahead the rumour spread that someone had tried to get rid of Edward Langtry. How much truth there was in the rumour is uncertain. But there can be no doubt that Edward Langtry's death would have suited Lillie very well. Not long before, she had had to abandon her idea of marrying Prince Louis Esterhazy, an old fop who was the military attaché to the Austrian embassy in London, for two reasons: one was that the Austrian Emperor, Franz Josef I, would almost certainly have refused to grant the necessary permission for the marriage; the other was that there were serious doubts about the validity of Lillie's Californian divorce. Had she been a widow, then at least one, or perhaps even two, of the objections to the match would have disappeared. And one knows how dearly Lillie would have loved to have become a princess.

Moreover, by this time – October 1897 – Lillie had already met the man whom she *would* soon marry; or might already have married had her divorce been valid. Langtry's death would have cleared up any uncertainties about her eligibility.

On the other hand, Edward Langtry spoke a great deal of nonsense during the two days that he was wandering about Crewe station. To some witnesses it seemed as though he were drunk; to others that he was concussed. Apparently he did not know what he was doing there, nor where he was meant to be going. To the policeman who, at one stage, took him to the police station, Langtry spoke of the subject uppermost in his mind: that his wife, to whom he had been married for twenty-five years (it was actually twenty-three) had recently divorced him, and that she had had to go 'to the colonies'[34] to get the divorce.

Eventually Langtry was committed by the magistrate to the Upton Asylum, near Chester. There, ten days later, on Friday 15 October 1897, he died. A post mortem examination revealed that he had died of an 'effusion of blood on the brain'[35] brought on by his fall on board ship, two weeks before.

That Lillie Langtry had anything to do with her husband's death is unlikely; there is much more substance in the accusation that she allowed him to die in penury. Edward Langtry died with eleven and a half pence to his name. Pointing up, even more vividly, the contrast between the wealthy Mrs Langtry and her impoverished husband was the fact that, just a couple of days before his death, she had won a handsome sum on the Cesarewitch with her horse Merman. And it was she who had married Langtry for *his* money.

To quell the rising tide of criticism, Lillie moved swiftly to get George Lewis to issue a statement on the subject. 'Mrs Langtry states with reference to the report that Mr Langtry was found with only a few pence in his pocket, that Mrs Langtry had since her separation from her husband many years ago, regularly made him an adequate allowance. As soon as she heard of his condition she at once forwarded to the authorities at Chester sufficient money for his immediate wants. The allowance paid by Mrs Langtry was in addition to the income which Mr Langtry derived from his Irish property.'[36]

Nowhere does Lillie mention a divorce; merely a separation. There was no longer any need to bring that up.

When Edward Langtry was buried in the Chester cemetery, a great crowd massed about the cemetery gates in the hope of catching a glimpse of the famous Mrs Langtry. But she did not appear. She contented herself with sending a wreath of lilies of the valley tied not, as is often alleged, with a ribbon in her racing colours of fawn and blue, but with a conventional purple ribbon. On the attached card was written, 'In Remembrance – Lillie Langtry.' She could hardly have said less; or more.

'In an evil hour,' observed the *Daily News* on the day of Edward Langtry's funeral, 'he was caught in the whirlwind of London fashion, and being anything but a swimmer, and having no artificial supports in fortune, he was quickly on his way to ruin. Those who remember him years ago, a gentlemanlike nobody, with a genial confiding manner that seemed to mark him one of the crew of The Good Intent, can but lament his miserable end.'[37]

Twenty years earlier Edward Langtry had watched his wife drop her first curtsey to the Prince of Wales at Sir Allen Young's supper party. How directly had that graceful obeisance led to his lonely and penurious death in the Chester Lunatic Asylum?

By now – the year 1897 – the Prince of Wales's great love for Lady Warwick was waning. As restless, fickle and immature as ever, the fifty-five-year-old Bertie seemed incapable of sustaining a permanent relationship. His behaviour towards Daisy remained warm and protective, but she no longer obsessed him to the extent that she had once done. For some time now their relationship had been platonic. The Prince appears to have been finding his sexual satisfaction elsewhere.

Daisy would not have minded this unduly. She had never been in love with him. In a frank moment she even admitted to a friend that she had found the Prince 'boresome as he sat on a sofa holding my hand and goggling at me'.[38] What she had enjoyed was her position as royal favourite. Daisy had always relished the idea of being a woman, not only of importance, but of influence.

In any case, not for several years had Lady Warwick been able to give the Prince her undivided attention. Ever since her friendship with Stead and her 'conversion' by Blatchford, she had been flinging herself, with customary ardour, into various worthy causes. She was then going through what she afterwards called her 'intermediate' or transitional stage: 'my middle-class period . . . that was my Board of Guardians, philanthropic, educational, lady-gardening period. I was a reformer, if you like, but not yet an avowed Socialist.'[39] She was still part-lady bountiful, part-radical feminist.

While leading as lavish a social life as ever (in spite of all Blatchford's strictures, she went to the Duchess of Devonshire's famous fancy dress ball in 1897 dressed, once again, as Marie Antoinette), she served on a bewildering number of committees and inaugurated countless progressive schemes. She started, among other things, a home for crippled children, a co-educational technical school, and the 'Lady Warwick Agricultural Scheme for Women' – a quaint project in which pairs of unmarried women would set up home together and devote themselves to working the land.

Try as he might, the Prince of Wales could not interest himself in these high-minded activities. Although, in her memoirs, Daisy is very anxious to create the impression that she had won the Prince's 'whole-hearted sympathy' for her various causes (he never stayed at a great country house, she assures us, without 'writing his name in the visitors' book'[40] of the local workhouse) and that he was the driving force behind such things as the Prince of Wales's Hospital Fund, there is no doubt that he found her enthusiasms tiresome. On one occasion he was obliged to sit in embarrassed silence in a cramped cottage parlour while one of her 'discoveries' – the aged founder of the Agricultural Labourers' Union – treated him, not to a customary show of deference, but to a diatribe on the injustices of the social system and the iniquities of the upper classes.

But what probably accelerated the end of their liaison was Lady Warwick's discovery that, at the age of thirty-five and well over twelve years since the birth of her last child, she was again pregnant. In March 1898, Daisy gave birth to a son, to whom she gave her maiden name of Maynard. On this particularly beautiful child she was to heap the sort of affection notably lacking in her dealings with her other two children, the fifteen-year-old Guy and the thirteen-year-old Marjorie.

Two months before that, however, she brought her nine-year affair with the Prince of Wales to a tidy and eminently satisfactory close. Appreciating that not even Queen Victoria could live much longer, Daisy was anxious to ensure that she would retain at least the friendship of the future King and, even more important, that she would once again become socially acceptable to the future Queen. Budding feminist, socialist and humanitarian Daisy might be, but not to be a member of society, with a capital S, was unthinkable.

So she sat down to write two very skilful letters: one to the Prince, the other to the Princess. In her formally phrased letter to the Prince – a letter clearly intended to be shown to Alexandra – Daisy stressed the fact that their relationship was now platonic, expressed the hope that the Princess would forgive her for past misunderstandings, and made much of her anxieties about losing the Prince's friendship. In her letter to Alexandra – that 'noble and gracious woman' – Daisy hoped that her 'enemies' had not poisoned Her Royal Highness's ears with spiteful gossip.

Her letters achieved their goals admirably; or so she thought. Bertie, having passed her 'beautiful letter' on to his wife, lost no time in putting Daisy's mind at rest. The Princess, he assured her, had been moved to tears; she was quite sure that 'out of evil good would come'; any enemies of Lady Warwick's were no friends of hers; she had quite forgiven the past; and, most important of all, she was ready to 'receive' Lady Warwick once more. The Prince felt sure that if the two women were to work together on some charitable venture, they would soon become good friends.

'The end of your beautiful letter touched me more than anything,' he continued, 'but how can you, my loved one, imagine that I should withdraw my friendship from you? On the contrary I mean to befriend you more than ever, and you cannot prevent my giving you the same love as the friendship I have always felt for you.

'Certainly the Princess has been an angel of goodness throughout all this, but then she is a Lady, and never could do anything that was mean or small.

'Though our interests, as you have often said, lie apart, still we have that sentimental feeling of affinity which cannot be eradicated by time . . .'[41]

Princess Alexandra's answer, if less fulsome, was no less reassuring. After all, she could afford to be magnanimous now. But she was not quite as magnanimous as her husband imagined. Alexandra was never the 'angel of goodness' of popular legend. To forgive – or to appear to forgive – her husband's ex-mistress was one thing; to work hand-in-hand with her on some project, no matter how charitable, was quite another. 'In case you should hear from Lady Warwick asking you to become President of a Charity of hers, refuse it,' wrote Prince George, Duke of York, to his wife. 'Motherdear has done so and wishes you to do the same.'[42]

Yet, according to Lady Warwick, it was from Princess Alexandra that she received 'a small crucifix wrapt in a piece of paper on which was written these words: "From one who has suffered much and forgives all." '[43]

Part Three

'BELOVED ALICE'

The Hon. Mrs George Keppel

FOR THE British monarchy, the summer of 1897 was particularly brilliant. On 20 June that year Queen Victoria celebrated the sixtieth anniversary of her accession, her Diamond Jubilee. Although, in private, the Prince of Wales was sometimes heard to grumble about the inordinate length of time he was being kept waiting for the throne, he actually took an immense pride in the span, success and splendour of his mother's reign. With his taste for pageantry, the Prince was determined that the Jubilee celebrations should be as memorable as possible.

He heartily agreed with the Colonial Secretary, Joseph Chamberlain, that the occasion should be in the nature of a festival of empire. Whereas Queen Victoria's Golden Jubilee, ten years before, had been marked by a mustering of European royalty, her Diamond Jubilee was designed to be an imperial fanfare, a manifestation of Britain's imperial power. Colonial prime ministers, rather than Continental crowned heads, would be the principal guests. And although Bertie did not share his mother's aversion to what she called 'the Royal Mob' (the thought of all those kings and emperors strutting about Buckingham Palace was more than the seventy-eight-year-old Queen could bear) he was delighted to know that his nephew, the braggardly Kaiser Wilhelm II, would not be present.

'Sir Arthur Bigge may tell the Prince of Wales,' wrote Queen Victoria to her private secretary early that year, 'that there is *not* the slightest fear of the Queen's giving way about the Emperor William's coming here in June. It would *never* do . . .'[1]

There was, though, no shortage of lesser royals. Princes and princesses from every court in Europe came swarming into London. 'Buckingham Palace is like a beehive,' reported Bertie's sister Vicky, the Empress Frederick, 'the place is so crammed we do not see very much of each other.'² And as the Queen resolutely refused to be inconvenienced for the sake of these foreign royals, it fell to the Prince of Wales to see that they were suitably entertained. He was no less responsible for the visiting prime ministers. The Prince even arranged for Daisy Warwick – with whom he had not, at that stage, yet ended his affair – to invite the colonial prime ministers to Warwick Castle. Seeing it as an opportunity to do something for the great imperial ideal, Daisy was only too delighted to oblige. The occasion was not a success. Of the eleven premiers then in Britain, only three turned up. Perhaps these less worldly colonials did not approve of the idea of being entertained by the Prince of Wales's mistress.

Into the preparations for the various Jubilee events the Prince flung himself with gusto. His Royal Highness, noted one official, 'loved detail, no matter how small'³ and there was no aspect of the celebrations, be it orders of precedence or stands for school-children, with which he did not concern himself. His energy, his enthusiasm, his attention to minutiae astonished those who had hitherto regarded him purely as a sybarite.

Nothing could more impressively have illustrated both Queen Victoria's position as head of a great imperial family and Britain's policy of 'splendid isolation' than the Queen's Jubilee procession through the streets of London on 22 June 1897. With the Princess of Wales sitting in the carriage opposite her and the Prince, in a field-marshal's uniform, riding his horse alongside, Queen Victoria processed through the streets in the midst of a swaggering parade of troops drawn from every quarter of her great empire. The watching crowds had never seen such a variety of races and peoples. While Alexandra leaned forward, every now and then, to press the Queen's hand, Bertie would bend down to draw her attention to this or that point of interest along the way. It was, in fact, at his suggestion that the Queen drove through the poorer districts south of the Thames as well as along the great processional ways.

'No one ever, I believe, has met with such an ovation as was given to me, passing through those six miles of streets . . .' wrote the gratified Queen. 'The crowds were quite indescribable, and their enthusiasm truly marvellous and deeply touching. The cheering was quite deafening, and every face seemed to be filled with real joy.'⁴

Climax of this triumphant procession was the short open-air service of thanksgiving conducted on the steps of St Paul's Cathedral, with the lame old Queen remaining firmly in her carriage. 'The scene in front of St Paul's was most impressive,' reported the Empress

Frederick, 'and when the bells pealed out from the dark old Cathedral, and the cheers rang out again, and the sun shone on all the glitter of the escort and carriages and the countless spectators, it was as fine a sight as you could wish to see.'5

And who had better reason to bask in any reflected glory than the heir to all this magnificence – the Prince of Wales?

Unlike Queen Victoria, who kept her public appearances to a minimum, the Prince revelled in all the activities of Jubilee year. He attended the great naval review where 173 warships, the largest battle fleet that had ever been assembled in peacetime, loomed like great grey castles on the sparkling waters of the Solent. Wearing the uniform of Grand Master of the Knights Hospitaller of Malta, he danced at the Duchess of Devonshire's costume ball. To his immense gratification, his horse Persimmon, which had won the Derby the year before, won the Ascot Gold Cup that summer. His racing earnings amounted to over £15,000 in 1897 and he was placed second on the list of winning owners.

Between the luncheons, dinners, garden parties, soirées and balls, the Prince was able to wedge the occasional less ephemeral activity, such as the summoning of a committee to establish (with Lady Warwick's encouragement) the 'Prince of Wales's Hospital Fund'. Princess Alexandra, too, felt compelled to mark the Jubilee by some philanthropic gesture; or rather, by some impulsive act of generosity. She suggested to the Lord Mayor of London that a fund be opened to provide a meal 'for the poorest of the poor in the slums of London'.6 To launch this typical scheme of Victorian charity, the Princess enclosed a sizeable donation. For some reason or other, the appeal did not catch on. Only by the intervention of the rich tea-merchant, Thomas Lipton (who was never averse to currying a little royal favour) was the Princess's project saved from abandonment: Lipton wrote out a hefty cheque to bring the sum up to the required amount.

For the Prince and Princess of Wales Jubilee year ended, as always, at Sandringham. Christmas found them standing side by side in front of the glittering tree in the ballroom, handing out gifts to the members of their household. 'It was all so beautifully done,' remembers one of their secretaries, 'and the pleasure of giving seemed never to leave [them], as it often does with rich people.'7 On New Year's Eve the royal couple observed the usual ritual of 'first footing'. The house was completely emptied of guests and servants so as to allow the Prince and Princess, standing in the cold outside, to be the first to open the door after the stroke of midnight. This was guaranteed to bring them good luck in the coming year.

It was almost possible to believe, as the genial, portly, cigar-puffing Prince and his smiling, soignée, apparently ageless Princess entered their favourite home together, that they were the best-suited, most affectionate couple in the world. But the new year, which marked the end of the Prince's affair with Daisy Warwick, did not usher in a new period of marital harmony between the Prince and Princess of Wales. On the contrary, it brought the Prince not only a new mistress, but the greatest love of his life: Alice Keppel.

There is some doubt as to when exactly in 1898 the Prince of Wales first met the Hon. Mrs George Keppel. According to the not always reliable memory of the Baroness de Stoeckl, it was she who presented Alice Keppel to the Prince during his customary spring holiday on the French Riviera. Knowing something of the Prince's taste in women and thinking that he might be 'amused' by the young Mrs Keppel, the Baroness arranged a small luncheon party. 'He saw her then for the first time,' she maintains stoutly, 'and from that day started their friendship.'[8]

Another version is supplied by the writer, Anita Leslie. Mrs Keppel, she tells us, was a close friend of her grandfather, Sir John Leslie, and it was by him that Anita Leslie was told of the Prince's first meeting with 'the delectable Alice'. While inspecting the Norfolk Yeomanry, of which the Prince was colonel-in-chief and in which Mrs Keppel's husband served as an officer, His Royal Highness first noticed Alice. He immediately asked Lord Leicester to present her. A few days later, at the Sandown races, the Prince again spotted Mrs Keppel, this time on the arm of John Leslie. On being summoned by the Prince, Leslie – about to present Mrs Keppel to His Royal Highness – was assured that they had already met.

'Then, in the most gracious way possible,' reports Anita Leslie, 'H.R.H. gave Leslie to understand that his presence was no longer required. Whimsically, my grandfather used to describe that certain look – blending shrewd appraisement and admiration – that crossed the Prince's face as his eyes travelled over Mrs George Keppel's lovely face and fashionably curved figure.'[9]

Sir Philip Magnus, in his life of King Edward VII, claims that the Keppels first entertained the Prince to dinner (by which time, presumably, they had been formally presented) on 27 February 1898.

But wherever or whenever the two of them met, there can be no doubt at all about the momentous effect of that meeting. Between the Prince and Mrs Keppel an 'understanding', as Magnus so tactfully describes it, 'arose almost overnight'.[10] That understanding, or to put it more bluntly, that strong physical attraction, very quickly developed into a full-blown love affair. Within a matter of weeks, Alice Keppel had been established as the Prince of Wales's new official mistress.

That the fifty-six-year-old Prince had been so strongly attracted to the twenty-nine-year-old Mrs George Keppel is not surprising. Alice Keppel was exceptional, both in looks and in personality. She was one of those women who, if not exactly beautiful, give an illusion of beauty. Her luxuriant chestnut hair was piled high onto her head, her skin was flawless and glowed with good health. She had large, lustrous, blue-green eyes. When, with studied slowness (for she was no fool), she lifted the veil of one of her ostrich-feather laden hats, the watching gentleman seemed, according to one witness, 'to catch his breath a little as he beheld her beautiful face'.[11] She was very proud of possessing those prized Victorian attributes – small hands and feet.

With her short but generously proportioned figure, Alice Keppel exuded an unmistakable sensuousness; there was a warm, almost Mediterranean quality about her appearance. This same exotic aura characterised her manner. She was vivacious, extrovert, expansive. Her voice was low and seductive. In old age one admirer remembered her as having a 'deep throaty voice like Garbo'.[12] Even in those less emancipated days she smoked, using a long cigarette holder; it emphasised her air of sophistication. She dressed with great panache and, after becoming the Prince of Wales's mistress, with greater panache still.

To attribute a certain Mediterranean quality to Alice Keppel's appearance and personality is not being too fanciful, for she had had a Greek grandmother. Her maternal grandfather, when British Governor of the Ionian Islands, had married a beautiful Greek girl; their daughter, in turn, had married Admiral Sir William Edmonstone, a descendant of a long line of Scottish baronets. Edmonstone had taken his half-Greek bride back to Scotland, to live in Duntreath Castle in Stirlingshire, not far from Glasgow. 'From Ithica to Kelvinside! What an odyssey!' exclaimed one of Lady Edmonstone's granddaughters in later life. 'How she must have loathed and resented the indefatigable rain, the sulphrous fogs, the grim bewhiskered elders!'[13]

But Lady Edmonstone apparently adapted to the change and bore her husband nine children, of whom the youngest, born in 1869, was Alice. Being the youngest did not, as far as Alice Frederica Edmonstone was concerned, mean being the least significant. According to one observer, her 'superabundant vitality'[14] ensured that she was never overshadowed by some of her more forceful sisters. In fact, in common with the Prince of Wales's other loves, Lillie Langtry and Daisy Warwick, Alice was something of a tomboy in girlhood, with this same tomboyishness developing into the high spirits and air of independence which the Prince always found so alluring.

Duntreath Castle, where Alice grew up, had been the home of the Edmonstone family since the fifteenth century. Set amid rugged moorland and against two austere, bald hills, it was an uncompromising, four-square structure, built around a courtyard with a pepper-pot tower at each corner. But this somewhat forbidding exterior belied the elegance and comfort within. Duntreath had been almost completely renovated fifteen years before Alice's birth and was, for its time, an unexpectedly civilised home.

'I have completely misled you,' writes one member of the family, 'if you imagine that Duntreath was a dour Scottish fastness, reeking of Balmorality; it was nothing of the kind. It was romantic, of a standard of luxury without equal in those days; gay with a touch of Frenchness in its *salons en enfilade,* and premeditated perspectives. One fled from terror to enchantment. The atmosphere of the place was complex: half-medieval, half-exotic. The Greek goddess wedded to the Scottish ogre.'[15]

The masculinity of the castle, as characterised by the gun room, the billiard room, the armoury, the dungeons and even the haunted Oak Room, was compensated for by the overpowering scent of the tuberoses, grown in the greenhouse, with which Alice's mother kept the rooms filled throughout the year, and by the fact that of the Edmonstones' eight surviving children, seven were girls. Even Archie, the only boy, was not quite as manly as might have been wished. 'He detested sport, winced through the glorious 12th, took little or no interest in fishing,' writes one of his nieces. Archie was much happier closeted in his turret-room studio, painting 'shepherds and shepherdesses, fêtes galantes, saucy harlequins, wistful pierrots'.[16]

Alice and Archie, the two youngest, were like twins. 'Their love for each other had the beauty of a theme in a Greek legend,' runs one honeyed account of their close relationship. 'Both had a great sense of family affection, but neither emotion transcended the white flame of their love for each other.'[17] Brother and sister complimented one another perfectly. Where Archie was gentle, sensitive, submissive, Alice was vital, outspoken, assertive. 'Oh, look,' wailed Archie, as the two of them once watched a funeral cortège passing the windows of their Edinburgh home, 'look at that great black coach, those great black horses, all those black people!'

'Never mind, Archie,' came Alice's brisk reply, 'the coachman's alive!'[18]

Although brother and sister shared a love of gardening, Archie did not have Alice's passion for outdoor sports. A tireless walker, she was seldom happier than when striding across the moors at Duntreath, or when joining the gillies in a wild game of cricket. 'Rin, Allus, rin!' – Run, Alice, run – they would yell encouragingly as, with lustrous hair flying, she raced down the pitch. Family picnics, on the banks of Loch Lomond, were another delight; she even climbed Ben Lomond.

Her sense of humour was sharp; in later life she was to become celebrated for her witty turns of phrase. She would often tell the anecdote about one of her older, vaguer sisters who, at the time of the defeat of the British by the Boers at the battle of Majuba, once asked her, 'Alice, dear, who *is* Majuba Hill?'[19]

As she matured, Alice Edmonstone – in spite of her Latin looks – appeared to be developing into a typically aristocratic young Scots-woman: honest, energetic, practical. She had, as they would say, her head screwed on correctly. But there was more to her than this. Alice Edmonstone had a genuinely kind heart; her nature was without pettiness, prejudice or malice. She never spoke ill of anyone; she almost never lost her temper. Even as a girl, her tact was remarkable. It was always she who kept the peace between her frequently bicker-ing sisters; who formed the bridge between those who were dogmatic and those who were diffident. Her impartiality, her willingness to make allowances, were to become proverbial.

'She not only had a gift of happiness but she excelled in making others happy,' wrote one witness. 'She resembled a Christmas-tree laden with presents for everyone.'[20] Fulfilling, in time, one of the most notoriously difficult roles in society – that of a King's mistress – Alice was to be unique in that it is almost impossible to find anyone with a bad word to say about her.

Allied to her seductively good looks and lively manner, Alice Ed-monstone's strength of character and generous nature ensured that, by the time she reached womanhood, she was a very desirable *parti* indeed. The one thing she lacked was money. Sir William Edmonstone's

Scottish estates might have been extensive but they were not particularly profitable. What Alice needed was a rich husband. But if,
in the years ahead, the one criticism that would be levelled against her
was that she was somewhat 'grasping', there was no indication of this
in her choice of a husband. Alice Edmonstone married for love.

The Hon. George Keppel, third son of the 7th Earl of Albemarle,
might have been well-born, handsome, charming and even-tempered
but he was not rich. He, no less than Alice, should have been on the
lookout for a moneyed partner. But love, in their case, conquered all,
and the young couple were married in 1891, when he was twenty-six
and she twenty-two.

'At their wedding,' writes one of their daughters, 'the combined
beauty of my father and mother had been sensational. In an age of
giants he stood six foot four inches high, and in his Gordon Highland-
er bonnet, at nearly eight feet. Like her, he had eyes of bright blue. But
whereas she had chestnut hair, his was black. And his magnificent
breadth was a foil to her slender figure.'[21]

Marrying for love was one thing; trying to live in London society in
the 1890s without money was quite another. Before many years had
passed, the increasingly worldly Alice Keppel had come to appreciate
that there was only one sure way by which a married but impoverished society woman could hope to get the bills paid. This was by
adopting that easy-going attitude towards adultery characteristic of
the Marlborough House set: she must take a wealthy lover. It has been
said that the father of her first daughter, Violet, born in 1894, was the
rich Ernest William Beckett, the future Lord Grimthorpe.

True or not, the child grew up to be the celebrated Violet Trefusis
who, in 1918 was to win notoriety by embarking on a turbulent love
affair with Vita Sackville-West. It was Vita Sackville-West who,
many years later, told the writer Philippe Jullian that Beckett was
probably Violet's father.

Violet, on the other hand, would always lay claim to much more
illustrious ancestry than this. When she was not boasting about the
Edmonstones (were they not direct descendants of Robert the Bruce?)
or the Keppels (the handsome and nobly-born young Arnold Joost
Keppel, having accompanied William of Orange to England had been
created Earl of Albemarle by his adoring sovereign) or even, in more
imaginative flights of fancy, the Stuarts or the Bourbons or the
Medicis; when she was not boasting about these, Violet Trefusis
would hint that her father had been the future King Edward VII.

This cannot be true. Not unless one is prepared to believe that the

Prince of Wales had really met Alice Keppel in 1893 – five years before the generally accepted date of the meeting – and that, on being introduced to her in 1898, he pretended, for some reason or other, that they had not yet met.

No, the claim that the Prince of Wales first met Alice Keppel in the early months of 1898 is probably correct. And whether or not they met on the parade ground or the racecourse, it would have been in the Keppels' Wilton Crescent home that the young couple first entertained the Prince to dinner. Even allowing for His Royal Highness's taste in women, and for Alice's eye for the main chance, would either of them have guessed, as they sat above the sparkling silverware and the glancing candlelight of the dinner table, that she was shortly to become his mistress and, within three years, the Pompadour of the Edwardian court?

Alice Keppel proved to be the ideal mistress for an ageing man. She was attractive enough to interest him sexually; entertaining when he was bored, patient when he was cantankerous, sympathetic when he was ill, unobtrusive when he appeared in public. In his company she was amusing, even-tempered, uncomplaining. Like all successful mistresses, Alice was part-lover, part-wife, part-mother. An added attraction, in the Prince's eyes, was that she was an accomplished bridge player. For the Prince was reaching the age when a man values a good partner at the bridge table as highly as a good partner in bed. Before long, Alice Keppel had become an indispensible part of the Prince's life: a brilliant thread running through the fabric of his days.

To live in a style worthy of her new status, Alice Keppel, like Lillie Langtry before her, was obliged to move house. The Keppels – George, Alice and their little daughter Violet – left Wilton Crescent to set up home in 30 Portman Square. It was in this house, in its elegant eighteenth-century square, that much of Alice's affair with the Prince of Wales, afterwards King Edward VII, was conducted.

By today's standards, it was a highly inconvenient home. It was on six stories, up and down whose narrow stairs – carpeted for the drawing room and main bedroom floors, linoleumed for the upper and basement floors – the servants toiled all day. It had few of the amenities which were already being installed in comparable houses, such as central heating or the telephone, and food had to be kept cool in an outhouse in the area yard. Yet it did boast some modern conveniences: it was lit by electricity instead of gas, and husband and wife had a bathroom each – an almost unheard-of luxury for a London house. For most homes had no bathroom at all. Where, in some of the grandest country houses, there were one or two bathrooms, they were invariably huge, icy caverns situated at the end of unheated corridors.

In most houses hot water would still have to be carried up by maids, to be tipped into hip-baths in the bedrooms. Writers of memoirs, recalling the joys of steaming and scented hip-baths in front of roaring fires in their bedrooms, rarely gave a thought to the servants who had to lug cans of water from a cauldron in the kitchen up several flights of stairs, and who had then to carry the dirty water down again.

In fact, in no area of domestic life has there been a more complete change since the turn of the century than in the matter of servants. To run their home, the Keppels, who were far from rich, employed what they considered to be the absolute minimum: a butler, a cook, a governess and a nanny for their daughter, two maids and a boy who acted as a general dogsbody. The butler and the boy slept in rooms in the basement, the governess and the nanny on the nursery floor, the cook and the maids in the attic. They ate in what was grandly called the 'servants' hall' which was simply a room in the basement.

By the standards of their time and class, the number of servants kept by the Keppels – two for each member of the family – was regarded as a very modest ratio. Four to one was more usual; wealthier families had as many as eight for each member. At Eaton Hall in Cheshire, the Duke of Westminster employed over three hundred indoor and outdoor servants. The Duke of Portland employed even more. When the Prince of Wales brought an especially large party to stay with Lord Derby for the Grand National one year, his lordship remained unflustered. 'That makes sixty extra servants,' he calculated, 'and with the thirty-seven who live in, nothing could be simpler.'[22]

Not that one needed to be especially wealthy or well-born to keep servants. A bank manager or a doctor usually had three – a cook, a parlourmaid and a kitchenmaid – and even the humblest tradesman could afford a 'skivvy' or maid-of-all-work. For a thirteen-year-old skivvy in a tradesman's home the wages were usually a shilling a week. The average annual wage for a housemaid, working for a family whose income could be in the region of £30,000 a year, was £20.

It was no wonder that the great majority of aristocratic households could afford to employ a small army of indoor servants: housekeeper, cook, lady's maid, nurse, housemaids, kitchen maids, scullery maids, laundry maids, maids-of-all-work, as well as a butler, under-butler, valets, footmen, pantry boys, lamp boys, odd–job–men and kitchen porters. And all these in addition to the outdoor staff – the coachmen, grooms, stable-lads, gardeners and game keepers. By the end of the nineteenth century nearly one and a half million people worked as domestic servants. They formed the largest group of the working class.

The life of the average housemaid was little better than slavery. From the time that she rose, usually in a dark, cold room at six in the morning, until the time that she went to bed, at about eleven at night, she drudged almost without stop. She tidied grates, laid and lit fires, swept, dusted and polished the downstairs rooms, served morning tea, carried cans of hot water, made beds, emptied slops, scalded chamber pots, washed windows and paintwork, carried coals, swept, dusted and tidied the bedrooms, put away clothes, checked soap and changed towels, answered doorbells, went on errands, served meals and, in the evenings, turned down beds, drew curtains, prepared warming pans or hot-water bottles, carried up yet more hot water and tidied the downstairs rooms.

As, in a well–ordered household, no housemaid should ever be seen at work, all housework except for the bedrooms had to be done very early in the morning, before the family or guests came downstairs. In some households, housemaids were never seen at all. The tenth Duke of Beaufort, who died in 1893, would instantly dismiss any woman servant who crossed his path after twelve noon, by which time her work was supposed to have been done; while the third Lord Crewe stipulated that no housemaids were to be seen at any time of the day, except in chapel. Masters and servants, explained Lady Cynthia Asquith blandly, 'knew their places, and kept to them as the planets to their orbits.'[23]

Worked almost beyond endurance, hedged about with regulations, at the mercy of intimidating mistresses or tyrannical upper servants, poorly and often irregularly paid, enjoying no long-term prospects, pension rights or job security, living in fear of dismissal without a reference for minor misdemeanours, frequently seduced by the master of the house or his sons, thrown out if found to be pregnant, the average female servant lived the most wretched of lives.

'Poor little devils,' said the butler at Cliveden of the scullery maids, 'washing up and scrubbing away at the dozens of pots, pans, sauce-pans and plates, up to their elbows in suds and grease, their hands red raw with the soda which was the only form of detergent in those days. I've seen them crying with exhaustion and pain, the degradation too, I shouldn't wonder. Well, let's hope they get their reward in heaven.'[24]

It was small wonder that girls sometimes turned to prostitution or became pregnant by the first handsome soldier who happened to treat them with kindness.

Of course, there were exceptions. Upper servants often lived very comfortable lives and even housemaids, if they worked for a good-natured employer or in congenial company, could occasionally enjoy themselves. But the widely accepted vision of a Victorian below-stairs world full of jolly, contented servants devoted to their employers and working for the same family for generation after generation, is wildly inaccurate. In the year 1898 the average length of service in one household was a mere eighteen months. Most girls would far rather find employment in shops or factories.

By all accounts, Alice Keppel was an exceptionally considerate employer. According to the, possibly rose-tinted, memories of her two daughters (a second, Sonia, was born after the Keppels moved to Portman Square) the atmosphere throughout the house was well-ordered but cheerful. There might be the occasional altercation between the French governess and the English nanny but Mr Rolfe, the butler, and Mrs Wright, the cook, were both 'corpulent, smiling figures, given to kind teasing and fat laughter'.[25] Alice Keppel was a very capable woman, adroit in her handling of people and, as a frequent hostess to the Prince of Wales, would have been well aware of the advantages of a contented and smoothly-run household. She was the kind of fair-minded and warm-hearted mistress that servants appreciated.

As well as having a staff worthy of her royal lover, Alice Keppel needed rooms worthy of him. A certain boldness of taste ensured that she avoided much of the frivolity and fussiness that characterised *fin de siècle* decoration. Nor was the sunlight filtered through layers of curtaining. 'Femininity in her drawing room was less challenging and more conciliatory than in many,' says one observer. 'Solidly comfortable chairs had their place there; and the curtains were not drawn until the daylight faded.'[26]

Osbert Sitwell, who, as a young man, often visited Mrs Keppel, has left a description of the grander Grosvenor Street house to which she subsequently moved, but one can safely assume that her Portman Square home was not so very different. 'Within existed an unusual air of spaciousness and light, an atmosphere of luxury, for Mrs Keppel possessed an instinct for splendour, and not only were the rooms beautiful, with their grey walls, red lacquer cabinets, English eighteenth-century portraits of people in red coats, huge porcelain pagodas [a gift from her royal lover], and thick, magnificent carpets, but the hostess conducted the running of her house as a work of art in itself.'[27]

The same 'atmosphere of luxury' pervaded her bedroom. Its mounds of pillows, its cut-glass vases filled with lilies and malmaisons and its rich velvet curtains drawn, in this instance, against the daylight, all helped to create a suitably seductive setting for her extramarital assignations. With George Keppel having obligingly gone off to his club – and later his job – for the afternoon, and with the staff remaining discreetly downstairs, the Prince and Mrs Keppel would be certain of a couple of hours to themselves.

Vita Sackville-West, who was friendly with the young Violet Keppel even as a child, used often to see a 'discreet little one-horse brougham' waiting outside when she arrived at the house. Gently but firmly Mr Rolfe, the butler, would push the visiting girl into a dark corner of the hallway with a murmured 'One minute, miss, a gentleman is coming downstairs.'[28]

Trailing a whiff of freshly-applied *eau de Portugal*, the gentleman would descend the stairs and, having collected hat, gloves and cane from the obsequiously bowing Mr Rolfe, would cross the pavement to the waiting brougham and go spinning away in the direction of Marlborough House.

A legend persists, to this day, that the attitude of Alexandra, as Princess and Queen, towards her husband's affair with Alice Keppel was one of saintly forbearance. She is popularly believed to have displayed all those qualities of charity and forgiveness for which she was renowned. This is not quite accurate. In the first place, Alexandra was never the saint of popular imagination: she had many attractive qualities but she could be stubborn and selfish. Her supposed acceptance of her husband's mistress could simply have been a manifestation of her own self-absorbtion. And secondly, there were times when, far from approving of Mrs Keppel, Alexandra revealed an active dislike of her.

It is true that the Princess of Wales preferred Alice Keppel to Daisy Warwick. She would have agreed with the Duchess of Sutherland that her husband was 'a child, such a much pleasanter child since he changed mistresses'.[29] (The fact that Millicent Sutherland was half-sister to Daisy Warwick gives her opinion added weight.) And

Alexandra would have approved of the fact that Mrs Keppel did not flaunt her position to the extent that Daisy Warwick had once done. She would also have been grateful to Alice Keppel for keeping the Prince in a good temper. But this did not mean that she found her almost continual presence any less irksome.

The royal family certainly appreciated the Princess's feelings. Mrs Keppel's presence at the annual regatta at Cowes, for instance, was always guaranteed to upset Alexandra.

'How are things going on in general?' wrote Princess Alexandra's daughter-in-law, Princess May, to her husband Prince George one Cowes week. 'I mean, does peace reign or have you had a difficult time?'

Peace had reigned between his father and mother, answered Prince George, but 'Mrs K. arrives tomorrow and stops here in a yacht, I am afraid that peace and quiet will not remain.'

'What a pity Mrs G.K. is again to the fore!' commented Princess May. 'How annoyed Mama will be.'[30]

There can be no doubt that the constant presence of Mrs Keppel was one of the reasons why Alexandra played a less public role than might have been expected. While the Prince enjoyed what one observer called 'a good many small "Mrs George" dinners'[31], the Princess remained at Sandringham or else travelled abroad – to her native Denmark or on Mediterranean cruises. 'When she gets *stuck* at Sandringham it is difficult to move her . . .' complained Princess May. 'It does not look good for her so constantly to leave *him* alone as she does.'[32]

With two of her daughters married (in 1896 Princess Maud married a Danish cousin who later became King Haakon VII of Norway), Alexandra clung, ever more possessively, to her remaining daughter, Princess Victoria. This daughter never married. In fact, from the increasingly embittered Princess Victoria, Alexandra demanded all the attention, companionship and loyalty so signally denied her by her husband.

But there were occasions when Alexandra's sense of fun, never far below the surface, overcame her sense of grievance. One day at Sandringham, on looking out of the window, she happened to see her husband and his mistress returning from a drive. The sight of this couple sitting sedately side by side in an open carriage like two plump pigeons (for Alice Keppel, unlike Alexandra, was putting on weight) greatly amused the childish Alexandra. Beckoning to her lady-in-waiting to join her at the window, she dissolved into peals of helpless laughter.

As always with the affable Prince of Wales, the emergence of a new love never meant the disappearance of an old. In the summer of 1898, for instance, he was asking Lady Sackville if she would invite not only Mrs Keppel, but Lady Warwick, to her large garden party at Knole. Bravely, Lady Sackville refused. She would far rather, she explained tactfully, 'ask some of the County ladies, especially as the Princess [of Wales] was coming'. His Royal Highness, she says, 'acquiesced and was very nice about it'.[33]

The Prince was also looking after the interests of his other old flame, Lillie Langtry. By this time Lillie's daughter Jeanne-Marie, who had been fathered by Prince Louis of Battenberg, was nearing her eighteenth birthday and Lillie was very anxious for the girl to be properly launched into society. Although Jeanne-Marie by now knew that Lillie Langtry was her mother and not her aunt, she – and most other people – believed that her father had been the late Edward Langtry. So there was no apparent reason why the young woman could not be presented at court, always provided a suitable sponsor could be found to do so.

At almost eighteen, Jeanne-Marie Langtry was a slender, attractive young woman. A reporter of the *Sketch* had described her, a couple of years earlier, as 'a simple well-bred looking girl, strongly recalling one or two of her mother's early portraits – those taken when Mrs Langtry was just bursting upon the world, the fairest among a world of fair women, and a dream of loveliness.'[34] The fact that the reporter reserved his superlatives for Lillie indicates that the daughter, no matter how attractive, could not match the mother's marvellous beauty. About this, the forty-five-year-old Lillie would not have been unduly perturbed.

To arrange the complicated business of Jeanne-Marie's presentation, Lillie appealed to the Prince of Wales. He, with his penchant for protocol and his readiness to grant a favour, immediately put his mind to the problem. On meeting Gladys, Countess de Grey at a dinner party, he asked her to go and see Lillie – 'so as to give you advice about your girl going out into society'. Between the three of them, and after a series of letters between Lillie in London and Bertie in Cannes (where, in the spring of 1899, he was holidaying with Alice Keppel) the matter was resolved. Lady de Grey would present the daughter-in-law of one of Lillie's brothers, a 'Mrs H. Langtry', at a Drawing Room, at which, in turn, Mrs H. Langtry would present her cousin-by-marriage, Miss Jeanne-Marie Langtry. 'All you tell me,' wrote the Prince on receiving Lillie's final report on the plans, 'seems very satisfactory . . .'[35]

With Jeanne-Marie safely launched that season, Lillie made her own bid for respectability. Her husband's death in the Chester Lunatic Asylum, eighteen months before, had removed all obstacles to her remarriage and, after the obligatory year of mourning, Lillie felt free to find herself another husband.

The choice, even for her, was unconventional. Not only was Hugo de Bathe poor and foolish but he was eighteen years her junior: twenty-eight to her forty-six. His nickname was Suggie. On the other hand, Lillie, as a successful actress and racehorse owner, no longer needed to marry for money; nor, with women like Lord Randolph Churchill's widow, the forty-five-year-old Jennie, about to marry the twenty-five-year-old George Cornwallis West, did the age difference seem so remarkable. And then Suggie had, for Lillie, one overwhelming advantage: his father was a baronet. When old Sir Henry de Bathe died, his son would inherit his title and Lillie would become Lady de Bathe. For this alone, Lillie was apparently prepared to put up with the ineffectual, if not bad-looking, young man.

The ill-matched couple were married, very quietly, on 27 July 1899 in St Saviour's church in Jersey: the church where her father had been Dean and where, twenty-five years before, she had married Edward Langtry. So secret was the wedding that Lillie received, it is said, only one telegram. It was from the Prince of Wales, congratulating her on her horse Merman winning the Goodwood Cup that afternoon.

Lillie did not waste much time on a honeymoon. Within days she was back in London rehearsing a new play, while Suggie was heading for a stay at Carlsbad, 'for health reasons'.[36] Before the end of the year he had sailed for South Africa to fight in the Boer War which had broken out that October. 'My heart is on its way to South Africa,' declaimed Lillie dramatically to a clutch of reporters; only the most naive amongst them would have believed her.

Lillie Langtry's new play was *The Degenerates*, a relatively outspoken piece in which she played an abandoned society woman whose career, it was maintained, closely resembled her own. So shocked, it appears, were London audiences by the low moral tone of the play that it did excellent business. When Lillie opened in it in New York early the following year, audiences were even more shocked, with the happy result that it did even better business.

Among the snowstorm of abusive reviews through which Lillie

Langtry was obliged to battle as she toured the United States in *The Degenerates* was one which, in many ways, is a not entirely unfair summing-up of her theatrical ability. 'She does well enough when she has only to be conversational, graceful and slightly playful,' wrote the influential Arthur McEwan in the *North American*, 'but when more is demanded of her, passion, maternal feeling, agitation even, there is no response to the demand. She remains an amateur after all her years on the stage. One may not write truthfully of Mrs Langtry without seeming to be cruel, for it is impossible not to treat of the woman instead of the character she tries to assume. Mrs Langtry would offend in any play, not to speak of one for which she had supplied the least chaste materials.

'It is not as an actress that Mrs Langtry appears on the stage – her personal notoriety, not her talents, constitutes her claim upon the interest and pockets of the public in her country and ours. And Mrs Langtry knows this, and has always known it.'[37]

By now the Prince of Wales's other ex-mistress, Daisy Warwick, had embarked on a new love affair. In 1898, at the age of thirty-six, the irrepressible Daisy fell deeply in love with a thirty-one-year-old army captain named Joseph Laycock. Well-born, wealthy, Laycock was one of those not particularly handsome men who none the less possess a strong animal magnetism that can be very attractive to women. He was powerfully built and exceptionally energetic, with all the sporting enthusiasms of his type and class. Although Laycock epitomised, in many ways, the sort of conservative, landowning aristocrat against whose iniquities Lady Warwick so tirelessly campaigned, she was besotted by him. She 'worshipped' him, as she put it, 'wildly'.[38]

For Daisy, this was a very different love affair from her one with the Prince of Wales. 'If,' says Lady Warwick's biographer, Margaret Blunden, 'with the Prince of Wales, he had been the captive, she the conquering, he the adoring, she the adored, the reverse was nearer the truth with Laycock. Lady Warwick could still be imperious, was seldom less than demanding, but Laycock was ultimately in the happy position of being the one most desired, the one more loved than loving.'[39]

It was true that at the start of their stormy relationship the young captain was dazzled by the beautiful and celebrated Countess of Warwick and that he gave her the customary 'wedding ring' (one assumes that she took off the Prince's wedding ring first). He also tried to interest himself in her various humanitarian schemes, even to the extent of making generous donations towards them.

These contributions were particularly welcome as Daisy's own finances were in a precarious state. For some – to her – inexplicable reason, her annual income had fallen from £30,000 to £6,000. That this should have been the direct result of her lavish entertaining and no less lavish philanthropy was something which she refused to believe. She, one of the most richly dressed women in society, would blithely protest that she cared not one jot for clothes and that she was able to make her money 'go further than most'.[40]

Laycock's departure to fight in the Boer War meant a period of anxiety for the lovelorn Daisy. It was an anxiety which paled into insignificance in comparison with the anguish which beset her on his return. For an accident on the hunting field, at which the injured Laycock was tended by the lovely Lady Downshire, led directly to a romance between them. Married, with three children, and eleven years younger than Lady Warwick, the Marchioness of Downshire proved a formidable rival. Daisy's letters to Laycock became progressively more frantic as his love for Kitty Downshire became more apparent. Torn by jealousy, sick with longing, driven to despair, poor Daisy poured forth her soul in page after page to her unfaithful lover. 'Joe. My Joe –' she scribbled in one letter, 'if you could see how my hand shakes when I write your name . . .'[41]

Daisy became more incoherent still when she heard that the Marquess of Downshire was about to divorce his wife for adultery, naming Laycock as co-respondent. Convinced that Laycock would marry Kitty Downshire once she were free, Daisy used every argument to prevent the 'ill-fated, *impossible* marriage'.[42] She even appealed to her old love, the Prince of Wales, who had by that stage, become King.

'My darling –' she reported to Laycock one day in October 1902, 'I have such a rush to get home (to the Guild) – only just to say that the King more than nice to me – agrees about it all – only he says (as *we* do) you *must* go away for a bit then "things will be alright" and "a pity a man's life should be ruined" etc (He is very down on poor Lady D, but that I can *tell you* . . .)'[43]

But not even this hint of royal intervention could dissuade Laycock. In November that year he married Kitty Downshire. The embittered Daisy had to content herself with writing him a scathing letter for having forgotten her birthday on 10 December. From friends all over the world, she declared, she had received gifts and telegrams; even the

King had sent her a diamond and turquoise bracelet. Only from Joe, to whom she had given everything – beauty, adoration and intellectual companionship – had she received nothing.

In spite of all this emotional turmoil, Lady Warwick still found time to attend to her manifold activities on behalf of the under-privileged: her work for the trades unions, for progressive education, for the physically handicapped. The nineteenth century, she declared ringingly on one occasion, 'has proved one thing to us, and that is that men will not rest content in the positions in which they were born.'[44]

One of her new enthusiasms was for an Anglo-American alliance. Encouraged by her mentor, W.T. Stead, and inspired by her hero, Cecil Rhodes, both of whom favoured the idea, Lady Warwick worked towards the fostering of an understanding between these two great nations. With the Stars and Stripes floating above the ramparts of Warwick Castle, the châtelaine guided American tourists through its halls and invited American dignitaries to spend the night. She blithely suggested to Stead that he go to America 'to find a millionaire who simply wants a motive given him for spending his hoards'. These hoards could then be used 'to found an ideal union between the whole English-speaking race'.[45]

Inevitably, Daisy tried to embroil the Prince of Wales in the enterprise. His Royal Highness refused to touch it. Although the Prince favoured an end to his country's policy of 'splendid isolation', it was towards Europe rather than the United States that he felt Britain should be looking for allies. Heartily as he might wish for an entente with America, replied the Prince tactfully, he could not give the scheme his open support. Not even Lady Warwick's tea party, at which the American wives of English aristocrats did their utmost to charm the susceptible Prince, could win him over. In any case, the Prince was in no position to implement, or even influence, British foreign policy. This was something which Lady Warwick never fully appreciated.

There were other occasions, though, when the Prince of Wales was still prepared to involve himself in Lady Warwick's affairs. When her eldest son, the seventeen-year-old Guy, persisted in going out to fight in the Boer War, the Prince – although deploring the fact that anyone so young should be on active service – suggested ways in which the youth could be usefully and safely employed. And throughout the war he took a kindly interest in the boy's doings. The Prince also supported Daisy in her efforts to dissuade her husband, the forty-five-year-old Earl of Warwick, from enlisting in the Imperial Yeomanry in order to go and serve in South Africa.

As the war in South Africa dragged on, the Prince wrote often to Lady Warwick. These letters 'would have to be quoted from, or given in full,' she claims, 'to get their flavour.'[46] In fact, Daisy was a great admirer and, unfortunately, hoarder of, the Prince's letters. 'They reveal qualities that are none too common in any class, but rare indeed in Royalty,' she writes. 'They were essentially unselfish letters. The writer always makes light of his own troubles and discounts his own qualities and ability. He was, if anything, too humble about himself, and was always ready to praise other people and willing to believe that they were better than he. He would give the most detailed care to the consideration of other people's troubles and problems, was always ready to help and was full of wise counsel. Every letter reflected a kindly, generous, loyal nature. He gave to his private friendships the practical insight that might so well have served the State.'[47]

Early in 1899 the Prince, although by then deeply in love with Alice Keppel, wrote Daisy 'a charming letter reminding me of the tenth anniversary of our friendship'. Its contents were wide-ranging but 'the main theme was the reality and sincerity of our friendship which he averred nothing could alter'.[48]

If only the Prince had known that one day his darling Daisy was to use these affectionate letters to blackmail his son, King George V, he would have expressed himself with rather more circumspection.

'It would be wrong to assume,' wrote Margot Asquith, 'that the [Prince of Wales's] only interest in women was to have an "affaire" with them. That he had many "affaires" is indisputable, but there were a great many other women in his life from whom all he sought was a diverting companionship.'[49]

It is, perhaps, in this light that the Prince's strange relationship with Miss Agnes Keyser must be viewed. He first met the forty-five-year-old Miss Keyser in February 1898, about the same time as he met Alice Keppel. The daughter of a wealthy stockbroker, Charles Keyser, Agnes Keyser was an attractive and intelligent woman, with that strongly individual streak which the Prince always found so irresistible. It was this independence – allied to her financial independence – which led Agnes Keyser, in spite of her charm and beauty, to reject the conventions of her time and to take up nursing as a career. With the passing years she developed into a brisk, efficient, somewhat intimidating nursing sister, highly respected in her profession.

That the Prince should have been attracted to this nanny-like figure, so different from the sumptuously dressed and seductively mannered women in whose company he usually delighted, is revealing. Indeed, it was precisely these nanny-like qualities that appealed to him. In her comfortable home in Grosvenor Crescent, the Prince could be assured of the calm that was so conspicuously lacking in his daily life. With head sympathetically tilted, Agnes Keyser would listen to his troubles, discuss his health and advise him on personal problems. Serene and unaffected, she gave him a sense of security. In her reassuring company, the Prince felt completely at ease. She even tried to improve his eating habits. The Prince would often dine with Agnes Keyser, sometimes at a small table laid in front of a glowing fire, and instead of stuffing him with *ortolans rôtis sur canapés* or *gâteau punch granit au champagne*, she fed him with what, in those days, was considered healthy food: Irish stews and rice puddings. At least it was plain and wholesome, redolent of the nursery.

An added attraction, as far as the Prince was concerned, was that Agnes Keyser was an accomplished bridge player. Quite often she and her sister would join the Prince and Alice Keppel in a game. With his appreciation both of female company and of good bridge, the Prince greatly enjoyed these evenings.

When the Boer War broke out in 1899, Agnes Keyser decided to convert her Grosvenor Crescent house into a nursing home for officers. As not even her substantial private income could meet all the costs of equipping the hospital, she appealed to the Prince of Wales for help. He immediately set up a trust and coerced his many rich friends, such as Ernest Cassel, Arthur Sassoon and Nathaniel Rothschild, into subscribing to it. As the ineffable Rosa Lewis – the kitchenmaid who ended up presiding over the famous Cavendish Hotel in Jermyn Street – put it, the Prince 'got his snob friends to dole out'.[50] After the Prince's accession to the throne, Agnes Keyser's nursing home, which she ran as matron, became known as King Edward's Hospital for Officers.

For twelve years, from 1898 until he died in 1910, King Edward VII kept up his close relationship with Agnes Keyser. Quite clearly, he was devoted to her. Whether or not it was anything more than an *amitié amoureuse* one does not know. Perhaps, for one of the greatest libertines of the time who never lacked sexual opportunity, it was enough that Agnes Keyser should be a comforting, understanding, all-forgiving presence – the quintessential mother-figure.

★

The Prince's relationship with his own mother, Queen Victoria, had greatly improved over the years. Time had mellowed them both. The Queen was more ready to concede her heir's good points and the Prince to appreciate his mother's attitudes. He was always very grateful when, during his all too frequent spells of trouble, she gave him active support. By now the Queen had finally allowed her heir access to official papers, with the result that one of his deepest causes of resentment had been removed. Max Beerbohm's famous cartoon – showing the adult Prince being made to stand in a corner by the tight-lipped Queen and captioned 'The Rare, the Rather Awful Visits of Albert Edward, Prince of Wales, to Windsor Castle' – no longer had quite the same validity. Although mother and son remained at odds over some things, they were in complete accord on others. Both, for instance, were ardent imperialists, very conscious of the importance of upholding British prestige throughout the world. This shared imperialism was a very strong bond indeed.

They had even learned to take pleasure in each other's company. The Queen's entry in her Journal, after her son had been to stay with her at Balmoral one year, has a strangely touching quality. 'An early luncheon,' she wrote, 'after which dear Bertie left, having had a most pleasant visit, which I think he enjoyed and said so repeatedly. He had not stayed alone with me, excepting for a couple of days in May '68, at Balmoral, since he married! He is so kind and affectionate that it is a pleasure to be a little quietly together.'[51]

But that the Prince should have felt an increasing frustration with the length of time he was being kept waiting for the throne can be appreciated. In December 1900 he entered his sixtieth year; he must, in darker moments, have agreed with the member of his household who afterwards claimed that 'the best years of a man's life, say from forty to sixty were to a great extent wasted, and King Edward came to the throne with a vitality already debilitated by the years of waiting.'[52]

On occasions, the Prince even gave voice to this sense of frustration. There is a story that once, in Paris, at the end of a long day, he turned to a companion and said, 'You Frenchmen are always talking of your Eternal Father, but I can see that you don't know what it is to possess an Eternal Mother.'[53]

Perhaps he said no such thing for, in the ordinary way, the Prince had far too highly developed a sense of majesty to make such a remark, but it would have been understandable if he had.

On this score of Queen Victoria's longevity, the Prince's great friend, the Portuguese ambassador, the Marquis de Soveral, used to tell an amusing anecdote. One evening, in the course of the usual cheerless dinner party at Windsor Castle, the old Earl of Clarendon with, one suspects, a touch too much gallantry and a glass too much wine, turned to Queen Victoria and asked, 'Ma'am, can you tell me the secret of your eternal youth?'

Her Majesty's reply was unequivocal. 'Beecham's pills,'[54] she snapped.

But not even this panacea could keep the old Queen alive forever and by the middle of January 1901 it was clear that she did not have much longer to live. On 18 January the Prince received a message advising him to come to Osborne, where the Queen was slowly dying, as soon as he could. That evening – his last in London before going to Osborne – he spent, not with his new mistress, the scintillating Alice Keppel, but with his new friend, the sympathetic Agnes Keyser. The eminently practical Miss Keyser would have known exactly how to hearten the Prince at this troubled time.

At dawn the following morning the Prince caught a special train to the Isle of Wight. Four days later, on 22 January 1901, Queen Victoria died and the Prince of Wales became King.

'So the Queen is dead . . .' wrote young Winston Churchill from Canada to his mother. 'A great and solemn event: but I am curious to know about the King. Will it entirely revolutionise his way of life? Will he sell his horses and scatter his Jews or will Reuben Sassoon be enshrined among the crown jewels and other regalia? Will he become desperately serious? Will he continue to be friendly to you? Will the Keppel be appointed Ist Lady of the Bedchamber?'[55]

La Favorita

'IF YOU ever become King,' Queen Victoria had once warned the Prince of Wales, 'you will find all these friends *most* inconvenient, and you will have to break with them *all*.'[1]

Here was yet another piece of maternal advice that King Edward VII had no intention of following. Far from turning his back on his somewhat racy circle of friends, the King ensured that they were all made welcome at the new Edwardian court. Buckingham Palace and Windsor Castle, for so long noted for their hushed, cathedral-like air, were suddenly filled with cigar-smoking financiers, dashing men-about-town and soignée, animated women. The rooms echoed to the sounds of lively conversation and the strains of Lehar and von Suppé. Whereas at Queen Victoria's table no one had ever spoken above a whisper, dinners were now, observed one astonished official, 'like an ordinary party'[2] – all talk and laughter.

'The White Drawing Room where for the last two years of her life the Queen sat after dinner,' lamented one of Victoria's ladies-in-waiting, 'is now used as a card room, one table being for whist and the other for bridge. The King delights in the last-named game and plays every evening, Sundays included, till between 1 and 2 in the morning.'[3]

Indeed, the old Queen's ladies-in-waiting, in their grey or mauve half-mourning, were pensioned off; as were scores of those attendants whose duties had become fossilised during the long years of Queen Victoria's seclusion. Out, too, went the accumulated memorabilia of half a century: the yellowing photographs, the elephants' tusks, the marble busts, the cumbersome mahogany furniture. Electric light, central heating and new bathrooms were installed. The state rooms were thoroughly overhauled: repainted, recurtained, recarpeted and refurnished. The chandeliers were electrified; the walls fitted with

enormous looking-glasses. Even at sacrosanct Balmoral the drawing
room walls were stripped of their tartan covering.

Not only did the new King instigate all these changes, he took an
active interest in them. With his fox terrier trotting at his heels, he
bustled from room to room, advising, directing, deciding. 'Offer it
up,'[4] he would command when someone suggested the hanging of a
picture here or the placing of a cabinet there, and he would make an
immediate decision. The effect of Edward VII on the court was, as one
of his grandsons has put it, 'much as if a Viennese hussar had suddenly
burst into an English vicarage.'[5]

This is not to say that the new court lacked dignity. On the
contrary, it gained as much in majesty as it did in animation. With his
highly developed sense of showmanship, the King saw to it that he
created an atmosphere worthy of his status. His refurbishing of the
various palaces made them not only more convenient but more
magnificent. Furniture and porcelain assembled by that great royal
connoisseur, George IV, were brought out of storage; gilding was of
the richest, carpeting of the deepest, fabrics of the most luxurious. On
gala occasions, great pyramids of roses, hydrangeas and carnations
decorated the main rooms.

Manners might have been more relaxed but dress became more
formal, with the women obliged to wear tiaras and the men court
dress with decorations. Once, when the young Duchess of Marlborough appeared at dinner wearing a diamond crescent instead of the
prescribed tiara, she was sternly rebuked. And when Lord Rosebery
arrived at an evening reception at Buckingham Palace in trousers
instead of knee-breeches, the King was furious. 'I presume,' he said in
his guttural voice, 'that you have come in the suite of the American
Ambassador.'[6]

As Edward VII remained the most punctilious of men, everything
was done with the utmost precision. 'Nothing,' confirmed one of his
Continental nieces, 'is more perfect in every detail than the King of
England's court and household, a sort of staid luxury without ostenta-
tion, a placid, aristocratic ease and opulence which has nothing showy
about it. Everything is run on silent wheels that have been perfectly
greased; everything fits in, there are no spaces between, no false note.
From the polite, handsome and superlatively groomed gentleman-in-
waiting who receives you in the hall, to the magnificently solemn and
yet welcoming footman who walks before you down the corridor,
everything pleases the eye, satisfies one's fastidiousness . . .'[7]

The ceremonial aspect of the monarchy was not only restored but expanded. Queen Victoria's sedate afternoon Drawing Rooms were replaced by brilliant evening Presentation Courts. State occasions such as the opening of parliament, the Garter ceremony, the investitures and the levées, were all conducted with a hitherto unheard-of splendour. In Queen Victoria's day, visiting royals had to put up in London hotels; now they were lavishly entertained at Buckingham Palace. Whereas the late Queen had not paid a formal visit to a foreign capital for almost half a century, Edward VII's reign was to be notable for a series of the most spectacular state visits ever undertaken by a modern monarch.

Inevitably, there was criticism. Lord Esher, who was to become, in time, one of Edward VII's most trusted confidants, lamented the passing of 'the mystery and awe of the old court'.[8] Henry James, too, regretted the disappearance of 'little mysterious Victoria' and the succession of that 'arch vulgarian, Edward the Caresser'.[9] The King, reported Lady Curzon to her husband, 'was miserable in the company of any but his few bridge friends as he feels himself so hopelessly out of it with intelligence or intellect – on the whole he has begun *badly*.'[10]

It was true, of course, that the tone of the new court was somewhat philistine. The King might have had an eye for a splendid setting but his taste – in pictures, plays and books – remained undeveloped. Paintings had to be strictly representational. He went to the theatre to see light opera, musical comedies or the sort of contemporary play about upper-class society in which Lillie Langtry so often starred. Music provided by bandmasters like Sousa and Gottlieb was what he preferred. *East Lynne* by Mrs Henry Wood is said to have been the only book he ever finished; and when he wanted to furnish his library shelves, he simply left the choice of books to a man from Hatchards. On being told, at a literary gathering, that a certain writer was an authority on Lamb, he was astounded. 'On *lamb?*'[11] he exclaimed.

The King was not, for all his gregariousness, a gifted talker. Not only could he discuss nothing in depth, or at length, he was not even a good raconteur. He tended to repeat the same jokes. A dozen words were usually his limit; often these were in the form of an abrupt question or a bantering remark. Although essentially kind-hearted, his tone was often chaffing, teasing, even insulting. In short, the art of conversation flourished no more than any of the other arts at Edward VII's court.

Yet, in the final analysis, none of this really mattered. Constitutional monarchs need not be intellectuals. They need not even be particularly intelligent. To this day, the undeniable success of the institution of monarchy in Britain is not due to the exceptional mental capacities of the members of the reigning dynasty. It is far more important that monarchs be gracious, conscientious, self-confident and dignified; and that they have a taste and talent for the showier aspects of their calling. In all these respects, Edward VII was eminently well-equipped for kingship. No European monarch had more panache.

With time, he was to prove himself in other ways as well. He was to reveal himself as wiser, more knowledgeable and more politically aware than he had ever been given credit for. But at the start of the reign it was enough that, with monarchy everywhere enjoying a period of almost unparalleled splendour – a last great flowering before being cut down by the First World War – Edward VII should preside over the most magnificent court in Europe.

On his accession Edward VII did not break with Alice Keppel, any more than with other members of his coterie. Those who had imagined that she would be discarded, or at least kept discreetly in the background, were proved very wrong. Not only did she maintain her position as *maîtresse en titre,* she became one of the leading personalities of his court. Throughout the ten years of Edward VII's reign, Alice Keppel was an accepted, respected and highly visible member of the royal entourage. She remained, in the widely used phrase, 'La Favorita'.

There were several reasons for her pre-eminence. The chief one was that the King was devoted to her. Physically, mentally and socially, Alice Keppel met his every requirement. He not only adored but admired her. It was noticed that whenever they were in company together, he never took his eyes off her, and was edgy if he noticed her talking to another man. This adoration was to have an echo in the love of his grandson, the future Edward VIII, for Wallis Simpson. He, too, would keep a constant watch on his beloved and, if she left the room, would look anxious and fretful until she returned.

So attractive, so chic, Alice Keppel was a decorative addition to the King's circle. In many ways she epitomised the Edwardian society woman – worldly, witty, light-hearted. Unlike her royal lover, she was very articulate. 'I liked greatly to listen to her talking,' remembers Osbert Sitwell, 'if it were possible to lure her away from the bridge table, she would remove from her mouth for a moment the cigarette which she would be smoking with an air of determination, through a

26. Duntreath Castle, Stirlingshire, birthplace of Alice Edmonstone (afterwards Keppel).

27. Alice Keppel and her eldest daughter Violet, at the time of her meeting with the Prince of Wales.

28. The King's Mistress: the astute and fascinating Mrs Keppel, at the height of her fame.

29. King at last: a portrait of Edward VII at the time of his accession.

30. *(left)* With an eye ever open for the ladies, Edward VII hosts a garden party.

31. *(right)* The Hon. George Keppel, gentlemanly *mari complaisant*.

32. *(below)* A rare photograph of the King and Mrs Keppel on a golf course in the South of France.

33. The King, with Alice Keppel sitting erect on his left hand, enjoying private theatricals at a Chatsworth house party.

34. Edward VII, presumably accompanied by Mrs Keppel, goes boating on Ascot Sunday.

35. Edward VII, who rarely missed one of Lillie Langtry's first nights, in a specially constructed royal box.

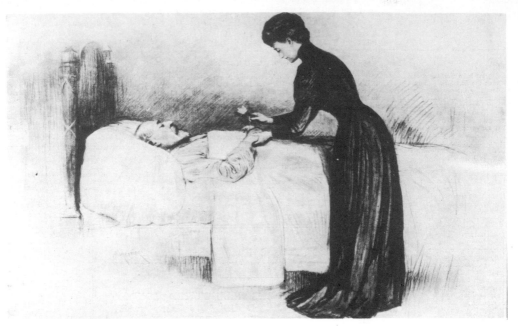

36. An idealised representation of Queen Alexandra at her husband's deathbed. The public knew nothing of the extraordinary scene which had taken place earlier.

37. The mistresses in old age. From the left, Lillie Langtry at Monte Carlo; Daisy Warwick at Easton Lodge; Alice Keppel at l'Ombrellino.

long holder, and turn upon the person to whom she was speaking her large, humorous, kindly, peculiarly discerning eyes. Her conversation was lit by humour, insight and the utmost good nature: a rare and valuable attribute in one who had never had – or, at any rate, never felt – much patience with fools. Moreover a vein of fantasy, a power of enchantment would often lift what she was saying, and served to emphasise the exactness of most of her opinions, and her frankness. Her talk had about it a boldness, an absence of all pettiness, that helped to make her a memorable figure in the fashionable world.'[12]

Her outspokenness even extended to the King. Alice was one of the few people in the world to stand up to him. At the bridge table, where the King was known for his high stakes, daring bids, short temper and dislike of losing, she refused to be cowed. 'God save the King,' she once drawled when her bidding had left him with a particularly difficult hand to play, 'and preserve Mrs Keppel from his rage.'[13] And on another occasion, when he barked at her for having played the wrong card, she boldly answered that she 'never could tell a King from a Knave'.[14]

She knew exactly how far she could go with him. Alice always handled the notoriously impatient monarch with great expertise. When the King's niece, the young Princess Alice of Albany, once complained to Alice Keppel about her difficulty in keeping up a dinner-table conversation with the King – a difficulty made worse by his habit of fiddling with the cutlery as one spoke – 'the charming and tactful Mrs Keppel' reassured her. 'Don't worry about that,' replied Alice Keppel, 'we all experience that trouble. He likes to join in general conversation injecting remarks at intervals, but he prefers to listen to others rather than to talk himself. Often he starts a discussion, but as soon as he can get others involved in it he is content to listen and make occasional comments.'[15]

Her tact, her skill in keeping the King amused and diverted was greatly appreciated by his entourage. 'Thank God,' Sir Arthur Nicolson once exclaimed on joining the monarch on a cruise, 'Alice will be on board.'[16]

Nicolson had good reason to fear his sovereign's peppery temper. When, as British ambassador at St Petersburg, Sir Arthur was summoned aboard the 'Victoria and Albert' to brief the King before a meeting with Tsar Nicholas II, His Majesty seemed more interested in the ambassador's decorations than his briefing.

'What is that bauble?' he finally demanded.

With some pride Nicolson explained that it was the 'badge of Nova

Scotia Baronetcy', the only hereditary order in England, conferred on his ancestors in 1637.

The King was not impressed. 'Never wear that bauble again,'[17] he growled.

Not only was Alice Keppel a soothing and cheerful companion, but her interests also coincided with those of her royal lover. No more cultured than he, no more knowledgeable about books or paintings or music, she was very well informed on those subjects which interested him. The Duchess of Marlborough, having paid tribute to Mrs Keppel's looks, geniality and approachability, goes on to claim that 'she invariably knew the choicest scandal, the price of stocks, the latest political move; no one could better amuse [the King] during the tedium of the long dinners etiquette decreed.'[18]

On one point, all those who knew Alice Keppel are agreed: she was never malicious. Even those who accused her of being an adventuress had to admit that she was extremely good natured. 'One of the secrets of her success,' says one witness, 'was that she could be amusing without malice; she never repeated a cruel witticism.'[19] The King once asked Margot Asquith if she had ever known 'a woman of kinder and sweeter nature' than Alice Keppel, and even the normally acidulous Margot had to admit that she had not. 'She is a plucky woman of fashion,' notes Margot, 'human, adventurous and gay who, in spite of doing what she liked all her life, has never made an enemy . . . her desire to please has never diminished her sincerity.'[20]

Alice watched over her ageing lover's health with an almost mater-nal solicitude. Some years before, while visiting Waddesdon, Baron Ferdinand de Rothschild's grandiose château-like country place, the Prince of Wales had fallen down a spiral staircase. He was discovered at the foot of the stairs, groaning with pain, by his current mistress, Daisy Warwick.

'I think I have broken my leg,' he gasped, 'please get someone to help me.'

He had, in fact, cracked his knee-cap. But refusing to have a doctor summoned from London, the Prince had returned to town by special train. 'The Prince,' says Daisy, 'had great fortitude and no man ever made less of physical pain.'[21] Since then, the knee had given him constant trouble. This, and the King's characteristic refusal to do anything about it, worried his new mistress, Alice Keppel, consider-ably.

'I want you to try and get the King to see a proper doctor about his knee,' she once wrote to her lover's great friend, the Marquis de

Soveral. 'Perhaps the Queen could make him do so. He writes that it is
very painful and stiff and that massage does it no good or rather harm
as there is a slight "effusion" on it . . . do try and do what you can with
your famous tact and, of course, don't tell anyone *I* wrote to
you . . .'[22]

This motherly, almost domestic facet of their relationship was
enhanced during the King's frequent, at times daily, visits to Alice's
home in Portman Square. (The King's green brougham, complained
Lady Curzon, was *always* outside Mrs Keppel's house.) Not all their
time there together was spent in bed. Sometimes Alice would entertain His Majesty to tea in the drawing room and, on these occasions,
her two daughters might be allowed to come down. Alice Keppel's
second daughter, Sonia, had been born on 24 May 1900 two years after
she had first met the Prince of Wales. One must assume that George
Keppel was Sonia's father, although the title which, almost sixty years
later, Sonia Keppel gave to her memoirs – *Edwardian Daughter* – has
the smack of a *double entendre*.

Just ten days before Sonia's birth, the high-spirited Alice Keppel
had celebrated the Relief of Mafeking by sitting astride a lion in
Trafalgar Square. 'I never doubted her story,' remembers Sonia.
'From my earliest childhood she was invested for me with a brilliant,
goddess-like quality, which made possible anything she chose to say
or do. It seemed quite right that she should bestride a lion . . .'[23]

To Violet and Sonia Keppel, their mother's lover was known as
'Kingy'. He was, remembered Violet, 'very kind to us children. He
had a rich German accent and smelt deliciously of cigars and *eau de
Portugal*. He wore several rings set with small cabochon rubies and a
cigarette case made of ribbed gold, no doubt by Fabergé.'[24]

Before ushering the girls into the drawing room, their nurse would
hiss, 'Always curtsey to the King, dear.' But for little Sonia, who was
six years younger than Violet, this was easier said than done. She
could not always distinguish between the King and another of her
mother's friends, Sir Ernest Cassel. Cassel, who modelled himself on
the monarch, was also portly, bearded, be-ringed, watch-chained and
cigar-smoking; more often than not Sonia, playing safe, curtsied to
him as well.

With Kingy, Sonia would play a fascinating game. On his outstretched and immaculately trousered legs, she would place two
pieces of bread, buttered side down. Bets of a penny each would
be laid on which piece of bread would slide down more quickly;
the winning piece always being the more buttery. 'The excitement

was intense while the contest was on,'[25] she remembers.

The King must indeed have been very fond of Sonia – or of her mother, rather – to have allowed this messy game to be played on his trousers. For, in the ordinary way, he was obsessively careful about his clothes; he could not bear to have anything spilt on them. Once at dinner, when a spot of spinach was splashed onto his starched white shirt, the King was so incensed that he plunged both hands into the serving dish and smeared the spinach all over his shirt-front. With a booming laugh, he left the table and thudded upstairs to change.

The fact that Sir Ernest Cassel was so often to be found in Alice Keppel's drawing room is significant. One reason is that, together with the Marquis de Soveral, and Alice Keppel herself, Cassel was a member of Edward VII's inner circle. So it was only natural that he and Alice should be friends. But for Alice, Cassel had another attraction: he was extremely rich.

A humbly-born German Jew, Cassel had, through his financial acumen, turned himself into a multi-millionaire. He was, in fact, the sort of self-made entrepreneur for whom Edward VII always had the greatest admiration. He admired him still more when, as his financial adviser, Cassel handled the royal investments in such a way as to increase the King's income most gratifyingly. For these services (and not, as has so often been assumed, because he gave the King money) Sir Ernest Cassel was handsomely rewarded by his grateful sovereign. He not only showered him with the honours that Cassel so dearly coveted but also, by parading their friendship, made him socially acceptable.

By now Cassel was one of the leading figures at the Edwardian court. Had he seen *The Importance of Being Earnest*, the then Prince of Wales had once asked the Marquis de Soveral. 'No,' replied the quick-witted diplomat, 'but I have seen the importance of being Sir Ernest.'[26]

Edward VII attended the wedding of Cassel's only daughter into the English aristocracy and stood godfather to his granddaughter, Edwina Ashley. With the subsequent marriage of Edwina Ashley to Lord Louis Mountbatten (who was not only a great-grandson of Queen Victoria but a half-brother to Lillie Langtry's daughter by Prince Louis of Battenberg) the Cassel star rose very high indeed. Yet Sir Ernest remained, despite this royal patronage, a modestly-mannered man: quietly spoken, austere, introvert.

Aware of the depth of the King's feelings for Alice, Sir Ernest Cassel was only too ready to grant whatever she might need for her task of keeping the monarch happy. And Alice would have been only too ready to take what was going. Cassel helped her, not so much with gifts of money but with financial advice and in kind. He always, for instance, lent her an entire floor of the Villa Eugenie at Biarritz each year so as to enable her to be near the King. And it would be through Cassel that Edward VII was to make provision for his mistress in the event of his death.

It was this close association with Cassel that led to talk of Alice Keppel's love of money; that, and her obvious interest in the stock market. Mrs Keppel, says the Duchess of Marlborough with a hint of disapproval, 'knew how to choose her friends with shrewd appraisal.'[27] And Lord Esher always considered her to be 'rapacious'.[28]

Sir Harold Acton, who was to become friendly with Alice Keppel in later years, based his claim that she was not 'snobbish' on the fact that 'no snob could have won the confidence of the big bankers and merchants who had surrounded King Edward . . . Mrs Keppel was fascinated by the power of capitalism.'[29]

In her *roman à clef, The Edwardians*, Vita Sackville-West modelled her character Romola Cheyne on Alice Keppel. Describing her as 'mercenary' and 'materialistic', she writes of 'the financial shrewdness of Mrs Cheyne, a lady . . . who cropped up constantly in the conversation; Romola Cheyne, it appeared, had made a big scoop in rubber last week – but some veiled sneers accompanied this subject, for how could Romola fail, it was asked, with such sources of information at her disposal?'[30]

This fiction was firmly rooted in fact. For it was well known, in Edward VII's circle, that the King had given Mrs Keppel a number of shares in a rubber company which, in time, earned her £50, 000. Some of the monarch's gifts were more immediate than this. The courtesan Skittles, with whom the King still kept in touch, once told Wilfrid Scawen Blunt that His Majesty had recently paid a £5000 dress bill for Alice Keppel.

But who, after all, can blame Alice Keppel for looking after her own interests? Life with her fat, ageing, often irritable lover could not have been one of unalloyed joy. That she should want to make as much hay as she could while her particular sun shone is perfectly understandable. In any case, being the mistress of a man such as Edward VII, who liked his women well-dressed and his surroundings luxurious, was an expensive business. It was also a precarious business. She could never be certain of retaining the King's affections: there was always the chance that she might be supplanted, as Lillie Langtry and Daisy Warwick had been supplanted. The King might be devoted to her but he was by no means sexually faithful to her. He could well fall in love with someone else. And although he was still in his early sixties during the first years of his reign, Edward VII was not really well: he suffered from recurrent bronchial trouble. Where would she be if he were suddenly to die?

This possibility was made frighteningly clear in the summer of 1902. A few days before the Coronation – set for 26 June – the King was taken ill. Although insisting, to his worried doctors, that he would be crowned if it killed him, Edward VII was finally obliged to postpone the ceremony and to undergo an operation for appendicitis. It seemed doubtful that he would survive the ordeal. The surgeon afterwards told the King's unmarried daughter, Princess Victoria, that 'his firm conviction was that His Majesty would die during the operation'.[31]

This, apparently, had been the King's conviction as well. He suspected that he might have cancer of the stomach, as both his brother, Prince Alfred, and his sister, the Empress Frederick, had recently died of cancer. It was when he was in this apprehensive state that he wrote a letter to Alice in which he said that if he were dying, he felt sure that 'those about him would allow her to come and see him'.[32]

The operation was a complete success. On the day after, the King was sitting up in bed, reading a newspaper and smoking a cigar. Relief, not only in the palace but throughout Britain and the Empire, was profound. And by few was it more genuinely felt than by Alice Keppel.

Yet, ever practical, Alice kept the King's letter. Very carefully, she filed it away. She was to put it to good use at a later date.

With Edward VII making no secret of his love for Alice Keppel or of his determination that she should be received in public, society found itself in a dilemma. Should Queen Alexandra and Mrs Keppel be invited to the same parties? Hostesses knew that the Queen would be irritated, or insulted, if Mrs Keppel were invited; and that the King would be in a bad mood if she were not. A *cri de coeur* from the Duchess of Westminster to the Marquis de Soveral (who managed to remain on friendly terms with the King, the Queen and Mrs Keppel) sums up this general quandary. 'I want the King to be happy, but I don't want to annoy the Queen, so please tell me what would be best,'[33] she begged on one occasion.

But not every host or hostess was similarly torn. For although even Queen Alexandra was obliged to receive Alice Keppel, not only in the official royal residences but in her own home, Sandringham, others felt no such obligation. Those pillars of Victorian and Edwardian rectitude, Lord Salisbury, the Duke of Portland and the Duke of Norfolk kept the doors of their houses – Hatfield, Welbeck and Arundel – firmly closed against the King's mistress.

The good-natured and worldly-wise Alice Keppel never allowed herself to be put out by these social embarrassments. Quite often, she triumphed over them. Once, when Lord Salisbury was entertaining the sovereigns at Hatfield, from which Alice was barred, she accepted an invitation to spend the weekend at nearby Knebworth, the home of Lord Lytton. The result, reports Count Mensdorff, the ambassador for Austria-Hungary, from Knebworth, was that 'all the guests (from Hatfield) came over here to tea – naturally, because *La Favorita* is here'.[34]

Yet so exquisitely mannered were both Queen Alexandra and Alice Keppel that on the many occasions that they were invited together, there was never any suggestion of animosity. Daisy, Princess of Pless, a daughter of Edward VII's old flame, Patsy Cornwallis West, was a guest at a huge house party given by the Duke of Devonshire (another of the King's old friends, Harty-Tarty, who had by now succeeded to the title) at Chatsworth in January 1904. While the King and Mrs Keppel – 'with lovely clothes and diamonds' – played bridge in a separate room, the Queen – 'charming and beautiful as always' – was entertained with songs and music in the spacious corridor.

'The last evening there was very cheerful,' writes the Princess of Pless, 'the Queen danced a waltz with Soveral, and then we each took off our shoes to see what difference it made to our height. The Queen took, or rather kicked, hers off and then got into everyone else's, even into Willie Grenfell's old pumps. I never saw her so free and cheerful but always graceful in everything she does.'[35]

For however much, in private, Alexandra might resent her husband's infidelities, in public she always presented an untroubled image. She was sustained by the knowledge that she was immensely popular. Alexandra brought so many things to the monarchy. The general public knew very little about her failings; to them she was a decorative, socially accomplished Queen with a reputation for boundless sympathy for those in suffering. She was appreciated for being virtuous and vivacious, dignified and natural, caring and *insouciant*. They called her the Queen of Hearts.

One of Alexandra's minor, but not insignificant, contributions to the monarchy was her way of dressing. It was to influence royal fashion for the following three-quarters of a century. Ignoring the fashion changes of the Edwardian era – the loosely-knotted hair, the outsize hats, the high waists, the narrow skirts – Queen Alexandra stuck resolutely to the style which she had decided suited her best. Her high-dressed, tightly-curled wig would be crowned by an elaborate toque; her slender neck would be encircled by a jewelled 'dog-collar'; her waist would be laced to its narrowest. Her clothes never looked anything less than opulent; she dressed as though she were on stage. There seemed nothing incongruous about her opening a row of workers' cottages wearing a toque of parma violets, a mauve ostrich feather boa, a dress of silver-embroidered lace, ropes of pearls, clusters of diamonds, and pale satin shoes.

In this way Queen Alexandra set a style in royal dressing. It had nothing to do with fashion but everything with effect. Her example was followed by the two queens who came after her: George V's consort, Queen Mary and George VI's consort, Queen Elizabeth. All three women perfected, and remained faithful to, a strongly personal style. When, in 1938, Queen Elizabeth accompanied George VI on his state visit to Paris, the verdict of that fashion-conscious city was that although she was not chic, she dressed like a queen. Her achievement is not as unimportant as it may seem. This art of royal dressing – an art which has now been lost – provides the monarchy with several, not inconsiderable advantages: a touch of essential theatricality, an instantly recognisable image, and a stable, dependable, unchanging air.

Never was Queen Alexandra's highly developed personal taste more in evidence than at the postponed Coronation, on 9 August 1902. Ignoring both tradition and fashion, she announced that she would wear 'exactly what I like and so will all my ladies – *Basta!*'[36] She was proved right. In a dress of golden Indian gauze, shimmering with diamonds and pearls, and trailing a richly-embroidered, ermine-lined train, she looked magnificent.

Even at that age of fifty-seven, Alexandra had no need to fear competition from younger women. She outshone them all. In Westminster Abbey that day was a bevy of the King's specially invited women friends, including Alice Keppel and Sarah Bernhardt, all sitting in a pew irreverently referred to as 'the King's loose box'.[37]

What Queen Alexandra thought of this collection of her husband's
women friends one does not know, but one of her ladies-in-waiting
leaves no doubt about her own feelings. To her 'the well-named loose
box' was 'the one discordant note in the Abbey – for to see the row of
lady friends in full magnificence did rather put my teeth on edge – *La
Favorita* of course in the best place, Mrs Ronnie Greville, Lady Sarah
Wilson, Feo Sturt, Mrs Arthur Paget and that ilk . . .'[38]

Nor, apparently, was this the first time that the King had invited a
selection of his old flames to witness him in his new regal state. 'King
Edward, it appears, goes among his lady friends as "Edward the
Caresser",' writes Wilfrid Scawen Blunt. 'When he succeeded to the
throne he wrote to divers of these ladies to say that though called to
other serious duties he hoped still to see them from time to time. They
had all gathered in the Ladies Gallery of the House of Lords when he
made his speech from the Throne and there was much speculation as
to whether he would address any part of it to them. He looked up
twice, but maintained his solemnity . . .'[39]

Yet another of Edward VII's old lady loves, who was attending the
Coronation ceremony in her own right, as a peeress, was Daisy
Warwick. She had arrived alone in the cumbersome family coach as
her husband, the Earl of Warwick, had decided that he would prefer to
travel to the Abbey in his new 'motor-brougham', having first applied
to the police for permission to do so. 'I was agreeably surprised to
learn that they would welcome it,' he writes, 'as old coaches were so
difficult to move out of the way.'[40]

For 'stately grace and absolute beauty', decided the watching Lord
Rosebery, Lady Warwick's entry into the Abbey 'was next to that of
Queen Alexandra'.[41]

Of all the memorable moments in the Abbey that day, it is not
altogether surprising that the scene which most impressed the King
was an exclusively feminine one. It came just after the Queen had been
crowned, when all the peeresses, in one graceful, fluid, simultaneous
movement, placed their coronets on their own heads.

'Their white arms arching over their heads', the King afterwards
declared, had resembled 'a scene from a beautiful ballet'.[42]

On 30 June 1902, four days after the original date of Edward VII's
Coronation, Lillie Langtry's daughter Jeanne-Marie married the Honourable Ian Malcolm at St Margaret's, Westminster.

Lillie could hardly have wished for a more socially acceptable match. The credentials of the thirty-three-year-old Ian Malcolm were, by the standards of the time, impeccable. Heir to the hereditary chieftainship of the Clan MacCullum and to a vast estate in Scotland, Malcolm led not only a privileged but a useful life. Eton and Oxford had been followed by a spell in the diplomatic corps, where he had served as an attaché in the British embassies in Paris and Berlin. Since 1895 he had been Conservative member of parliament for Stowmarket in Suffolk. Together with four other young Conservative members, among them Winston Churchill, he had formed a mildly rebellious group; in fact their name, 'The Malcolmtents', acknowledged him as their founder. Cultivated and capable, Ian Malcolm seemed set for a successful parliamentary career. In time, he would be knighted, and Jeanne-Marie would become Lady Malcolm.

As the King was recovering from his operation a few days before, there was no question of his attending the fashionable wedding ceremony, although it was reported that he had sent the bride a valuable piece of jewellery. Less easily explained was the absence of the bride's step-father, Lillie's new husband, Hugo de Bathe. Perhaps the fact that he was younger than the bridegroom was one explanation; the lack of rapport between him and Lillie might have been another. But then this outwardly conventional wedding was beset with irregularities; not least by the fact that by now Lillie and Jeanne-Marie were barely on speaking terms.

The relationship between mother and daughter had never been harmonious. A gentler, more reserved person than Lillie, Jeanne-Marie had never really approved of her mother's flamboyant way of life. She had once been heard to say, on being told by some ageing Lothario that he had known her mother in younger days, that yes, a great many elderly men had told her the same thing. But the chief reason for Jeanne-Marie's antipathy towards her mother was the discovery, not long before her marriage, that she was illegitimate: that her father had not been the late Edward Langtry but Prince Louis of Battenberg.

She had, it seems, first heard this astonishing news from Margot Asquith. What, asked Margot, had Jeanne-Marie's father given her for her recent birthday? When the bemused girl protested that her father was dead, the always outspoken Margot told her that, on the contrary, her father was still very much alive. He was Louis Battenberg. Surely her mother had told her this?

Jeanne-Marie was appalled. For a girl who had spent the first half of her life believing that her father had been one of Lillie's brothers and that Lillie was her aunt, and the second believing him to be Edward Langtry, the news came as a severe shock. Hurrying home, she confronted her mother with the allegation. Lillie, who happened to be sitting at her dressing table when her distraught daughter burst in, did not even, it is said, turn round to face her. 'You shouldn't believe everything you're told,'[43] she said coolly. But Jeanne-Marie would not be fobbed off in this way, and attacked her mother for her duplicity. It was in the course of a heated exchange that Lillie asked Jeanne-Marie if she did not prefer a father like Prince Louis to 'a drunken sot'[44] like Edward Langtry.

But Jeanne-Marie refused to be mollified. Once her wedding, followed by a reception at the Hotel Windsor, was over, she broke with her mother. At first, Lillie seems not to have appreciated the finality of the break. Not until over three months later, after she had written to Jeanne-Marie to demand 'some sort of explanation' for her long silence, was Lillie made aware of the strength of her daughter's feelings.

'I think I have always shown my intense love for you,' Lillie had written, 'and to be in the same town with you and not see you makes me so wretched that I am quite ill. Please darling, write me a nice letter . . .'

Jeanne-Marie's reply was chilling. Having reminded her mother of their row about her parentage, Jeanne-Marie goes on to say, 'What I suffered the last days under your roof, knowing this change to have come upon me, yet feeling powerless to alter it . . . Had it not been for the support of the pure love and devotion of the strong man who wished to make me his wife, in spite of all, I think I should have gone mad . . . I have felt within the last year or two that our tastes are widely different. Therefore in future we had best live our own lives apart. In conclusion, please believe that, painful as I know it must be for you to receive this letter, the necessity of writing it causes the most intensive misery to your daughter – Jeanne.'[45]

From that time on, Jeanne-Marie had nothing more to do with her mother. 'Lillie's name was not mentioned in our household . . .' claims Jeanne-Marie's daughter, 'my mother was unrelenting and would not receive her.'[46]

Another of Lillie's bids for respectability – by the marriage of her daughter into a conventionally upper-class family – had turned to ashes.

But rising from the ashes was something at which Lillie excelled, and she wasted no time on regrets. She was already well launched on her latest venture: the leasing and restoring of the old Imperial Theatre, Westminster. At considerable expense she had the interior gutted, the stage lowered, the walls lined with Italian marble, new plush seats put in, electricity installed and the boxes hung with satin curtains in what she fancifully calls 'the colours of nature's spring garb – purple, green and gold.'[47]

Unfortunately, her performances never matched the splendour of her surroundings, and the venture was not a great success. One flop followed another. Not even the presence of King Edward VII and Queen Alexandra at a command performance of *The Crossways* on 8 December 1902 could save the situation. The theatre closed.

So it was back to touring the United States where, as usual, she did good business and where, again as usual, she never hesitated to use Edward VII's name for publicity purposes. In 1905 she ventured even further afield: she toured South Africa. She was hardly back from this strenuous journey before she was persuaded to join a vaudeville show due to tour the United States. Vaudeville, usually regarded as a third-rate form of entertainment, had recently been made respectable by the likes of Sarah Bernhardt. This fact, allied to the size of the salary offered by the impresario, B. F. Keith, overcame Lillie's scruples and she agreed to do a performance of a piece called 'Between Nightfall and Light'.

But she remained uneasy about it. 'For heaven's sake,' she instructed the flock of reporters who greeted her arrival in New York in September 1906, 'please don't ever refer to my playlet as a sketch! That sounds too vaudevillainous for words. I could not stand it. I call my endeavour "a tabloid tragedy".'[48]

It was while performing her tabloid tragedy in Cincinnati on 6 January 1907 that Lillie heard that her father-in-law, Sir Henry de Bathe, had died and that her husband, Hugo, had inherited the title. She was now Lady de Bathe. It was, in a way, a moment of triumph. Yet when Keith, the impresario, suggested that she change her name on the billing, she refused. She had become famous as Mrs Langtry; she had no intention of being billed as Lady de Bathe, particularly as the title was all that the impecunious Hugo had inherited.

'Everything is precisely as it was,' she explained to a friend. 'I'm still supporting my dear husband.'[49]

In common with those other cuckolded husbands – Edward Langtry and Lord Warwick – George Keppel was obliged to turn a blind eye towards his wife's liaison with the King. Indeed, of the three of them, Keppel behaved with the greatest good nature. Where Langtry took to drink and Warwick to fishing, George Keppel remained devoted to his wife.

The word most commonly used by his contemporaries to describe George Keppel is 'gentleman'. He certainly looked like everyone's idea of a gentleman. Six foot four inches tall, with an upright carriage, an upswept moustache (it had to be curled, with tongs, every morning) a carnation in the button-hole of his frock-coat and a gleaming top hat on his dark hair, George Keppel cut an impressive figure. 'One could picture him waltzing superbly to the strains of "The Merry Widow",'[50] says one observer.

Gentlemanly, too, were his manners and conversation. 'Kind-hearted, spontaneous, he was easily pleased, easily appeased, willing to believe the best of everyone, the best of life. He was what the French call *bon public*, an optimist,'[51] writes one of his daughters. His attitudes were conventional. A patriot, a lover of tradition and an uncritical friend, George Keppel was very much a product of his time and class.

Once, on discovering someone reading a book about Oscar Wilde, Keppel professed himself deeply shocked. 'A frightful bounder,' he muttered. 'It made one puke to look at him.' Did Alice Keppel ever remind him, muses Harold Acton, 'that he was descended from William III's minion [Arnold Joost Keppel] who was created Earl of Albemarle for his *beaux yeux*?'[52]

In no respect was George Keppel more of a 'gentleman' than in his attitude towards his wife's infidelity. He was the ideal *mari complaisant*. Keppel not only accepted the situation philosophically but with great grace and dignity. He never complained, he never showed a vestige of jealousy, he was never anything other than discreet. 'So you're a Keppel,' a grand duke once remarked at Baden. 'Are you related to the King's mistress?'[53] To this studied insult, Keppel paid not the slightest attention.

Indeed, to some members of society, George Keppel seemed to be too tolerant by half. 'Had Keppel been put up for membership at some London clubs,' confided one Edwardian survivor to the writer Gordon Brooke-Shepherd, 'the black balls would have come rolling out like caviare.'[54]

Keppel was even obliged, in order to keep up a style of life appropriate to his wife's new position, to suffer the ultimate Victorian and Edwardian humiliation: to 'go into trade'. He was given a job by the King's yachting companion, Sir Thomas Lipton. From an office in

Wigmore Street, George Keppel worked as a salesman in Lipton's 'Buyers' Association'. Lady Curzon reported to her husband that Lipton had been given 'a high class Victorian order'[55] by his grateful sovereign for making Keppel his American agent and sending him off for a spell in the United States.

Nor, it was rumoured, was the King Alice Keppel's only lover. Daisy, Princess of Pless, attending a luncheon party given by Alice, professed herself shocked by the candour with which her fellow women guests admitted to having had 'several lovers'.[56] Already it was being said that George Keppel had fathered neither of Alice's two daughters, and the indefatigable Lady Curzon reported to her husband, in September 1901, that 'Mrs Favourite Keppel is bringing forth another questionable offspring! Either Lord Stavordale's or H. Sturt's!!' Lord Stavordale, she goes on to say, was about to be married as 'Mrs Keppel made a promise to Lady Ichester to *allow* him to marry at the end of this summer'.[57] (The fact that Alice Keppel did not have another child indicates that this might all have been unsubstantiated gossip.)

Alice's happy-go-lucky attitude towards marital fidelity was graphically borne out when, three or four years after Edward VII's death, she one day suggested to Winston Churchill's young wife Clementine that, in order to help Winston in his career, Clementine should find herself a rich and influential lover. Alice, who was quite prepared to assist her in the search for a suitable candidate, considered it positively selfish of Clementine to refuse to help Winston in this fashion.

To what extent George shared his wife's attitude one does not know. Perhaps his imperturbable public face hid a private melancholy; perhaps not. They seem, from all accounts, to have been very attached. So tactful in her dealings with others, Alice Keppel was never more so than in her handling of her husband. He, who was the simpler of the two, remained attentive and loving. To their children – and children are quick to sense an atmosphere of strain – they seemed an ideally matched couple. Theirs was 'a companionship of love and laughter',[58] claims Sonia Keppel. Moving easily in and out of each other's bedrooms, delighting in dressing up and going out, devoted to their two little daughters, they epitomised marital happiness. Both were great tellers of bedtime stories. But whereas his would be conventional adventure tales, more suitable for boys than girls, hers would be altogether more exotic. 'Once upon a time,' Alice would start in her husky, seductive voice, 'there was a Manchu princess, who kept a singing cricket the price of a Derby winner . . .'[59]

This admirably adjusted relationship lasted all their lives. There was never any question of the marriage breaking up. In fact, far from resenting his wife's affair with Edward VII, George Keppel basked in its reflected glory, both at the time and in later years. He even, towards the end of his life, became as celebrated a figure as she, in spite of the fact that the precise reason for his renown was not always clear. In Tuscany – where the couple lived until their deaths, within two months of each other, in 1947 – the Italian guides would solemnly inform the tourists that the tall, straight-backed, bristlingly moustached Englishman had been 'the last lover of Queen Victoria'.[60]

La Maîtresse Du Roi

I<small>F THERE WAS</small> one place in which Alice Keppel reigned supreme, it was the French seaside resort of Biarritz. Lying on the Atlantic coast close to the Spanish border, Biarritz had been popularised by the Spanish-born Empress Eugenie during the Second Empire. The imperial residence, the Villa Eugenie, had been the Osborne of Napoleon III's court. This royal, or imperial, patronage had now been revived by Edward VII. For a month or so each year, from early March to early April, the King spent a holiday there. As neither Queen Alexandra nor George Keppel ever accompanied their spouses to Biarritz, the King and Mrs Keppel were able to live the life of a married couple, free of the social embarrassments that so often beset their relationship at home. During those weeks at Biarritz, writes one of Edward VII's biographers, 'Alice Keppel *was* Queen.'[1]

It was only to be expected that France should be the country to provide the King with the setting for his annual spell of domestic bliss. The French understood this sort of thing so well: official mistresses, even royal official mistresses, were very much in the French tradition. And then France had always been Edward VII's favourite Continental country; it was the foreign country in which he felt most at home, in which he had enjoyed some of the most hedonistic days of his protracted youth.

As Prince of Wales he had invariably spent these early spring weeks on the Riviera (at a carnival in Nice, noted an astonished French detective, the middle-aged Prince, masked and costumed, had behaved '*comme un jeune homme*'[2]) but as King he preferred Biarritz. Its bracing Atlantic breezes seemed not only to relieve his chronic bronchial troubles but to discourage the sort of smart society that flocked to the South of France. 'I no longer go to Cannes and Nice,' he once explained to his French bodyguard, 'because you meet too many princes there. I should be obliged to spend all my time in paying and receiving visits, whereas I come to the Continent to rest.'³

Biarritz was mercifully free not only of visit-exchanging royals, but of the statesmen, politicians and diplomats who crowded those other Continental resorts favoured by Edward VII – Bad Homburg in the German Empire and Marienbad in the Austro-Hungarian Empire. Not that the King minded this blend of social and political activity; on the contrary, he revelled in it. In Marienbad particularly (in which, since 1903, he spent several weeks from mid-August onwards) much of the King's time was given over to informal talks with other holidaying or cure-seeking political figures. Indeed, it was as much through these casual discussions, often with no British minister in attendance, as through his more spectacular state visits that Edward VII gained his somewhat exaggerated reputation as an accomplished royal diplomat. In so-called spa diplomacy, which was such a feature of political life before the First World War, Edward VII had great faith.

But at Biarritz it was different. Here the King's days, if no less active, were entirely given over to recreation. At the beginning of March each year, having spent a few days in Paris *en route,* the King would settle into a suite of rooms at the Hotel du Palais. Accompanying him would be a doctor, two equerries, two valets and two footmen. Compared with Queen Victoria, who used to be accompanied by scores of people and who would take over an entire hotel for her annual stay in the South of France, Edward VII's suite was very modest.

Waiting for him in Biarritz would be Mrs Keppel. She never, for some reason, accompanied her royal lover to Marienbad. It has been suggested that whereas, in tolerant and republican France, her presence was quite acceptable, in the Austro-Hungarian Empire, where Edward VII was a visitor to the domain of the stiff-backed old Emperor Franz Josef, she would have been less welcome. It was true that Franz Josef had a long-standing mistress of his own, Katharine Schratt, but unlike Mrs Keppel, Frau Schratt was never openly paraded. And Edward VII thought too highly of Alice to subject her to the indignity of a clandestine existence, even for a few weeks. Mrs Keppel's presence in Biarritz might not actually have been announced in the court circular but the King made no secret of the fact that she was there.

Alice Keppel's journey to Biarritz for her annual 'Easter holiday' would be conducted with almost as much precision as the King's.

Accompanied by her two daughters, their governess, their nurse, a ladies' maid and a courier supplied by the palace, she would leave in a specially reserved carriage from Victoria station. Her huge studded wardrobe trunks, tall enough to stand up in and always stored upright, would be put in the van, while her smaller luggage – hat-boxes, shoe-boxes, overnight suitcases, food hampers, medicine chest, hold-all, rugs, cushions and, most important of all, her travelling jewel-case – would be stored in the carriage.

On the boat there was always a special suite of cabins reserved for the family and, on arrival in Calais, Mrs Keppel would be formally received by the *chef-de-gare* who would personally escort her through customs. Her luggage was *never* searched. To avoid the stares of the curious (for by now, of course, all the passengers would know that the fashionably dressed lady in the private carriage was Madame Keppel, *la maîtresse du Roi*) Alice would insist that the family keep well away from the restaurant car and that they eat their meals from baskets in their compartments.

Before going to sleep the beautiful Alice would be transformed into an almost unrecognisable creature. Her voluptuous body would be hidden under a shapeless nightgown; her chestnut hair would be pushed into an outsize mob-cap; her face and neck would be liberally creamed; and her lustrous, blue-green eyes would be covered by 'night-spectacles'. She would then take a powerful sleeping draught and, as the *wagon-lits* went hurtling south through the dark French countryside, she would sleep as though dead. 'Sometimes,' remembers her daughter Sonia, 'I would peer over the edge of my berth at Mama and, in the weird, blue ceiling-light, her white face, with its black-bandaged eyes, looked ghastly.'[4]

But, on alighting at Biarritz station the following day, Alice Keppel would look her usual glamorous self. For the sake of appearances she would neither be met by the King nor accommodated in his hotel. Her host would be Sir Ernest Cassel, who would have rented the luxurious Villa Eugenie – the restored seaside residence of the Second Empire court – which would be run for him by his widowed sister. Alice Keppel would have a floor to herself, her daughters being accommodated in the nursery wing which had once housed the late Prince Imperial. The girls were always hard put to keep up with Sir Ernest Cassel's beautifully-dressed granddaughters, Edwina and Mary Ashley. Could *they* not have real lace on their knickers, like the Ashley girls, begged Mrs Keppel's daughters.

'Mrs Ashley can afford it,' was Alice's brusque answer, 'I can't.'[5]

As Edward VII led no less highly organised a life at Biarritz than anywhere else, Alice would have to adjust her life to his. They would meet, each day, at a quarter past twelve exactly. By then the King, who always rose at seven no matter how late he had gone to bed the night before, would have had his warm bath and his glass of milk, been dressed in one of his immaculate suits, enjoyed a breakfast of boiled eggs, grilled bacon, freshly-caught trout and milky coffee, and spent a couple of hours at his writing desk.

For even on holiday the sovereign is never free of constitutional duties. No matter where he or she might be, the monarch must attend to the 'boxes' – that collection of cabinet minutes, memoranda, despatches, reports, letters, departmental statements, documents for signature, petitions, appeals and protests. Each morning, at Biarritz, Edward VII would be faced by three large canvas bags brought over by special government messenger. 'The King,' writes one observer, 'examined all the despatches, studied them, annotated them, wrote to the prime minister in his own hand, himself treated all important questions, directed how the others were to be dealt with and divided the work between his equerries.'[6]

Alice Keppel would join him at a quarter past twelve and together they would stroll along the promenade. The sight of this elegantly dressed couple – the King sporting one of his many walking sticks, all monogrammed with an E surmounted by a crown, and Mrs Keppel in a large veiled hat – was a familiar one to the people of the resort. At Biarritz, in marked contrast to Marienbad where the demented mayor was driven to nailing posters on every tree along the *Kreuzbrunnen* begging the public to leave their illustrious guest in peace, the inhabitants respected the King's wish for privacy. Indeed, some illustrated French papers even went so far as to airbrush out the features of Mrs Keppel whenever she was photographed walking by the side of her royal lover.

There were a couple of locals, though, who made certain that the King was never ignored. These were two blind beggars who positioned themselves, at precisely noon each day, beside the road that led from the Hotel du Palais to the beach. The King never failed to drop a handful of coins into their begging bowls and to greet them with a reassuring 'Till tomorrow!' One day, however, there was only one beggar to be seen. The worried King was very relieved to find, the following morning, that the man was back in his place.

'Were you ill yesterday?' asked the King.

'No, monsieur le Roi,' answered the man.

'Then you were late?'

'Excuse me, monsieur le Roi,' stammered the embarrassed beggar. 'I beg your pardon. You were early.'

The King was highly amused. 'A thousand apologies,'[7] he declared.

Always accompanying the King and Alice Keppel on their walk was his long-haired white fox terrier, Caesar. Edward VII doted on Caesar: on his collar the dog bore the proud inscription, 'I am Caesar, the King's dog.' Whenever Caesar accompanied his master to the Villa Eugenie, where the King enthusiastically joined Alice's daughters in their games, the excited dog would gnaw the chairlegs or rip the curtains. But no one, least of all the King, ever punished him.

'His Majesty,' reports Charles Stamper, the King's chauffeur, 'never beat Caesar. The dog and he were devoted to one another, and it was a picture to see him standing shaking his stick at the dog, when he had done wrong. "You naughty dog," he would say very slowly. "You naughty, naughty dog." And Caesar would wag his tail.'[8]

The King and Mrs Keppel usually lunched together in his suite at the Hotel du Palais. The hotel waiters would wheel the trolleys of food to the door of the royal suite but it would be served by Edward VII's two personal footmen. Lunch invariably consisted of hard-boiled plover's eggs sprinkled with paprika, followed by fish – trout, salmon or soles – which was in turn followed by a meat dish. As His Majesty disliked red meat, this was usually chicken or game, with an occasional slice of lamb. His favourite vegetable was asparagus and his favourite fruit strawberries. With his meal the King would drink chablis and Perrier water, dry champagne and occasionally claret. He would always finish the meal with a balloon of Napoleon brandy and a Corona y Coronas cigar. A fast eater, he disliked spending longer than thirty minutes at table.

Most of all, the King enjoyed his afternoon, or even day-long excursions with Alice Keppel. In his fleet of claret-coloured cars, which had been driven from England to be awaiting his arrival at Biarritz, the royal party would set out. With His Majesty always demanding change and variety, there was hardly an area of the surrounding countryside, including nearby Spain, that Alice Keppel did not come to know. Together, they would watch the pelota matches at Anglet or the races at La Barre; they would go lurching along the little mountain roads above Cambo and St-Jean-Pied-de-Port; they would cross the flat landscape lying to the north towards Bordeaux or negotiate the hazardous passes through the Pyrenees. Occasionally, to ensure an afternoon's complete privacy with Alice,

the King would arrange for his 'double', Sir Ernest Cassel, to imper-
sonate him by leaving the hotel in one of the royal cars.

Unfortunately, and inexplicably, His Majesty had a preference for
picnicking by the side of the road. Once he had chosen the spot,
everyone would pile out and the footmen would set out table, chairs,
linen table cloths, napkins, plates, glasses and silver. Cold food would
be unpacked from hampers, hot food from deep dishes sunk into a
large, heavily-padded box, and iced cup served from silver-plated
containers. But as even in those more tranquil days the roads out of
Biarritz were often crowded with cars and carriages, the party would
be subjected to the stares of passers-by and to clouds of white dust.
Gamely Alice Keppel would sit under her jewel-handled parasol (for
to be tanned by the sun was unthinkable) while the King, happily
oblivious to the fact that he was being recognised by every person who
drove by, delighted in his anonymity.

The ever-present Alice provided Edward VII not only with the
pleasure of her company, but with a measure of protection from
predatory females. In Biarritz he was relatively safe from the sort of
adventuress who wanted to boast that she had slept with the King of
England (in Marienbad one such huntress professed herself ready to
settle for His Majesty's secretary if His Majesty himself were not
available) but he remained in danger of those who wanted to claim
him as a friend. One such social climber was a relentless American by
the name of Mrs Moore. 'There are three things in life which one
cannot escape,' the King used to sigh, '*l'amour, la mort* and *La Moore.*'9

Untiring, but unsuccessful, in her efforts to gain admission to the
magic circle, Mrs Moore finally hit upon a way of doing so. She
bribed one of His Majesty's drivers (one can only assume that it was
not an official royal chauffeur) to feign a break-down on the way back
to Biarritz from St-Jean-de-Luz. As the monarch sat fuming in his
stationary car, a distant cloud of dust heralded the approach of another
vehicle. The equerry flagged it down. Out clambered Mrs Moore, her
motoring veil tied firmly under her chin. Could she possibly give His
Majesty a lift to the Hotel du Palais? She could. And the citizens of
Biarritz were presently treated to the sight of King Edward VII sitting
in the back of an open car beside a triumphantly beaming Mrs Moore.
It was her finest hour. When next she invited the King and Mrs Keppel
to play a little bridge, he could hardly refuse.

Other excursions brought other dilemmas. Once, when Alice
Keppel decided to go shopping in nearby Bayonne, the King was
talked by the thirteen-year-old Violet Keppel into taking her to the

carnival in San Sebastian. Both masked, the corpulent old man and the slender young girl were soon swallowed up by the surging, confetti-flinging crowd. Presently Violet noticed that Kingy was in trouble: his face was scarlet and his breathing laboured. Tearing off his mask, the frightened girl shouted, '*Es el Rey*! Can't you see it's the King? You're suffocating him!' But at first the crowd refused to take her seriously; it was some time before they realised who he was and before a path could be cleared to allow him to reach his car and his distraught chauffeur.

Alice was waiting for them on the steps of the Villa Eugenie. 'I was sent straight to my room,' reports Violet. 'As for the poor King, it was decidedly the last time that he gave in to one of my childish whims.'[10]

The afternoon's excursions – whether successful or not – over, the King would spend another period at work with his equerries and then dress for dinner. This would be served at eight-fifteen, again in the royal suite and would be a full dress occasion – the men in white tie and tails, the women in evening dress and jewels. Never more than ten sat down to the meal; often Alice was the only woman present. The menu would again be, as one guest tactfully puts it, 'pretty copious'.[11] After dinner there would be bridge, with Alice always playing at the King's table. Towards midnight the party would break up.

But perhaps one may be allowed to imagine Alice remaining behind for a further half-hour while the King drinks his last whisky and soda and smokes his last cigar on the canopied balcony outside his suite. Sometimes in April, along this usually bracing Basque coast, comes a balmy night, rich with the promise of summer, with a full moon reflected in the inky waters of the Atlantic; on such a night, in the company of his beloved Alice, the normally fidgety, perennially restless King of England is able to enjoy a period of blissful contentment.

Any hopes that the Countess of Warwick might have harboured of becoming an *éminence grise* of the Edwardian reign were soon dashed. A matter of months after Edward VII had ascended the throne, Daisy was visited by Viscount Esher, the true *éminence grise* of the new reign. In his charming, tactful fashion, this polished courtier told her, she says, 'that he thought it would be as well for all concerned if my close association with great affairs were to cease, as it was giving rise to hostile comment which distressed Queen Alexandra.' Just before Esher's visit, continues Daisy, the Queen 'had written me a letter – a very kind letter – to the same effect.'[12]

Although Daisy had never been as closely associated with 'great affairs' as she would like us to believe, it was quite clear that Queen Alexandra wanted the King to have nothing more to do with her. Having fondly imagined that her carefully composed letter of renunciation, written to her royal lover at the end of their affair, would ensure her continued access to him, Daisy was proved wrong. Queen Alexandra had had quite enough of Lady Warwick: of her immoral reputation and her radical opinions. Yet, in her memoirs, Daisy is at pains to point out that the Queen's attitude merely confirmed her own; that it was she who had refused to take advantage of her continuing friendship with the King. 'I had been most scrupulous, since he came to the throne,' she asserts, 'in seeking nothing for myself or my friends.' Her noble withdrawal, she claims, astonished the King's circle. One of his rich friends – and here she surely means Cassel – even went so far as 'to ask me bluntly why, in a season when so many favours were being dispensed, I remained so quietly in the background'.[13]

Yet Edward VII, as was his way, never completely broke with Daisy Warwick. They continued to see each other from time to time and always exchanged gifts and greetings on their birthdays. But she was never again to have any influence over him.

The fact that Lord Esher's courteously worded warning was delivered in 1901 and that Daisy Warwick did not officially become a socialist until late in 1904 gives the lie to two frequently repeated claims: that Edward VII broke with Lady Warwick because she joined a socialist party, and that Lady Warwick joined the socialists because she was annoyed with the King for having deserted her for Alice Keppel. The truth is that their affair had ended before the Prince of Wales met Alice Keppel and that not until six years later did Lady Warwick join the Social Democratic Federation.

Until then, despite her humanitarian activities, Daisy Warwick had regarded herself as standing above party politics. But having finally joined the Social Democratic Federation – the most radical and militant of the contemporary left-wing groupings, well in advance of the Independent Labour Party – she worked for it with unflagging enthusiasm. There always remained, though, something paradoxical about her position. Despite her proletarian sympathies, Lady Warwick was still very much the grand lady. Swathed in furs, she would address co-operative society meetings; roped in pearls, she would entertain trade unionists in her Italianate London home. In her forty-horse-power Wolseley she would tour the country campaigning for free meals for children; in her special train she would travel to workers' rallies. From Nawton Towers, the luxurious country house of her son-in-law Viscount Helmsley, prospective Conservative candidate, she would sally forth to make speeches on behalf of the local Labour candidate.

She was of immense value to the cause. 'We are having fine meetings with the Countess of Warwick as a speaker or in the chair,' reported one leading socialist to a friend. 'There is of course a lot of snobbery in this, but what matter? People would come to see and hear her who would never come to see or hear you or me. Last Friday at the Memorial Hall on a *frightful* night the place was packed with over 2000 people, many, perhaps the majority, of the well-to-do class.'[14]

Indeed, in common with Edward VII's other old flame, Lillie Langtry, Daisy Warwick had the ability to draw an audience. Like Lillie, too, she was making her own mark in the world, quite independent of her status as a royal mistress.

Leading such an active political life, Daisy was understandably surprised to discover, in the year 1904, that she was to give birth to another child. 'Oh, Mercy!' the forty-two-year-old Lady Warwick exclaimed on realising that she was once again pregnant; and Mercy was the name that she gave to her daughter. But to Mercy, Daisy was able to give even less attention than she had to her other children. The girl was left in the care of nurses while the mother went off to campaign on behalf of those other mothers with a dozen children and no food, let alone nurses.

One of the ways in which Daisy Warwick differed from Lillie Langtry was that she had no head for figures. By 1907, at the age of forty-five, she was experiencing considerable financial difficulties. Short of money and harried by creditors, she was obliged to sell off properties and close down some of her charitable institutions. There was, of course, one way by which she could have recouped her losses: by writing her memoirs. It was at this time, she says, that she was 'approached with offers of very large sums of money'[15] for her reminiscences. This is hardly surprising. As the one-time mistress of the reigning sovereign, the intimate friend of many prominent men, the lover of many others, a celebrated society hostess, a fashionably dressed beauty, a repository of a great deal of gossip and a peeress who had become a socialist, Daisy Warwick had more than enough material to write a bestseller.

But she resisted the temptation. With almost all her circle, including Edward VII, still alive, the undertaking would be fraught with difficulties; and no publisher was going to advance her those 'very large sums of money' for a compilation of tame social chit-chat and tedious socialistic moralising. The idea was shelved. Times would have to become more difficult still before Lady Warwick would be ready to convert her secrets into hard cash.

Another setting against which Edward VII's love affair with Mrs Keppel was played out was Paris. The Biarritz holiday over, the King and the Keppels would move on to the French capital. Here, with Edward VII in his usual suite at the Hotel Bristol, Alice and her family would stay in Sir Ernest Cassel's spacious apartment in the Rue du Cirque. In Paris Alice Keppel, like Lillie Langtry and Daisy Warwick before her, was able to shop at Worth.

'I have vivid memories of the first time I accompanied my mother to the dressmaker, where she was received like a goddess,' writes Violet Keppel, 'Monsieur Jean (Worth) supervising her fitting in person, the *vendeuses* quite shamelessly forsaking their other clients to vie with each other in flattering epithets. *Il y avait de quoi.* My mother had everything that could most appeal to them, lovely, vivacious, fêted, fashionable, with a kind word for each of the anonymous old crones who had been for years in the establishment . . .'[16]

And although Violet does not say so, her mother's chief attraction for these fluttering *vendeuses* was her status as *la maîtresse du Roi*.

Again, like her predecessors, Alice would be taken to Edward VII's favourite Parisian restaurants. But whereas in his days as Prince of Wales, he could occasionally give his French detectives the slip, now he was kept under close and constant surveillance. Yet knowing how much the King hated to be watched, this surveillance was kept as discreet as possible. On one occasion the King, Mrs Keppel and a party of friends were lunching in a garden restaurant at St Cloud. As they sat there in the leaf-dappled sunlight, Alice, always concerned about her lover's well-being, became more and more nervous about the apparent lack of police protection. Eventually she confided her fears to one of the King's secretaries, Frederick Ponsonby. Anyone, she whispered, could come in through the open garden gate; the diners on either side of the royal table looked very suspicious; one of them had a particularly 'villainous' face. She felt sure that the police had been given the wrong name of the restaurant at which the King would be lunching and that he was now at the mercy of any assassin.

To set her mind at rest, Ponsonby went to seek out the manager of the place. On his way he spotted M. Lépine – head of the French police and responsible for the monarch's safety – calmly eating his own *déjeuner*. To Lépine Ponsonby repeated Mrs Keppel's fears about the unguarded gate and the diners close to His Majesty's table. Lépine was able to reassure him. The gardener working beside the open gate was a policeman. The diners on either side of the royal table were policemen with their wives. The diner with the particularly villainous face was 'one of the best and most trusted detectives in the force'.[17]

Returning to the table, Ponsonby whispered to Alice that all was well and, after luncheon, was able to tell her what Lépine had said. She was both highly amused and deeply impressed.

Alice Keppel's position as royal favourite brought her into contact with many notable people who might not, in other circumstances, have befriended her. One of these was the ex-Empress Eugenie. By now in her eighties, the Empress remained an alert and forceful personality. Once, while Alice was staying at a hotel in Fontainebleau, her maid burst into her room.

'Madam! Madam!' cried the girl. 'The wife of Napoleon the First is waiting to see you downstairs; she says she has only just discovered you were staying here.'

The reason why the wife of the late Napoleon the *Third* had called on Mrs Keppel was to suggest that they join the guided tour of the nearby palace. Alice was intrigued. Was it insensitivity, or curiosity to hear the republican version of Napoleonic history, that was prompting the Empress to revisit the palace where she had once held court?

Unrecognised, the black-clad Empress, with Alice Keppel in tow, joined the group as they followed the guide through the sumptuous rooms. In the salon in which Napoleon I had signed his Act of Abdication, the guide held up a pen and declared, 'And this is the pen he used.'

'*Pardon, Monsieur,* you make a mistake,' interrupted the Empress. Stepping forward, she crossed to the desk, pressed an invisible spring and from a secret drawer which leapt out, produced a pen.

'This, I happen to know, is the pen His Imperial Majesty used,'[18] she announced to the astonished tourists.

If one reason for Eugenie's friendship with Alice Keppel was that the old Empress delighted in the company of lively and good-looking young women, another was that she was devoted to Edward VII. His championship of the French imperial family, through good times and bad, had never wavered; for this the Empress was deeply grateful. Eugenie was always made welcome at Edward VII's court and if the two of them happened to be in Paris at the same time, the King never failed to call on the Empress.

There were times, though, when their shared passion for travelling incognito had its drawbacks. One day, on calling at the Empress's hotel, the King asked the clerk at the desk if the Comtesse de Pierrefonds would receive the Duke of Lancaster.

'Wait a moment,' answered the unsuspecting clerk, 'I am sorting the mail.'

After a minute or two, the King could contain himself no longer. With a voice like thunder he demanded, *'Sa Majesté l'Impératrice Eugenie peut-elle recevoir le Roi d'Angleterre?'*[19]

He was shown up immediately.

After a week together in Paris, the King and Mrs Keppel would separate: she to return to her husband in London, he to join Queen Alexandra on a spring cruise in the Mediterranean. In the course of these annual cruises, Edward VII would meet his fellow sovereigns: sometimes Alfonso XIII of Spain, sometimes Victor Emmanuel III of Italy, invariably Queen Alexandra's brother, George I of the Hellenes.

It was because of these long periods abroad (he never spent less than a quarter of each year on the Continent or cruising its waters) that Edward VII came to be so closely identified with Europe. With his life-long interest in the politics, diplomacy and richly varied way of life of the Continent, the King had been able to establish a great many social and political contacts and to accumulate a considerable knowledge of European affairs. This he could now put to good use.

Always interested in foreign affairs – which, at the time, meant European affairs – Edward VII was passionately concerned with the momentous shift that was taking place in British foreign policy: the abandonment of its position of 'splendid isolation' and its commitment to Europe. He not only presided over, but actively encouraged, his country's new series of alliances: the *entente cordiale* with France, the agreement with Spain, the convention with Russia. Indeed, the Triple Entente, by which Britain became allied to France and Russia, was generally regarded as 'the triumph of King Edward's policy'.[20]

Although the King was in no position to initiate any of these policies, his ministers found him invaluable when it came to making the first advance or creating a sympathetic atmosphere. By a series of magnificent state visits – and no monarch enjoyed a full-blown state visit more than Edward VII – he was able to prepare public opinion for some proposed agreement or set the seal on some convention already signed.

Who, as they watched the lavishly uniformed, self-confident King of England passing in spectacular cavalcade through the streets of Paris or Berlin or Rome, could doubt that he was a figure of considerable international importance? And who, as they saw him in earnest conversation with some foreign statesman or diplomat beneath the pleached linden trees of some spa, could deny that he was discussing a point of great political significance?

And despite the fact that King Edward VII was never as powerful, influential or even astute a figure as was popularly imagined, he came to be regarded as a supreme royal diplomat – 'The Peacemaker of Europe' or, even more fulsomely, as 'The Arbiter of Europe's Destiny'.

To what extent was Alice Keppel fulfilling the political role to which Daisy Warwick had once aspired? Alice's social and sexual contributions to Edward VII's well-being were only too apparent; it was her political usefulness that was more difficult to assess. Indeed, with the political position of a British constitutional monarch being a somewhat nebulous one, any political influence on such a monarch must of necessity be more nebulous still.

That great analyst of the British constitution, Walter Bagehot, once defined the monarch's three rights as the right to be consulted, the right to encourage and the right to warn. The extent to which these rights are exercised depends very much on the individual monarch. Some monarchs are more assertive than others, some more politically aware, some more experienced. A sovereign such as Queen Elizabeth II, who has reigned for over thirty-five years, not unnaturally develops into a person of undeniable influence and authority.

At his first Privy Council, Edward VII had announced that he was 'fully determined to be a constitutional sovereign in the strict sense of the word'.[21] He was equally determined, though, not to be anything less. The King was very conscious of his rights: any minister who ignored these soon earned the rough edge of the monarch's tongue. He insisted on being kept fully informed on every matter, great or small. He was not going to be 'a mere signing machine'.[22]

Although the King applied himself, with all the conscientiousness of his nature, to his daily work on the 'boxes', it was in the course of his regular meetings, usually with prime ministers but sometimes with other political figures, that he was able to bring his influence to bear. He in turn was influenced and advised by a number of people, principally by his private secretary, Francis Knollys, but also by a coterie of close associates which included, of course, Alice Keppel.

In politics Alice Keppel, in common with a surprising number of others close to the King, was a Liberal. 'To be a Liberal in high society is rare,' declared Margot Asquith, whose husband became Liberal prime minister in 1908, 'indeed I often wonder in what society they are to be found; I do not meet them among golfers, soldiers, sailors or servants; nor have I seen much Liberalism in the Church, the Court or the City; but Alice Keppel was born in Scotland and has remained a true Liberal.'[23]

Alice's Liberalism was not merely tribal. It could manifest itself in very practical ways. On one occasion, for instance, she taught her Portman Square neighbour, the wealthy Lord Alington, a salutory political lesson. Lord Alington, who greatly admired her and delighted in being seen in her company, used often to take Alice driving – to Hampton Court or Richmond Park in the summer and to picture galleries or exhibitions in the winter. One day, on asking her where she would like to go, she suggested Hoxton. Hoxton, in East London, was then a notorious slum: a slum in which Lord Alington, who had never seen it, owned a great deal of property.

The drive was anything but entertaining. As Lord Alington's smart carriage passed along the dingy streets, it was jeered, or stared sullenly at, by wretchedly-dressed children and dull-eyed men and women. Through the occasionally open doorways were glimpses of depressing squalor. 'Many of the window-frames had lost their glass, and the holes had been stuffed up with old rags or newspaper or just left empty,' reported Alice. 'The afternoon was cold and rather foggy, and few of the chimneys boasted smoke.'

It was an extremely chastened and embarrassed Lord Alington who finally dropped Alice at her home three hours later. 'I do think it was charming of you to let me see Hoxton as it is *now*,' said Alice meaningfully. 'Next time I go there I shan't recognise it.'[24]

The value of such gestures is difficult to assess; with a man like Lord Alington, who knew that Mrs Keppel had the ear of the King, they could have been considerable.

A lesser woman than Alice might well have used her unique position as the King's confidante to press her own views or to make political mischief. But being both astute and good-natured, such influence as she was able to exert on her royal lover was always beneficial. The remarkable tribute paid to her by Charles Hardinge, permanent head of the Foreign Office and later, as Lord Hardinge of

Penshurst, Viceroy of India, is worth quoting in full.

'I take this opportunity to allude to a delicate matter upon which I am in a position to speak with authority,' he wrote in a private memorandum soon after King Edward VII's death. 'Everybody knew of the friendship that existed between King Edward and Mrs George Keppel, which was intelligible in view of the lady's good looks, vivacity and cleverness. I used to see a great deal of Mrs Keppel at that time, and I was aware that she had knowledge of what was going on in the political world.

'I would like here to pay a tribute to her wonderful discretion, and to the excellent influence which she always exercised upon the King. She never utilised her knowledge to her own advantage, or to that of her friends; and I never heard her repeat an unkind word of anybody. There were one or two occasions when the King was in disagreement with the Foreign Office, and I was able, through her, to advise the King with a view to the policy of the Government being accepted. She was very loyal to the King, and patriotic at the same time.

'It would have been difficult to find any other lady who would have filled the part of friend to King Edward with the same loyalty and discretion.'[25]

Herbert Asquith, when he became Liberal Prime Minister in 1908 and had to take the unprecedented step of travelling to Biarritz in order to kiss hands in the Hotel du Palais (a step for which the King was widely criticised: the monarch should have received his new Prime Minister in Britain) was similarly grateful to Alice Keppel. In a letter written to her after his return from Biarritz, he thanked her for 'your kind words and wise counsels, which I shall treasure and (I hope) profit by'.[26] One may be sure that, if nothing else, Alice would have advised Asquith on how to handle the King.

Often, Edward VII would ask Alice Keppel to do a little diplomatic scouting on his behalf; or she might decide to do some reconnoitring of her own. In 1907 Kaiser Wilhelm II, having paid a state visit to King Edward VII, prolonged his stay with a visit to Highcliffe Castle on the Isle of Wight. Count Mensdorff, the Austro-Hungarian ambassador, was staying at nearby Crichel Down as a member of another large house party which included, as he puts it, 'La favorita Keppel with her "lady-in-waiting", Lady Sarah Wilson [Lord Randolph Churchill's sister]'. One evening the Kaiser came over to dinner.

In spite of Wilhelm II's imperviousness to feminine charm in general and his aversion to Edward VII's mistresses in particular, and with a complete disregard for all rules of precedence, the Kaiser found that Mrs Keppel had been placed beside him at table. Only at the express wish of Edward VII would this extraordinary *placement* ever have been considered. 'The *Favorita* was seated next to the Kaiser,' decided Mensdorff, 'so she might have the opportunity of talking to him. I would love to know what sort of report she sent back to Sandringham!'[27]

On another occasion Mensdorff, having discussed the latest Balkan crisis with Alice Keppel at yet another house party, was disconcerted to find himself taken to task a couple of days later by Sir Edward Grey, the British Foreign Secretary, for what Grey considered to be Mensdorff's prejudiced opinion on the subject. Quite clearly, Alice had lost no time in reporting the conversation to the King; or the King in reporting it to Grey.

Yet Alice Keppel always denied that she was *au fait* with confidential political matters. She realised that this would be constitutionally improper. Years later, when Margot Asquith published her book 'More Memories', she was roundly attacked by Alice for having given the impression that Alice had been the late Edward VII's political confidante. She had never been told a cabinet secret in her life, declared Alice hotly, and Margot's assertions had 'got her into endless trouble with George V'.[28]

'Kingy was such a Wonderful Man'

EDWARD VII might have been devoted to Alice Keppel but he was certainly not faithful to her. The habits of a lifetime's philandering could not be changed overnight. The King was too old and licentious a dog to learn any new tricks of fidelity now; he continued to take his pleasures wherever and whenever he found them. And Alice, as a woman of the world who was fond of, but not in love with, the ageing libertine, let him have as much rein as he wanted.

In his sixties, the King's interest in the opposite sex was undimmed. 'Night after night as I sat in my stall at the opera and saw him coming into the omnibus box and taking up his opera glasses to survey the glittering women in the first and ground tier boxes,' remembers Robert Hitchens, 'I saw a man who looked, I thought, extremely genial and satisfied with his position in the scheme of the world.'[1]

As well he might be. In the majority of cases the King needed only to find out the name of some beauty who had caught his eye for a subsequent meeting to be arranged. There was even an occasion when the beauty who had captured the royal interest was not of the opposite sex. Prince Felix Youssoupoff who, a decade later, was to become famous as the murderer of Rasputin, was generally regarded as one of the most beautiful young men of his day. One evening at the Théâtre des Capucines in Paris, as he sat in the stalls dressed as a woman (he always, he assures us, dressed as a schoolboy by day and as 'an elegant woman' by night) Youssoupoff noticed an elderly gentleman in a box eyeing him persistently. When the lights went up for the interval, he saw that his admirer was King Edward VII. Yousoupoff's brother Nicholas, who had accompanied him to the theatre, came back from smoking a cigarette in the foyer with the news that he had been approached by one of the King's equerries: His Majesty wished to know the name of the lovely young woman he was escorting.

'I must confess,' says Youssoupoff, 'that this conquest amused me enormously and greatly flattered my vanity.'[2]

If, as a monarch, Edward VII had to behave with rather more circumspection at home than he had as Prince of Wales, no such considerations inhibited him when he travelled abroad. It was true that on his various cruises Queen Alexandra was able to keep an eye on him, and at Biarritz Alice Keppel could do the same; but during his late summer sojourn at Marienbad and during his frequent stays in Paris, the King flung himself into amorous adventures with as much gusto as ever. 'I got so mixed up with the King's incessant gaieties, for which his energy and appetite are alike insatiable,' complained Sir Henry Campbell Bannerman, the Liberal Prime Minister, from Marienbad, 'that it was no rest or holiday for me. Thus when at last he was gone . . . my Dr ordered me to bed and absolute rest for forty-eight hours.'[3]

For the King's equerries, it was worse. They never knew who His Majesty was going to take up next. Amongst what one observer calls the 'semi-déclassé ladies'[4] were an overblown Parisian adventuress married to a bogus Baron years younger than herself; Mrs Dale Lace with 'short skirts and a murky past';[5] Mrs Hall Walker who would prepare her hotel room for the King's afternoon visits by filling the vases with flowers, spraying the air with scent and, most important of all, drawing the curtains. Then there was a Mrs X whom he would either visit in her Marienbad home or else drive out to the Café Nimrod, tucked away in the woods. For this particular excursion he would dispense even with an equerry; it would be left to a single Austrian policeman to plod among the dripping trees while the King of England took his pleasure within.

The American actress Maxine Elliot, realising that it would be almost impossible to meet the King socially in London, decided to go to Marienbad instead. Exquisitely dressed, she sat decorously one morning reading her book on a bench in the *Kreuzbrunnen*. As the King and his entourage passed by on their way to the Kurhaus for their first glass of mineral water, she glanced up. His Majesty glanced back. The party strolled on but within a few minutes one of the King's companions returned with a message for Miss Elliot. His Majesty would be delighted with her presence at a dinner party that evening; a formal invitation would, of course, be delivered to her hotel later. Miss Elliot was only too delighted to accept.

Their association blossomed and after a further visit to Marienbad the following year, Miss Elliot felt so confident of the King's interest that she bought herself a house outside London. At considerable expense she prepared a suite of rooms above her own which she would always refer to as 'the King's suite'.[6]

Even more worrying for Edward VII's staff was the sort of public escapade that could so easily get into the newspapers. He once asked for the English dancer, Maud Allen, to perform at a dinner party to be given in his honour. As Miss Allen usually appeared wearing only 'two oyster shells and a five-franc piece'[7] his entourage was understandably apprehensive. But as in those days journalists could be trusted to keep royal secrets if asked to do so, the newspaper corps were sworn to secrecy and the performance went ahead. His Majesty, by all accounts, was enraptured by Miss Allen's only too obvious talents, and no word of the entertainment found its way into the press.

Yet there were limits, it seems, even to Edward VII's taste for titillation. He once walked out of a theatre during a skit about a licentious countess who entices a monk to take off his robes. It was not so much that he was shocked: he felt that he should not have been publicly exposed to such smut. And on another occasion he again left the theatre during a performance of lewd songs by a touring Viennese cabaret company. This time, the King had been more bored than outraged.

When news of the King's walk-out reached England, the Bishop of Ripon felt moved to write him a fulsome letter of congratulation for having taken a public stand against obscenity. But the King was no hypocrite. When his secretary asked him how he should reply to the Bishop's letter, Edward VII said, 'Tell the Bishop the exact truth. I have no wish to pose as a protector of morals, especially abroad.'[8]

Paris, so long the King's happy hunting ground, had by now been rendered somewhat less happy because of that increased emphasis on security by the French police. His clandestine meeting with one beauty in the Jardin des Plantes was completely spoiled when His Majesty recognised one of the plain-clothes policemen who had been assigned to keep an eye on him. The King was furious. It was absurd, he thundered, that 'in Paris of all places'[9] he should be shadowed. But any subterfuge to evade the police – such as publicly ordering his car for four o'clock and then secretly sending for it at three – was in vain; the police never let him out of their sight.

There were other ways, though, of enjoying feminine company without police surveillance. One evening, while staying incognito at the Hotel Meurice, the King returned to the hotel early to find his equerry, Arthur Paget, in the dining room with an attractive young woman. The King promptly joined them.

'Dear boy,' he said to Paget over coffee, 'I have worked you much too hard today; go and get some rest.'

'I am feeling fine, Sir,' replied the uncomprehending equerry.

Over cognac the King tried again. 'You are looking *very* tired,' he said.

'But I can assure you, Your Majesty . . .' persisted Paget.

The King ordered a second cognac. 'I *advise* you to go up to bed immediately,'[10] he commanded.

This time Paget understood. Hastily draining his cognac he disappeared, leaving the King alone with his conquest.

There are countless other anecdotes. Two more will suffice. As late as 1940 a faded Edwardian beauty, the half-French Mrs Hope Vere, would sometimes astonish her listeners with a casual remark like, 'One morning the King said to me, "Put on your dressing gown and come and watch the squadron passing." '[11] And an officer on board the royal yacht once heard, as he walked past the porthole of the King's cabin, the monarch's guttural voice saying, 'Stop calling me Sir and put another cushion under your back.'[12]

Hand-in-hand with these stories of Edward VII's insatiable sexual appetite goes the recently revealed theory that he was impotent during the last years of his life. In his secret diary, Wilfrid Scawen Blunt reports a conversation he had with the courtesan Skittles on the subject. Blunt had asked her if the King's death, in 1910, had had anything to do with sexual overindulgence. 'Oh no,' answered Skittles, 'the King has been impotent for the last fifteen years.'[13] As an ex-lover and life-long friend of Edward VII (for years the King had written to her, paid her an annual allowance and, when she was ill, arranged for his doctor to attend her) she was probably in a position to know. In fact, the King regarded his letters to Skittles as so confidential that, when it was thought she might be dying of cancer in 1908, he sent his private secretary, Francis Knollys, to collect and destroy three hundred of them.

Skittles's contention seems to be borne out by something which the Archbishop of Canterbury, Randall Davidson, once told the Earl of Crawford and Balcarres. The King's affair with Alice Keppel, believed the Archbishop, had always been platonic. His Majesty indicated this by 'always placing her beside the Archbishop at table: something he would never have done if she had, as generally supposed, been his mistress. It would have been an insult to the Church and utterly unlike him.' The subtlety of this approach, said the Archbishop, 'was very characteristic of the King'.[14]

On the other hand, it might not have been nearly as subtle as His Grace imagined. It may be true that by the last years of the King's life his affair with Alice Keppel had become platonic (just as his affair with Daisy Warwick had been platonic in its last stages) but his high regard for Alice's intelligence and a determination not to slight her might have provided stronger reasons for placing her beside the Archbishop, just as he had placed her beside the Kaiser. Nor could all those well-documented and widely discussed stories of his amorousness have been pure invention; surely, for instance, he did not go to such extraordinary lengths to evade the police in order to enjoy nothing more exciting than a little polite conversation?

Impotence, of course, can mean many things. If Edward VII was indeed impotent, one can only assume that his impotence was of the type in which erection, but not ejaculation, is possible.

There was certainly no suggestion of impotence in earlier days. In later life Lillie Langtry once repeated an exchange between her royal lover and herself which leaves the question of his virility in no doubt.

'I've spent enough on you to buy a battleship,' he complained to Lillie.

'And you've spent enough in me to float one,'[15] came her deft reply.

But an apocryphal story going the rounds towards the end of Edward VII's life seems to bear out the rumours of his particular type of impotence. At Cowes the King and Mrs Keppel had retired to the cabin of the royal yacht for an after-luncheon siesta. Suddenly steps were heard on the companionway.

'Pst, there's someone coming,' whispered the King.

'Well,' answered Alice, 'it's certainly not Your Majesty.'[16]

In October 1908 Lillie Langtry, or, as she was now styled, Lady de Bathe, turned fifty-five. Although still an exceptionally handsome and stylishly dressed woman, she was beginning to look matronly: her air was assertive, imperious, almost intimidating. Except for the occasional British or American tour, her stage career was virtually over. She might still deport herself like a famous actress but she now tended to divide her time between various hotels on the Riviera, which she loved, and Regal Lodge, her home near Newmarket. Racing remained her great passion. It remained, also, her one link with Edward VII. In fact, their shared interest in the turf was responsible for their last intimate meeting.

On 26 May 1909, the King's horse Minoru won the Derby. Having won the Derby twice before, the King was overjoyed by this third victory. The crowds were hardly less ecstatic. To a spontaneous singing of 'God Save the King', followed by frantic shouts of 'Good old Teddy! Teddy boy! Hurrah! Hurrah!' a beaming Edward VII led in his horse. In some ways, it was the happiest day of his life.

Yet just over a month later, Lillie, at Regal Lodge, received a telephone call from Richard Marsh, the King's trainer at nearby Egerton House. Could he come and see her at once? On arriving, he told her that Lord Marcus Beresford, who managed the King's stables, had received a curt note from His Majesty to say that he intended to shut up Egerton and move all his horses to Blackwells, a training establishment in Newmarket itself. And this in spite of the fact that Minoru had been trained at Egerton. Nothing that either Beresford or Marsh could say would make him change his mind. Marsh was in despair: the King's racing stables at Egerton were his whole life. Could Lillie speak to His Majesty about it?

She demurred. Surely there were others who could argue more forcefully? 'They know nothing of racing,' answered Marsh, 'and have no influence in that direction.' She promised to do what she could.

At the July meeting at Newmarket she met the King in the Jockey Club enclosure. Tactfully, she raised the subject of his proposed move. 'As I expected,' she says, 'he shut me up.' But he did suggest that he visit her at Regal Lodge the following day.

Having inspected the various improvements that Lillie had made to the house since his visit the year before, they retired to her boudoir. Amongst its chintzy and lacy furnishings and over a bottle of chilled hock and a dish of peaches, Lillie plucked up the courage to discuss the forbidden subject, 'as sportsman to sportsman'. He explained that the Egerton establishment had become too expensive; he would save hundreds a year by moving to Blackwells.

Employing all the charm that had melted his heart over thirty years before, and the common sense that could impress him still, Lillie set out to persuade him not to move. He would lose, she argued, not only the advantages of those private gallops which had helped Minoru win the Derby but also his own privacy whenever he visited his stables. Against these considerations, the saving of a few hundred pounds would count for very little.

In the end, she convinced him. He went home to tell Marsh that he could remain at Egerton.

That afternoon on the course, Lillie met Beresford and Marsh. Both were beaming. 'You're a brick!'[17] exclaimed Beresford.

As always with Edward VII, a woman's word had carried most weight.

With Daisy Warwick, too, there was to be one last meeting. She saw her old lover for the last time early in 1910. This was in the London home of her brother-in-law, the Duke of Sutherland. 'It was a sad interview,' she says, 'for I was shocked at the change in the King.'[18] He complained of the effect of the influenza injections he had been given; they made him feel ill and depressed. Usually the two of them would discuss current events and the latest gossip, but on this occasion his mind seemed filled with thoughts of the past. He spoke about Paris in the days – over twenty years before – when he had first taken her there. 'All the glamour has gone,' he sighed. 'I don't mind if I never cross the Channel again.'[19] Every second sentence, claims Daisy, seemed to start with the words 'Do you remember?'[20]

The King was due to dine at the home of an American friend that evening but when the worried Daisy tried to dissuade him from going, he would not hear of it. 'How I wish I could give it up,' he said, 'but I do shrink from disappointing my host.'[21] That, says Daisy, was very typical.

One of the most persistent myths adding lustre to the saga of the British royal family is about Queen Alexandra sending for Mrs Keppel to bid the dying King Edward VII goodbye. Rising, claims one of Alexandra's biographers, 'to the full height of her generous nature',[22] the Queen arranged – during one of her husband's conscious moments – for Mrs Keppel to go alone into the sickroom to see the King for the last time. What, generations of royal historians have asked, could have been nobler, more self-sacrificing than that?

The truth is rather different. A refutation of this touching scene has now come from two independent sources: the private papers of Viscount Esher, who was in the palace the day the King died, and the unpublished secret diary of Wilfrid Scawen Blunt, who had the story from Skittles who, in turn, had it from the King's doctor, Sir Francis Laking.

Before the King set off on his annual jaunt with Alice Keppel to Biarritz on 6 March 1910, he appears to have had an altercation with the Queen: 'It was about Mrs Keppel and the affront put on [the Queen] by his going openly with her . . .'[23] But as the King had no intention of denying himself the pleasure of Alice's company, the couple set off, separately as always, for Biarritz. Edward VII travelled – again, as usual – by way of Paris. Here, after sitting in an overheated theatre to see Edmond Rostand's new play *Chantecler* ('I never saw anything more stupid and childish,'[24] he reported to his son, Prince George) he caught a chill. But never one to let his health stand in the way of his pleasures, the King continued on his social round and arrived in Biarritz on 9 March.

Within a few days he had caught another chill and was confined to his rooms at the Hotel du Palais. 'The King's cold is so bad that he can't dine out,' wrote Alice to the Marquis de Soveral, who was also in Biarritz, 'but he wants us all to dine with him at 8.15 at the Palais, SO BE THERE.

'I am quite worried *entre nous* and have sent for the nurse . . .'[25]

But after a week, with Alice constantly in and out, he felt better and was able to enjoy his customary walks and drives. Queen Alexandra wrote suggesting that he leave 'that horrid Biarritz'[26] – by which she undoubtedly meant that horrid Mrs Keppel – and join her on a Mediterranean cruise in the new royal yacht 'Alexandra'. For many reasons, not least because he had to be close to home to deal with a threatened political crisis concerning a conflict between the House of Commons and the House of Lords, the King refused. So Alexandra, accompanied by her unmarried and long-suffering daughter, Princess Victoria, set off without him. She made for Corfu. Here, as the guest of her brother, King George of the Hellenes, she was able to enjoy one of those unsophisticated family holidays in which she revelled.

As the King was not, in fact, obliged to hurry home for political reasons, he remained in Biarritz for almost seven weeks. He seemed loath to leave. By his side, during all those picnics, race-meetings, drives and excursions (there was even a visit to Lourdes) was Alice Keppel. It was the longest continuous period that they had ever spent in each other's company: was it rendered even sweeter by the King's premonition that it might be the last? He was certainly in a strange mood on the day that he finally left Biarritz. Going out onto his balcony he stood gazing at the familiar view across the promenade and out to the shimmering sea. 'I shall be sorry to leave Biarritz,' he sighed, 'perhaps for good.'[27]

He arrived back in England on 27 April. For the following nine days, in spite of having caught another chill, which turned to bronchitis, while inspecting some alterations at Sandringham, he insisted on carrying on as usual. Nothing could undermine that ingrained sense of duty. He granted audiences, he worked at his papers, he fulfilled various social obligations. On the evening of 2 May he dined out and played bridge with Alice Keppel and 'the Keyser girls'[28] – Agnes Keyser and her sister. But he looked so ill – so grey-faced, so short of breath, so racked by coughing – that Alice insisted that he go home to bed at half-past ten.

He would not leave the palace alive again. By now the doctors were so worried that they had sent for the Queen. She and Princess Victoria came hurrying back from Corfu and arrived home on the evening of 5 May. Only on seeing her shrunken husband did Alexandra appreciate how ill he was. That same night the country was told that the King was ill with bronchitis and that his condition was causing some anxiety.

By the following morning – Friday 6 May 1910, the last day of his life – the King was much worse. Yet he insisted on being dressed in formal clothes and on receiving various people. Sir Ernest Cassel came at noon and the King, who realised by now that he was dying, discussed what the circumspect Cassel describes as 'other matters'[29] – presumably the private financial arrangements to be made, not least for Alice, after the King's death.

During the afternoon the King, still sitting fully dressed in an armchair, suffered a series of heart attacks. But he refused to go to bed. 'No, I shall not give in,' he protested. 'I shall go on: I shall work to the end.'[30]

It is from this point on that the generally accepted accounts of Edward VII's last hours are at variance with what actually happened. Queen Alexandra did not, in a gesture of touching magnanimity, send for Alice Keppel to take leave of the King. According to the royal doctor, Sir Francis Laking, who was in constant attendance that day, Alice had been in and out of the palace until the Queen's arrival home and had since sent Alexandra the letter which the King had written to her at the time of his appendix operation in 1902: it was the letter in which he had said that 'if he were dying, he felt sure that those about him would allow her to come to him.'[31] That, combined with the King's request that Alice be sent for, is what forced the reluctant Queen into agreeing that Mrs Keppel should be summoned.

There now followed an extraordinary scene. On arrival, the distraught Alice curtseyed to the Queen and Princess Victoria and was then asked by the King to sit down beside him. Stroking her hand, he told her not to cry. Calling to Alexandra, who was standing at the window with her back to this little tableau, the King said, 'You must kiss her. You must kiss Alice.' Fighting down, one imagines, her distaste, the Queen presented her cheek to Mrs Keppel, although she was afterwards to deny that she had done any such thing. Both women then sat down beside the King. His mind, says Laking, was by now beginning to wander. He began fumbling for his false teeth and seemed uneasy at not having them in. Suddenly, quite forgetting that he was in the company of the Queen, Princess Victoria and Mrs Keppel, he said, 'I want to p ——.'

'What is that he said?' demanded the deaf Alexandra.

'He is asking Ma'am for a pencil,' was Laking's adroit reply.

Mercifully, at this point, the King slumped into another bout of unconsciousness. Getting up, Alexandra drew Laking aside and hissed, 'Get that woman away.'[32]

This was easier said than done. By now Alice Keppel was hysterical. Nothing would induce her to leave the side of her dying lover. Only on being told, very firmly, that His Majesty had asked to be left alone with the Queen, did the demented Alice allow herself to be led out by Princess Victoria. Shrieking at the top of her voice for 'all the pages and footmen in the passage' to hear, Alice kept repeating, 'I never did any harm, there was nothing wrong between us. What is to become of me?' All Princess Victoria's efforts to soothe her were hopeless; in 'a wild fit of hysterics' Alice was carried into Frederick Ponsonby's room. She remained there for several hours.

'Altogether,' wrote an indignant Lord Esher, 'it was a painful and rather theatrical exhibition, and ought never to have happened.'[33] It must also have been an extremely macabre one.

King Edward VII died just before midnight. He was in his sixty-ninth year.

When it was over Alexandra, 'in a terrible state of despair', blurted out her feelings about Mrs Keppel, and about the King, to Sir Francis Laking.

'I would not have kissed her,' she said, 'if he had not bade me. But I would have done anything he asked of me. Twelve [sic] years ago, when I was so angry about Lady Warwick, and the King expostulated with me and said I should get him into the divorce court, I told him once for all that he might have all the women he wished, and I would not say a word; and I have done everything since that he desired me to do about them. He was the whole of my life and, now he is dead, nothing matters.'[34]

And Lord Esher, invited by Alexandra to take a last look at her husband's body a few days later, has some interesting observations to make on her attitude to the King's death. He notes, 'The Queen talked for half an hour, just as she always talked to me, with only a slight diminution of her natural gaiety, but with a tenderness which betrayed all the love in her soul, and oh! so natural feeling that she had got him there *altogether to herself* [author's italics]. In a way she seemed, and is, I am convinced, happy. It is the womanly happiness of complete possession of the man who was the love of her youth, and – as I fervently believe – all her life.'[35]

After all, Alexandra is reputed to have said to a friend after Edward VII's death, 'he always loved me the best.'[36]

As for the legend about her saintly gesture towards Alice Keppel: how did that originate? Not with the Queen. Not even with those devoted members of her entourage who were always anxious for 'the beloved lady' to be presented in the best possible light. It originated with Alice Keppel.

Once her lover had died, Alice, in an effort to safeguard her future, had hurried to Marlborough House to sign her name in the book. But the new monarchs, King George V and Queen Mary, were having none of her: 'orders had been given that she should not be allowed to do so . . .'[37] Seeing the way the wind was blowing, the astute Alice put about the story of how the all-forgiving Queen had summoned her to the dying King's bedside, of how Alexandra had 'fallen upon her neck and wept with her', and of how she had promised that the royal family would 'look after her'.

'Mrs Keppel,' declared Esher, who had heard the truth from Edward VII's secretary, Francis Knollys, 'has lied about the whole affair.'[38]

Among the hundreds of sanctimonious tributes heaped upon the head of the dead Edward VII, Wilfrid Scawen Blunt's comments strike a refreshingly honest note.

'Today,' runs the unexpurgated version of his diary entry for 20 May 1910, 'the King was buried and I hope the country will return to comparative sanity, for at present it is in delirium. The absurdities written in every newspaper about him pass belief. He might have been a Solon [the Greek Sage] and a Francis of Assisi combined if characters drawn of him were true. In no print has there been the slightest allusion to Mrs Keppel or to any of the 101 ladies he has loved, or to his gambling or to any of the little vices which made up his domestic life. It is not for me or perhaps any of us to censure him for these pleasant wickednesses, but his was not even in make-believe the life of a saint or of an at all virtuous or respectable man, and according to strict theology he is most certainly at the present moment in hell. Yet all the bishops and priests, Catholic, Protestant and Non-conformist, join in giving him a glorious place in heaven . . .'

Edward VII's particular qualities – his showmanship, his conscientiousness, his diplomatic achievements – 'doubtless made him a wiser and a better King than most of ours have been,' continues Blunt, 'and he may even rightly share with Solomon the title of the "Wise". They each had several hundred concubines and, as we know, "The knowledge of women is the beginning of wisdom". At least it teaches tolerance for the unwisdom of others.

'Of all this the newspaper writers say no word, being virtuous men and fools.'[39]

Having recovered her habitual composure, Alice recovered her habitual good sense. Her best bet would be to lie low. Overnight she and her husband left their Portman Square home to move in with friends in Grafton Street. The children followed a day or two later. The gossips lost no time in saying that she had had to flee her creditors; whereas, of course, Edward VII had left her very handsomely provided for. It was to escape publicity that Alice moved house.

Her youngest daughter, the nine-year-old Sonia, bewildered by the sudden flight from Portman Square and by her mother's abstracted air, appealed to her father for enlightenment. 'Why does it matter so much, Kingy dying?' she asked.

'Poor little girl,' answered George Keppel. 'It must have been very frightening for you. And for all of us, for that matter. Nothing will ever be quite the same again. Because Kingy was such a wonderful man.'[40]

At least Mrs Keppel received an invitation to the King's funeral. She went to it in full mourning 'like a widow',[41] reports Blunt; but she was obliged to slip into St George's Chapel by a side door. As discreet as she had ever been, Alice was determined to do nothing to upset the palace. When she invited a few old friends, Soveral among them, to dinner one evening, she took the precaution of dropping a line to Lady Knollys, wife of the late monarch's private secretary, to explain that she was *not* giving a 'dinner party': it was simply a matter of having a few people in for a quiet evening to talk about old times.

'How people can do anything I do not know,' she continued, 'for life with all its joys have [sic] come to a full stop, at least for me . . .'[42]

In the end, Alice decided that it would be best for her to get right out of the country: away from the embarrassments of her position, from the inevitable changes at court and in society, and from the all-too-obvious disapproval of the new sovereigns. She would travel to the Far East. She would stay away for at least as long as the official mourning period lasted. In fact, Alice Keppel was to be abroad, in Ceylon and China, for almost two years.

By the time they set out, Alice had regained much of her celebrated verve and sparkle. When her excited daughters wanted to know why they were going to Ceylon, her reply was richly typical.

'In my opinion,' she explained airily, 'no young lady's education is complete without a smattering of Tamil.'[43]

'A WELL-REMEMBERED FRIEND'

Memories for Sale

ONE DAY IN the mid-1960s the writer Theo Lang, visiting friends in Switzerland, was shown an old family deed box. In it, among a fusty accumulation of papers and photographs, was a bundle of envelopes and a couple of photographic plates. Coming across this dossier was, as Lang puts it, 'one of those lucky accidents which come as a rare bonus in a writer's life'.[1] For what he had uncovered were the carefully preserved details of a hitherto secret series of negotiations: the attempt by the Countess of Warwick to blackmail King George V.

By the summer of 1914, four years after the death of Edward VII, the fifty-two-year-old Daisy Warwick was in a desperate financial plight. Her debts – to a variety of moneylenders and friends – amounted to something like £90,000. She had had to talk her husband into letting Warwick Castle, both the Warwick and Easton estates were heavily mortgaged and her valuables had been either sold or impounded. Her various, and increasingly frenetic, money-making schemes had all proved abortive. Not by writing scripts for the cinema, producing weekly columns for the *Daily Express*, editing women's pages for the *Daily Sketch* or giving lectures in the United States was she able to keep her persistent creditors at bay. Her long-suffering husband, the Earl of Warwick, was proving equally unsuccessful. His investments were disastrous; his grandiose schemes, for mining gold or growing timber, utterly impractical.

And as not even Lady Warwick, with her aristocratic disdain for vulgar moneylenders, could stave off impending bankruptcy forever (the full realisation of her predicament came, it seems, when a shopkeeper in Leamington finally refused to grant her any more credit) she decided that there was only one way by which she could save herself: she must make use of King Edward VII's love letters.

Valuable enough in themselves, these letters had been rendered even more valuable by virtue of the fact that, in his will, the late King had left instructions for all his private and personal correspondence to be destroyed. One knows that, even before his death, Edward VII had had all his letters to Skittles returned and burned (although his annual allowance to her continued after his death) and it was left to his two trusted associates, Lord Knollys and Lord Esher, to destroy everything that might be regarded as in any way compromising. Their lordships carried out their task with regrettable efficiency: all available traces of Edward VII's irregular private life were successfully obliterated.

Not that all the King's private correspondence was necessarily compromising. 'Do right by all men and don't write to any woman,'[2] Lillie Langtry used to say; and although Edward VII could not resist writing to his lady-loves, he usually had the good sense to keep these letters discreet and not to sign them with anything more revealing than a phrase like 'Your only love'. But by both the handwriting and the content, the letters were unmistakably his. Such of his letters as have survived – to Lillie Langtry and Alice Keppel – are innocuous enough: catalogues of the weather, the sport and the other members of the house party. Only the fact that they were written by, first, the heir apparent and then the monarch, to his women friends, makes them significant. But one may be sure that his more intimate letters to them were destroyed. Many years after Lillie Langtry's death, the writer Alison Adburgham came across an aged relation of Lillie's whose task it had been to burn a suitcase-full of Edward VII's love letters.

In 1914, though, Daisy Warwick still had all his letters to her. Addressed to his 'Darling Daisy Wife', they were not only love letters, rich in intimacies and endearments, but they were full of the sort of political information and comment that should never have been passed on by someone in his position. So what Lady Warwick had in her possession were letters which, having escaped the general conflagration after the King's death, were both rare and indiscreet.

Fully alive to the potential of these letters, Daisy, by the summer of 1914, had decided that she must use them to clear her £90,000 debt. But throughout the protracted and complicated negotiations which followed her decision, one clear fact emerges: unbeknown to all those with whom she had dealings, Lady Warwick had no intention of publishing these letters. What she was selling was not her secrets but her silence. Daisy wanted to be paid for *not* publishing her royal lover's letters. And the payment was to come from her lover's son, George V.

With consummate skill, Daisy put her plan into action. Her first approach was to that notorious contemporary figure, Frank Harris. By now this braggardly charlatan, his various literary adventures having failed, had been forced to leave England as an undischarged bankrupt and was living, as much by his wits as ever, in France. So when Lady Warwick suggested that he help her write her memoirs, Harris was all ears. Provided King Edward VII's letters were included, claimed Harris, he would be able to sell her memoirs for £100,000 in the United States alone. He, of course, would receive a share of the royalties.

Having had her letters thus valued, Daisy made her next move. She arranged a meeting with her financial adviser – and creditor – Arthur du Cros. No two men could have been less alike than Frank Harris and Arthur du Cros. A Conservative member of parliament, a millionaire, founder of the Dunlop Rubber Company and of the Junior Imperial League, du Cros was a model of integrity and respectability. He was also, as Lady Warwick well knew, a man of unquestioned loyalty to King and Country.

Arthur du Cros had recently lent Daisy £16,000 and it was his refusal to allow her any more time to pay the long overdue interest on his loan that led her to arrange a meeting with him. His insistence on payment, she claims, drove her to consider publishing her reminiscences.

It was, of course, nothing of the sort. By the time Daisy Warwick met Arthur du Cros in a borrowed house in Eaton Square on 25 June 1914, her plan of campaign was underway. Already, in her letter to du Cros suggesting the meeting, Daisy had hinted that she had in her possession certain information which, if made use of, would earn her £100,000. Du Cros had been sceptical. But his scepticism did not last long. Within a few minutes of meeting Lady Warwick, he was being told, as an 'understanding friend', that she had been forced into writing her autobiography in order to clear her debts. She realised that this would 'blast her reputation'[3] but what else could she do?

Du Cros needed only to be shown one of Edward VII's letters, and to be told that the notorious Frank Harris would be collaborating with Lady Warwick on the project, for him to become seriously alarmed. Had she considered the harm which the publication of the letters would do to 'the interests of the Royal Family and the nation'?[4] She had. But had the Royal Family and the nation ever considered her? That she was in such a dire financial predicament was entirely due, she said unblinkingly, to the fact that she had had to spend so much money on entertaining her royal lover and his circle.

Du Cros advised delay. That would be impossible, countered Daisy. Her creditors would wait no longer and she was due to meet Frank Harris in Paris in ten days' time to finalise the deal. At least then, begged du Cros, let him speak to someone about the matter. To this, with a great show of indifference, Daisy agreed. She had all along appreciated that du Cros was the sort of socially ambitious man who would be only too willing to be of service to the Crown. When du Cros left – headed, she had no doubt, for the palace – Daisy knew that her plan was working.

The worried du Cros went, if not exactly to the palace, to one of George V's equerries, the Earl of Albemarle, who happened to be, in this royal merry-go-round, a brother of Alice Keppel's husband, George. Albemarle went, in turn, to the King's private secretary, Lord Stamfordham. And Lord Stamfordham went to the King.

In contacting the palace, Arthur du Cros had come up against that elaborate stockade which encircles the monarch. Self-preservation is one of the monarchy's chief concerns and the discreet, courteous and apparently honourable gentlemen with whom du Cros now found himself dealing were all past-masters in the art of protecting the royal image. Once they had convinced themselves that du Cros was not in league with Lady Warwick, Stamfordham and the King's solicitor, the equally urbane Charles Russell, decided to make use of the loyal du Cros to serve their own ends. If blackmail were indeed being considered by Lady Warwick, then let du Cros be the one to carry out any distasteful negotiations. What was to be avoided at any cost was a royal scandal.

Would Mr du Cros, they now asked politely, go back to Lady Warwick 'to ascertain the monetary value she attached to [the letters] with a view to their purchase'?[5]

The highly gratified Lady Warwick put the monetary value of the letters at £85,000. This was increased to £100,000 at a subsequent meeting at the Ritz Hotel in Paris between herself, du Cros and Frank Harris. Out of this she would get £85,000, Harris £15,000.

On their way back from Paris, Lady Warwick indicated to du Cros that she did not, in fact, mind who paid her the money: if a loyal and patriotic man like himself felt like serving his sovereign by footing the bill, she would be quite happy to settle for that. And just before taking leave of her travelling companion at Charing Cross station, Daisy handed him a written ultimatum. Unless the money were forthcoming, Harris would shortly be leaving for New York to market both her memoirs, in which the letters would be incorporated, and, after publication, the letters themselves. From this she hoped to make £200,000.

But it would never, Daisy imagined, come to that. Before then, either the palace or du Cros himself would hand over the £100,000 she was demanding.

In all good faith, du Cros reported back to the King's men, Stamfordham and Russell. If they were prepared to meet Lady Warwick's debts, he told them, she would hand over the letters. Assuming that his part in the affair was now over, du Cros was somewhat surprised to hear that the courtiers wanted him to continue negotiations with the lady for a while longer: there were still, they said, some loose ends to be tied up.

At this point, Lady Warwick lost patience. Enlisting the services of yet another intermediary, Bruce Logan – one of those handsome and athletic young men for whom she had such a *penchant* – Daisy tried to pressure du Cros into making an immediate payment. Unless she were paid, promptly and in cash, an American deal would be finalised. She also took the precaution of lodging the precious letters in the safe of a London insurance broker. In mounting agitation, du Cros tried to stall Lady Warwick. It was, she warned him, '*practically* too late' – by which she meant that as she had not yet signed the American agreement, there was still time for the palace to buy her off.

When du Cros, on 31 July 1914 – the last day before Europe was plunged into war – reported yet again to Russell, he was greeted with some astonishing news. An interim injunction had been served on Lady Warwick, restraining her from publishing the letters.

Quite unsuspected by du Cros, the palace had been contemplating this action all along. They had never even considered paying Lady Warwick for the letters. For weeks, their detectives had been trailing all the parties concerned; du Cros had simply been used to stall Lady Warwick until such time as the palace authorities had ensured that the letters had not been given to Frank Harris or sent to America. They knew, by now, that she had lodged them with an insurance broker.

The injunction forbidding publication of the letters had been applied for in the strictest secrecy; in all documentation, Edward VII was referred to simply as 'The Testator'. And the fact that the injunction had been applied for 'in Chambers' instead of in open court ensured that the identity of 'The Testator' was never revealed.

Except for Lady Warwick and Frank Harris, only a handful of people – all of them utterly loyal to the monarch – knew about the injunction. And as Britain had declared war on Germany on 4 August 1914, the palace authorities were able, by invoking the extraordinary powers of the Defence of the Realm Act, to threaten Lady Warwick even more effectively. She now stood in danger of being arrested – although how the suppression of the late Edward VII's love letters could in any way defend the realm is difficult to imagine.

Lady Warwick, beaten at her own game by the palace professionals, was incensed. But she was not cowed. If she was not allowed to publish the letters, she would publish something equally revealing. Once more poor du Cros was visited by Lady Warwick. This time she threatened him with a manuscript which contained not only the full story of the way in which the palace had tried to silence her but a great deal of defamatory information about other prominent national figures. She even hinted, to the increasingly discomforted du Cros, that she knew one or two things about his past which he would probably prefer to be kept dark. In panic, du Cros suggested a couple of wildcat schemes whereby she might be able to make some money and, at a later stage, even went so far as to release her from paying back all the interest she owed him.

The injunction against the publication of the letters had been a temporary measure, and the business was finally settled on 5 July 1915. The action against Lady Warwick was stayed on condition that the letters were destroyed. She was forced to comply. Edward VII's love letters, on which she had hoped to raise £100,000, were handed over.

'I am handing back with splendid generosity,' runs her self-righteous statement of defence, 'the letters King Edward wrote me of his great love, and which belong absolutely to me. I have done nothing with these letters, and have never dreamed of publishing such things. My memoirs are my own affair, and every incident of these ten years of close friendship with King Edward are in my brain and memory . . .'[6]

It was, in short, a warning. They need not think that because she had been prevented from publishing the letters, she could be prevented from one day writing her memoirs.

The palace, in its anxiety to sweep the whole scandalous business under the carpet, went to the extraordinary lengths of removing all traces of the legal action from the records. The affair must be kept absolutely secret. And so it was, until the day that Arthur du Cros's own meticulously detailed account was discovered by Theo Lang in that deed box in Switzerland, half a century later.

In the end, the irrepressible Daisy Warwick did not do too badly out of the affair. For this, the well-meaning du Cros was responsible. Having already agreed that she need not repay the interest on his loan, he released her from paying back the £16,000 loan itself. He then, in a gesture of extreme generosity, took over all her outstanding bills, amounting to £48,000. Perhaps du Cros had taken her threats of exposing his past seriously; perhaps he simply wanted to put an end to the whole wretched business; perhaps he still saw it as a way of serving his sovereign.

So what Daisy Warwick finally obtained – obliquely – for Edward VII's love letters was £64,000. What du Cros obtained, a year later, was a baronetcy. Frank Harris, apparently, got nothing.

By the time she finally came to publish her autobiography, fifteen years later, Lady Warwick seems to have convinced herself that her discreditable attempt at blackmail had never happened. Her friends, she claims, had expected her memoirs to be full of confidential information. But how, she asks piously, could she possibly betray those 'great ones' who had been her 'intimates'? The fact that 'they' were dead was all the more reason for her silence; 'those' who remained trusted her to keep silent.[7]

One summer evening during the First World War, the gardens of Easton Lodge were the setting for an interesting encounter. Two of the late Edward VII's mistresses, Daisy Warwick and Lillie Langtry, were to be seen strolling arm-in-arm among the famous roses. With Lillie in her early sixties and Daisy in her mid-fifties, both were undeniably middle-aged, but whereas Lillie was merely plumper than she had once been, Daisy was frankly fat. Of the sylph-like shape that had so enchanted the Prince of Wales, no trace remained. Yet there were traces, in both women, of their once celebrated beauty. And it was about this that they were talking as they moved through the sweet-scented garden.

'Whatever happens, I do not intend to grow old!' announced Lillie. 'Why shouldn't beauty vanquish time?'

'I forgot what I answered,' writes Daisy, 'for I was busy analysing what she had said. I stole a glance at her, and certainly Time's ravages, although perceptible to the discerning eye of one who had known her at the zenith of her beauty, were disguised with consummate artistry, while her figure was still lovely.

'But it came to me then that there was tragedy in the life of this woman, whose beauty had once been world-famous, for she had found no time in the intervals of pursuing pleasure to secure content-ment for the evening of her day. Now that she saw the evening approach, Lillie Langtry could only protest that it was not evening at all, but just the prolongation of a day that was, in truth, already dead.'[8]

There was something in what Daisy Warwick said. Lillie Langtry was growing old any way but gracefully. It was not that she behaved indecorously – she was far too dignified for that – it was simply that she bitterly resented the passing of time. Again and again, those who knew Lillie during the last dozen or so years of her life (she was to die in 1929) speak of her sadness, her loneliness, her inability to come to terms with the fact that her day was over.

'Lillie Langtry interested me,' wrote the publisher, Newman Flow-er, who used to visit her in her London hotel in the early 1920s, 'because of the manner in which she strove to keep herself alive, after that particular Social World, which she had queened, was dead. She always appeared to be a lingering leaf on an autumn tree which hangs on and will not die nor perish beneath the blast of Winter, because it has once belonged to a never-to-be-forgotten Summer. She could not let go. She fought in order not to let go.'[9]

Yet he, again like many others who knew her, paid tribute to Lillie's remarkable intelligence. Under all the theatricality, under all those anecdotes, impersonations and jokes, lay a bedrock of good sense. 'I discovered, stage by stage,' writes Flower, 'how deep-thinking was her mind. No one ever gave Lillie Langtry credit for her cultured mind. But she acquired something untaught from Life. She drew knowledge unto herself and stored it, and brought it out at the required moment.'[10]

Occasionally, she would speak to him about Edward VII, as Prince of Wales. They had only had one serious difference throughout their relationship, she claimed. It had been 'a most stupid' quarrel. 'I wore a dress of white and silver at two balls in succession. I did not know that he was going to be present at both balls, but he was. He came up to me on the second night and exclaimed: "That damned dress again!"'

'He walked away in a temper . . . It took me a long time to make it up . . . That was the only quarrel we ever had.'[11]

It was, of course, exactly the sort of trivial thing that annoyed the Prince.

Not long after the war, Lillie sold her various English houses and bought a villa, overlooking Monte Carlo, which she named Le Lys.

Set in a flowery garden, against pine-covered slopes and with a view over the glittering Mediterranean, Le Lys was something of a show-place. Occasionally Lillie's husband Suggie, the dapper and ineffectual Sir Hugo de Bathe, was to be seen in her company but a more constant companion was a Mrs Mathilde Peate, who acted as part-housekeeper, part-secretary and part-confidante. Lillie's days were spent in strolling along the promenade, gambling in the casino, meeting friends for tea and giving or attending little dinner parties. Always well dressed and regally mannered, she remained, amongst the fashionable crowd that thronged the Riviera, very much of a celebrity in her own right.

It was, quite naturally, as the one-time mistress of King Edward VII that Lillie Langtry was chiefly celebrated. And although, in private conversation, she was ready to tell the odd anecdote about their association, she was careful not to commit anything to paper. Yet as long ago as the 1890s publishers had been pestering her to write her memoirs. 'I would go up to £40,000 and it would be worth it,' one publisher assured the journalist William Colley, 'if she would write all the truth and all she knows.'

'Mr Colley,' exclaimed an amused Lillie on hearing about the offer, 'you don't really think I would ever do such a thing as to write my *real* reminiscences, do you?'

'No,' admitted Colley, 'I don't.'[12]

Lillie then gave him, says Colley, her reasons for not writing her '*real* reminiscences'; these, he says nobly, he would never disclose.

But her well-known reluctance did not stop other publishers, or newspaper editors, from trying to get her to change her mind. 'Her frank reminiscences,' one journalist told Lord Northcliffe, 'would provide the best Sunday reading for many a long day.'[13]

Newman Flower came closer than most. After he had been begging her for months to write her autobiography, Lillie one day invited him to her London house to discuss it. 'I was shown into a room where the litter of lunch still lingered – two used table-napkins thrown across the table, two stained glasses, an empty bottle, a cigarette-end still smouldering in a glass ash-tray . . .

'She came in presently. There was no make-up on her face. She was depressed and unhappy. Restive. She pulled out a chair, and sat corner-wise on it. She pushed the plates and glasses aside in a noisy clatter.'

'Oh, the book,' she remarked as if, says Flower, they had met to discuss the Scriptures. 'Oh, yes, the book. Now I'll tell you . . .'

She drummed her fingers on the table. 'What you've got to do –' she began.

'What *I've* got to do?' asked Flower.

'Yes. *You,*' she explained. 'You've got to get all the cuttings about me that have ever appeared in the Press. You can get the record of all my horses. You can put the whole lot together and I shall sign them. There's the book.'

'It's not quite like that,' he protested. 'I mean, books aren't made like that.'

'Well, come into the drawing room and have coffee.'

'We went into the drawing room,' writes Flower. 'We had coffee. We never talked about the book again.'[14]

Yet in 1925 – the year of Queen Alexandra's death – Lillie Langtry published an autobiography entitled *The Days I Knew*. The book could hardly have been more innocuous or imprecise. It is remarkable more for what it leaves out or glosses over than for what it reveals. Whole areas of Lillie's life are ignored; others are presented in a haphazard, unchronological fashion. Her succession of lovers are either not mentioned or else dismissed in a sentence. Freddie Gebhard, the young American multi-millionaire who provided her with, among other things, her famous railway carriage 'Lallee', is referred to as 'what Americans designate a clubman, which gave rise to a great deal of newspaper gossip'.[15] George Alexander Baird – 'the Squire' – who bought her a yacht and bequeathed her a string of racehorses, is described as 'an eccentric young bachelor with vast estates in Scotland . . . and with more money than he knew what to do with'.[16] Prince Louis of Battenberg is not mentioned at all; nor is there any indication that Lillie ever had a daughter, whether by Prince Louis or not. Her husband, Edward Langtry, after a few condescending references, very soon fades out of the picture altogether.

What Lillie calls her 'friendship' with the Prince of Wales is treated with great circumspection. Although she could not resist parading her relationship with her royal lover, both as Prince of Wales and as King, she is careful not to give away too much. Her tone, in dealing with him, is reverent and sycophantic, yet it must have been patently clear to any reader of her memoirs that the bond between the two of them had been physical. Why else should the heir to the throne have taken up with a woman so far removed from his usual social orbit? There was no need, though, for her lover's son, George V, to lose any sleep about Lady de Bathe's revelations. No secret injunctions against publication were issued on this occasion.

On the contrary, George V remained very kindly disposed towards Lillie Langtry. Captain Champion de Crespigny told the writer Ernest Dudley the story of how, one day in 1928, when Lillie was visiting London from Monte Carlo, she telephoned him in great excitement to say that the King had invited her to tea at Buckingham Palace. The King, she afterwards told de Crespigny, had been 'sweet'. He had arranged for an old footman, whom she had known in Edward VII's day, to be on hand. 'My lady,' said the footman, 'I've brought you the same sort of brandy-and-soda you used to like when you came to see King Edward.'

George V, in his chaffing way, had told Lillie not to hide herself away in Monte Carlo. 'That's what you pretty women are inclined to do when you feel you're not so young any more. It's a mistake, and I want you to come to London more often.'[17] She promised that she would.

She never did come back. Lillie Langtry died on 12 February 1929, at the age of seventy-five, in her Monte Carlo home. With her, at the end, was her faithful companion, Mathilde Peate. The value of Lillie's estate was £47,000. Of this she willed £5000 to each of her four grandchildren; Mathilde Peate inherited £10,000, the villa, the jewellery and such personal effects as were not otherwise bequeathed.

Lillie had asked to be buried in her parents' grave in the churchyard of St Saviour's, Jersey, but with snow-storms raging across the Continent, it was not until ten days later that her body, aboard the steamer 'Saint Brieuc', reached St Helier. The coffin lay in the church overnight. St Saviour's – lying a stone's throw from the Rectory where Lillie had grown up – was where her father had been Dean and where she had married both Edward Langtry and Hugo de Bathe. A prettier spot in which to be buried than the leafy, gently sloping churchyard of St Saviour's would be difficult to find.

Of the great and glittering world in which Lillie Langtry had been so celebrated an ornament, there was not a single member at her funeral on 23 February 1929. Mathilde Peate was her only close friend. Her family was represented by her daughter, Lady Malcolm, to whom she had not spoken for years and by her grandson, George Malcolm, whom she could not have known very well.

Lillie, who had always laid claim to the friendship, and love, of so many royals, was sent only one wreath from a member of a royal family. It came from Prince and Princess Pierre of Montenegro, who now lived in Monte Carlo. Prince Pierre was the least important son of Europe's least important royal house, which had anyway ceased to reign in 1922. His wife, Princess Pierre, had been born Violet Wegner in South Hackney, London, the daughter of a tram conductor.

No one could ever accuse Daisy Warwick of clinging to her yesterdays. Throughout the 1920s and 1930s, when she was in her sixties and seventies, she remained as active, as forward-looking, as politically aware and involved as she had ever been. 'The way not to admit age, not to brand oneself as a back number, is to keep heart and faith and enthusiasms,' she pronounced. 'Let all your thoughts be hopeful. Study always. Keep as active mentally as you were physically active . . .'[18]

Advancing age made Lady Warwick no less controversial or capricious. She surrounded herself with a host of unconventional and progressively-minded people. In a steady stream of articles, she pontificated on every aspect of modern life. A committed socialist, she was a hard-working supporter of the Labour Party. In 1923 she stood as a Labour candidate in a by-election in her own constituency of Warwick and Leamington. Her Conservative opponent was the young Anthony Eden, to whom she happened to be doubly related through the marriages of two of her children. Although Daisy came a poor third, after the Liberal candidate, the Labour Party did very well nationally and, in 1924, was able to take office as the first Labour government. Lady Warwick's gratification was somewhat tempered by the fact that on 15 January 1924, her understanding husband 'Brookie', the Earl of Warwick, died at the age of sixty-eight.

As Lord Warwick had died a comparatively poor man and Lady Warwick was in her perennially impecunious state (which not even the sale of a great deal of land had been able to alleviate) she decided to combine philanthropy with expediency by a *grand geste*: she would allow the Labour Party the use of her home, Easton Lodge. Although she would live on there (Warwick Castle had passed to her eldest son) the Party, provided it paid certain expenses, could have free run of the house and grounds.

It sounded like an excellent idea, but in the end it proved no more successful than her other enterprises. Neither as a centre for conferences and study groups, nor as a venue for summer schools, or a Labour college under the auspices of the Trades Union Congress, did her plans for Easton Lodge fully materialise. Yet, for several years, its over-furnished rooms and spacious park were the setting for various Labour gatherings. The arrangement was not really a comfortable one. Beatrice Webb considered the house 'far too gorgeous in its grandiose reception rooms and large extravagantly furnished bedrooms',[19] and her sister Kate felt that the less sophisticated party members must feel repelled by this show of 'degenerate luxury'.[20] The grounds swarmed with Lady Warwick's bizarre collection of birds and animals, tame and wild.

But most discomforting of all was the hostess herself. Shelf-bosomed, tightly corseted, picture-hatted and opulently gowned, Lady Warwick made a striking contrast to the short-skirted, shingled and cardiganed women members of the party. They found her manner, for all her good-heartedness and open-mindedness, to be autocratic and intimidating. 'When I first knew her,' writes one young socialist, 'though she had grown fat, her face still had the fixed pink-and-white attractions which one associates with the Lillie Langtry era, and an "electric light" smile which was turned on in a brilliant flash and gone again. She had a gushingly affectionate manner of greeting, with her wonderfully curled head on one side and her smile blazing, which was none the less perfectly sincere "period"; she trailed about with a string of revolting Pekingese dogs and she had quick and sudden gusts of temper . . .'[21]

Her outspokenness astonished the students attending the summer schools. Making no secret of her adulterous love affair with Edward VII, Lady Warwick would lead them through her 'Friendship Garden', where most of the flowers seem to have been planted by the Prince of Wales, and would point out the heart-shaped plaques with their inscriptions: 'Lily of the Valley. Planted by H.R.H. The Prince of Wales. Nov 18, 1892.'[22] Conspicuously absent would be any flowers planted by the Princess of Wales. With almost every room sporting its photograph of the late King, Lady Warwick would regale her embarrassed listeners with risqué stories about their intimate relationship. Unselfconsciously, she would point out, to tight-lipped Nonconformists, the great four-poster bed which she had shared with her royal lover.

She was still, in fact, hoping to turn her royal memories into hard cash. Two things – other than her reluctance to get down to work and her inability to get on with various collaborators – made her task more difficult: Frank Harris appears to have stolen some of her papers, and a fire at Easton, in 1918, destroyed a great many others. The fire, she would hint darkly, had not been accidental. Appreciating the lengths to which the palace had gone to prevent her from making use of Edward VII's love letters, she suspected that the same 'authorities' might have had a hand in this destruction of her papers.

But eventually, after innumerable false starts and complicated agreements with collaborators and publishers, Lady Warwick produced two books of autobiography: *Life's Ebb and Flow* appeared in 1929 and *Afterthoughts* in 1931. Like Lillie Langtry's memoirs, they were selective, highly coloured and inaccurate, but they were given weight by Daisy's interesting account of her conversion to, and ardent belief in, socialism. 'So much,' she felt able to write, 'has changed for the better.'[23]

About her 'friendship' with the Prince of Wales, Lady Warwick was very discreet. Quite clearly, she was not prepared to risk another prosecution. From her pages he emerges as a wise, magnanimous and lion-hearted gentleman. While admitting that he had 'no sympathy whatever with my enthusiasm for Socialism', she implies that he was otherwise ready to 'put himself out . . . in anything, everything' to please her. That the two of them were very closely associated for a number of years must have been obvious to even the most naive reader, and in *Life's Ebb and Flow* Daisy goes so far as to give her chapter on the Prince of Wales the title 'The Heart of a Friend'. To this she adds, as that other woman to capture the heart of another Prince of Wales – the Duchess of Windsor – was to add to the title of her book of memoirs: 'The heart has its reasons about which reason knows nothing.'[24]

By the late 1930s, Daisy, Countess of Warwick was becoming increasingly eccentric. Too fat, reports Robert Bruce Lockhart who visited her in 1937, to get out of her chair, she ate like a wolf: 'for breakfast she had two sausages, a fish-cake, and bacon.'[25] Swathed in a feather boa, she would wander through the gardens tending to the assortment of birds and animals – peacocks, pigeons, ponies, donkeys, monkeys, dogs and cats – to which she had given a home. To her various other interests, she had by now added spiritualism: she threw herself into this latest obsession with characteristic ardour. Her old friend, Elinor Glyn, remembering Lady Warwick in her heyday – as a beautiful and sophisticated leader of society – was shocked to tears on visiting this odd and impoverished old lady. She could have saved her tears. 'I am a very happy woman,'[26] said Lady Warwick simply.

And so she was. Even if most of her ambitious schemes had crumbled to dust, her idealism, her belief in a fairer tomorrow, had survived. While her aristocratic contemporaries were bemoaning the passing of their privileged world, she had already embraced a new, more egalitarian age. 'I am going to devote my afterthoughts to the old days,' she wrote in the preface to her second book of memoirs, 'in the hope that the present generation will see, as I see, that conditions are far better for the great majority of people than ever they were before, and that we have made astounding progress.'[27]

This gallant, unpredictable, highly romantic figure died, at the age of seventy-six, on 26 July 1938. Her body was taken from Easton to Warwick where she was buried beside her husband in the family vault. She, who at the age of three had been an heiress worth £30,000 a year, left a mere £37,000 in property to her surviving son, Maynard. To her faithful housekeeper at Easton, Nancy Galpin, went a small annuity, five hundred birds and thirteen dogs. It was a not entirely welcome legacy.

'I fear,' remarked Miss Galpin, 'the dear Countess did not know it cost £8 a week to keep them.'[28] And that was only the *birds*.

Discreet to the last, Alice Keppel published no memoirs. Although she outlived her royal lover by almost forty years, she seems to have felt no compulsion to put their relationship on record. In any case, Alice Keppel was never one for dwelling on the past. 'She made the best of what she found,' claims her daughter Violet, 'she did not, as the French say, "seek for midday at fourteen o'clock".'[29] Life, for Alice Keppel, was for the living.

On her return to London two years after Edward VII's death, the Keppels bought number 16 Grosvenor Street. Now freed both of financial constraints and of any need for circumspection, Alice entertained lavishly. The spacious, superbly furnished rooms of her Grosvenor Street house swarmed with guests: writers, dancers, politicians, Continental royals. The outbreak of the First World War brought only a slight diminution of this brilliant social life. Although George Keppel joined his regiment and Alice spent periods helping her great friend Lady Sarah Wilson run her hospital in Boulogne, she still played hostess to an assortment of guests, with as many as seventy sitting down to luncheon. 'Mama dominated the big table,' remembers her daughter Sonia, 'where usually it was tacitly understood that the conversation should remain on a light level with the darker shades of war excluded from it.'[30]

But darker shades, of a more personal nature, threatened Alice Keppel towards the end of the war when her daughter Violet embarked on a turbulent love affair with Vita Sackville-West, who was by now married to Harold Nicolson. Alice, who was more disturbed by the possibility of scandal than by the unconventionality of the liaison, suggested the conventional remedy: Violet must get married. But Violet Keppel's marriage to Denys Trefusis in the summer of 1919 solved nothing; the Violet-Vita love affair became more stormy still. When Violet threatened to divorce her husband, Alice Keppel tried a second conventional remedy: she would cut her daughter off without a penny. This solution seems to have proved more successful; at any rate, it was from this point on that the affair began to die a death.

At one stage during this three-year upheaval, when Violet had been threatening to go off and live with Vita, Alice Keppel had said, 'Very well, but wait until Sonia is married: a scandal like this and her wedding will never take place.'[31] Violet agreed, and in the autumn of 1920 Sonia Keppel married Roland Cubitt, the son of Baron Ashcombe and heir to the Cubitt building fortune.

Lord Ashcombe had been somewhat disconcerted to find that, on arriving at Grosvenor Street to discuss the marriage settlement with George Keppel, it was with Alice Keppel that he was obliged to do business. Alice proved herself more than a match for his lordship. Visibly shaken by the size of the settlement to which Mrs Keppel had forced him to agree, Lord Ashcombe said that he hoped that this expensive marriage would endure. 'My dear Lord Ashcombe,' drawled Alice, 'neither you nor I can legislate for the future.'[32]

In 1927 the Keppels sold their Grosvenor Street house (Alice was able to up the price by agreeing to leave behind her celebrity-studded visitors' book) and moved to Italy. Here they bought the Villa dell'Ombrellino on Bellosguardo, above Florence. For the following two decades, with the exception of the war years, this was to be their home. Although Alice improved the house almost beyond recognition and furnished it in her usual sumptuous style, it was for its views – one across the domes and towers of the city, the other across the vines and cypresses of the countryside – that the villa was chiefly remarkable. At l'Ombrellino, says Alice Keppel's neighbour, Sir Harold Acton, 'none could compete with her glamour as a hostess.' Celebrated as the ex-mistress of Edward VII, as an international *grande dame* and as a matchless party-giver, Alice Keppel reigned like a queen over Florentine society. Her chestnut hair, by now, had turned white; her figure, always voluptuous, had become majestic.

'A fine figure of a woman, as they used to say, more handsome than beautiful, she possessed enormous charm, which was not only due to her cleverness and vivacity but to her generous heart,' writes Harold

Acton. 'Her kindnesses were innumerable and spontaneous. Altogether she was on a bigger scale than most of her sex; she could have impersonated Britannia in a *tableau vivant* and done that lady credit.'

George Keppel, continues Acton, 'spent much of his leisure compiling booklets of contemporary dates for his sight-seeing guests. Naturally he acted as cicerone to the prettiest debutantes – "such a little cutie" he said fondly of more than one.'[33]

Although Alice Keppel seldom dwelt on her past association with Edward VII, there were occasions when her listeners were sharply reminded of the position she had once enjoyed. She happened to be in the dining room of her favourite hotel, the Ritz in London, on the day that King Edward VIII abdicated his throne in order to marry Mrs Wallis Simpson. To Alice Keppel the whole thing was incomprehensible. That the King should want to sleep with Wallis Simpson was perfectly understandable, but why on earth should he want to *marry* her? With, according to the journalist Janet Flanner, 'all London' dining at the Ritz that evening, Mrs Keppel's opinion went reverberating through the room. 'Things were done much better,' she announced in her deep voice, 'in *my* day.'[34]

Within four years Mrs Keppel was back at the Ritz on a more permanent basis. In 1940 the entry of Italy into the war forced the Keppels to leave Florence and to find their way back to Britain. In France they were caught up in the familiar mêlée but, as always, Alice kept her head. In Biarritz she was greeted like a returning heroine and, on boarding the Royal Navy troopship off Saint-Jean-de-Luz, was given the only available private cabin – the captain's. The greatest danger faced by the refugees during the crossing seems to have been physical discomfort; yet Alice Keppel's friend, the inimitable Mrs Ronald Greville, was heard afterwards to say that 'To hear Alice talk about her escape from France, one would think she had swum the Channel, with her maid between her teeth.'[35]

On arrival in England, the Keppels went to stay with their daughter Sonia Cubitt in the country; but preferring, as Alice put it, 'bombs to boredom',[36] they soon moved back to London and into the Ritz. Here they remained for the rest of the war.

In no time, Alice Keppel had established herself as the leading, personality of the Ritz Hotel. 'The most jovially optimistic of my friends,' writes Harold Acton of these war-time years, 'was Mrs George Keppel, who was empress of the Ritz at this period. Wherever she pitched her tent she appeared to rule. She created her own aura of grandeur in the suitably Edwardian lounge, far more regal than poor King Zog and Queen Geraldine of Albania, who had taken refuge in the same caravanserai. Traditionally better informed than anyone else – and when the fact failed her she would embellish it with plausible fancy – she divulged the latest Florentine gossip . . .'[37]

Her sense of humour remained as sharp as ever. On one occasion, during these years, she visited the Bishop of Wells in his picturesque moated palace.

'And what, Bishop,' asked the socially accomplished Alice in an effort to fill an awkward pause in the conversation, 'are your favourite books?'

'Well,' replied his lordship, 'my idea of a perfect afternoon is to relax on that sofa with my favourite Trollope.'[38]

It became one of Alice's pet anecdotes.

The diarist 'Chips' Channon has left a telling pen-picture of Alice Keppel towards the end of the war, when she was already seventy-four. 'I gave a dinner party at which Mrs Keppel was the "show-piece"; she looked magnificent in black sequins and jewels, and her fine white hair and gracious manners are impressive: she is so affectionate and grande dame that it is a pity she tipples, and then becomes garrulous and inaccurate in her statements . . .'[39]

This is not the only time that 'Chips' Channon mentions Alice's 'tippling'; nor is he the only one to do so. She was often to be seen, during these years, holding uproarious court to gatherings of equivocal young men in London pubs.

During this period in Britain, Alice and her daughter Violet once paid a visit to that other *grande dame* with whom she had so often come in contact in her days as Edward VII's mistress: his daughter-in-law, Queen Mary. Now also in her seventies, the dowager Queen was spending the war at Badminton House in Gloucestershire. What these two old matriarchs discussed one does not know (although Queen Mary was more worldly than was generally imagined) but Violet, herself almost fifty by now, was studiously ignored by the old Queen. Only on making her farewell curtsey was Violet rewarded with a remark.

'Very good Violet,' pronounced Queen Mary on her curtsey, 'you hold yourself as straight as ever.'[40]

Throughout these years at the Ritz, George and Alice Keppel had, as they put it, 'buried' the Villa dell'Ombrellino. They never harked back to their home above Florence. But one day, late in 1944, Major Hamish Erskine, freshly arrived from the triumphant Allied campaign in Italy, came bursting into the hotel.

'Mrs Keppel, Mrs Keppel,' he exclaimed. 'I can't wait to tell you that the Villa is safe, everything is intact, even the Chinese pagodas.'

Alice remained imperturbable. 'Those, my dear Hamish,' she declared, 'were the *common* pagodas.'[41]

The uncommon pagodas – the pagodas given to her by Edward VII – were safely stored away.

In 1946 the Keppels returned to l'Ombrellino. Now seventy-seven, Alice was beginning to show signs of failing health. She was suffering from sclerosis of the liver. For a while though, the delights of her Italian home, with its warm sunshine, its statue-lined terrace, its orange and lemon trees in tubs and its 'jangle-tangle of bells'[42] restored her. And her optimism, her tendency to look ahead, remained as marked as ever. When someone asked her how she regarded the prospect of turning eighty, her reply was characteristic. 'Oh, eighty is such a *dull* age!' she laughed. 'Now ninety, on the other hand, is rather chic. So I shall start counting from ninety.'[43]

But she did not even live to be eighty. By the summer of 1947 it was clear that she was dying. While poor George Keppel wandered disconsolately about the hushed villa, Alice's illness took its long, slow course. 'Look darling,' her daughter Violet once said in an effort to cheer her up, 'look at the view from your window. Surely you love nature?'

'Yes,' answered Alice, 'the nature of the Ritz.'[44]

Alice Keppel died, at the age of seventy-eight, on 11 September 1947. She was buried under the cypresses of the Protestant cemetery in Florence. Two months later, the heartbroken George Keppel also died. 'Always the most courteous of men,' says their daughter Violet, 'it was as though he were loth to keep her waiting.'[45]

Although all the obituaries of Mrs George Keppel linked her, with consummate tact, to 'the intimate circle of the Edwardian court'[46], it was as a contemporary figure that she was chiefly remembered. 'It was difficult to think of her as an old lady,' wrote Sir Osbert Sitwell in *The Times*, 'since she retained unimpaired her bold, vigorous and enterprising personality.' Another friend described her as 'one of the most vivid of beings, no one could ever have enjoyed life more, or provided greater enjoyment for those who surrounded her.'[47]

In short, Alice Keppel was not simply an Edwardian ghost. No more than with Lillie Langtry or Daisy Warwick did her fame rest solely on the fact that she had once been a mistress of King Edward VII. Like them, Alice was a woman of intelligence and independence, very much a personality in her own right.

Yet there was no denying the fact that when Alice Keppel died, the most colourful living reminder of Edward VII's scandalous love life died also. For if, by 1947, the leading representative of the official side of Edward VII's career was his eminently respectable grandson, George VI, then the leading representative of his unofficial, immoral, profligate side had been Alice Keppel.

But then she had never been able, Alice once said, to tell a king from a knave.

Notes

CHAPTER ONE

1 Russell, *Collections*, p 132
2 Magnus, *Gladstone*, p 267
3 *Ibid*, p 209
4 *Ibid*, p 209
5 Nicolson, *George V*, p 82
6 Holden, *Charles*, p 257
7 Magnus, *Edward VII*, p 7
8 *Ibid*, p 75
9 Hamilton, *Halcyon Era*, p 73
10 Magnus, *Gladstone*, p 211
11 *Ibid*, p 209
12 *Ibid*, p 213
13 *Ibid*, p 214
14 *Ibid*, p 215
15 *Ibid*, p 216
16 *Ibid*, p 215
17 Grey, *Twenty-one Years*, p 15
18 Hibbert, *Edward VII*, p 98
19 Lee, *Edward VII*, p 179
20 Jullian, *Edward*, p 13
21 Magnus, *Edward VII*, p 21
22 Nicolson, *George V*, p 14
23 Benson, *Edward VII*, p 21
24 Martin, *The Prince Consort*, Vol 4, p 206
25 Hibbert, *Edward VII*, p 37
26 *Ibid*, p 37
27 Battiscombe, *Alexandra*, p 29
28 Hibbert, *Edward VII*, p 48
29 Victoria, *Dearest Mamma*, p 43
30 *Ibid*, p 43
31 Battiscombe, *Alexandra*, p 41
32 *Ibid*, p 39
33 Victoria, *Dearest Mamma*, p 180
34 Bagehot, *English Constitution*, p 53
35 Victoria, *Dearest Mamma*, p 186
36 Brooke-Shepherd, *Uncle of Europe*, p 54
37 Hibbert, *Edward VII*, p 73
38 Battiscombe, *Alexandra*, p 70
39 Ponsonby, *Henry Ponsonby*, p 87
40 Battiscombe, *Alexandra*, p 85
41 St Aubyn, *Edward VII*, p 152
42 Noel, *Alice*, p 172
43 Magnus, *Edward VII*, p 442
44 Cavendish, *Diary*, Vol 2, p 80

CHAPTER TWO

1 Michael, *Tramps*, p 130
2 Warwick, *Life's Ebb*, p 46
3 Asquith, *More Memories*, p 31
4 Langtry, *Days I Knew*, p 47
5 *Ibid*, p 39
6 *Ibid*, p 39
7 *Ibid*, p 40
8 *Ibid*, p 17
9 *Ibid*, p 17
10 *Ibid*, p 16
11 Dudley, *Gilded Lily*, p 101
12 *Ibid*, p 101
13 *Ibid*, p 33
14 Langtry, *Days I Knew*, p 27
15 *Ibid*, p 36
16 Gerson, *Langtry*, p 18
17 Langtry, *Days I Knew*, p 19
18 *Ibid*, p 31
19 Gerson, *Langtry*, p 20

20 *Ibid*, p 23
21 Lambert, *Unquiet Souls*, p 99
22 Langtry, *Days I Knew*, p 35
23 *Ibid*, p 37
24 *Ibid*, p 38
25 *Ibid*, p 42
26 Gerson, *Langtry*, p 38
27 Brough, *Prince and Lily*, p 122
28 Langtry, *Days I Knew*, p 53
29 *Ibid*, p 44
30 Brough, *Prince and Lily*, p 123
31 Asquith, *Remember*, p 64
32 Langtry, *Days I Knew*, p 46
33 *Ibid*, p 35
34 Churchill, *Reminiscences*, p 105
35 Langtry, *Days I Knew*, p 48
36 *Ibid*, p 49
37 *Ibid*, p 70
38 *Ibid*, p 60
39 James, *Rosebery*, p 57
40 Langtry, *Days I Knew*, p 72
41 *Ibid*, p 72
42 *Ibid*, p 73
43 Warwick, *Life's Ebb*, p 172
44 Ponsonby, *Recollections*, p 272
45 *Ibid*, p 272
46 Beddington, *All That*, p 25
47 Leslie, *Edwardians*, p 221

CHAPTER THREE

1 Gerson, *Langtry*, p 8
2 Hamilton, *The Times* 16/8/1986
3 Gerson, *Langtry*, p 9
4 *Ibid*, p 9
5 Langtry, *Days I Knew*, p 46
6 *Ibid*, p 45
7 *Ibid*, p 138
8 *Ibid*, p 135
9 *Ibid*, p 57
10 *Ibid*, pp 59–60
11 *Ibid*, pp 59–60
12 *Ibid*, p 73
13 Windsor, *King's Story*, p 34
14 Brough, *Prince and Lily*, pp 168–71
15 Langtry, *Days I Knew*, p 140
16 *Ibid*, p 77

17 Battiscombe, *Alexandra*, p 138
18 Brough, *Prince and Lily*, p 295
19 Warwick, *Life's Ebb*, p 48
20 Langtry, *Days I Knew*, pp 74–75
21 St Aubyn, *Edward VII*, p 132
22 Langtry, *Days I Knew*, p 78
23 *Ibid*, p 299
24 *Ibid*, p 153
25 *Ibid*, p 76
26 Cresswell, *Eighteen Years*, pp 169–171
27 Langtry, *Days I Knew*, p 81
28 *Ibid*, p 34
29 *Ibid*, p 75
30 *Hughenden Papers*, Disraeli to Victoria
    7/1/1880
31 Langtry, *Days I Knew*, p 114
32 *Ibid*, p 110
33 *Ibid*, p 235
34 Warwick, *Life's Ebb*, p 172
35 Ziegler, *Diana Cooper*, p 18
36 Lambert, *Unquiet Souls*, p 143

CHAPTER FOUR

1 Private information
2 Vanderbilt, *Farewell*, pp 121–2
3 Peel, *Stream of Time*, p 182
4 Ponsonby, *Henry Ponsonby*, p 132
5 Langtry, *Days I Knew*, p 105
6 *Ibid*, p 104
7 *Ibid*, p 108
8 *Ibid*, p 109
9 *Ibid*, p 107
10 *Ibid*, p 107
11 *Ibid*, p 114
12 Ponsonby, *Recollections*, p 238
13 Langtry, *Days I Knew*, p 116
14 *Ibid*, p 116
15 Longford, *Victoria R.I.*, p 331
16 Blunt, *Secret Diary*, MS9 4/6/1909
17 Magnus, *Edward VII*, p 132
18 Langtry, *Days I Knew*, p 137
19 Warwick, *Life's Ebb*, p 38
20 Langtry, *Days I Knew*, p 137
21 *Ibid*, p 81
22 *Ibid*, p 104
23 *Ibid*, p 157

24 Dudley, *Gilded Lily*, p 22
25 *The Times*, 30/11/1977
26 Gerson, *Langtry*, p 70
27 *Ibid*, p 71
28 Hyde, *Wilde*, p 47
29 *Ibid*, p 48
30 Langtry, *Days I Knew*, p 87
31 *Ibid*, p 97
32 Hyde, *Wilde*, p 48
33 Robertson, *Time Was*, p 70
34 *Reynolds Newspaper*, 20/2/1870
35 *Town Talk*, August to October 1879
36 Private information
37 *The Times*, October, 1879

CHAPTER FIVE

1 Blunt, *Secret Diary*, MS 9, 10/3/1880
2 Langtry, *Days I Knew*, p 120
3 *Ibid*, p 122
4 Barwick, *Century*, p 53
5 Cavendish, *Diary*, p 235
6 Langtry, *Days I Knew*, p 121
7 *Ibid*, p 123
8 Brough, *Prince and Lily*, p 211
9 Warwick, *Life's Ebb*, p 47
10 Asquith, *More Memories*, p 31
11 Blunt, *Secret Diary*, MS 43,
   13/3/1880
12 Brough, *Prince and Lily*, p 213
13 Langtry, *Days I Knew*, p 52
14 Hough, *Louis and Victoria*, p 70
15 *Ibid*, p 81
16 *Ibid*, p 94
17 Nicholas II, *Letters*, p 189
18 *The Times*, 30/11/1977
19 Langtry, *Days I Knew*, p 140
20 *Ibid*, p 142
21 *Ibid*, p 144
22 *New York Times*, 6/11/1880
23 *Town Talk*, 21/5/1881
24 Langtry, *Days I Knew*, p 162
25 *Ibid*, p 143
26 *The World*, 22/11/1881
27 Bancroft, *On and Off*, p 277
28 *The Times*, 16/12/1881
29 Brough, *Prince and Lily*, p 250

30 Langtry, *Days I Knew*, p 173
31 *Ibid*, p 41
32 *Gladstone Papers* 44207/193.
   8/1/1882
33 Magnus, *Gladstone*, p 293
34 Gladstone, *Diaries*, Vol III, p XLVII
35 Blunt, *Secret Diary*, MS 333,
   17/5/1885
36 *Gladstone Papers*, 44207/195,
   14/1/1882
37 Marlow, *Mr and Mrs Gladstone*,
   pp 217–8
38 Langtry, *Days I Knew*, pp 176–7
39 *Ibid*, pp 176–7
40 Hibbert, *Edward VII*, p 71

CHAPTER SIX

1 Dangerfield, *Victoria's Heir*, p 223
2 Gwynn, *Dilke*, Vol 1, p 392
3 St Aubyn, *Edward VII*, p 203
4 *Ibid*, p 204
5 Lee, *Edward VII*, Vol 1, p 584
6 Hough, *Advice*, p 56
7 Wortham, *Delightful*, p 162
8 Alice, *Grandchildren*, pp 25–26
9 Warwick, *Life's Ebb*, p 16
10 Warwick, *Afterthoughts*, p 58
11 Warwick, *Life's Ebb*, p 17
12 Cornwallis-West, *Hey-Days*, p 5
13 Warwick, *Life's Ebb*, p 28
14 *Ibid*, p 24
15 *Ibid*, p 26
16 *Ibid*, pp 46–7
17 *Ibid*, p 27
18 *Ibid*, p 32
19 *Ibid*, p 33
20 *Ibid*, p 32
21 *Ibid*, p 34
22 *Hughenden Papers*, Rowton to
   Disraeli, 11/5/1880
23 *Ibid* 12/5/1880
24 Warwick, *Life's Ebb*, p 34
25 *Ibid*, p 38
26 *Ibid*, p 38
27 *Ibid*, p 38
28 *Ibid*, p 39

29 *Ibid*, p 34
30 Blunden, *Warwick*, p 43
31 Warwick, Earl of, *Memories*, p 233
32 Warwick, *Afterthoughts*, p 168
33 Warwick, *Life's Ebb*, p 40
34 *Ibid*, p 182
35 Hibbert, *Edward VII*, p 73
36 Magnus, *Edward VII*, p 120
37 Warwick, *Afterthoughts*, p 79
38 *Ibid*, pp 40–41
39 Warwick, Earl of, *Memories*, p 75
40 Alice, *Grandchildren*, p 75
41 Warwick, *Life's Ebb*, p 77
42 Hibbert, *Edward VII*, p 154
43 Pearson, *Edward the Rake*, p 120
44 Battiscombe, *Alexandra*, p 74
45 Jullian, *Edward*, p 134
46 Warwick, *Life's Ebb*, p 178
47 Glyn, *Romantic*, p 136
48 Blunden, *Warwick*, p 48
49 Warwick, *Life's Ebb*, p 189
50 Warwick, Earl of, *Memories*, p VI
51 Warwick, *Afterthoughts*, p 66
52 Blunden, *Warwick*, p 65
53 *Ibid*, p 66
54 *Dic. of Nat. Biography*
55 Lang, *Darling Daisy*, p 40
56 Blunden, *Warwick*, p 67
57 *Pearsons*, October 1916
58 Blunden, *Warwick*, p 68
59 *Pearsons*, October 1916

CHAPTER SEVEN

1 Warwick, *Afterthoughts*, p 16
2 Lang, *Darling Daisy*, p 65
3 Warwick, *Life's Ebb*, p 156
4 *Ibid*, p 159
5 *Pearsons*, October 1916
6 Warwick, *Afterthoughts*, p 40
7 *The World*, 6/5/1891
8 Warwick, *Life's Ebb*, p 149
9 Lacey, *Majesty*, p 332
10 Warwick, *Afterthoughts*, p 161
11 Warwick, *Life's Ebb*, p 65
12 *Pearsons*, October 1916
13 Tannahill, *Sex in History*, p 336

14 Glyn, *Romantic*, p 66
15 Warwick, *Afterthoughts*,
   pp 15–16
16 Warwick, Earl of, *Memories*, p 265
17 Glyn, *Elinor Glyn*, p 74
18 Warwick, *Afterthoughts*, p 97
19 Arthur, *Not Worth Reading*,
   p 32
20 Ponsonby, *Recollections*, p 221
21 Jullian, *Edward*, p 43
22 Warwick, *Afterthoughts*, p 39
23 Glyn, *Romantic*, pp 74–75
24 *Ibid*, p 73
25 Warwick, *Afterthoughts*, p 39
26 Lang, *Darling Daisy*, p 87
27 St Aubyn, *Edward VII*, p 85
28 Warwick, *Life's Ebb*, p 42
29 Hough, *Advice*, p 56
30 Hibbert, *Edward VII*, p 159
31 *The Times*, 10/6/1891
32 Magnus, *Edward VII*, p 227
33 *Ibid*, p 231
34 Warwick, *Life's Ebb*, p 42
35 Battiscombe, *Alexandra*, p 55
36 *Ibid* p 55
37 Hibbert, *Edward VII*, p 68
38 Brooke-Shepherd, *Uncle of Europe*,
   p 42
39 Langtry, *Days I Knew*, p 117
40 Warwick, *Afterthoughts*, p 256
41 Peel, *A Hundred*, p 66
42 Nicholas II, *Letters*, p 173
43 Warwick, *Life's Ebb*, p 77
44 Warwick, *Afterthoughts*, p 96
45 Forbes, *Memories*, p 66
46 Ponsonby, *A Memoir*, p 5
47 Cresswell, *Eighteen Years*, pp 169–70
48 Bisset, *Sport and War*, p 123
49 Warwick, Earl of, *Memories*, p 91
50 Windsor, *Family Album*, p 43
51 Churchill, *Reminiscences*, p 231
52 Hayward, *Essays*, p 395
53 Blunden, *Warwick*, p 75
54 Magnus, *Edward VII*, p 232
55 Hibbert, *Edward VII*, p 162
56 Blunden, *Warwick*, p 76
57 Lang, *Darling Daisy*, p 26

CHAPTER EIGHT

1 Dudley, *Gilded Lily*, p 89
2 *Ibid*, p 107
3 Michael, *Tramps*, p 130
4 Brooke-Shepherd, *Uncle of Europe*, p 57
5 Langtry, *Days I Knew*, p 237
6 Hyde, *Cleveland Street*, pp 97–8
7 *Ibid*, pp 97–8
8 Langtry, *Days I Knew*, p 97
9 Brooke-Shepherd, *Uncle of Europe*, p 58
10 Hibbert, *Edward VII*, p 283
11 Fulford, *Votes for Women*, p 10
12 Michael, *Tramps*, p 138
13 Robertson-Scott, *Life and Death*, p 192
14 Glyn, *Romantic*, p 75
15 Warwick, *Afterthoughts*, p 16
16 Marie, Queen, *Life*, Vol I, p 43
17 Antrim, *Recollections*, p 221
18 Blunt, *Secret Diary*, MS 9, 7/2/1909
19 Warwick, *Afterthoughts*, p 41
20 Marie, Queen, *Life*, Vol 1, p 43
21 St Aubyn, *Edward VII*, p 103
22 Nicolson, *George V*, p 70
23 Hyde, *Cleveland Street*, p 99
24 *Ibid*, p 90
25 *Ibid*, p 96
26 *Ibid*, p 55
27 *Ibid*, p 59
28 *Ibid*, p 122
29 *Ibid*, p 59
30 *Ibid*, p 60
31 Pope-Hennessy, *Queen Mary*, p 208
32 Battiscombe, *Alexandra*, p 188
33 Hyde, *Cleveland Street*, p 244
34 Battiscombe, *Alexandra*, p 191
35 Whyte, *Stead*, Vol II, p 107
36 *Review of Reviews*, July 1891
37 Whyte, *Stead*, Vol II, p 104
38 St Aubyn, *Edward VII*, p 219
39 Hibbert, *Edward VII*, p 109
40 St Aubyn, *Edward VII*, p 253
41 Blunden, *Warwick*, p 95
42 Warwick, *Life's Ebb*, p 155

CHAPTER NINE

1 Warwick, Earl of, *Memories*, p 12
2 Warwick, *Life's Ebb*, p 260
3 Blunden, *Warwick*, p 97
4 Warwick, *Life's Ebb*, p 91
5 *Ibid*, p 91
6 *Ibid*, pp 91–2
7 *Ibid*, pp 91–2
8 Langtry, *Days I Knew*, p 285
9 Dudley, *Gilded Lily*, p 131
10 Langtry, *Days I Knew*, p 235
11 *Ibid*, p 288
12 Dudley, *Gilded Lily*, p 134
13 Warwick, *Afterthoughts*, p 166
14 *Ibid*, p 167
15 Magnus, *Edward VII*, p 254
16 Brooke-Shepherd, *Uncle of Europe*, p 59
17 Warwick, *Life's Ebb*, p 129
18 *Ibid*, p 130
19 *Ibid*, p 130
20 Whyte, *Stead*, Vol II, p 108
21 Warwick, *Life's Ebb*, p 124
22 Roberts, *Cecil Rhodes*, p 112
23 Warwick, *Life's Ebb*, p 124
24 *Ibid*, pp 107–8
25 Whyte, *Stead*, Vol II, p 106
26 *Ibid*, p 106
27 *Ibid*, p 106
28 Warwick, *Life's Ebb*, p 113
29 *Ibid*, p 113
30 *Chester Chronicle*, 20/10/1897
31 *Ibid* 20/10/1897
32 Dudley, *Gilded Lily*, p 159
33 *Chester Chronicle*, 20/10/1897
34 *Ibid*, 20/10/1897
35 *Ibid*, 20/10/1897
36 Dudley, *Gilded Lily*, p 158
37 *Chester Chronicle*, 30/10/1897
38 Robertson-Scott, *Life and Death*, p 195
39 Warwick, *Life's Ebb*, p 193
40 *Ibid*, pp 225–6
41 Lang, *Darling Daisy*, pp 81–2
42 Battiscombe, *Alexandra*, p 208
43 Warwick, *Life's Ebb*, p 185

CHAPTER TEN

1 Victoria, *Letters*, Third Series, Vol III, p 127
2 Victoria, Empress, *Empress to Sophie*, p 207
3 Cust, *Edward VII*, p 167
4 Victoria, *Letters*, Third Series, Vol III, p 174
5 Victoria, Empress, *Empress to Sophie*, p 207
6 Battiscombe, *Alexandra*, p 210
7 Ponsonby, *Recollections*, p 153
8 Stoeckl, *Not All Vanity*, p 69
9 Leslie, *Edwardians*, p 230
10 Magnus, *Edward VII*, p 260
11 Keppel, *Edwardian*, p 28
12 Leslie, *Edwardians*, p 236
13 Trefusis, *Don't Look*, p 17
14 Keppel, *Edwardian*, p 25
15 Trefusis, *Don't Look*, p 27
16 *Ibid*, p 27
17 Keppel, *Edwardian*, p 48
18 Trefusis, *Don't Look*, p 28
19 Keppel, *Edwardian*, p 50
20 Trefusis, *Don't Look*, p 16
21 Keppel, *Edwardian*, p 21
22 Jullian, *Edward*, p 235
23 Streatfield, *Day Before*, p 102
24 Aslet, *Last Country*, p 98
25 Keppel, *Edwardian*, p 8
26 *Ibid*, p 7
27 Sitwell, *Great Morning*, p 21
28 Nicolson, *Portrait*, p 27
29 Lees-Milne, *Enigmatic*, p 206
30 Battiscombe, *Alexandra*, p 209
31 *Ibid*, p 228
32 Pope-Hennessy, *Queen Mary*, p 361
33 Alsop, *Lady Sackville*, p 142
34 *Sketch*, June 1895
35 Brooke-Shepherd, *Uncle of Europe*, p 59
36 Dudley, *Gilded Lily*, p 161
37 *Ibid*, p 171
38 Blunden, *Warwick*, p 130
39 *Ibid*, p 161
40 *Ibid*, p 134

41 Leslie, *Edwardians*, p 178
42 *Ibid*, p 175
43 *Ibid*, p 178
44 Blunden, *Warwick*, p 151
45 Warwick, *Life's Ebb*, p 110
46 *Ibid*, p 153
47 *Ibid*, p 154
48 *Ibid*, p 157
49 Minney, *Edwardian Age*, p 72
50 Leslie, *Edwardians*, p 238
51 Victoria, *Letters*, Third Series, Vol I, pp 354–5
52 Cust, *Edward VII*, p 259
53 Pearson, *Edward the Rake*, p 121
54 Lees-Milne, *Enigmatic*, p 173
55 Churchill, *W.S. Churchill*, Vol I, p 545

CHAPTER ELEVEN

1 Hibbert, *Edward VII*, p 172
2 Esher, *Letters*, Vol I, p 291
3 Mallet, *Life*, p 224
4 Cust, *Edward VII*, p 34
5 Windsor, *King's Story*, pp 45–6
6 Magnus, *Edward VII*, p 364
7 Marie, Queen, *Life*, Vol II, p 211
8 Esher, *Letters*, Vol I, p 292
9 Hibbert, *Edward VII*, p 191
10 Curzon, *Letters*, p 130
11 Hibbert, *Edward VII*, p 175
12 Sitwell, *Great Morning*, p 218
13 Jullian, *Edward*, p 278
14 St Aubyn, *Edward VII*, p 379
15 Alice, *Grandchildren*, p 124
16 Jullian, *Edward*, p 184
17 Nicolson, *Carnock*, p 271
18 Balsan, *Glitter*, p 120
19 Acton, *More Memoirs*, p 65
20 Asquith, *Autobiography*, p 280
21 Warwick, *Life's Ebb*, pp 146–7
22 Brooke-Shepherd, *Uncle of Europe*, pp 143–4
23 Keppel, *Edwardian*, p 3
24 Trefusis, *Don't Look*, p 33
25 Keppel, *Edwardian*, p 23
26 Jullian, *Edward*, p 142

27 Balsan, *Glitter*, p 120
28 Lees-Milne, *Enigmatic*, p 206
29 Acton, *More Memoirs*, p 60
30 Sackville-West, *Edwardians*, pp 17–18
31 de Stoeckl, *Not All Vanity*, p 98
32 Lees-Milne, *Enigmatic*, p 206
33 Brooke-Shepherd, *Uncle of Europe*, p 140
34 *Ibid*, p 143
35 Pless, *Private Diary*, pp 126–7
36 Esher, *Letters*, Vol I, p 318
37 Magnus, *Edward VII*, p 299
38 Antrim, *Louisa*, p 97
39 Blunt, *Secret Diary*, MS 6, 28/3/1901
40 Warwick, Earl of, *Memories*, p 225
41 Leslie, *Edwardians*, p 177
42 Magnus, *Edward VII*, p 299
43 Mary McFadyean to the author
44 Birkett, *Langtry*, p 4
45 Letters in poss. of Mary McFadyean
46 Birkett, *Langtry*, p 4
47 Langtry, *Days I Knew*, p 278
48 Dudley, *Gilded Lily*, p 194
49 Gerson, *Langtry*, p 225
50 Acton, *More Memoirs*, p 66
51 Trefusis, *Don't Look*, p 9
52 Acton, *More Memoirs*, p 66
53 Jullian, *Trefusis*, p 9
54 Brooke-Shepherd, *Uncle of Europe*, p 139
55 Curzon, *Letters*, p 81
56 Pless, *Private Diary*, p 98
57 Curzon, *Letters*, p 130
58 Keppel, *Edwardian*, p 13
59 Trefusis, *Don't Look*, p 20
60 Acton, *More Memoirs*, p 66

CHAPTER TWELVE

1 Brooke-Shepherd, *Uncle of Europe*, p 270
2 Hibbert, *Edward VII*, p 311
3 Paoli, *Royal Clients*, p 225
4 Keppel, *Edwardian*, p 43
5 *Ibid*, p 41
6 Paoli, *Royal Clients*, p 224
7 *Ibid*, p 230

8 Stamper, *What I Knew*, pp 72–3
9 Jullian, *Edward*, p 234
10 Jullian, *Trefusis*, p 17
11 Paoli, *Royal Clients*, p 227
12 Warwick, *Afterthoughts*, pp 275–6
13 *Ibid*, pp 275–6
14 Blunden, *Warwick*, pp 175–6
15 *Daily Mail*, 30/12/1907
16 Trefusis, *Don't Look*, p 44
17 Ponsonby, *Recollections*, p 216
18 Trefusis, *Don't Look*, p 45
19 Jullian, *Edward*, p 286
20 Hardinge, *Old Diplomacy*, p 157
21 Lee, *Edward VII*, Vol II, pp 4–5
22 St Aubyn, *Edward VII*, p 392
23 Asquith, *Autobiography*, p 279
24 Keppel, *Edwardian*, pp 29–30
25 Magnus, *Edward VII*, p 260
26 Jullian, *Trefusis*, p 11
27 Brooke-Shepherd, *Uncle of Europe*, p 142
28 Bennett, *Margot*, p 376

CHAPTER THIRTEEN

1 Hitchens, *Yesterday*, p 123
2 Youssoupoff, *Lost Splendour*, p 90
3 Hibbert, *Edward VII*, p 245
4 *Ibid*, p 244
5 Ponsonby, *Recollections*, p 231
6 Hibbert, *Edward VII*, p 245
7 Brooke-Shepherd, *Uncle of Europe*, pp 229–30
8 Ponsonby, *Recollections*, p 241
9 *Ibid*, p 217
10 Jullian, *Edward*, p 183
11 *Ibid*, p 234
12 *Ibid*, p 184
13 Blunt, *Secret Diary*, MS10, 13/5/1910
14 Hibbert, *Edward VII*, p 170
15 Morgan, *Maugham*, p 209
16 Lockhart, *Diaries*, p 291
17 Langtry, *Days I Knew*, pp 296–7
18 Warwick, *Afterthoughts*, p 22
19 *Ibid*, p 20
20 *Ibid*, p 22
21 Warwick, *Life's Ebb*, p 158

22 Battiscombe, *Alexandra*, p 271
23 Blunt, *Secret Diary*, MS 10, 13/5/1910
24 Magnus, *Edward VII*, p 450
25 Brooke-Shepherd, *Uncle of Europe*, p 350
26 Magnus, *Edward VII*, p 450
27 Lee, *Edward VII*, Vol II, p 709
28 Blunt, *Secret Diary*, MS10, 13/5/1910
29 Lee, *Edward VII*, Vol II, p 717
30 *Ibid*, Vol II, p 717
31 Lees – Milne, *Enigmatic*, p 206
32 Blunt, *Secret Diary*, MS 11, 14/12/1910
33 Lees-Milne, *Enigmatic*, p 206
34 Blunt, *Secret Diary*, MS 11, 14/12/1910
35 Esher, *Letters*, Vol III, pp 1–2
36 Battiscombe, *Alexandra*, p 71
37 Blunt, *Secret Diary*, MS 10, 13/5/1910
38 Lees-Milne, *Enigmatic*, p 206
39 Blunt, *Secret Diary*, MS 10, 20/5/1910
40 Keppel, *Edwardian*, p 54
41 Blunt, *Secret Diary*, MS 10, 14/12/1910
42 Brooke-Shepherd, *Uncle of Europe*, p 359
43 Trefusis, *Don't Look*, p 56

CHAPTER FOURTEEN

1 Lang, *Darling Daisy*, p 17
2 Dudley, *Gilded Lily*, p 52
3 Lang, *Darling Daisy*, p 104
4 *Ibid*, p 24
5 *Ibid*, p 113
6 *Sunday Times*, 5/12/1965
7 Warwick, *Life's Ebb*, p 274
8 Warwick, *Afterthoughts*, p 179
9 Flower, *Just As*, p 132

10 *Ibid*, p 131
11 *Ibid*, p 132
12 Colley, *News Hunter*, p 69
13 *Ibid*, p 69
14 Flower, *Just As*, p 133
15 Langtry, *Days I Knew*, p 223
16 *Ibid*, p 285
17 Dudley, *Gilded Lily*, p 219
18 *Daily Express*, 7/9/1928
19 Webb, *Diaries*, p 21
20 *Ibid*, p 22
21 Cole, *Growing Up*, p 146
22 Lockhart, *Diaries*, p 224
23 Warwick, *Afterthoughts*, p 279
24 Warwick, *Life's Ebb*, p 145
25 Lockhart, *Diaries*, p 224
26 *Daily Express*, 13/4/1937
27 Warwick, *Afterthoughts*, p XIV
28 *Daily Express*, 22/9/1938
29 Trefusis, *Don't Look*, p 212
30 Keppel, *Edwardian*, p 119
31 Jullian, *Trefusis*, p 49
32 Keppel, *Edwardian*, p 199
33 Acton, *More Memoirs*, p 65
34 Bryan, *Windsor Story*, p 281
35 Channon, *Diaries*, p 323
36 Trefusis, *Don't Look*, p 156
37 Acton, *More Memoirs*, p 182
38 Trefusis, *Don't Look*, p 174
39 Channon, *Diaries*, p 464
40 Jullian, *Trefusis*, p 108
41 Trefusis, *Don't Look*, p 183
42 *Ibid*, p 183
43 Brooke-Shepherd, *Uncle of Europe*, p 60
44 Trefusis, *Don't Look*, p 231
45 *Ibid*, p 232
46 *The Times*, 15/9/1947
47 *Ibid*, 20/9/1947

Bibliography

Acton, Harold, *More Memoirs of an Aesthete*, Methuen, London, 1970

Alice, Princess, Countess of Athlone, *For My Grandchildren*, Evans, London, 1966

Alsop, Susan Mary, *Lady Sackville*, Weidenfeld & Nicolson, London, 1978

Andrews, Allen, *The Splendid Pauper*, Harrap, London, 1968

Antrim, Louisa, Lady, *Recollections*, The King's Stone Press, Shipston-on-Stour, 1937

Antrim, Louisa, Lady, *Louisa, Lady in Waiting* (ed. Elizabeth Longford) Jonathan Cape, London, 1979

Arthur, Sir George, *Not Worth Reading*, Longmans Green, London, 1938

Aslet, Clive, *The Last Country Houses,* Yale University Press, New Haven & London, 1982

Asquith, Cynthia, *Remember and Be Glad*, James Barrie, London, 1952

Asquith, Margot, *More Memories*, Cassell, London, 1933

Asquith, Margot, *The Autobiography of Margot Asquith* (ed. Mark Bonham Carter), Eyre & Spottiswoode, London, 1962

Bagehot, Walter, *The English Constitution,* Kegan Paul, London, 1898

Balsan, Consuelo Vanderbilt, *The Glitter and the Gold,* Heinemann, London, 1953

Bancroft, Mr & Mrs, *On and off the Stage,* Richard Bentley, London, 1888

Barwick, Sandra, *A Century of Style,* Allen & Unwin, London, 1984

Battiscombe, Georgina, *Queen Alexandra*, Constable, London, 1969

Beddington, Mrs Claude, *All that I have Met*, Cassell, London, 1929

Bennett, Daphne, *Margot: A Life of the Countess of Asquith and Oxford,* Gollancz, London, 1984

Benson, E.F., *King Edward VII*, Longmans Green, London, 1935

Birkett, Jeremy & Richardson, John, *Lillie Langtry: Her Life in Words and Pictures*, Rupert Shuft, Channel Islands, 1979

Bisset, Major-General, *Sport and War,* John Murray, London, 1875

Blake, Robert, *Disraeli,* Eyre & Spottiswoode, London, 1966

Blunden, Margaret, *The Countess of Warwick,* Cassell, London, 1967

Booth, Horace H., *The Astonishing Mrs Langtry*, Geo. H. Doran, New York, 1930

Brooke-Shepherd, Gordon, *Uncle of Europe,* Collins, London, 1975

Brough, James, *The Prince and the Lily,* Hodder & Stoughton, London, 1975

Bryan, J. & Murphy, C.J.V., *The Windsor Story,* Granada, London, 1979

Cavendish, Lady Frederick, *The Diary of Lady Frederick Cavendish* (ed. John Bailey), 2 vols. John Murray, London, 1927

Channon, Sir Henry, *Chips: The Diaries of Sir Henry Channon* (ed. Robert Rhodes James), Weidenfeld & Nicolson, London, 1967

Chetwynd, Sir George, *Racing Reminiscences,* Longmans Green, London, 1891

Churchill, Lady Randolph, *Reminiscences,* Edward Arnold, London, 1908

Churchill, Randolph S., *Winston S. Churchill*, vols. 1 & 2, Heinemann, London, 1966

Cole, Margaret, *Growing up into Revolution*, Longmans Green, London, 1926

Colley, William, *News Hunter,* Hutchinson, London, 1936

Cornwallis West, George, *Edwardian Hey-Days,* Putnam, London, 1930

Cowles, Virginia, *Edward VII and His Circle*, Hamish Hamilton, London, 1958

Cozens-Hardy, H.T., *The Glorious Years,* Robert Hale, London, 1953

Cresswell, Mrs George, *Eighteen Years on the Sandringham Estate,* Temple, London, 1888

Croft-Cooke, Rupert, *Bosie: Lord Alfred Douglas,* Bobbs-Merrill, New York, 1963

Curzon, Lady, *Lady Curzon's India: Letters of a Vicereine* (ed. John Bradley), Weidenfeld & Nicolson, London, 1985

Cust, Sir Lionel, *King Edward VII and His Court*, John Murray, London, 1930

Dale, Alan, *Familiar Chats with Queens of the Stage,* Dillingham, New York, 1890

Dangerfield, George, *Victoria's Heir: The Education of a Prince,* Constable, London, 1941

Donaldson, Frances, *Edward VIII*, Weidenfeld & Nicolson, London, 1974

Dudley, Ernest, *The Gilded Lily,* Oddhams Press, London, 1958

Escott, T.H.R., *Society in London*, Chatto & Windus, London 1886

Esher, R.B.B., Viscount, *Letters and Journals* (ed. M.V. Brett), 4 vols., Nicolson Watson, London, 1934–38

Esher, R.B.B., *The Influence of King Edward and Essays on other Subjects,* John Murray, London, 1915

Evans, Richard J., *The Feminists,* Croom Helm, London, 1977

Flower, Newman, *Just as it Happened,* Cassell, London, 1950

Forbes, Lady Angela, *Memories and Base Details*, Hutchinson, London, 1921

Fryer, Peter, *The Birth Controllers*, Secker & Warburg, London, 1965

Fulford, Roger, *Votes for Women*, Faber & Faber, London, 1957

Gaunt, William, *The Pre-Raphaelite Dream*, Jonathan Cape, London, 1943

Gerson, Noel B., *Lillie Langtry*, Robert Hale, London, 1972

Gladstone, W.E., *The Gladstone Diaries* (ed. M.R.D. Foot & H.C.G. Matthew), 9 vols., Clarendon Press, Oxford 1968–1986.

Glyn, Anthony, *Elinor Glyn*, Hutchinson, London, 1955

Glyn, Elinor, *Romantic Adventure*, Ivor Nicholson & Watson, London, 1936

Grey, Viscount, of Fallodon, *Twenty-five years*, 2 vols., Hodder & Stoughton, London, 1925

Gwynn, S.L., *The Life of the Rt. Hon. Sir Charles Dilke*, John Murray, London, 1917

Hamilton, Lord Ernest, *The Halcyon Era*, John Murray, London, 1933

Hamilton, Lord Frederic, *The Vanished World of Yesterday*, Hodder & Stoughton, London, 1950

Hardinge, Charles, Baron, *Old Diplomacy*, John Murray, London, 1947

Harrison, Michael, *Clarence*, W.H. Allen, London, 1972

Harrison, Michael, *Painful Details*, Max Parrish, London, 1962

Hayward, Abraham, *Selected Essays*, Longmans Green, London, 1879

Hayward, Abraham, *Correspondence*, (ed. Henry E. Carlisle), John Murray, London, 1886

Hibbert, Christopher, *Edward VII: A Portrait*, Allen Lane, London, 1976

Hicks, Seymour, *Between Ourselves*, Cassell, London, 1930

Hitchens, Robert, *Yesterday*, Cassell, London, 1947

Holden, Anthony, *Charles, Prince of Wales*, Weidenfeld & Nicolson, London, 1979

Holland, Bernard, *Life of the Duke of Devonshire*, Longmans, London, 1911

Hollis, Patricia, *Women in Public 1850–1900*, Allen & Unwin, London, 1979

Horn, Pamela, *The Rise and Fall of the Victorian Servant*, St Martin's Press, New York, 1975

Hough, Richard, *Louis and Victoria*, Hutchinson, London, 1974

Hough, Richard, *Advice to a Grand-daughter*, Heinemann, London, 1975

Hyde, H. Montgomery, *The Cleveland Street Scandal*, W.H. Allen, London, 1976

Hyde, H. Montgomery, *Oscar Wilde*, Eyre Methuen, London, 1976

James, Robert Rhodes, *Rosebery*, Weidenfeld & Nicolson, London, 1963

Jullian, Philippe, *Edward and the Edwardians*, Sidgwick & Jackson, London, 1963

Jullian, Philippe & Phillips, John, *Violet Trefusis*, Hamish Hamilton, London, 1976

Kennedy, A.L. (ed.), *My Dear Duchess: Social and Political Letters to the Duchess of Manchester*, John Murray, London, 1956

Keppel, Sonia, *Edwardian Daughter*, Hamish Hamilton, London, 1958.

Lacey, Robert, *Majesty*, Hutchinson, London, 1977

Lambert, Angela, *Unquiet Souls*, Macmillan, London, 1985

Lang, Theo, *My Darling Daisy*, Michael Joseph, London, 1965

Langtry, Lillie, *The Days I Knew*, Hutchinson, London, 1925

Langtry, Lillie, *All At Sea*, Hutchinson, London, 1909

Lee, Sir Sydney, *King Edward VII*, 2 vols., Macmillan, London, 1927

Lees-Milne, James, *The Enigmatic Edwardian*, Sidgwick & Jackson, London, 1986

Leslie, Anita, *Mr Frewen of England*, Hutchinson, London, 1966

Leslie, Anita, *Edwardians in Love*, Hutchinson, London, 1972

Lockhart, Sir Robert Bruce, *Diaries 1915–1938* (ed. Kenneth Young), Macmillan, London, 1973

Longford, Elizabeth, *Victoria, R.I.*, Weidenfeld & Nicolson, London, 1964

Longford, Elizabeth, *A Pilgrimage of Passion*, Weidenfeld & Nicolson, London, 1979

Magnus, Philip, *King Edward VII*, John Murray, London, 1964

Magnus, Philip, *Gladstone*, John Murray, London, 1954

Mallet, Marie, *Life with Queen Victoria*, John Murray, London, 1968

Marcus, Steven, *The Other Victorians*, Weidenfeld & Nicolson, London, 1966

Marie-Louise, Princess, *My Memories of Six Reigns*, Evans, London, 1956

Marie of Romania, Queen, *The Story of My Life*, Cassell, London, 1934

Marlow, Joyce, *Mr and Mrs Gladstone*, Weidenfeld & Nicolson, London, 1977

Martin, Sir Theodore, *The Life of H.R.H. The Prince Consort*, 5 vols., Smith, Elder, London, 1875–1880

Mayhew, Henry, *London's Underworld*, (ed. Peter Quenell), William Kimber, London, 1950

Menzies, Amy Charlotte Stuart, (A Woman of No Importance), *Further Indiscretions*, Herbert Jenkins, London, 1918

Michael, Edward, *Tramps of a Scamp*, T. Werner Laurie, London, 1928

Millais, John Guille, *Life and Letters of Sir John Everett Millais*, Methuen, London, 1905

Minney, R.J., *The Edwardian Age*, Cassell, London, 1965

Morgan, Ted, *Somerset Maugham*, Jonathan Cape, London, 1980

Nevill, Lady Dorothy, *Under Five Reigns*, Methuen, London, 1910

Nicholas II, Tsar of Russia, *The Letters of Tsar Nicholas and Empress Marie* (ed. E.J. Bing), Ivor Nicholson & Watson, London, 1937

Nicolson, Harold, *King George the Fifth*, Constable, London, 1937

Nicolson, Harold, *Sir Arthur Nicolson, Bart, First Lord Carnock*, Constable, London, 1930

Nicolson, Nigel, *Portrait of a Marriage*, Weidenfeld & Nicolson, London, 1973

Noel, Gerard, *Princess Alice: Queen Victoria's Forgotten Daughter*, Constable, London, 1974

Onslow, Richard, *The Squire: A Life of George Alexander Baird,* Harrap, London, 1980

Paoli, Xavier, *My Royal Clients,* Hodder & Stoughton, London, N.D.

Pearson, Hesketh, *The Life of Oscar Wilde,* Methuen, London, 1946

Pearson, John, *Edward the Rake,* Weidenfeld & Nicolson, London, 1975

Peel, Mrs C.S., *A Hundred Wonderful Years,* Bodley Head, London, 1926

Peel, Mrs C.S., *The Stream of Time,* John Lane, London, 1931

Peters, Margot, *Mrs Pat,* Bodley Head, London, 1984

Pless, Daisy, Princess of, *From My Private Diary,* John Murray, London, 1931

Pless, Daisy, Princess of, *What I Left Unsaid,* Cassell, London, 1936

Plimpton, Margaret, *The Life and Loves of Lillie Langtry,* Dumont, London, 1931

Ponsonby, Arthur, *Henry Ponsonby: His Life from His Letters,* Macmillan, London, 1930

Ponsonby, Sir Frederick, *Sidelights on Queen Victoria,* Macmillan, London, 1930

Ponsonby, Sir Frederick, *Recollections of Three Reigns,* Eyre & Spottiswoode, London, 1951

Ponsonby, May, *A Memoir, Some Letters and a Journal,* John Murray, London, 1927

Pope-Hennessy, James, *Queen Mary,* Allen & Unwin, London, 1959

Porter, H.T., *Lillie Langtry,* Société Jersiaise, Jersey, 1973

Portland, Duke of, *Men, Women, and Things,* Faber & Faber, London, 1937

Raeburn, Antonia, *Militant Suffragettes,* New English Library, London, 1973

Roberts, Brian, *Cecil Rhodes and the Princess,* Hamish Hamilton, London, 1969

Roberts, Brian, *The Mad Bad Line,* Hamish Hamilton, London, 1981

Robertson, W. Graham, *Time Was,* Hamish Hamilton, London, 1931

Robertson Scott, J.W., *The Life and Death of a Newspaper,* Methuen, London, 1952

Rose, Kenneth, *King George V,* Macmillan, London, 1983

Russell, G.W.E., *Collections and Recollections,* Smith, Elder, London, 1899

Sackville-West, Victoria, *The Edwardians,* Hogarth Press, London, 1933

St Aubyn, Giles, *Edward VII,* Collins, London, 1979

Sebright, Arthur, *A Glance into the Past,* Eveleigh Nash, London, 1922

Sewell, J.P.C., *Personal Letters of King Edward VII,* Hutchinson, London, 1931

Sharpe, Henrietta, *A Solitary Woman: A Life of Violet Trefusis,* Constable, London, 1981

Sitwell, Osbert, *Great Morning,* Macmillan, London, 1948

Skinner, Cornelia Otis, *Madame Sarah,* Michael Joseph, London, 1967

Soames, Mary, *Clementine Churchill,* Cassell, London, 1979

Stevens, Joan, *Victorian Voices: An Introduction to the papers of Sir John Le Couteur,* Société Jersiaise, Jersey, 1969

Stoeckl, Baroness de, *Not All Vanity,* John Murray, London, 1950

Streatfield, Noel (ed.), *The Day Before Yesterday,* Collins, London, 1956

Suffield, Lord, *My Memories 1830–1913* (ed. Alys Lowth), Herbert Jenkins, London, 1917

Sykes, Christopher, *Four Studies in Loyalty,* Collins, London, 1946

Tannahill, Reay, *Sex in History,* Hamish Hamilton, London, 1980

Terriss, Ellaline, *Just a Little Bit of String,* Hutchinson, London, 1955

Terry, Ellen, *The Story of My Life,* Hutchinson, London, 1922

Todd, Ann, *The Eighth Veil,* Kimber, London, 1980

Trefusis, Violet, *Don't Look Round,* Hutchinson, London, 1952

Vanderbilt, Cornelius, *Farewell to Fifth Avenue,* Gollancz, London, 1935

Victoria, German Empress, *Letters of the Empress Frederick* (ed. Sir Frederick Ponsonby), Macmillan, London, 1928

Victoria, German Empress, *The Empress Writes to Sophie* (ed. A. Gould-Lee), Faber & Faber, London, 1955

Victoria, Queen, *Leaves From the Journal of Our Life in the Highlands 1848–1861,* Smith, Elder, London, 1868

Victoria, Queen, *The Letters of Queen Victoria: A Selection of Her Majesty's Correspondence,* 9 vols., John Murray, London, 1907–1932

Victoria, Queen, *Further Letters,* Thornton Butterworth, London, 1938

Victoria, Queen, *Dearest Child: Letters between Queen Victoria and the Princess Royal* (ed. Roger Fulford), Evans Bros, London, 1964

Victoria, Queen, *Dearest Mamma: Letters between Queen Victoria and the Crown Princess of Prussia* (ed. Roger Fulford), Evans Bros, London, 1968

Victoria, Queen, *Your Dear Letter: Private Correspondence of Queen Victoria and the Crown Princess of Prussia* (ed. Roger Fulford), Evans Bros, London, 1971

Warwick, Frances, Countess of, *Life's Ebb and Flow,* Hutchinson, London, 1929

Warwick, Frances, Countess of, *Afterthoughts,* Cassell, London, 1931

Warwick, Fifth Earl of, *Memories of Sixty Years,* Cassell, London, 1917

Webb, Beatrice, *Diaries 1924–1932,* Longmans, London, 1956

Webster, Margaret, *The Same Only Different,* Gollancz, London, 1969

Whyte, Frederick, *The Life of W.T. Stead,* Jonathan Cape, London, 1925

Williams, Florence, (Mrs Hwfar Williams), *It Was Such Fun,* Hutchinson, London, 1935

Williams, Montagu, *Later Leaves,* Macmillan, London, 1891

Windsor, H.R.H. Duke of, *A King's Story,* Cassell, London, 1951

Windsor, H.R.H. Duke of, *A Family Album,* Cassell, London, 1960

Wortham, H.E. *The Delightful Profession: Edward VII, a Study in Kingship,* Jonathan Cape, London, 1931

Youssoupoff, Prince Felix, *Lost Splendour,* Jonathan Cape, London, 1953
Ziegler, Philip, *Lady Diana Cooper,* Hamish Hamilton, London, 1981

Newspapers, Magazines and Reference Books
Burke's Royal Families of the World, The Chester Chronicle, Daily Express,
Daily Mail, Dictionary of National Biography, Graphic, Jersey Evening
Post, Illustrated London News, New York Times, Pall Mall Gazette,
Pearson's Magazine, Reynolds Newspaper, Review of Reviews, Sketch,
Sunday Times, The Telegraph, The Times, Town Talk, Whitehall Review,
Woman's Own, The World.

Index